The collection is a truly global exploration of anti-fascism that both explores its local variants and traces the networks that connected activists and institutions on six continents. Expanding our vision of anti-fascism well beyond Europe, the case studies highlight the crucial, complex and understudied intersection of anti-imperialism and anti-fascism.

Lisa A. Kirschenbaum, Professor of History, West Chester University, USA

Anti-fascism has long been considered synonymous with Soviet communism. In fact, as this book so amply and ably demonstrates, anti-fascism was a global force representing diverse ideologies. The chapters chart the international and transnational nature of anti-fascism, moving way beyond the Eurocentric approach of most previous studies. At the same time, they show that anti-fascism was a hugely diverse phenomenon, with movements coming from all sections of the liberal left. In globalizing and disaggregating anti-fascism, the book is bold, innovative and hugely thought-provoking. An essential read for all scholars of fascism and its opponents.

Dan Stone, Professor of Modern History, Royal Holloway, University of London

ANTI-FASCISM IN A GLOBAL PERSPECTIVE

This book initiates a critical discussion on the varieties of global anti-fascism and explores the cultural, political and practical articulations of anti-fascism around the world.

This volume brings together a group of leading scholars on the history of anti-fascism to provide a comprehensive analysis of anti-fascism from a transnational and global perspective and to reveal the abundance and complexity of anti-fascist ideas, movements and practices. Through a number of interlinked case studies, they examine how different forms of global anti-fascisms were embedded in various national and local contexts during the interwar period and investigate the interrelations between local articulations and the global movement. Contributions also explore the actions and impact of African, Asian, Latin American, Caribbean and Middle Eastern anti-fascist voices that have often been ignored or rendered peripheral in international histories of anti-fascism.

Aimed at a postgraduate student audience, this book will be useful for modules on the extreme right, political history, political thought, political ideologies, political parties, social movements, political regimes, global politics, world history and sociology.

Kasper Braskén is a Postdoctoral Researcher at Abo Akademi University, Turku, Finland.

Nigel Copsey is Professor (Research) in Modern History at Teesside University, UK.

David Featherstone is a Senior Lecturer in Human Geography at the University of Glasgow, UK.

ROUTLEDGE STUDIES IN FASCISM AND THE FAR RIGHT

Series editors: Nigel Copsey, Teesside University, UK and Graham Macklin, Center for Research on Extremism (C-REX), University of Oslo, Norway.

This new book series focuses upon fascist, far right and right-wing politics primarily within a historical context but also drawing on insights from other disciplinary perspectives. Its scope also includes radical-right populism, cultural manifestations of the far right and points of convergence and exchange with the mainstream and traditional right.

Titles include:

Lost Imperium
Far Right Visions of the British Empire, c.1920–1980
Paul Stocker

Hitler Redux
The Incredible History of Hitler's So-Called Table Talks
Mikael Nilsson

Researching the Far Right
Theory, Method and Practice
Edited by Stephen D. Ashe, Joel Busher, Graham Macklin and Aaron Winter

The Rise of the Dutch New Right
An Intellectual History of the Rightward Shift in Dutch Politics
Merijn Oudenampsen

Anti-Fascism in a Global Perspective
Transnational Networks, Exile Communities, and Radical Internationalism
Edited by Kasper Braskén, Nigel Copsey and David Featherstone

British Fascism After the Holocaust
From the Birth of Denial to the Notting Hill Riots 1939–1958
Joe Mulhall

For more information about this series, please visit: www.routledge.com/Routledge-Studies-in-Fascism-and-the-Far-Right/book-series/FFR.

ANTI-FASCISM IN A GLOBAL PERSPECTIVE

Transnational Networks, Exile Communities, and Radical Internationalism

Edited by Kasper Braskén, Nigel Copsey and David Featherstone

Routledge
Taylor & Francis Group
NEW YORK AND LONDON

First published 2021
by Routledge
2 Park Square, Milton Park, Abingdon, Oxon OX14 4RN

and by Routledge
52 Vanderbilt Avenue, New York, NY 10017

Routledge is an imprint of the Taylor & Francis Group, an informa business

British Library Cataloguing in Publication Data
A catalogue record for this book is available from the British Library

Library of Congress Cataloging-in-Publication Data
A catalog record has been requested for this book

ISBN: 9781138352186 (hbk)
ISBN: 9781138352193 (pbk)
ISBN: 9780429058356 (ebk)

Typeset in Bembo
by Taylor & Francis Books

CONTENTS

CONTRIBUTORS

Kasper Braskén is a Postdoctoral Researcher at Abo Akademi University, Turku, Finland. He is a historian specialising in 20th-century transnational and global history, and the history of international communism, fascism and anti-fascism. Braskén is leading a 36-month Academy of Finland research project 'Towards a Global History of Anti-Fascism: Transnational Civil Society Activism, International Organisations and Identity Politics Beyond Borders, 1922–1945'. He is the author of *The International Workers' Relief, Communism, and Transnational Solidarity: Willi Münzenberg in Weimar Germany* (2015), and co-editor of the volume *Anti-Fascism in the Nordic Countries* (2019).

Nigel Copsey is Professor (Research) of Modern History at Teesside University, UK. He specialises in historic and contemporary forms of fascism and anti-fascism. He is currently working on a comparative study of militant anti-fascism in the US and Britain. He is the author of *Anti-Fascism in Britain* (2017), and co-editor of *Varieties of Anti-Fascism: Britain in the Inter-War period* (2010) and *Anti-Fascism in the Nordic Countries* (2019).

David Featherstone is a Senior Lecturer in Human Geography at the University of Glasgow. He has strong interests in the histories and geographies of the left and in the intersections between anti-colonialism and anti-fascism. His publications include *Resistance, Space and Political Identities: the Making of Counter-Global Networks* (2008) and *Solidarity: Hidden Histories and Geographies of Internationalism* (2012).

Bernhard H. Bayerlein is a Senior Researcher at the Institute of Social Movements, University of Bochum, Germany. He holds a German PhD degree and a French Habilitation à diriger des recherches. He is the Editor of *The*

International Newsletter of Communist Studies http://incs.ub.rub.de and additional journals. He has published widely in many languages on European history, Socialism and Communism and Portuguese and Spanish studies including *'Stalin, the Traitor Is You!!' – 1939–1941* and *Germany–Russia–Komintern*, 3 vols (in German, Aufbau, 2008 and De Gruyter, 2014/2015). See http://ruhr-uni-bochum.academia.edu/BernhardHBayerlein. He is editor of the International Willi-Münzenberg-Forum (Berlin) and acts as secretary general of the Association for the Promotion of Archives (VfA), successor of The International Committee for the Computerization of Comintern Archives (Council of Europe). Email: dr.bayerlein@uni-koeln.de; bernhard.bayerlein@ruhr-uni-bochum.de.

Cathy Bergin is Course Leader for History, Literature & Culture at the University of Brighton. She is the author of *Bitter with the Past, but Sweet with the Dream: Communism in the African American Imaginary* (2015) and *African American Anti-Colonial Thought, 1917–1937* (2016). She is co-editor with Anita Rupprecht of a special Issue of *Race & Class*: 'Reparative Histories: Radical Narratives of "Race" and Resistance' (2016). Recent publications include 'Reparative Histories: Tracing Narratives of Black Resistance and White Entitlement' (with Anita Rupprecht) in *Race & Class* (2018) and 'The Russian Revolution and Black Radicalism in the United States' in *Soundings* (2018).

João Fábio Bertonha is Professor at the State University of Maringá (Brazil). He has been a visiting researcher in numerous countries and universities, mainly in Latin America, Europe and North America. His latest books are *Aventureros, utopistas, emigrantes. Del Imperio Habsburgo a las Américas* (as coeditor – 2017); *Italianos e austro-húngaros no Brasil: nacionalismos e identidades* (2018); *Plínio Salgado: biografia política* (2018) e *La Legione Parini. Gli italiani all'estero e la guerra d'Etiopia* (2018). http://joaofabiobertonha.com.

Federico Ferretti received his PhD from the Universities of Bologna and Paris 1 Panthéon-Sorbonne in 2011. After research and teaching in Italy, France, Switzerland and Brazil, he became Associate Professor in the School of Geography at University College Dublin, Ireland. His interests lie in philosophy and history of geography and in cultural and historical geography, as well as in the international circulation of geographical knowledge through critical and anarchist approaches, with a special focus on Latin America. He is Secretary/Treasurer/Webmaster for the Commission History of Geography of the International Geographical Union and Secretary of the History and Philosophy of Geography Research Group of the RGS-IBG.

Hugo García is Associate Professor of Modern History at the Universidad Autónoma de Madrid (Spain). He is the author of, among other works, *The Truth about Spain! Mobilizing British Public Opinion, 1936–1939* (Sussex Academic Press,

2010), as well as co-editor of *Rethinking Antifascism: History, Memory, and Politics, 1922–1945* (Berghahn, 2016) and sole editor of the collection *Transnational Anti-Fascism: Agents, Networks, Circulations*, published as a special issue of *Contemporary European History* in November 2016.

Jonathan Hyslop is Professor of Sociology and African Studies at Colgate University, Hamilton, New York and Extraordinary Professor at the University of Pretoria. He worked for many years at the University of the Witwatersrand, Johannesburg, where he was Deputy Director of the Wits Institute for Social and Economic Research (WISER) and a member of the committee of the History Workshop. Hyslop has published widely on late Nineteenth and Twentieth Century southern African social and political history, on British imperial history and on maritime history. In 2015–2016, he was a fellow at the Re:work program, *Humboldt-Universität zu Berlin*. Email: jhyslop@colgate.edu.

Ariel Mae Lambe is Assistant Professor of History at the University of Connecticut where she teaches Latin American, Caribbean, and US History courses. Her book *No Barrier Can Contain It: Cuban Antifascism and the Spanish Civil War* was published by University of North Carolina Press in December 2019. Dr Lambe earned a BA in History from Yale College and a PhD in Latin American and Caribbean History from Columbia University.

Michele L. Louro is an Associate Professor at Salem State University specializing in modern South Asia, the British Empire, and international history. She is author to *Comrades against Imperialism: Nehru, India and Interwar Internationalism* (Cambridge University Press, 2018), and her new book project traces the local and global history of the Meerut Conspiracy Case (1929–1935), a legal trial in colonial India. Louro is also co-editor and contributor to *The League against Imperialism: Lives and Afterlives* (Leiden, 2020). She also serves as the Treasurer of the World History Association and President of the Society for Advancing the History of South Asia.

Sandra Pujals, PhD, is Professor of History at the University of Puerto Rico. She has a MA in Russian Area Studies and a PhD in Russian History, both from Georgetown University in Washington DC. Her main research interests include Soviet revolutionary culture and Soviet Russia's cultural relationship with Latin America and the Caribbean (1920s–1940s). Her forthcoming and recent publications include articles in several collections for Routledge Publishers, Indiana University Press and Slavica Publishers; Manchester University Press; McGill-Queen's University Press; and *Cuadernos de Historia Contemporánea* of the Complutense University of Madrid. Her book *Un Caribe soviético: el comunismo internacional en Puerto Rico y el Caribe*, will be published next year. She is currently working on her second monograph titled *Su Casa Es Mi Casa: The Caribbean Bureau of the Comintern and the Forging of a Soviet Caribbean, 1930–1936.*

Sana Tannoury-Karam, PhD, is a historian of the modern Middle East, writing on the intellectual and social history of the Left in the Levant during the Mandate period. She is an Early Career Fellow at the Arab Council for the Social Sciences and a lecturer in the Humanities Department at the Lebanese American University. Most recently, she had completed a post-doctoral fellowship at Rice University. She has various publications on the Arab left and communism including in the *Journal of World History* and as a co-editor of the volume *The League Against Imperialism: Lives and Afterlives* with Leiden University Press.

ACKNOWLEDGEMENTS

This edited volume is the result of a collaborative research effort that started in 2016. Like many collections of this kind, international academic conferences have offered a vital forum to develop exciting new ideas and visions. Several of the chapters included here were initially presented at one of three interlinked panels on global anti-fascism convened by the editors. The first was organised by Kasper Braskén at the European Social Science History Conference (ESSHC) in Valencia, Spain. The second was co-organised the next year by Braskén and Nigel Copsey at the 2017 ENIUGH Congress in Budapest, Hungary. The final panel was co-organised by Braskén and David Featherstone at the 2018 ESSHC in Belfast, Northern Ireland. We wish to thank all participants who contributed to the vibrant discussions: A special thanks goes to Christopher Vials (Connecticut), Fraser M. Ottanelli (South Florida), Maria Framke (Rostock), Andrea Acle-Kreysing (Leipzig & Munich), Holger Weiss (Åbo/Turku), and Benjamin Zachariah (Trier). Several new authors joined the volume in late 2018 who made invaluable contributions to the final product. Lastly, Kasper Braskén wishes to acknowledge the Academy of Finland for funding the project 'Towards a Global History of Anti-Fascism: Transnational Civil Society Activism, International Organisations and Identity Politics Beyond Borders, 1922–1945', which is based at Abo Akademi University, Finland (2017–2020).

INTRODUCTION

Towards a global history of anti-fascism

Kasper Braskén, David Featherstone and Nigel Copsey

On 7 October 1934, a major street battle between fascists and anti-fascists took place in the centre of Sao Paulo. It became a landmark for Brazilian anti-fascism and is commonly remembered as the 'See Square Battle (Batalha da Praça da Sé)'. An anti-fascist protest action was staged on that day against a major demonstration organised by the country's largest fascist party, Brazilian Integralist Action (*Ação Integralista Brasileira*). The confrontation led to violent street fighting that managed to close down the fascist protest. It left several wounded and some dead, predominantly on the fascist side.[1] Four years later, fascist Blackshirts in Johannesburg, South Africa, were responsible for escalating levels of violence perpetrated against both leftist movements and Jewish institutions. On 27 November 1938, the rising political tensions culminated in a violent battle between Blackshirts and anti-fascists in central Johannesburg, causing one of the largest disturbances in the city since the early 1920s.[2] Many memorialise the Battle of Cable Street,[3] when anti-fascists in London successfully halted the demonstration of Oswald Mosley and the British Union of Fascists in 1936, but all too few have knowledge of analogous events beyond European frameworks.

These two examples, from Brazil and South Africa, expose how the histories and geographies of anti-fascisms remain uneven. Our aim with this volume is to initiate a critical discussion on the varieties of global anti-fascism and to explore the cultural, political and practical articulations of anti-fascism around the world. Through a number of interlinked case studies, this volume examines how different forms of global anti-fascisms were embedded in various national and local contexts during the interwar period and we investigate the interrelations between local articulations and the global movement. Through doing so, this book is a gateway into the diverse trajectories, agency and solidarities shaped by anti-fascist political activity and provides space to African, Asian, Latin American, Caribbean and Middle Eastern anti-fascist voices that have often been ignored or rendered peripheral in international histories of anti-fascism.

Like any global approach, the aim of this volume is to neither establish homogeneity nor force historical coherence. Our aim, instead, is to reveal the abundance and complexity of anti-fascist ideas, movements and practices. This volume is not disconnected from developments in Europe, but it does strive to expand our horizons and enhance our understanding of global anti-fascism and fascism. It seeks to explore the historical and intellectual implications of bringing together cases and examples from Latin America, the Caribbean, North America, Scandinavia, Spain, the Middle East, Ethiopia, South Africa, India and Australia. All too often anti-fascism is understood as a monolith, mainly connected to Stalinism or Soviet communism, which grossly misrepresents the varieties of anti-fascist resistance. We find it of outmost importance to re-visit these histories and to reveal their diverse trajectories based on the very latest research findings. Political myths and misrepresentations of anti-fascist histories are constantly used in contemporary debates and political struggles around the world, which highlights the importance of understanding these histories and legacies beyond simplistic narratives. We also contend that engagement with these diverse histories can help to animate contestation of the far right in the present.

Firstly it must be acknowledged that the state of 'anti-fascism studies' is directly connected to the emerging global and comparative history of fascism.[4] As Benjamin Zachariah argues, there is a resilient 'prejudice that fascisms in general are strictly European phenomena and that non-Europeans only produced inadequately understood imitations'.[5] Such limits continue to circumscribe the terms on which anti-fascism is understood and theorised. Thus recent calls to 'rethink anti-fascism' have made an important attempt to recover the importance and diversity of anti-fascist politics.[6] Such work has, however, continued to underplay the intersections between anti-fascism and anti-colonialism/anti-imperialism which is of crucial relevance in the global arena. This means that major mobilisations like those against Mussolini's invasion of Ethiopia in 1935 often get written out of work on anti-fascism as do many of the actors involved in the formation of such resistance and solidarity.[7]

Most international histories of anti-fascism are based on European thinkers and activists, and partly as a result a serious analysis of the intersections and commonalities between fascism and colonialism are all too seldom. Thus Richard Iton notes that Giorgio Agamben 'cites Nazism and the Holocaust as crucial markers of modernity's 'hidden matrix' in his book *Homo Sacer* while 'paying little attention to the broader phenomenon of colonialism'.[8] He contrasts Agamben's omission of the articulations of fascism, anti-fascism and colonialism with the work of key intellectuals associated with the Black radical tradition such as W. E. B. Du Bois, Oliver Cox, George Padmore and C. L. R. James, and the film-maker Ousmane Sembène, who foregrounded 'the colonial factor' and made 'connections between this history and the events that took place in Europe leading up to and during World War II'. Thus George Padmore, the key anti-colonialist, noted for example in 1938 that the Government of Trinidad and Tobago was 'inaugurating a policy which savours of Colonial Fascism, and which, if not challenged immediately, is bound to deprive the workers of their most elementary civil rights, such as freedom of the press, speech and assembly'.[9] Padmore's articulation of 'Colonial Fascism' was an innovative intervention which directly asserted the co-production of fascism and colonialism.

Such interventions challenge the construction of fascism as a distinctly European phenomenon and positions it as emerging at the intersections of colonial and metropolitan political networks and exchanges. Padmore, as Leslie James has noted, arguably made the case that 'European rule in its colonies was itself fascist' and did so 'more vehemently than anyone else at the time'.[10] Although Padmore was vocal in his articulations, he was far from the only anti-colonialist to seriously embrace the concept of fascism beyond European frameworks. In a similar way, the Indian National Congress and its president Jawaharlal Nehru defined fascism and imperialism as 'blood brothers' during the mid-late 1930s. From an Indian horizon, as Michele Louro reveals in Chapter 6 of this volume, fascism and imperialism were perceived as dual symptoms of world capitalism, responsible for fierce oppression and exploitation on a global scale.[11] Besides Padmore's concept of 'colonial fascism', the Cuban communists Julio Antonio Mella and Rubén Martínez Villena explicitly defined Gerardo Machado's dictatorial regime in Cuba as a form of 'tropical fascism' during the 1920s. Sandra Pujals demonstrates in Chapter 3 how such interventions were enriched by pivotal local experiences, encounters and practices that have since then fallen into neglect. Despite this they not only deserve their place in the emerging global history of anti-fascism, but can offer different routes into understanding the solidarities and internationalisms shaped through these global histories.

Different anti-fascist traditions

For several European countries key literature on anti-fascism is available as recent examples from Britain, France, Germany, Italy, Spain and the Nordic Countries demonstrate.[12] Comparative and transnational research efforts still remain the exception, although the emerging literature suggests that there is great promise in such approaches.[13] Hugo García argues convincingly that transnational history forms the new paradigm for 'anti-fascist studies', but it still must be remembered that the transnational turn does not itself lead to the abandonment of Eurocentrism.

Recent work by Christopher Vials and Susan D. Pennybacker, for example, offer vital new perspectives on the way we need to de-colonise and globalise these histories. Vials's discussion of the contributions to the CPUSA affiliated journal *The Fight Against War and Fascism*, for example, argues that the journal reveals 'the ways in which US-based communists and non-communists worked together, for a time, to forge a democratic language that confronted hierarchies of race, class, and empire, and in a manner that did not neatly follow any "party line" directed from Moscow'. Pennybacker depicts how anti-colonial activists played a huge role in European metropolitan spaces, where people from India or Africa rallied together with British and European anti-fascists and anti-colonialists against the injustices of Empire.[14]

Breaking out of a European centred lens also enables us to focus on the different and contested articulations between anti-colonialism and fascism/anti-fascism. Even so, new studies which engage with anti-fascism in more transnational ways still somehow manage to marginalise such questions. Michael Seidman's book *Transatlantic Antifascisms* adopts a very narrow usage of the transatlantic in the title employing it in a restricted way to refer predominantly to relations between the US, France and Britain. Seidman is also dismissive of the importance of transnational organising in relation to China and Ethiopia: 'Neither Japanese aggression against China (1931–1933) nor the Italian conquest of Ethiopia (1935–1936) aroused the same level of international emotion and commitment as the Spanish Civil War and Revolution.'[15] Downplaying the significant transnational anti-fascisms shaped in opposition to Italy's invasion of Ethiopia has important consequences in limiting understandings of anti-fascism, particularly in terms of recognising diverse articulations with anti-colonialism. It also hinders an engagement with the differing and conflictual perspectives of anti-fascists on empire. As Tom Buchanan has argued it was not only the political right, but also elements of the left that were silent on articulations of anti-fascism and anti-colonialism.[16]

With the outbreak of the Second World War, many anti-colonialists were forced to make the painful choice, at least momentarily, to put aside their anti-colonial agenda and double down on fighting fascism first. However, some anti-colonialists were instead prepared to abandon anti-fascism and to strive in alliance with Nazi Germany to fulfil their mission to bring down the British and French empires.[17] Many anti-colonialists on the left who had admired and adhered to the Communist International's (Comintern) anti-imperialist agenda were, during the mid-1930s, disillusioned with the communist turn to popular front politics. Like George Padmore, they disdained the Soviet Union's new path towards appeasement and collaboration with European empires to forward anti-fascist popular fronts and collective security, rather than continuing the efforts to disrupt the colonial empires from within.[18] The Axis Powers actively utilised this dilemma during the Second World War and, as Evan Smith notes, 'it encouraged the indigenous populations in the British and (former) French and Dutch colonies to view the Axis Powers (particularly Japan) as liberators of these people from colonial tyranny'. Such perspectives were strongly opposed by Moses Kotane of the South African CP and the African American communist James Ford. Ford argued in 1942 that it was a 'hideous lie' that Japan could be the 'champion of the darker races'. According to Ford, such ideas came 'from the lips of a gang of fascists who betrayed Ethiopia and took their places besides Mussolini and his wholesale murder of this peaceful Negro nation in Africa'.[19]

The existing scholarship on anti-fascism has had a tendency to narrowly focus on the international communist movement. This collection will extend the reach, covering the broader global left, including not only communists, but anarchists, social democrats, left-intellectuals and anti-colonialists. In many cases, these activists and left-intellectuals moved through different political affiliations during the course of the interwar period, passing from socialism to communism, left-socialism and to independent left-opposition groups. Some leaped over to the fascist side, while others found an enforced anti-totalitarian world-view in the common rejection of Stalinism and Nazism.

The history of communist anti-fascism has contributed to a substantial literature on Soviet anti-fascism and the Comintern's debates on the nature of fascism.[20] While such studies remain valuable in many respects, they have in most cases been limited to perspectives 'from above' that discuss the twists and turns at the highest political levels in Moscow, but say very little about local anti-fascist responses around the world. In this regard a core contribution of this collection is to apply some of the methodologies associated with work on transnational subaltern histories to work on anti-fascist solidarities and internationalisms.[21] This is a productive approach which can open up different understandings and ways of recognising who was important in shaping anti-fascist politics and different understandings of the labour involved in so doing.

Recent global histories of communism have noted that anti-fascism became fundamentally integrated into the global communist identity during the 1930s, but no comprehensive study beyond European frameworks has been produced. Studies on global communism tend to be either limited to national case studies or restricted to discussing anti-fascism in the context of the Comintern's Popular Front period (1935–1939) and the Spanish Civil War (1936–1939). In general, the Spanish Civil War has formed a major subfield of international anti-fascism studies, sometimes even erroneously understood to be the *only* relevant field of anti-fascism studies. The war in Spain was quickly understood as an event of global significance, and major studies from around the world have also been produced.[22] As the chapters in this volume show, Spain did not only attract volunteers to fight, but included groups of medical volunteers as revealed by Ariel Lambe in Chapter 14, dealing with the story of Cuban medical aid. Cathy Bergin (Chapter 13) highlights again the role of black internationalism and anti-fascism that inspired many African Americans to join the international brigades in Spain. Constant movement across borders and continents seems to be the most striking aspect of this global history in the making, emphasising the vast opportunities for intercultural learning and transnational transfers of anti-fascist practices that enabled inventive thinking about the common fascist menace. Following such an argument, it was no surprise that Spain became in the minds of the many the 'world capital of anti-fascism' as Hugo García fittingly maintains in his contribution to the volume.

Relevant for the history of global communist anti-fascism, several recent works have revealed much new information about international communist-led organisations. They offer vital new knowledge on the inner workings of international communist organisations such as the International Red Aid, the League against Imperialism, the International Workers' Relief, the International Trade Union Committee of Negro Workers, or the International of Seamen and Harbour Workers and their relations to Moscow. Such international organisational histories offer an important way to look beyond national frameworks and to establish global links and transnational transfers.[23] However, as Joachim C. Häberlen notes in an effective critique of the historiography on global communism it has been difficult for researchers to move beyond two dichotomic perspectives that either emphasise a perspective 'from below' or limits itself to a perspective 'from above.' While the former underlines the importance of local contexts and experiences, the latter emphasises the control and influence of the Comintern and Moscow's clandestine services. In a similar way, the research of US communism has been divided between 'traditionalists' who emphasise the subversive Moscow connection, while 'revisionists' have commonly approached the history of communism from the perspective of local actors and contexts and connected it to the rise of civil rights movements and questions of social and racial justice.[24]

For sure, the deeply permeating effects of Stalinism on global anti-fascism cannot be overlooked, as Bernhard H. Bayerlein's chapter on Comintern policy in Brazil and Ethiopia shows (Chapter 11). At the same time, the gaze at the top levels of the world movement must not lead to losing touch with various local developments, and the vital anti-fascist activity carried on by independent communists, anarchists, syndicalists, lefts socialists, trotskyists, socialists and progressive liberals within the global left. Still, one needs to be careful not to treat uncritically concepts such as the 'global left'. As discussed by Hugo García in Chapter 12, the global left was indeed a fragile construct during the interwar period with many internal contradictions and incoherent factors. And so it is perhaps even more remarkable that it still could produce such powerful and empathic global bonds of solidarity, although they usually could only be upheld momentarily. Through many of these histories, left-solidarities reveal themselves as remarkably transformative ideas that enabled the global connection and unification of people from various backgrounds and geographical locations that was of vital importance for the history of anti-fascism.[25] In this way, one could argue that global anti-fascism was not as much a product of the global left, as the global left was a product of anti-fascist mobilisation on a world wide scale.

Pivotal moments in the history of fascism, such as Mussolini's rise to power in 1922, the establishment of the Third Reich in 1933, the Italo-Ethiopian war in 1935–1936, the Spanish Civil War, 1936–1939, and Nazi Germany's attack on the Soviet Union in summer 1941, all gave rise to significant, but separately distinct global waves of anti-fascist responses. The establishment of fascist regimes in Italy and Germany was pre-dated and followed by violent attacks against the labour movement and everything anti-fascist, which led to the establishment of anti-fascist exile communities around the world.[26] The flows of political refugees and exiles from Italy and later Germany had direct global repercussions. For the 1920s, as both Federico Ferretti (Chapter 9) and Nigel Copsey (Chapter 1) illustrate, Italian anarchists became pivotal transnational actors and organisers. The anarchist and anti-fascist Camilo Berneri crisscrossed the European continent, and Italian anti-fascist radicals (either as exiles or apart of the pre-existing Italian global immigrant communities) made during the 1920s significant interventions against the spread of fascism in for example Brazil, the USA, Canada, Britain and Australia.

As a consequence of the German catastrophe in 1933 a new wave of anti-fascist exiles emerged when Weimar Germany's transnational left was dislocated to Europe, America and around the world. In Chapter 10, writing on transatlantic anti-fascism, Kasper Braskén demonstrates how in 1933 German exiles in Paris launched together with French and British intellectuals, socialists and communists completely new global solidarity networks for the benefit of the victims of German fascism. Such efforts not only revealed the true menace of German fascism, but emphasised the need to fight every form of fascism both locally and globally.

If the lessons of the 'Italian catastrophe' in 1922 had not awakened the world's public to the menace of international fascism, the rise of Nazi Germany represented the ultimate signal. Even so, most governments prioritised the need for good foreign relations with Germany and officially withheld sharp criticism of German 'internal affairs' such as the bloody crackdown of Europe's strongest labour movement and anti-Semitic persecution. For many smaller countries the new Nazi government demanded an awkward *quid pro quo* where good relations were conditional on restricting anti-fascist press coverage and demonstrations.

For the anti-fascist movement, the lessons of the Italian and German catastrophes played a significant role in the transnational anti-fascist 'space of experience' and 'horizon of expectation'.[27] The rapid rise of Mussolini's *fasci di combattimento* ('fighting leagues'), founded in March 1919, was a telling and devastating example for all anti-fascists that motivated and demanded constant vigilance. As a consequence, anti-fascism often articulated the need for pre-emptive strikes against the rise of the extreme right. As early as 1923, the *grand old lady* of German socialism and communism Clara Zetkin argued at an international anti-fascist conference in Frankfurt am Main that it was their duty to hammer into the consciousness of every worker that the fate of the Italians would become their own if they did not commence an energetic, revolutionary anti-fascist struggle. They had to crush every emerging fascist organisation in the world, before it was too late.[28]

The research on the global Italian and German immigrant diaspora communities have produced significant contributions to the global history of anti-fascism. In most cases anti-fascism and fascism have been secondary themes within larger immigration histories and in most cases the German and Italian experiences have been written within their own national boxes, in separate research environments, often inhibiting the possibilities for comparative approaches. For the USA, the research on Italian-Americans' relation to fascism and anti-fascism has been most prominent and diverse, as recently shown by Marcella Bencivenni in her study of Italian immigrant radical culture. The relation between the Italian foreign office and the Italians' relation to fascism/anti-fascism has been further developed in pioneering studies that show that Italy was deeply involved in maintaining the global Italian diaspora loyal and supportive of their native home country.[29] Still, Italian diasporic nationalism remained heterogeneous despite the fascist regime's efforts to steer it. Those Italians around the world who supported or were sympathetic to Italian fascism did not in the end have hegemony on what it meant to be Italian.[30] In a similar fashion the German anti-fascist exiles in Latin and North

America argued that they represented the 'other Germany' ('Otra Alemanias' or 'Das Andere Deutschland') that directly challenged the marriage of Nazism and German national identity.[31] However, despite the traditionally strong marriage between exile studies and anti-fascism there is a significant risk that the perspective overlooks or downplays the role of other groups and actors whose primary experience was not that of exile, but of working class solidarity, black internationalism, or anti-colonialism.

Just as nationalism and fascism were inherently entangled, so too radical anti-fascist internationalism, which in many cases was deliberately based on national frameworks and understandings. The symbolical meaning of originating from a fascist country and yet being proudly Italian, German or Spanish was of outmost importance in showing that there were alternative, anti-fascist paths and ways to embrace nationalism. Research on the ambivalent relation between the labour movement and nationalism has demonstrated that the meaning and relevance of nationalism could differ greatly between radical and more reformist labour movements around the world. Moreover, labour cannot automatically be perceived as free from prejudice and ethnic stereotyping, racism or xenophobia. The efforts to keep the labour movement 'white' was persistent in Australia, the USA and South Africa, for example, where 'non-white colonised peoples and ex-slaves' were perceived as inferior.[32]

Examples from around the world show that despite anti-racists intentions, not even radical left movements that officially endorsed anti-racism and interracial solidarity managed to completely abolish prejudices within their movements.[33] Moreover, segregation in the metropoles of the world caused major, although not insurmountable, obstacles to inter-ethnic co-operation and solidarity.[34] Despite these contrasts, anti-fascism could in its time result in unprecedented 'interracial' demonstrations, like in New York City where Italian and African-Americans marched together in solidarity in protest against the Italian invasion of Ethiopia.[35] Clearly the resistance against fascist Italy was not only a matter for Italians, just as resistance against Nazi Germany was not something restricted to Germans. Similarly, the persecution of the Jews in Germany was not merely a concern for the Jewish diaspora, but a general human rights issue of major concern for any ethnic or religious minority facing the repression of the majority rule, or those who shared socialist, liberal or progressive mind-sets.

We hold that anti-fascism cannot be analysed as a rigid ideology, but as a cultural and political project that above all manifested itself in the formation of a left-liberal political identity that was neither defined by a nation, a people, a race, nor a party. Anti-fascist campaigns had the potential to at least momentarily unite communists, anarchists, socialists, democrats, liberals and anti-colonialists against fascism across borders and in diverse metropolitan spaces.

But just as class and national belonging were crucial factors in the forging of anti-fascist alliances, so too was the question of gender. Women, irrespective of their national background or social class could agree on the need to protest against fascist and Nazi gender models. The debate about the role of women in society played a vital role for anti-fascists as fascism proscribed a very limited role to women by placing them back in the home environment as mothers and caretakers. A vital global mission of the anti-fascist movement was thus connected to the female question.[36] As revealed by Sana Tannoury-Karam in Chapter 7, on anti-fascism in Syria and Lebanon, the writer and poet Maqbula al-Shalaq raised in the name of Arab women the question 'what kind of woman who has a heart does not resent fascism?' It shows how liberal-left Arab women were, in inventive ways, pairing anti-fascism with the quest 'for national independence from colonialism, democracy, progress, and women's rights'.[37]

Just as the role of women was contested, so to was the fascist promulgation of an extremely militarised ideal of masculinity in the form of new fascist virility.[38] This was especially so in relation to young men who were militarised to the extreme in fascist societies where young boys were disciplined and drilled, idolised as soldiers and bred into loyal servants of the fascist leader. The question of how fascism was breeding war, or even *needed* war to survive, naturally connected anti-fascism to anti-war movements during the 1930s. Still, it is important to keep in mind that anti-fascism was by no means a pacifist mission as it advocated the right to defend society against fascist aggressions, by violent means if necessary. This preparedness could take expression in local street battles against fascist bands, whether in Sao Paulo, Johannesburg or London, but it could also inspire young men and women to make their way to Spain to fight fascism directly. In the process, a highly militarised anti-fascist iconography was also created that was directly connected to a vision of communist/leftist masculinity. Typically the anti-fascist male figure was showing his muscles, he was equipped with a resolute will, and armed with the tools of his craft – hammers, tools, or perhaps only with his clenched fists, as posters and illustrations from around the world show.[39]

According to Thierry Pillon, the image of the 'strong, masculine workforce, ready for labor and fighting' became a fundamental feature of the early 20th century imaginary of the working class.[40] The German Communist Party (KPD) formed a party culture where the 'male productive labor and male physical prowess' was made into the revolutionary ideal, which was also seen as a model around the world. In the worst case this led to the representation of women as passive objects, oppressed and functioning as representations of capitalist exploitation. Although the image of the passive woman was recurrent, the communists also depicted them as active fighters, as mothers and proletarian versions of the emancipated new woman of the 1920s.[41] The communists' militaristic ethos was intensified by the direct interaction with the Nazis and it idealised street combat and constructed an image of a combative and heroic male proletarian.[42] Although violent confrontations were an important element of a certain 'culture of radicalism', one should be careful to make too literal translations of anti-fascist visual representations: The depiction of workers physically 'fighting fascism' did not necessarily mean that fascism had to be *physically* crushed, just that there was a militant preparedness to defend themselves. Moreover, violence was never more than *one* of several anti-fascist practices, and not necessarily the most important one.[43] The figurative smashing of the fascist enemy could equally be realised through an intense *cultural* battle, through humour, satire and the 'de-masking' of fascist slogans and solutions. Throughout the interwar period, the anti-fascist movement had a strong belief in the power of propaganda and 'political education': if the cultural and political battle was fought successfully, it could have the power to disintegrate the fascist appeal and eradicate the need for physical confrontation.

The structure of the book

The chapters in the volume have been divided into two parts. In Part I, 'Globalising Anti-Fascist Geographies', we present a number of case studies localising anti-fascist histories in the USA, Canada, Australia, Brazil, the Caribbean, the Nordic Countries, South Africa, India, Syria and Lebanon. They bring to light new knowledge about anti-fascist practices, and the establishment and development of anti-fascist alliances beyond traditional Eurocentric parameters. By bringing together cases from such diverse, but often overlooked geographies, it forms a basis for new global comparisons. They also demonstrate the diverse articulations of anti-fascism in different contexts and permits a focus on connections which have often been ignored or downplayed.

Nigel Copsey (Chapter 1) opens the volume with an analysis of resistance to Mussolini's fascism among Italian immigrant and exile communities. This chapter maintains that in order to understand anti-fascism as a global historical phenomenon, historians should start with reactions to fascism in the 1920s, rather than the 1930s. Italy was the birthplace of the fascist and anti-fascist struggle, but as Copsey shows, this struggle soon had global reach, extending to Italian diasporic communities across several continents. Focusing on four cases from the English-speaking world (US, Canada, Britain, Australia), this chapter reveals how anarchists formed the vanguard of the earliest anti-fascist opposition. Copsey underscores the importance of radical fulcra, key figures emerging as anti-fascist figureheads. The networks created by immigrant anti-fascists such as Italians, Germans, Spaniards and Portuguese in Brazil are also central to João Fábio Bertonha's Chapter 2. It also develops a broader contribution in the way that it emphasises the bridge between national and international concerns and how the opposition against fascism in Brazil was both a national struggle and a global one.

In Chapter 3 Sandra Pujals follows anti-fascist trajectories to the Caribbean and examines the evolution of the Communist International's Caribbean Bureau and its anti-war effort in the Caribbean Basin during the first half of the 1930s. The discussion underscores the role of Comintern-supported, anti-imperialist initiatives in Latin America and the Caribbean as an inadvertent testing ground for future anti-fascist propaganda campaigns during the Spanish Civil War and the Second World War at both sides of the Atlantic. It also focuses on the transmission of ideas that subliminally equated the heinous nature of imperialism to that of fascism. The work contributes to the understanding of anti-fascism's labyrinthine complexities beyond the traditional ideological divide, as an example of the unexpected geographical dimensions of the so-called 'transnational world' of communist internationalism and its intricate interpersonal networks.

Jonathan Hyslop (Chapter 4) introduces us to the history of anti-fascism in South Africa where the Nazi seizure of power elicited a movement of protest and boycotts from mainly white leftist, liberal and Jewish organisations. He argues that the construction of anti-fascist politics in South Africa was fundamentally shaped by the racialised dynamics of the country and that while in some small liberal circles and united front movements people of different races came together in the main there were *different* black and white anti-fascisms. He argues that Black nationalists in particular mobilised the discourse of wartime anti-fascism for their own goals of national liberation and he signals the importance of relations between anti-fascist ideas and the struggles against apartheid.

In Chapter 5, Kasper Braskén brings the analysis to an often overlooked corner of Europe, where Hitler's seizure of power provided the impetus to stage one of the worlds' first, but almost completely overlooked, international anti-fascist conference in April 1933. The chapter shows that the establishment of the Third Reich, on the one hand, vitalised anti-fascism in Scandinavia but that it paradoxically, on the other, further sharpened communist critique of reformist social democracy and empowered social democratic anti-communism. Moreover, small neutral states, especially with social democratic governments, were confronted with an acute dilemma as the German foreign office made it clear that sharp critique of Nazi Germany and Hitler in the Nordic press and anti-fascism 'from below' had to be limited in order to maintain good bilateral relations.

Michele L. Louro's contribution (Chapter 6) positions India's independence struggle in relation to a wider world of anti-fascists and anti-imperialists. She focuses on the foreign department of the Indian National Congress which concentrated on developing and strengthening India's ties to anti-fascist movements abroad and providing support for struggles in Ethiopia, Spain, and China during the second part of the 1930s. Louro offers both a study of the ways the INC Foreign Department leveraged international connections to strengthen India's anti-colonial resistance, as well as the significant role played by India in the global anti-fascist struggle in the 1930s.

Sana Tannoury-Karam (Chapter 7) closes the first part of the volume with a significant analysis of Arab leftists who opposed Nazism and fascism during the 1930s and 1940s, examining how they organised against, debated, and rejected fascism and Nazism. It argues that the threat of fascism pushed leftists to re-examine the meaning of the 'national' and to reposition themselves vis-à-vis the rest of the world. Leftists who framed anti-fascism as an active form of the national liberation struggle saw the opposition to fascism as a natural product of a long Arab tradition of freedom, and as a protector to that tradition from all kinds of oppression. Her focus on the gendered politics of anti-fascism also draws attention to some of the imaginaries through which leftist struggles were articulated.

Part II of the volume, 'Transnational Lives, Radical Internationalism', offers a selection of chapters that analyse anti-fascist actors and intellectuals, international organisations, and trade unions that were vital for the circulation and mobilisation of local radical anti-fascist programs and internationalist practices across borders and continents.

In Chapter 8, David Featherstone investigates distinctive articulations of maritime spaces and organising and uses it to probe the relation between anti-fascist internationalisms and subaltern politics. It does this through engaging with the political trajectories of Black seafarers from the Caribbean and West Africa who were in contact with anti-colonial agitators such as Padmore and were integral to organisations such as the London-based Negro Welfare Association (NWA). The chapter engages in particular with activities connected to the ports of Cardiff, London and North Shields which were significant in relation to various transnational political networks around anti-fascism and anti-colonialism. It argues that some of the forms of organising shaped in relation to these ports offers potential for thinking about the global connections and trajectories that shaped anti-fascisms and some of the 'subaltern lives' that were articulated through such political activity.

Federico Ferretti (Chapter 9) uses a fine-grained engagement with life writing and radical internationalism to explore the important articulations between anarchism and anti-fascisms. He does this through addressing the life and works of Italian transnational anarchist and anti-fascist Camillo Berneri (1897–1937), murdered by Stalinist agents during the Bloody Week of Barcelona in May 1937. Berneri is here presented as an outstanding representative of an entire generation of Italian anarchists and anti-fascists. Ferretti argues that the analysis of spaces of exile and transnational solidarity networks are paramount for understanding the trajectories of anarchist anti-fascism between the two world wars.

Kasper Braskén's second chapter (Chapter 10) offers a new analysis of two communist-led, international organisations called the World Committee against War and Fascism and the World Relief Committee for the Victims of German Fascism. It shows how anti-Nazi activities were initially mobilised in the USA from 1933 to 1935 and reveals the transnational connections present in American anti-fascist movements. It shows the importance of the connections established between American anti-fascists and German, British and French anti-fascists before the beginning of the popular front period, especially highlighting the role of German exiles who played a significant role in inspiring local anti-Nazi activism across the USA.

In Chapter 11, Bernhard H. Bayerlein continues to examine the history of the Comintern and the Soviet Union and offers a closer analysis of two almost simultaneous but at first sight contradictory events that took place in Africa and Latin America in 1935. The chapter contends that both events mark a transformation process of the Soviet Union and international communism in the context of Mussolini's imperial war against Ethiopia. When it began in October 1935 it was unofficially backed by the Soviet Union and anti-fascism was only half-heartedly mobilised in defence of Abyssinia by the Comintern and efforts to react from below were squandered by the communists. It seems therefore a contradiction that one month later, the Comintern supported a military uprising in Brazil against the government of Getúlio Vargas. Bayerlein argues that the uprising of the *Aliança Libertadora Nacional* (ALN) in Brazil and the Abyssinian case finally revealed the abandonment of anti-fascism and anticolonialism by Soviet-style party communism.

Hugo García (Chapter 12) shifts the focus to the Spanish Civil War and examines the discourse and actions of the activists who supported – or refused to support – the Spanish Republic as combatants, relief workers or intellectuals, focusing on their conceptions of anti-fascism. Thus, it tries to move beyond existing international histories of the war to gauge the extent to which a transnational imagined community built on this notion operated throughout this period, its relations to parallel movements in various regions and its changing contours. While the often invoked 'Anti-fascist International' never achieved actual unity or a truly global reach, García argues that it served as an effective bond between disparate actors and projects and had a considerable performative force in sustaining Republican resistance throughout the conflict.

The intersections between international anti-colonial and anti-fascist struggle in relation to the Spanish Civil War are explored by Cathy Bergin in Chapter 13, based on the writings of African American radicals. The anti-colonial call which had been earlier mobilised in the face of fascist aggression in Ethiopia was seized upon in the context of Franco's Spain. By the late 1930s *The Crisis* could claim that in Harlem 'Spanish Freedom and Negro freedom were made to be synonymous' and nearly 100 African Americans joined what is now referred to as the Abraham Lincoln Brigade to fight for the Spanish Republic. The chapter shows that the links made between racism and fascism by black activists were informed by the lived experience of 'race' in the US and also by the ambitious and dynamic race/class politics of the black Left. As victims of the 'domestic fascism' of Jim Crow many of these activists pointed to their vanguard role in fighting fascism at home and abroad and presented an anti-fascist vision which was dependent on anti-racist transnationalism.

In the final chapter, Ariel Mae Lambe (Chapter 14) investigates Cuban medical volunteers on the side of the Republic during the Spanish Civil War. Cuba offered overall more volunteers than any other Latin America country and their international solidarity work produced a large, vibrant, domestically sited but transnationally linked movement of Cuban anti-fascism. Lambe presents the stories of six individual Cuban men and women who served as medical volunteers in Spain, and explores several broad and important themes of Cuban anti-fascism: the significance of Cuban anti-fascists' transnational identities and experiences, the way in which they situated their anti-fascism in Cuban domestic politics, and the nature of their connections to the international left during the Spanish Civil War.

The combined result of the chapters presented above is to demonstrate the urgent need to re-think anti-fascism from a global perspective. Although it is impossible to produce a total global overview in such a volume, the chapters certainly point the way for a comprehensive globalisation of 'anti-fascist studies' that finally breaks it free from Eurocentric perspectives that until now have hidden significant varieties of global anti-fascist articulations. In this respect we hope that the volume will open up new debates and stimulate related work on different articulations of anti-fascism.

After 1945

This book has a clearly defined pre-1945 focus but we accept that like fascism, anti-fascism did not die in 1945. After 1945, in the post-war reconstruction, anti-fascism was deployed instrumentally as a way to legitimate regime transition from fascism to democracy. As a result one of the key ways in which anti-fascism was understood during the Cold War, was through a lens of 'bifurcated' anti-fascism, where anti-fascism in the East meant something rather different to anti-fascism in the West. Such an imaginary of anti-fascism is captured by Stein Ugelvik Larsen who argued that, 'Anti-fascism in the East meant opposing fascism and capitalism, while anti-fascism in West meant opposing totalitarianism i.e. communism.'[44] Anti-fascism in Eastern Europe, continued to retain central importance as a mechanism for regime legitimation. In the West/Western Europe there were diverse articulations of anti-fascism and different attitudes to anti-fascist ideas and legacies. Thus significant pressures were exerted on the memory of anti-fascism which in many contexts became actively silenced in processes that are ongoing.[45] This was a particular issue in relation to the post-war rehabilitation of Franco's Spain and in relation to the fascist/reactionary dictatorships in Greece and Portugal.[46]

Anti-fascist ideas and solidarities were not, however, neatly contained within the polarising logics of the Cold War and shaped important transnational geographies of solidarity. The Czech dissident Jiří Pelikán, who was part of Dubcek's reforming government in the 1960s and went into exile in Italy after the Prague spring in 1968, argued after the coup against Salvador Allende's Popular Unity government in September 1973 that 'Fascism is simply fascism, no matter under which label it operates, whether it rages in Chile or Czechoslovakia'.[47] The lens of fascism was widely used to understand the regimes of Pinochet in Chile, Galtieri in Argentina – and also in central American contexts such as Guatemala.[48] The Southern Cone dictatorships (Argentina, Chile and Uruguay) fashioned themselves as the 'successors to interwar fascism' and welcomed also a number of ex-Nazis and far-right militants and encouraged co-operation with Italian, German and Spanish militant far right groups during the Cold War era. They believed themselves to be engaged in a 'Third World War' that continued the fight against the subversive forces of global communism.[49] The role of the USA in the establishment of right-wing authoritarian regimes not least in Latin and Central America, did not go unnoticed by the global left, where for example Noam Chomsky and Edward S. Herman developed during the 1970s a radical and controversial thesis on 'Third World Fascism' which fiercely denounced US neo-colonialism.[50]

Anti-fascism also became an influential framework for human rights campaigns for Chile. Kim Christeans argues that the idea of an anti-fascist struggle created a shared identity between Europe and Chile:

> Campaigns represented Pinochet and his uniformed soldiers as SS officers, and when the new Chilean ambassador to France arrived in Paris, activists hoisted the Nazi flag. Chilean exiles contributed to this connection: iconic figures of the Chilean opposition, such as Allende's widow and daughter, visited World War II memorials in the West and East, and when Chile Democrático launched appeals for international solidarity, it did this by calling for the formation of an 'anti-fascist front' after the example of the resistance against Nazi Germany.[51]

Attending to the diverse histories and geographies of connection which have shaped anti-fascist solidarities in different contexts is of particular relevance given the post-millennial rise of right-wing authoritarian populism has allowed anti-fascism to reclaim substance and impetus. As Geoff Eley notes in his essay 'Fascism Then and Now' in the *2016 Socialist Register*, the present

> contains a profoundly different order of crisis than the original ones of the interwar, with a different set of state/society relations, different categories of political actors, different types of possible political agency, different forms and processes of publicness (of the possible ways of becoming public) and a different surrounding environment of capitalism, all of which have the effect of calling up a different set of coercively authoritarian political interventions and modalities than before.[52]

In the USA, the surprise election of Donald Trump emboldened the far right, occasioning a surge in a militant counter-protest movement known as 'ANTIFA'. Taking the form of a loosely organised, autonomous global network of leftists – anarchists, communists, socialists – this movement, with its own aesthetic and subculture, ANTIFA has located its contemporary struggle in a history of popular anti-fascist resistance. Significantly, reference has been drawn to the symbols and iconography of the interwar period. Popular slogans of that era, such as 'No Pasaran!', derived from the battle-cry of 'Los fascistas no pasarán! NO PASARÁN!' attributed to a speech by Dolores Ibárruri on Radio-Madrid in July 1936, have been immortalised across the globe. Equating the anti-fascist cause with popular self-defence, ANTIFA claim that 'no platforming' through force is a legitimate act of self-defence.

Critics, however, take ANTIFA as a synonym for aggressive violence, or even, as in the case of Republicans in the US, seek to designate ANTIFA a domestic 'terror organisation'. Such 'anti-anti-fascist' definitions not only draw *false* moral equivalency between fascism and anti-fascism – there is lack of equivalence – they also negate the multifarious 'varieties of anti-fascism'[53] that are just as present today as they were in the 1920s and 1930s. This also speaks to a contemporary terrain of transnational solidarities emerging in response to the far right/fascism and making important connections between anti-fascist struggles in different contexts. In this regard Eley's essay largely stays in the confines of an understanding of fascism and anti-fascism within a broadly European/American centred frame. The current global political conjuncture, however suggests the importance of making connections between struggles against far-right and fascist leaders in different contexts whether this be Brazil, the US or India.[54] In this context exploring the transnational histories of anti-fascism is important in terms of articulations of different anti-fascist internationalisms/left solidarities. Understanding and recognising the diverse political trajectories of anti-fascism is an important political and intellectual project. For a century on from the founding of the first *fascio di combattimento*, it is clear that the history of fascism and anti-fascism is still to be resolved.

Notes

1 See further in Chapter 2, this volume.
2 See Chapter 4, this volume.
3 A good example is the fine song 'The Ghosts of Cable Street' by the English folk-punk band the Men They Couldn't Hang, which was released on their album *How Green is the Valley?* on RCA Records in 1986.
4 For edited volumes focused on fascism beyond Europe see, Francis R. Nicosia and Boğaç A. Ergene (eds), *Nazism, The Holocaust, and the Middle East: Arab and Turkish Responses* (New York: Berghahn Books, 2018); Gert Sørensen and Robert Mallett (eds), *International Fascism, 1919–45* (London: Frank Cass, 2002); Stein Larsen Ugelvik (ed.) *Fascism Outside Europe: The European Influence against Domestic Conditions in the Diffusion of Global Fascism* (New York: Columbia University Press, 2001).
5 Benjamin Zachariah, 'A Voluntary Gleichschaltung? Indian Perspectives Towards a non-Eurocentric Understanding of Fascism', *Transcultural Studies*, No. 2, 2014, pp. 63–100, quote on p. 61.
6 Hugo García, Mercedes Yusta, Xavier Tabet, and Cristina Clímaco (eds), *Rethinking Antifascism: History, Memory and Politics, 1922 to the Present* (New York: Berghahn Books, 2016).
7 For recent exceptions, see Joseph Fronczak, 'Local People's Global Politics: A Transnational History of the Hands off Ethiopia Movement of 1935', *Diplomatic History*, Vol. 39, No. 2, 2015, pp. 245–274; Neelam Srivastava, 'Anti-Colonialism and the Italian Left: Resistances to the Fascist Invasion of Ethiopia', *Interventions* Vol. 8, No. 3, 2006, pp. 413–429; Denise Lynn, 'Fascism and the Family: American Communist Women's Anti-fascism During the Ethiopian Invasion and Spanish Civil War', *American Communist History*, Vol. 15, No. 2, 2016, pp. 177–190.
8 Richard Iton, *In Search of the Black Fantastic: Politics and Popular Culture in the Post-Civil Rights Era* (Oxford, Oxford University Press, 2008), pp. 301–302n47, see also Paul Gilroy, *Against Race: Imagining Political Culture Beyond the Color Line* (Cambridge, MA: Harvard University Press, 2001); Robin D.G. Kelley 'Introduction', in Aime Cesaire, *Discourse on Colonialism* (New York: Monthly Review Press, 2000); Robbie Shilliam 'Ah, we have not forgotten Ethiopia: Anti-Colonial Sentiments for Spain in a Fascist Era', in Gurminder K. Bhambra and John Naryan (eds), *European Colonialism: Colonial Histories and Postcolonial Societies* (London: Routledge, 2016).
9 George Padmore, 'Fascism in the Colonies', 1938, online at www.marxists.org/archive/padmore/1938/fascism-colonies.htm1938. See further Chapter 8, this volume.
10 Leslie James, *George Padmore and Decolonization From Below: Pan-Africanism, the Cold War and the End of Empire* (London: Palgrave Macmillan), p. 43.

11 See also Michele L. Louro, *Comrades against Imperialism: Nehru, India, and Interwar Internationalism* (Cambridge: Cambridge University Press, 2018).
12 Stanislao Pugliese (ed.) *Italian Fascism and Antifascism: A Critical Anthology* (Manchester: Manchester University Press, 2001); Gilles Vergnon, *L'antifascisme en France de Mussolini à Le Pen* (Rennes: Presses universitaires de Rennes, 2009); Hugo García, *The Truth about Spain! Mobilizing British Public Opinion, 1936–1939* (Brighton: Sussex Academic Press, 2010); Hans Coppi and Stefan Heinz (eds), *Der vergessene Widerstand der Arbeiter: Gewerkschaftler, Kommunisten, Sozialdemokraten, Trotzkisten, Anarchisten und Zwangsarbeiter* (Berlin: Karl Dietz Verlag, 2012); Francis R. Nicosia & Lawrence D. Stokes (eds), *Germans against Nazism: Nonconformity, Opposition and Resistance in the Third Reich: Essays in Honour of Peter Hoffmann* (New York: Berghahn, 2015); Nigel Copsey, *Anti-Fascism in Britain* (Abingdon: Routledge, 2017).
13 Nigel Copsey, 'Communists and the Inter-War Anti-Fascist Struggle in the United States and Britain', *Labour History Review,* Vol. 76, No. 3, 2011, pp. 184–206.
14 Minkah Makalani, *In the Cause of Freedom: Radical Black Internationalism from Harlem to London* (Durham, NC: University of North Carolina Press, 2011); Christopher Vials, *Haunted by Hitler: Liberals, the Left, and the Fight against Fascism in the United States* (Amherst, MA: University of Massachusetts Press, 2014); Susan D. Pennybacker, *From Scottsboro to Munich: Race and Political Culture in 1930s Britain* (Princeton, NJ: Princeton University Press, 2009).
15 Micheal Seidman, *Transatlantic Antifascisms: From the Spanish Civil War to the End of World War II* (Cambridge: Cambridge University Press, 2018).
16 Tom Buchanan, '"The Dark Millions in the Colonies are Unavenged": Anti-Fascism and Anti-Imperialism in the 1930s', *Contemporary European History*, Vol. 25, No. 4, 2016, pp. 645–665.
17 Daniel Brückenhaus, *Policing Transnational Protest: Liberal Imperialism and the Surveillance of Anticolonialists in Europe, 1905–1945* (Oxford: Oxford University Press, 2017), pp. 194–207.
18 John Callaghan, 'Storm over Asia. Comintern Colonial Policy in the Third Period', in Matthew Worley (ed.) *In Search of Revolution: International Communist Parties in the Third Period* (London: I. B. Tauris, 2004), pp. 29–33.
19 Evan Smith, 'Against Fascism, For Racial Equality: Communists, Anti-Racism and the Road to the Second World War in Australia, South Africa and the United States', *Labor History*, Vol. 58, No. 5, 2017, p. 687–688. All quotes from Smith, p. 688.
20 Theo Pirker (ed.) *Komintern und Faschismus: Dokumente zur Geschichte und Theorie des Faschismus* (Stuttgart: Deutsche Verlags-Anstalt, 1965); David Beetham (ed.) *Marxists in Face of Fascism: Writings of Marxists on Fascism from the Inter-War Period* (Manchester: Manchester University Press, 1983); Larry Ceplair, *Under the Shadow of War: Fascism, Anti-Fascism, and Marxists, 1918–1939* (New York: Columbia University Press, 1987); Leonid Luks, *Entstehung der kommunistischen Faschismustheorie: Die Auseinandersetzung der Komintern mit Faschismus und Nationalsozialismus 1921–1935* (Stuttgart: Deutsche Verlags-Anstalt, 1985); Bernhard H. Bayerlein, 'Abschied von einem Mythos: Die UdSSR, die Komintern und der Antifaschismus', *Osteuropa,* Vol. 59, No. 7–8, 2009, pp. 125–148; Stanley G. Payne, 'Soviet Anti-Fascism: Theory and Practice, 1921–45', *Totalitarian Movements and Political Religions*, Vol. 4, No. 2, 2003, pp. 1–62.
21 See, for example, Jonathan Hyslop, 'German seafarers, anti-fascism and the anti-Stalinist left: the "Antwerp Group" and Edo Fimmen's International Transport Workers' Federation, 1933–1940', *Global Networks*, Vol. 19, No. 4, 2019, pp. 499–520.
22 Robert J. Alexander, *The Anarchists in the Spanish Civil War*, vol. 1 & 2 (London: Janus Publishing Company, 1998); Michael Alpert, *A New International History of the Spanish Civil War* (Houndmills: Palgrave Macmillan, 2004); Rob Stradling, 'English-speaking Units of the International Brigades: War, Politics and Discipline', *Journal of Contemporary History*, Vol. 45, No. 4, 2010, pp. 744–767; Nir Arielli, 'Induced to Volunteer? The Predicament of Jewish Communists in Palestine and the Spanish Civil War', *Journal of Contemporary History*, Vol. 46, No. 4, 2011, pp. 854–870; Dieter Nelles et al. (eds), *Deutsche AntifaschistInnen in Barcelona (1933–1939): Die Gruppe 'Deutsche*

Anarchosyndikalisten' (DAS) (Heidelberg: Verlag Graswurzelrevolution, 2013); David Featherstone, 'Black Internationalism, International Communism and Anti-Fascist Political Trajectories: African American Volunteers in the Spanish Civil War', *Twentieth Century Communism*, No. 7, 2014, pp. 9–40; Robin D. G. Kelley, *Race Rebels: Culture, Politics and the Black Working Class* (New York: Free Press, 1996); Lisa A. Kirschenbaum, *International Communism and the Spanish Civil War: Solidarity and Suspicion* (Cambridge: Cambridge University Press, 2015); Svend Rybner, 'Fairyland: Nordic Communism and the Spanish Civil War 1936–1939', in Åsmund Egge and Svend Rybner (eds), *Red Star in the North: Communism in the Nordic Countries* (Stamsund: Orkana Akademisk, 2015); Maria Framke, 'Political Humanitarianism in the 1930s: Indian Aid for Republican Spain', *European Review of History*, Vol. 23, No. 1–2, 2016, pp. 63–81; Adam Hochschild, *Spain in Our Hearts: Americans in the Spanish Civil War, 1936–1939* (Boston, MA: Houghton Mifflin Harcourt, 2017); Mark Falcoff and Fredrick B. Pike (eds), *The Spanish Civil War, 1936–39: American Hemispheric Perspectives* (Lincoln, NE: University of Nebraska Press, 1982); Ariel Mae Lambe, *No Barrier Can Contain It: Cuban Antifascism and the Spanish Civil War* (Chapel Hill, NC: The University of North Carolina Press, 2020).

23 See the contributions by Gleb J. Albert, Bernhard H. Bayerlein, Fredrik Petersson, Holger Weiss and Kasper Braskén in Holger Weiss (ed.), *International Communism and Transnational Solidarity: Radical Networks, Mass Movements and Global Politics, 1919–1939* (Leiden: Brill, 2017).

24 Bryan D. Palmer, 'American Communism in the 1920s: Striving for a Panoramic View', *American Communist History* Vol. 6, No. 2, 2007, pp. 139–149.

25 David Featherstone, Solidarity: *Hidden Histories and Geographies of Internationalism* (London: Zed Books, 2012); Kasper Braskén, *The International Workers' Relief, Communism, and Transnational Solidarity: Willi Münzenberg in Weimar Germany* (Basingstoke: Palgrave Macmillan, 2015); Sabine Dullin and Brigitte Studer, 'Communism + Transnational: The Rediscovered Equation of Internationalism and the Comintern Years', *Twentieth Century Communism*, No. 14, 2018, pp. 66–95.

26 Alexander de Grand, '"To Learn Nothing and To Forget Nothing": Italian Socialism and the Experience of Exile Politics, 1935–1945', *Contemporary European History*, Vol. 14, No. 4, 2005, pp. 539–558.

27 Reinhart Koselleck, *Futures Past: On the Semantics of Historical Time* (New York: Columbia University Press, 2004).

28 Kasper Braskén, 'Making Antifascism Transnational: The Origins of Communist and Socialist Articulations of Resistance in Europe, 1923–1924', *Contemporary European History*, Vol. 25, No. 4, 2016, p. 583.

29 Marcella Bencivenni, *Italian Immigrant Radical Culture: The Idealism of the Sovversivi in the United States, 1890–1940* (New York: New York University Press, 2011). See also Donna R. Gabaccia and Fraser M. Ottanelli (eds), *Italian Workers of the World: Labor Migration and the Formation of Multiethnic States* (Urbana, IL: University of Illinois Press, 2001); João Fábio Bertonha, 'Fascism and Italian Communities in Brazil and the United States', *Italian Americana*, Vol. 19, No. 2, 2001, pp. 146–157; Philip V. Cannistraro and Gerald Meyer (eds), *The Lost World of Italian American Radicalism: Politics, Labor, and Culture* (London: Preager, 2003); Pellegrino Nazzaro, *Fascist and Anti-Fascist Propaganda in America: The Dispatches of Italian Ambassador Gelasio Caetani* (Amherst, MA: Cambria Press, 2008); and Stefano Luconi, 'Fascism and Italian-American Identity Politics', *Italian Americana*, Vol. 33, No. 1, 2015, pp. 6–24.

30 Michael Goebel, 'Italian Fascism and Diasporic Nationalism in Argentina, Brazil, and Uruguay', in Nicola Foote and Michael Goebel (eds), *Immigration and National Identities in Latin America* (Gainesville, FL: University Press of Florida, 2014).

31 For the German speaking world there is a rich tradition of exile studies, pursued after 1945 by both East German and Western historians. Major works include Wolfgang Kießling, *Exil in Lateinamerika* (Leipzig: Verlag Philipp Reclam jun., 1980); Patrik von zur Mühlen, *Fluchtziel Lateinamerika: Die deutschen Emigration 1933–1945: Politische*

Aktivitäten und soziokulturelle Integration (Bonn: Verlag Neue Gesellschaft, 1988); Helga Grebing and Christl Wickert (eds), *Das 'andere Deutschland' im Widerstand gegen den Nationalsozialismus: Beiträge zur politischen Überwindung der nationalsozialistischen Diktatur im Exil und im Dritten Reich* (Essen: Klartext Verlag, 1994); Jean-Michel Palmier, *Weimar in Exile: The Antifascist Emigration in Europe and America* (London: Verso, 2006); Andreas Agocs, *Antifascist Humanism and the Politics of Renewal in Germany* (Cambridge: Cambridge University Press, 2017). Ongoing major projects dealing with German speaking exiles in Latin America promises to globalise the research topic even further, as shown by Andrea Acle-Kreysing, 'Shattered Dreams of Anti-Fascist Unity: German Speaking Exiles in Mexico, Argentina and Bolivia, 1937–1945', *Contemporary European History*, Vol. 25, No. 4, 2016, pp. 667–686.

32 Stefan Berger & Angel Smith, 'Between Scylla and Charybdis: Nationalism, Labour and Ethnicity Across Five Continents, 1870–1939', in Stefan Berger & Angel Smith (eds), *Nationalism, Labour and Ethnicity 1870–1939* (Manchester: Manchester University Press, 1999), pp. 1–30.; Oleksa Drachewych, *The Communist International, Anti-Imperialism and Racial Equality in British Dominions* (London: Routledge, 2019).

33 Joachim C. Häberlen, 'Between Global Aspirations and Local Realities: The Global Dimensions of Interwar Communism', *Journal of Global History*, Vol. 7, No. 3 (2012), pp. 415–437. See also Lucien van der Walt, 'The First Globalisation and Transnational Labour Activism in Southern Africa: White Labourism, the IWW, and the ICU, 1904–1934', *African Studies*, Vol. 66, No. 2/3, 2007, pp. 223–251.

34 Carl H. Nightingale, *Segregation: A Global History of Divided Cities* (Chicago, IL: The University of Chicago Press, 2012).

35 Gerald Meyer, 'Italian Americans and the American Communist Party', in Philip V. Cannistraro and Gerald Meyer (eds), *The Lost World of Italian American Radicalism: Politics, Labor, and Culture* (London: Preager, 2003), p. 221.

36 Lynn, 'Fascism and the Family'; Isabelle Richet, 'Women and Antifascism: Historiographical and Methodological Approaches', in Hugo García et al. (eds), *Rethinking Antifascism: History, Memory and Politics, 1922 to the Present* (New York: Berghahn Books, 2016), pp. 152–166.; Mercedes Yusta, 'The Strained Courtship between Antifascism and Feminism: From the Women's World Committee (1934) to the Women's International Democratic Federation (1945)', in Hugo García et al. (eds), *Rethinking Antifascism: History, Memory and Politics, 1922 to the Present* (New York: Berghahn Books, 2016), pp. 167–184.

37 Quotation from Chapter 7, this volume.

38 Johann Chapoutot, 'Fascist Virility', in Alain Corbin, Jean-Jaques Courtine & Georges Vigarello (eds), *A History of Virility* (New York: Columbia University Press, 2016), pp. 491–514.

39 Gerhard Paul, *BilderMACHT: Studien zur Visual History des 20. und 21. Jahrhunderts* (Göttingen: Wallstein Verlag, 2013), pp. 45–99.

40 Thierry Pillon, 'Working Class Viritlity', in Alain Corbin, Jean-Jaques Courtine & Georges Vigarello (eds), *A History of Virility* (New York: Columbia University Press, 2016), p. 515.

41 Eric D. Weitz, *Creating German Communism, 1890–1990: From Popular Protests to Socialist State* (Princeton, NJ: Princeton University Press, 1997), p. 189.

42 Ibid., pp. 200–204.

43 Tom Buchanan, '"Beyond Cable Street": New Approaches to the Historiography of Antifascism in Britain in the 1930s', in Hugo García, et al. (eds), *Rethinking Antifascism: History, Memory and Politics, 1922 to the Present* (New York: Berghahn Books, 2016), p. 69.

44 Stein Ugelvik Larsen, 'Overcoming the Past', in Stein Ugelvik Larsen (ed.), *Modern Europe After Fascism* (Boulder, CO: Social Science Monographs, 1998), p. 1787.

45 See the chapters in part II of Hugo García, et al. (eds), *Rethinking Antifascism: History, Memory and Politics, 1922 to the Present* (New York: Berghahn Books, 2016), especially those by Filippo Focardi, and Manuel Loff and Luciana Soutelo.

46 Helen Graham, *The War and its Shadow: Spain's Civil War in Europe's Long Twentieth Century* (Brighton, Sussex Academic Press, 2012); Neni Panourgiá, *Dangerous Citizens: The Greek Left and the Terror of the State* (New York: Fordham University Press, 2009).
47 Jiří Pelikán, *Socialist Opposition in Eastern Europe: the Czechoslovak Example* (London: Allison and Busby, 1976), pp. 208–209.
48 See Greg Grandin, *The Last Colonial Massacre: Latin America in the Cold War* (Chicago, IL: The University of Chicago Press, 2004); Vijay Prashad, *The Darker Nations: A People's History of the World* (New York: The New Press, 2007).
49 Kyle Burke, *Revolutionaries of the Right: Anticommunist Internationalism and Paramilitary Warfare in the Cold War* (Chapel Hill, NC: The University of North Carolina Press, 2018).
50 Noam Chomsky & Edward S. Herman, *The Washington Connection and Third World Fascism: The Political Economy of Human Rights: Volume I* (Chicago, IL: Haymarket Books, 2014).
51 Kim Christiaens, 'European Reconfigurations of Transnational Activism: Solidarity and Human Rights Campaigns on Behalf of Chile during the 1970s and 1980s', *International Review of Social History*, Vol. 63, No. 3, 2018, pp. 413–448.
52 Geoff Eley, 'Fascism Then and Now', *Socialist Register 2016* (London: Merlin Press, 2015).
53 See Nigel Copsey and Andrzej Olechnowicz (eds), *Varieties of Anti-Fascism: Britain in the Inter-War Period* (Basingstoke: Palgrave Macmillan, 2010).
54 In this respect there is a significant literature on the character of the Hindu right in India – see for example, Aijaz Ahmad, *Lineages of the Present: Ideology and Politics in Contemporary South Asia* (London: Verso, 2002); Jairus Banaji, *Fascism: Essays on Europe and India* (Three Essays Collective, 2013); Achin Vanaik *The Furies of Indian Communialism: Religion, Modernity and Secularization* (London: Verso, 1997) and the essays collected in Azad et al., *What the Nation Really Needs to Know: The JNU Nationalism Lectures* (Delhi: Harper Collins India, 2016).

PART I

Globalising anti-fascist geographies

1

RADICAL DIASPORIC ANTI-FASCISM IN THE 1920S

Italian anarchists in the English-speaking world

Nigel Copsey

Introduction

On 11 January 2018, at midday, a small group of people gathered on the corner of New York's Fifth Avenue and Fifteenth Street.[1] Passers-by were no doubt oblivious as to why this group was gathered there. Those who stopped to hear the group's speakers, and handed flyers, could learn that they were commemorating the colourful life of a fearless advocate of radical anti-fascism. At this very spot, some seventy five years earlier, Italian emigrant Carlo Tresca had been gunned down. Once described by Mussolini's political police as the '*deus ex machina* of anti-Fascism' in the United States, Carlo Tresca is now all but forgotten in his country of adoption. 'One of the greatest anti-Fascists and a man with a sole purpose, which was to rid the world of Fascism', Luigi Antonini eulogised at Tresca's funeral.[2] A tribute that suggests that Tresca deserves a place in the pantheon of Mussolini's enemies, alongside the likes of Giacomo Matteotti and Carlo Roselli, even if, in Tresca's case, he was seemingly slain by a city gangster rather than by a fascist.[3]

In the transnational vanguard of the very earliest opposition to fascism, the anarchist Carlo Tresca is emblematic of those among Italian diasporic communities who expressed their anti-fascism as radical *sovversivi* (subversives). Their anti-fascism, manifesting a decade or so before Hitler's appointment as Chancellor, should not pass without recognition. Yet historians of anti-fascism retain their blind spots when it comes to the 1920s. Christopher Vials's study of the anti-fascist tradition in the US starts *after* Hitler's accession to power in 1933;[4] Michael Seidman's *Transatlantic Antifascisms,* which claims to be the first comprehensive study of anti-fascisms in Spain, France, the United States and Britain, does not begin its account until as late as 1936.[5] And yet if we venture back to the early 1920s we find the United States as 'the first sanctuary of anti-fascism'.[6]

'He carried on a one-man war against Fascism long before the rest of the United States joined him', the *New York Times* opined when reporting on Tresca's murder.[7] Such was Tresca's anti-fascist prescience that freelance writer, Dorothy Gallagher, would dub Tresca 'the most premature of "premature" anti-Fascists'.[8] Yet his anti-fascist struggle was neither remarkably premature nor solitary. Tresca's struggle, in truth, formed part of a much wider effort spanning several continents. As João Fábio Bertonha has previously pointed out:

> The Italian communities scattered around the globe experienced a unique situation in the period between the wars. On the one hand, they were the target of extreme propaganda from the fascist regime, which tried to reinforce ties between Italy and its emigrants. This effort, in turn, provoked reaction and militancy from anti-fascist groups, which struggled for years to keep Italians outside of Italy immune to Mussolini's propaganda.[9]

Over the period 1876–1915 no fewer than 14 million Italians left their country of birth, followed by a further 4.5 million in the period 1916 to 1945. Not only did Italians settle in large numbers in Europe but also in both North and South Americas. Some ventured further still. According to the 1921 census there were 8,135 Italians in Australia.[10] Bertonha submits that 'All of the countries to which Italians immigrated – Brazil, Canada, France, the United States, and so on – experienced this conflict between fascism and anti-fascism.'[11] While this was not strictly true, it remains true enough that wherever Italian communities were established abroad, they became subject to the competing claims of fascists and anti-fascists. This struggle, as we shall see, could sometimes turn violent, and in some cases lethal. Between 1921 and 1932, according to figures cited by Luca de Capraiis, 45 fascists abroad were killed and 283 wounded.[12] In one of the most publicised incidents, in 1924 a young anarchist, Enrico Bonomini, shot dead a 'Fascist of the first hour', Nicola Bonservizi in a Parisian restaurant.[13]

Within Italian emigrant neighbourhoods, the stage for anti-fascist opposition was often set by the arrival of black-shirted fascists. Organised into sections of the *Partito Nazionale Fascista* abroad, emigrant devotees of Mussolini were quick to form local branches of so-called *fasci all'estero* (Abroad League).[14] It has been suggested that a London *fascio* was the very first (founded in June 1921),[15] but a New York *fascio* had already been established a month or so earlier. In the United States alone, by early 1923, 85 *fascio* branches had been formed.[16] By June 1924 it was reported that there were close to 300 *fasci all'estero* in existence outside Italy, with branches 'in nearly every corner of the world'.[17]

Needless to say, for Italian left-wing radicals, the *polarising prism* through which this 'world-wide expansion' of fascism was understood was the fascist repression being meted out on comrades in Italy. According to one study, during the first six months of 1921 black-shirted squads ransacked 141 Communist and Socialist party branches in Italy. Over 70 Socialists were killed.[18] Giacomo Matteotti, in his *The Fascisti Exposed: A Year of Fascist Domination*, chronicled fascist violence in Italy, ranging from murder and severe physical assault to attacks on property. There were hundreds of such incidents during May and November 1923, two typical months.[19] Against this backdrop, that some compatriots wanted to don black-shirts on foreign soil was, unsurprisingly, sufficient stimulus for diasporic anti-fascist opposition to emerge.

Although this anti-fascism, as Bertonha makes clear, was truly global in reach, my chapter limits its scope to the response of the radical Italian diaspora in the English-speaking world: primarily to the US, but also to Canada, Britain and Australia. Here, as a result of the emotional traction that the figure of Mussolini held for diasporic expressions of 'defensive nationalism', that is to say, ethnic consciousness, pride and self-respect, anti-fascists of every hue were in the minority. Not surprisingly, when confronted with (white) nativist discrimination, most migrant Italians responded positively to the perceived 'glories' of Fascist Italy. In the US, for example, anti-fascists 'numbered not more than 10 percent of the Italian American population, if that'.[20] This would present anti-fascists, particularly those left-wing radicals who favoured world-wide proletarian revolution with a dilemma: either express anti-fascism in strict ideological terms of international class solidarity and opposition to capital, or accommodate diasporic nationalism. There were other choices to be made too. What of the nature of their militant opposition: were fascists 'to be treated as they treated anti-fascists in Italy'?[21] Of the four examples discussed in this chapter, which responses were the most violent, and why?

As we shall see, each one of my examples taken from the English-speaking world had its fulcrum (a particular figure who played a central or essential role). In the US, it was Carlo Tresca; in Canada, Attilio Bortolotti; in Britain, Emidio Recchioni; and in Australia, Francesco Carmagnola. That all four were of anarchist/anarcho-syndicalist persuasion further problematises (revisionist) conflations of inter-war anti-fascism with Stalinism.[22] It might be difficult to resist, but for sure, as Enzo Traverso put it in 2004, 'Anti-fascism cannot be reduced to a simple variation of Soviet Communism.'[23]

Before I begin to consider my four cases, some conceptual clarification is needed. The subject of 'diaspora' (from Greek, *diaspeirein* 'disperse') is typically approached through three core features: the first is dispersal in space (dispersal from the ethno-national 'homeland'); the second is an orientation to this real or 'imagined' homeland; the third is a shared ethno-national cultural identity that cuts across the boundaries of the host society or societies.[24] Within Italian diasporic communities, we can further differentiate a specific sub-type: groups of Italian leftists who formed a *radical* diaspora. This diaspora shared the secondary characteristic of a radical political culture inherited from Italy and recreated within the host society. As in the case of the United States, as Marcella Bencivenni has revealed, this culture covered a wide spectrum of ideologies: communism, anarchism, syndicalism and socialism. Since this culture traversed ideological ground, it might make more sense to speak of a *family* of radicals, or an expatriate *milieu* of radicals. The *family* of *sovversivi*, for all their ideological differences, shared an insurgent desire to overthrow capitalism, free the workers, and thereby effect equality and social justice.[25]

Resisting the 'Black Death': Italian-American anti-fascism in the 1920s

> The final goal of the [North American Anti-Fascist] Alliance is to overthrow fascism in Italy so that the whole world will go immune from the fascist virus.
>
> *(Manifesto of the North American Anti-Fascist Alliance, 26 August 1926)*

According to Pellegrino Nazzaro, the Manifesto of the North American Anti-Fascist Alliance (*Alleanza Anti-Fascista di Nord America* – AFANA) gave expression to the 'first anti-fascist campaign in the western world'.[26] Yet within the field of anti-fascist studies few historians have ever reflected upon it, no doubt the result of the wider American left demonstrating more concern with the rise of Hitler than the rise of Mussolini who, according to one historian of anti-fascism, the American left 'barely noticed'.[27]

If no doubt correct in this broader sense, within the particular milieu of Italian–American radicalism Mussolini's rise had very obvious repercussions. For Italian–American radicalism now 'redirected much of its energy toward the anti-Fascist struggle, continually challenging, and in some case instances successfully contesting, the Fascist hegemony within the community'.[28] At the forefront of this struggle was Carlo Tresca who, following a brief sojourn in Lausanne, Switzerland, emigrated to the US in 1904. In Switzerland he had met a young socialist firebrand – Benito Mussolini no less. When Tresca boarded his train to Le Havre, his point of departure for New York, it was comrade Mussolini who bade him farewell.[29]

Tresca was just one of the millions of Italians who migrated to the United States between 1880 and 1920. Most of these migrants (more than three million by 1918) originated from rural southern Italy (approximately 80 per cent); they were also disproportionately male (at a ratio of 190 males to 100 females in 1910). As copious numbers settled in North America, so Italian communities – 'Little Italies' – were established across numerous metropolitan areas. New York City was home to the largest concentrations. By 1930 the Italian-American population in the New York metropolitan area numbered over one million.[30] Largely unskilled workers, not only were Italian migrants the most proletarianised of all European migrants in the US, they were also largely ignored by a Democratic Party machine dominated by Irish Americans. Italian neighbourhoods could therefore encourage radicalisation. So if Italian radicals of various stripes comprised the militant minority within these communities, they could form a significant one nonetheless.

Most radicals became denizens of New York (although others were active elsewhere, such as in Boston, Detroit, Chicago, and San Francisco). In New York City, described as the 'Mecca of the South Italians', *sovversivi* fiefdoms could be found in the Italian Chamber of Labor led by Arturo Giovannitti; specific Italian branches or locals of the clothing workers' unions, such as locals 48 and 89 of the International Ladies Garment Workers' Union (ILGWU), the latter led by Luigi Antonini; and in groups linked to the radical Italian-language press, such as Tresca's anarcho-syndicalist paper, *Il Martello* (The Hammer), which in April 1923 had a weekly circulation of 6,500.[31] The point that needs to be made here is that the radical culture from which anti-fascism first sprung in the US was not a culture of anti-fascist exile. Like Tresca, both Giovannitti and Antonini had emigrated before the First World War and so *before* fascism.

This is not to say that there was not an influx of anti-fascist exiles between 1919 and 1924, escaping the worst of the *squadristi* violence in northern and central regions of Italy. And some newcomers joined the ranks and took up the anti-fascist struggle with zeal, such as Comintern agent Vittorio Vidali.[32] Others, however, maintained a low profile to minimise the risk of possible retribution. Many anti-fascists entering the US in the 1920s did so illegally (Vidali assumed the false name of Enea Sormenti); the threat of deportation was ever-present (Vidali was deported in July 1927). Identification as an active anti-fascist also invited intimidation of family and relatives in the home country (Italian police would amass files on some 6,000 or so Italian-Americans 'affiliated to subversive parties').[33]

In 1921, the occasion for the first violent encounter between fascists and anti-fascists on American soil was the visit to the US of a prominent fascist, Guiseppe Bottai.[34] Bottai, who was supposedly promoting an ex-servicemen's charity, revealed to the American press that he also wanted to fight 'Bolshevism' among Italian-Americans. As Nunzio Pernicone tells it:

> That he should receive the red carpet treatment was galling enough but anti-Fascists were seething because a socialist deputy had recently been murdered by Fascists, a crime that prompted Bottai to boast at a local Fascist meeting that he personally had killed five communists in Rome.[35]

Tresca used Bottai's provocative visit to turn his fire on the leaders of the new New York *fascio* group, declaring defiantly that they would never be permitted to raise their heads.[36] In a series of stormy exchanges, Tresca took to holding open-air anti-fascist rallies across New York City's Italian neighbourhoods. By early 1923 he had inaugurated a *Comitato Generale di Difesa Contro Il Fascismo* (General Defence against Fascism Committee). The rationale behind this committee was to forge greater anti-fascist unity, but only among the most radical, revolutionary elements (Tresca remained suspicious of social-democrats in the Italian trade unions).

So rather than coming directly through Tresca, the Anti-Fascist Alliance of North America (AFANA) came about through the Italian labour unions. Led by Frank Bellanca, editor of the weekly of the Amalgamated Clothing Workers' Union (ACWU), AFANA was originally launched at New York's Italian Chamber of Labor on 10 April 1923. Its stated aim was to protect American labour and the unions of Italian workmen from the spread of fascism.[37] It promised 'an insistent and unflagging campaign of publicity to enlighten American public opinion on the nature and goals of Fascism in Italy and America'.[38] But this campaign soon faltered, in part because 'we thought that fascism would be a transient movement of collective madness'.[39] It would take the murder of Giacomo Matteotti in May 1924, and then the establishment of the Fascist League of North America in July 1925, to impart AFANA with fresh momentum.

Tresca, who up until this point, 'remained personally the most effective focus of anti-Fascist resistance', now put his weight behind AFANA.[40] Working alongside the Communist Vittorio Vidali, he was convinced that the consolidation of the Fascist regime, and the growing presence of fascism within the Italian-American community, demanded broader unity. He became, as Pernicone describes him, 'anti-Fascism's most outspoken advocate of a united front'.[41] So how did this particular 'united front', singled out by Nazzaro as 'the earliest expression of an organized United Front in the struggle against fascism',[42] *frame* its anti-fascism?

If the Manifesto of the Anti-Fascist Alliance of North America, published in New York on 26 August 1926, was 'the very first common attempt by anti-Fascist forces aimed at the condemnation of Fascism, its ideology, and its tactics', it becomes my obvious point of reference.[43] Tellingly, even if the Manifesto had some 'Marxist-sounding tones',[44] it made no appeal to international class solidarity, or to proletarian revolution. Rather, this anti-fascist struggle was projected as a democratic and civilisational one, not one defined by class struggle. At its core was an appeal to civil conscience and moral values. And here we detect the 'anti-fascist minimum' that I first spoke about in 2010, that is to say, a common denominator of political and moral opposition to fascism rooted in the *democratic* values of the Enlightenment tradition.[45]

In view of Mussolini's ruthless destruction of freedoms (press; association; thought; worship), the Manifesto charged fascism with crimes of high treason against the sovereignty and liberty of the Italian people. 'The constant moral decline of the individual and popular values are pursued', it declared, 'as means towards the triumph of the idea of the *immanent nation*'. But this fascist *Italianità* (sense of being Italian) was essentially *unpatriotic*, because 'all Italian liberties – the heritage and conquest of our ancestors, philosophers, poets, martyrs, and apostles – have been first outraged and violated, then abolished and destroyed'. The Manifesto also attacked the monarchy and held the King responsible for allowing the fascistisation of the Italian state. It declared him 'dethroned' and called for a Republic.

Significantly, this Manifesto revealed a republican anti-fascism infused not with revolutionary class politics but with an alternative national imaginary. Donna Gabaccia aptly describes the nationalism intrinsic to this permutation of diasporic anti-fascism as 'a twentieth-century Italian expression of national liberation'. In the US, Italian-American anti-fascism thereby accommodated 'diasporic nationalism' by becoming 'self-consciously nationalist'.[46] This was less a struggle over class allegiance than a struggle over ethnic allegiance (after all, the fascists defined anti-fascists as 'anti-Italian'). 'We are, it is true, all Italians, we love Italy immensely, but we spit on the face of the assassins of the Italians', as one anarchist was heard to shout at a fascist during a meeting in New Haven, Connecticut, in March 1923.[47]

On the other hand, the Manifesto also made sure to embed its anti-fascism in Americanism, defining opposition to fascism as a patriotic act that constituted a defence of the values of the country of adoption (the values of freedom and equality as vested in the Declaration of Independence). So not only was a true

Italian anti-fascist, a true American was anti-fascist too. The Manifesto called on all Americans to resist the fascist tyranny, which it said, was in the process of being transplanted onto American soil through propaganda, espionage, fascist organisation, diplomatic offices, embassies, consular agencies, and so on. Fascism was a '*Black Death*',

> attempting to proselytize in many European countries and in America as well. It is trying in Greece, Spain, Poland, France, England and in the United States of America. If this monster is not strangled soon – and it should be done before it comes of age – it will undermine all liberties.[48]

It was thus incumbent on America to expel any Fascist or pro-Fascist element. Although its nefarious centre was in Rome, Fascism was projected as a *global* menace to democracy.

Nonetheless, *sovversivi* anti-fascism remained conflicted. The careful crafting of the Manifesto could not conceal underlying ideological divisions; it did nothing to stop social-democrats leaving AFANA due to perceived Communist domination (Vidali had replaced Arturo Giovannitti as secretary). In early 1927 those who abandoned AFANA formed the Anti-Fascist Federation of North America for the Freedom for Italy, supported by the ILGWU, ACWU and the Italian Chamber of Labor. In August 1928, AFANA, now firmly under the grip of Communists,

> prepared a statement which declared that Fascism was a reaction against the proletariat which wished to free itself from the bondage of capitalism. The declaration contended that it was not sufficient to defeat Mussolini alone; the capitalist system which supported him had to be destroyed too.[49]

In June 1929, in the *Labor Defender*, the AFANA's then-secretary Tom De Fazio wrote:

> FASCISM is the instrument chosen by the capitalist class to supress the revolutionary aspirations of the working class, by destroying every branch of the labor movement and disarming the proletarian forces, making possible thereby the continuation of the rule of the bourgeoisie and the exploitation of the working masses upon which the rule of the bourgeoisie is based [...] Fascism is not a force above the classes as the social democrats try to make it appear.[50]

When Mussolini signed his Concordat with the Pope in 1929, one local AFANA branch declared Catholicism 'incompatible with modern civilisation and therefore the progress of the working classes'. For Madeline Goodman, 'In one sweeping gesture, these anti-fascists severed the ideology of anti-fascism from both nationalism and religion.'[51]

If the Manifesto's condemnation of fascism had been relatively moderate, limiting itself 'to condemnation of the anti-democratic fascist trend in Italy and of the underground activities carried on by the North American Fascist League in the United States',[52] it did not mean that anti-fascist mobilisation was any less fierce. Property was raided; violent clashes were common; protagonists were murdered. According to John P. Diggins, this fascist/anti-fascist encounter claimed 'altogether over a dozen lives'.[53] Feuds were especially violent in New York City where, as Travis Tomchuk puts it, 'Tresca was in the thick of it.'[54] One of Tresca's former comrades recalled that 'Carlo had groups in all parts of the country. Here in New York there were maybe several hundred. They'd break up fascist meetings with baseball bats'.[55] Vidali also had his own communist 'action squad', implicated in the double homicide of two fascists during a Memorial Day parade in New York in 1927.[56]

So why was this particular encounter so violent? Old World influences obviously loomed large: the *sovversivi* culture of direct action that Italian radicals brought with them from Italy had been sustained over many years, particularly through workplace agitation. Labour struggles would often turn violent (the 1913 Paterson Strike, for example), so transposing direct action from one arena to another would seem normal. Then, of course, passions were further stirred by ongoing developments in the homeland. Tresca cited the repression of his comrades in Italy: 'we say we'll debate (with the fascists) when our brothers in Italy have a free press and the right to speak and meet in the streets. Until then, we do our arguing with guns.'[57] A further aggravating factor was evidently the belligerent nature of the *fasci*: many were war veterans, and therefore accustomed to violence (some were even former *squadristi*). Their hubristic local leaders were also committed to the violent destruction of the anti-fascist opposition (notwithstanding the concerns of the Italian ambassador that violence would turn US public opinion against Italy). Tresca was an obvious target for their reprisals. He 'narrowly escaped being lynched, deportation to Fascist Italy (the equivalent of a death sentence); he was stabbed in the face, viciously beaten on a number of occasions, and was the target of an attempted bombing'.[58] There may have been a broader ethno-cultural dimension too. Violence was more socially acceptable in Italian-American neighbourhoods with violent crimes ranking relatively high among Italians in New York. Comparative crime records demonstrate that they were more likely than native-born to carry weapons, commit violent assault and homicide.[59]

So what of the effects of this militant opposition? Nunzio Pernicone contends that by the end of the 1920s, if the fascists wanted to hold public demonstations, they could only do so with police protection, and so 'Tresca and the antifascists did succeed in derailing Mussolini's grandiose plan for the fascistization of Italian America'.[60] The hammer blow to the Italian Blackshirts in the US did come in 1929, but not through any physical war of attrition with radical anti-fascists. The reality was that Mussolini finally ordered the dissolution of the Fascist League following a sensationalist exposé of its activities by the journalist Marcus Duffield in *Harper's Magazine*, which then led to calls for a congressional investigation. With anti-fascists (as well as fascists) feeding information to Duffield, Tresca could claim credit: 'it was inspired in large part by us', he wrote in *Il Martello* at the very end of

December 1929.[61] Yet fascism's dissemination did not suddenly stop. In the 1930s Mussolini simply shifted the focus away from the *fasci* to a programme of cultural propaganda supported by the active engagement of community elites (the *prominenti*). This reached its point of maximum efficacy during the Ethiopian war, which for Pernicone, marked 'the apogee of Mussolini's popularity among Italian Americans and the nadir of Italian anti-Fascism'.[62] But by this time, with the rise of Hitler, the anti-fascist movement in US had already morphed into a far broader socio-political concern. Mirroring developments elsewhere, anti-fascism now found wider expression in a series of left-wing/liberal common fronts, such as the Communist-initiated American League Against War and Fascism; and lawyer Samuel Untermeyer's Non-Sectarian Anti-Nazi League (to Champion Human Rights).[63]

North of the border

Moving north, the obvious point to make is that the Italian emigrant community was much smaller. In a Canadian population of just 8.7 million, there were, according to the 1921 census, 35,531 Italian born. From 1924 to 1929 a wave of new Italian migrants arrived, so that by 1931 the census recorded a figure or 42,578 Italian born (an increase of 20 per cent on 1921). Most Italian Canadians were drawn either to Montreal or Toronto. The first *fascio* appeared in Montreal in 1925 and a year later, the *Fascio Principe Umberto* formed in Toronto. However, as Angelo Principe points out, 'During this decade, fascists and their fasci in Canada were few, weak, and existed in a constant state of struggle.'[64] Their relative weakness more the result of community indifference than the consequence of anti-fascists winning out.

According to Principe, since Italians had been in the country for some time (80 per cent for 16 years or more by the late 1920s/early 1930s), they had become largely acculturated to democracy. At first therefore, most Italian Canadians were unresponsive to fascism.[65] 'Throughout the 1920s, fascism was as foreign to Toronto's Italians', Luigi Pennacchio maintains, 'as it was to the city's non-Italians'.[66] So the earliest anti-fascists in Canada operated in a climate where fascism, and so by extension, anti-fascism, was not a pressing community concern. And there were not that many committed anti-fascists either. Tellingly, the files of the Italian Central Political Records Office in Rome identified just 111 expatriate 'subversive' radicals in Canada (compared to the 6,000 or so in the US).[67] While this figure was almost certainly an under-estimate, numbers pale into insignificance when compared to the numbers of *sovversivi* south of the border.

Even so, certain areas could still garner a reputation for 'no-nonsense' anti-fascism. One such area was Windsor, Ontario. Here the anarchist Attilio Bortolotti, considered by Rome to be one of the most 'dangerous' anti-fascists in Canada, led a combative group of anti-fascists. For João Fábio Bertonha, given its Italian working-class demographic, strength of the local left, and lesser influence of the Catholic Church, the Windsor industrial area 'could be considered a true "Italian anti-fascist city'".[68] But this misses a significant point: in this locality the radical milieu developed an obvious *trans-border* dynamic. With the cities of Windsor and Detroit only separated by the width of the Detroit River, anti-fascists from both sides of the border would divide their time between the two, confronting their foe in both border cities.

Having departed Italy as sixteen-year old, a young Bortolotti joined his elder brother in Windsor in July 1920. Unlike Tresca, however, Bortolotti's politicisation occurred later, and on North American soil. He was introduced to anarchism through a small group of compatriots in Detroit. Travelling to Detroit every Sunday to attend meetings, Bortolotti recalled becoming 'an antifascist besides calling myself an anarchist' around the time of the March on Rome.[69] Significantly, the anarchist contingent in Detroit was not aligned to Tresca but to the *antiorganizzatori* of the New York anarchist publication *L'Adunata dei Refrattari* (The Call of the Incorrigibles). This wing was deeply critical of Tresca for his role in the AFANA, and for his collaboration with communists (and so there was no formal anti-fascist 'organisation' to speak of).[70]

Accounts of the finer details are thin on the ground, but Bortolotti recalled that the struggle against fascism in Windsor had become especially heated by 1926. While in Detroit,

> In 1926 Pietro Bedus called me from Windsor to let me know that the fascists had issued a manifesto stating that the Italian consul from Toronto would be coming down to Windsor to urge all young men who had not done their army service to regularize their position: we issued a manifesto of our own, urging every antifascist to turn out. The meeting was held in the basement of a Catholic school [...] His speech was loudly applauded ... I bounced up to the platform ... and spotted the poster of King Victor Emmanuel III: in a flash, I ripped it up, screwed it up into a ball and tossed it into the consul's face. At which point a ruckus erupted, the police stepped in and my brother said to me: 'We'd better get back to Detroit right away. Otherwise you can expect a beating and you'll be charged.'[71]

After returning to live in Windsor in 1927, Bortolotti was soon back in Detroit:

> Then in 1928 the inevitable happened. The fascists wanted to march in black shirts on Columbus Day and this celebration of Italian-ness was organized by dumb ultra-Italian businessmen – most of them scoundrels who charged twice the going rate. So we organized a counter-demonstration to stop the fascists from marching in their black shirts. But in the end only eighteen of us out of the hundreds of antifascists turned out to confront around fifty to sixty black-shirted rogues. When the band struck up we attacked them and one of them who was armed opened fire, killing comrade Barra and wounding Ventricchia. I had a fascist by the hair [...] and I hid under the crates of apples for an hour, then I was called out ... and, after an hour, I was still holding the fascist's black

> hair in my hand. In spite of all this, we carried on with our propaganda as best we could, even if the fascists were becoming stronger and stronger and besides, they had the backing of the Church.[72]

If the AFANA Manifesto appealed to an alternative construction of diasporic nationalism, were similar concessions to Italian nationalism made north of the border? Did the radical diaspora in Canada become 'self-consciously nationalist', offering an alternative *Italianità*? The picture is incomplete, although it is certainly worth taking note of Montreal's leading anti-fascist Antonio Spada's comments that 'I have never been a nationalist, and fascism was a rhetorical and pompous form of nationalism.'[73] In September 1929 a 'near-riot' broke out when the Italian vice-consul of Toronto was confronted by anti-fascists at two meetings in Windsor over the course of one weekend. At the first, one man was slashed across the forehead with a knife; at the second, fighting ensued after anti-fascists tore down the Italian flag, produced a 'Union Jack' (the national flag until 1965) and shouted, tellingly, 'We are Canadians, not Fascists.'[74] If anti-fascists did advance a different model of the Italian nation, then it had no impact on the fascists. Dubbed the community's '*cani sperduti*' (stray dogs),[75] they ridiculed anti-fascists as 'weaklings who, unlike most immigrants, could adapt to Canada only by abandoning their Italian and Catholic identity'.[76]

After 1929, Italian migrant communities in Canada turned increasingly receptive to fascism largely as a consequence of the work of Italian consular officials, their hegemonic control over community organisations, and endorsement from Italian parish priests (particularly in the wake of the 1929 Concordat). Nothing is more symbolic of the Italian Catholic parishes' support for fascism than the fresco of Mussolini on horseback painted on the vault of the church of the Madonna della Difesa in Montreal! One contemporary student of the Italian community in Montreal estimated that 90 per cent of the city's Italians supported fascism during the mid-1930s.[77] If French Canada was thought to be particularly pro-fascist, a not dissimilar picture emerges from English-speaking Toronto where, through most of the 1930s, anti-fascist protest went unheeded.[78]

'London calling'

In April 1931, a call to raise funds '*per la nostra guerra*' (for our war), i.e. for Mussolini's assassination appeared in New York's *L'Adunata dei Refrattari*. This call originated with the London-based anarchist Emidio Recchioni, the wealthy owner of the King Bomba delicatessen shop in London's Old Compton Street. Monies collected by *L'Adunata* were despatched to London, but fundraising efforts were in vain. As Kenyon Zimmer reveals:

> Some of this money financed Brooklyn anarchist Michele ('Mike') Schirru, a naturalized American citizen who plotted with Recchioni and others to kill Mussolini with bombs, but Schirru was under surveillance by Italian

> authorities and arrested in Rome before carrying out the plan. He was sentenced to death by firing squad, becoming another anarchist and anti-Fascist martyr.[79]

Born in 1864, Emidio Recchioni was already approaching his sixties when Mussolini came to power. Although dubbed 'a giant among anti-fascists', he was no Carlo Tresca. More a transnational facilitator and fundraiser than orator or street-fighter, his King Bomba emporium served as the covert meeting place for a small circle of London *sovversivi*, including Decio Anzani (who would be a victim of the *Arandora Star* tragedy in 1940), the anarchist Silvio Corio (life-long partner of Sylvia Pankhurst), and the freemason, Francesco Galasso. The London *sovversivi* were often joined by a scattering of English and American radical intellectuals too, such as George Orwell and Emma Goldman.

The formation of the London *Fascio* – their office in Soho at 25 Noel Street, just a third of a mile from his King Bomba delicatessen – led Recchioni's circle to launch a weekly Italian-language anti-fascist newspaper, *Il Comento* (The Comment) in 1922. Edited first by Francesco Galasso, and finally coming under the editorial control of the anarchist Vittori Taborelli, this journalistic endeavour proved short-lived. Blaming fascist intimidation of those buying advertising space in the paper, and a mysterious fire at the printing press, it ceased publication in 1924.[80] Anti-fascist activity then turned increasingly clandestine and conspiratorial; Recchioni setting his sights on assassinating Mussolini. By 1929 he had become convinced that since support for Mussolini relied on his cult of personality, assassinating *Il Duce* would bring the whole edifice crashing down.[81]

When considering the anti-fascist experience of Anglo-Italian communities in the 1920s, it is clear that this experience diverged significantly from the US. If in the US, fascist/anti-fascist conflict 'took on the character of an urban guerrilla war in which clubs were viciously swung, stilettos brandished, bullets fired',[82] there were no pitched battles on Soho's streets. As Judith Walkowitz says, 'political tensions between Italian Fascists and Italian anti-Fascists in Soho were more or less contained indoors in demarcated social and commercial spaces'.[83] So why was this so?

The size of the Italian migrant population was diminutive in comparison: in the 1921 census of England and Wales, 20,401 people were recorded as Italian born; in Scotland the figure was 5,559. The majority of Italians (15,000 or so by 1931) lived in London, for the most part concentrated in the London districts of Soho and Clerkenwell. Their occupational profile, in hotel and catering trades, did not lend itself to radical political subjectivities. Active anti-fascists within the Italian communities were very few in number. Even when Mussolini briefly visited London in December 1922, as he was welcomed off the boat-train at Victoria Station by sixty black-shirted Italians, there was no opposition. After Mussolini was hustled into a waiting car, 'the singing black shirts disappeared into the misty night in the direction of the shops and restaurants of the Soho district'.[84] Unlike the US, the Italian radicals in Britain did not pose any significant obstacle to fascists winning over the hearts and minds of Italian communities. In terms of raising anti-fascist consciousness, the forced closure of *Il Comento* was indicative of weakness. Moreover, most anti-fascist exiles chose refuge in other countries, such as the US, because they considered the British government too sympathetic to Mussolini.[85] Although some notable exiles did arrive, such as Gaetano Salvemini, their educative campaigns 'took place more in the cultural sphere than in the strictly political arena', as Stefania Rapello points out.[86]

A further factor which inhibited the scale of the anti-fascist response was the lack of fascist provocation on the streets. While harassment of known anti-fascists did take place, the Italian black-shirted presence was not especially visible. As a London witness from Richard Wright's study explained:

> In daily life, no. It was only visible – er, you never saw them, walking around London, you only saw them in Soho round about the fascio HQ, or the sports field in Edgware, in uniform, and that was on occasions like theatre or sports or something like that, they didn't walk around the streets, you wouldn't see one. I mean he might walk out in his uniform to go to a meeting but he had an overcoat over it and a hat.[87]

Wright's study also suggests that Anglo-Italian anti-fascism had negligible impact. Referencing this study, Judith Walkowitz makes the point that of those who recalled parental opposition to fascism, not one mentioned public opposition or participation in any anti-fascist organisation. Where there was anti-fascist sentiment, it was personal and familial.[88] For most Anglo-Italians, as was the case with migrant communities elsewhere in the English-speaking world, support for fascism was not overly ideological but more an expression of patriotic pride, where fascism and Italy simply became synonymous.

Anti-fascisti 'Down Under'

Last but not least, Australia, some 10,000 miles from the Italian peninsula, a vast distance that further underscores how the diffusion of anti-fascism abroad was emphatically global in reach. The Australian case, as we shall see, shares some similarities with our primary US example. But there are also key differences. In the first place, anti-fascism among Italian migrant communities 'down under' did not spring from those who had arrived before fascism; the *anti-fascisti* were largely formed from the ranks of migrants arriving *after* 1922.

If there were just over 8,000 Italians in Australia in 1921, a further 12,500 arrived during the period 1922–1925, and then 12,000 or so more by 1930. Italian migrants had been traditionally unorganised, lacking both state-wide or nation-wide representation. This was a consequence of the nature of their settlement (relatively few in number with many dispersed in the countryside), their occupation (working very long hours, often as agricultural labourers), their illiteracy, and their political isolation. Those who arrived later, and particularly so from the end of 1924, were more politically engaged. They had witnessed the rise of fascism first-hand, and many had been compelled to emigrate because of it. Anti-fascist Italians settled in areas such as the canefields in northern Queensland, the cities of Sydney and Melbourne, and mining towns (e.g. Broken Hill in New South Wales), which subsequently developed into centres of anti-fascist activity. If anti-fascism was a relative late-comer, so too was fascism: there were no Fascist party branches in Australia in 1923 and it would be 1926 before the first one officially opened in Melbourne, and it was 1927 before one opened in Sydney.

As we have seen, anti-fascism had its linchpins. Within the radical *sovversivi* in Australia, the anarchist Francesco Carmagnola performed that role; he was the pacesetter. Campagnola was a 'brook-no-compromise' militant, proclaiming that, 'A people that does not fight violence by means of violence, that bends its knees and cowardly tolerates the impositions of infamous mercenaries, is unworthy of such a name.'[89] Unsuprisingly, therefore, Carmagnola's name appeared in the security files in Rome alongside 232 of his compatriots in Australia. Of those listed (230 men, 3 women), 77 were identified as communist, 57 socialist, 31 anarchist, 11 Republican, 56 'anti-fascist' and one 'subversive'.[90] As the historian Gianfranco Cresciani points out, while the majority of migrants opposed to the regime were communists or socialists, it would be the anarchists who would become 'the unchallenged leaders of the anti-Fascist movement' in Australia during the 1920s.[91]

Carmagnola arrived in Australia in May 1922; thereafter taking up employment as a sugar cane worker in Ingham in northern Queensland. Within a few years he had emerged as the local champion of militant anti-fascism in North Queensland, an area that had experienced significant anti-fascist chain migration from the provinces of Vincenza, Treviso and Belluno.[92] In February 1925 an Italian fascist immigrant in Ingham was chased by a group of up to 150 of his compatriots; in nearby Halifax on the same evening, a newly arrived Italian immigrant was physically assaulted by anti-fascists after he refused to drink castor oil. A similar incident happened in Innisfail.[93] The following month, Carmagnola led a group of anti-fascists in the assault of three known fascists upon their arrival in Halifax. Such acts were essentially acts of *reprisal* – as Cresciani points out, the files in Rome 'contain undisputable evidence that many anti-Fascists, who had been victims of Fascist violence before emigrating to Australia, once they landed in this country committed violent acts of reprisal against known Fascists, Italian diplomatic staff and sympathisers of the Regime'.[94]

In 1926, after Carmagnola had moved to Sydney, he established the *Lega Anti-fascista* (the Anti-Fascist League). The League could count on the support of around 400 sympathisers, and it was followed-up with publication of the first Italian anti-fascist newspaper in Australia (*Il Risveglio – The Awakening*). Significantly, *Il Risveglio* openly espoused violence as an essential weapon in the anti-fascist struggle,

> only one way to fight, that is by letting our physical strength be experienced by the official and unofficial representatives of the fascist government abroad who are at the mercy of our blows. We can hinder, make difficult, if not prevent, the life of the diplomats of fascism, and for every crime which is committed in Italy against one of ours, we can take revenge on one of them abroad.[95]

One of the most favoured tactics was to assault members of Fascist organisations, making sure to rip the Fascist party badge from coats, which the anarchists called the 'nit'.

At the end of 1927, now in Melbourne, Carmagnola, along with other anarchists, formed the Matteotti Club. Its membership was said to comprise around 600. While trying to appeal to a broader radical-left constituency, the anarchists still forced the pace. In Melbourne in October 1929, as 100–150 black-shirted fascists celebrated the seventh anniversary of the March on Rome in the city's Temperance Hall, they were rushed by Carmagnola and his comrades. With several fascists injured, many fascists in Sydney were deterred from attending their own event two days later.[96] But this would be one of their last hurrahs: the diasporic anti-fascist movement suffered schism in 1930; and the Depression meant that many could no longer subscribe to the anti-fascist press or pay their membership dues to the Matteotti Club. According to Cresciani, by the end of 1932, 'the anti-Fascist movement in Australia had disappeared as an effective, aggressive force [...] Even Italian aggression in Abyssinia did not revive the anti-Fascist movement'.[97]

Placing the response in Australia in comparative perspective, it was similarly violent but not as lethal as the US (although possibly more by luck than by design – in one incident, in 1928, there was a gelignite attack on the homes of fascists in Broken Hill). However, and in contrast to the US, we have little sense of any 'united front' during this period. More moderate elements could find representation in Omero Schiassi and his Anti-Fascist Concentration (the Australasian branch of the Anti-Fascist Concentration based in Paris). Schiassi did not subscribe to violence and considered the anarchists of the Matteotti Club hot-headed rogues.[98] At the same time, the anarchists maintained their ideological monopoly over the politics of the radical diaspora. This was a credo defined by class warfare, revolution, anarchy and violence. There was, it seems, little attempt to seriously accommodate diasporic nationalism. Anti-fascists had, as Cresciani puts it, 'the disability of fighting a doctrine which ascribed to itself the right of being the sole dispenser of nationalism'.[99] Some anti-fascists might have protested that they were not anti-Italian, and appealed to the Republican tradition of Mazzini and Garibaldi, but such counter-claims were eclipsed by their politics of internationalism, class solidarity and violence. Tellingly, in early 1932, when Carmagnola was cross-examined during a trial related to his participation in a violent anti-fascist assault, he even admitted to feeling 'ashamed to call myself an Italian under the present Regime'.[100]

Conclusion

Was it really the case, as Donna Gabaccia maintains, that 'Worldwide, both fascism and antifascism became competing and transnational but self-consciously nationalist movements seeking to bind migrant Italians to Italy'?[101] This is a broad-brush characterisation which we clearly need to finesse. During the 1920s, in the

English-speaking world – with the exception of the US and even here this diasporic nationalism was relatively short-lived – ideologies of internationalism and class solidarity largely prevailed. Diasporic nationalism did allow for the establishment of 'united front' organisations (such as AFANA). It offered a common denominator to anti-fascists of various ideological stripes – an alternative definition of *Italianità* – based upon the values of Enlightenment humanism. Yet outside the US – in Canada, Britain and Australia – Italian anti-fascists do not appear to have so obviously anchored their struggle to competing notions of nation.

The British experience, as we have seen, was the solitary one of our four that was largely free from violence. And this in a country with a confrontational tradition of anti-fascism that dates back to the 1920s.[102] But where physical confrontations did occur, it was between native British fascist organisations and their opponents. 'Italian and British anti-Fascism seem not have encountered each other in this period', as Rampello recognises.[103] It may be that Anglo-Italian fascists limited their visibility in order not to invite unwanted attention from British anti-fascists. There is certainly some evidence to suggest that this may have been a factor.[104]

So when historians approach the history of global anti-fascism, their point of departure must be the 1920s not the 1930s. What is more, historians should not narrate their history solely in terms of Comintern-led responses. For sure, communists (and socialists) were involved, but as this chapter demonstrates, in the English-speaking world of the 1920s, it was *sovversivi* anarchists, *rebels* who comprised the vanguard of radical diasporic anti-fascism. Tresca in the US, Bortolotti in Canada, Recchioni in Britain, Carmagnola in Australia, and these people were the movement's early fulcrums. Come the 1930s, and as the nature of the anti-fascist offensive widened in response to the Nazi seizure of power, power relations within this family of radicals had definitively changed. Now under the Comintern-sponsored World Committee Against War and Fascism, a Committee for Co-ordinating Anti-Fascist Activities took the lead in Britain (established June 1934, an offshoot from the British Anti-War Movement); the American League Against War and Fascism in the US (established September 1933); a Canadian League Against War and Fascism (established October 1934); and the National and State Councils Against War and Fascism in Australia (established through 1933).

Let me end at where I began, by quoting from the memorial speech delivered by Stephen Cerulli at the corner of New York's Fifth Avenue and Fifteenth Street, on the 75th anniversary of Tresca's murder:

> During the War, in a speech to friends, Carlo stated: 'When I see young people who carry the struggle against Fascism and totalitarianism, then I am glad. For I know that my life work has not been lost; and the seeds I have sown are bearing fruit.'[105]

For today's ANTIFA, their progenitor's words seem as relevant now as they were all those decades ago.

Notes

1 See Stephen Cerulli, 'In Memory of Carlo Tresca, The Italian Vanguard of Anti-Fascism in New York', *La Voce di New York*, 13 January 2018, online at www.lavocedinewyork.com/en/people/2018/01/13/in-memory-of-carlo-tresca-the-italian-vanguard-of-anti-fascism-in-new-york (accessed 10 April 2019). One of those present was the historian Fraser Ottanelli, who when commenting on an earlier version of this paper presented in Budapest suggested widening its scope. I'm thankful to Fraser Ottanelli for his advice.

2 Nunzio Pernicone, *Carlo Tresca: Portrait of a Rebel* (New York: Palgrave Macmillan, 2005), p. 266.

3 Treca's killer was most likely the 'mobster' Carmine Galante.

4 Christopher Vials, *Haunted by Hitler: Liberals, the Left and the Fight Against Fascism in the United States* (Amherst, MA: University of Massachusetts Press, 2014).

5 Michael Seidman, *Transatlantic Antifascisms: From the Spanish Civil War to the End of World War II* (Cambridge: Cambridge University Press, 2018).

6 Pellegrino Nazzaro, 'The Manifesto of the North American Anti-Fascist Alliance, New York, August 26, 1926', *Labor History*, Vol. 13, No. 3, 1972, pp. 418–426 (quote at 419).

7 *New York Times*, 13 January 1943, p. 22

8 Dorthy Gallagher, *All the Right Enemies: The Life and Murder of Carlo Tresca* (New York: Penguin Books, 1989), p. 4. The idiom 'premature anti-Fascist' originated in the US – a critical term denoting the 3,000 or so left-wing Americans who had fought against Franco in the Spanish Civil War, but who had therefore fought fascism 'too early' as part of a Comintern-inspired effort (and hence supect in their loyalty to the US).

9 João Fábio Bertonha, 'Fascism and the Italian Immigrant Experience in Brazil and Canada: A Comparative Perspective', *International Journal of Canadian Studies*, Vol. 25, Spring 2002, pp. 169–196 (quote at 169).

10 Gianfanco Cresciani, *Fascism, Anti-Fascism and Italians in Australia 1922–1945* (Canberra: Australia National University Press, 1980), p. 3.

11 Bertonha, 'Fascism and the Italian Immigrant Experience in Brazil and Canada', p. 169.

12 See Luca de Caprariis, '"Fascism for Export"? The Rise and Eclipse of the Fasci Italiani all'Estero', *Journal of Contemporary History*, Vol. 35, No. 2, 2000, 151–183.

13 See Charles Delzell, *Mussolini's Enemies: The Italian Anti-Fascist Resistance* (New York: Howard Fertig, 1974), p. 46.

14 See Emilio Gentile ''I Fasci Italiani All'Estero: The Foreign Policy of the Fascist Party', in Stein Ugelvik Larsen (ed.) *Fascism Outide Europe* (Boulder: Social Science Monographs, 2001) pp.), pp. 95–115.

15 Baldoli, *Exporting Fascism*, p. 10.

16 See Pellegrino Nazzaro, *Fascist and Anti-Fascist Propaganda in America: The Dispatches of Italian Ambassador Gelasio Caetani* (Amherst: Cambria Press, 2008), p. 31.

17 de Caprariis, 'Fascism for Export?', p. 157.

18 On the Blackshirt 'orgy of violence' in 1921, see Tom Behan, *The Resistible Rise of Benito Mussolini* (London: Bookmarks, 2003), pp. 44–45.

19 See Giacomo Matteotti, *The Fascisti Exposed: A Year of Fascist Domination* (London: Independent Labour Party, 1924).

20 Pernicone, *Carlo Tresca: Portrait of a Rebel*, p. 137.

21 Cresciani, *Fascism, Anti-Fascism and Italians in Australia*, p. 100.

22 For further discussion of 'anti-anti-fascism' revisionism, see Enzo Traverso, 'Antifascism between Collective Memory and Historical Revisions', in Hugo García, Mercedes Yusta, Xavier Tabet & Cristina Clímaco (eds), *Rethinking Antifascism: History, Memory and Politics 1922 to the Present* (New York: Berghahn, 2016), pp. 321–338.

23 Enzo Traverso, 'Intellectuals and Anti-Fascism: For a Critical Historization', *New Politics*, Vol. 9, No. 4, 2004, online at https://newpol.org/issue_post/intellectuals-and-anti-fascism-critical-historization/?print=pdf (accessed 21 August 2019).

24 See Rogers Brubaker, 'The "diaspora" diaspora', *Ethnic and Racial Studies*, Vol. 28, No. 1, January 2005, pp. 1–19.
25 See Marcella Bencivenni, *Italian Immigrant Radical Culture: The Idealism of the Sovversivi in the United States, 1890–1940* (New York: New York University Press, 2011).
26 Nazzaro, 'Manifesto of the North American Anti-Fascist Alliance', p. 419.
27 Larry Ceplair, *Under the Shadow of War: Fascism, Anti-Fascism and Marxists, 1918–1939* (New York: Columbia University Press, 1987), p. 183.
28 Philip V. Cannistraro and Gerald Meyer, 'Italian American Radicalism: An Interpretive History', in Philip V. Cannistraro & Gerald Meyer (eds), *The Lost World of Italian American Radicalism* (Westport, CT: Praeger, 2003), p. 6.
29 Pernicone, *Carlo Tresca: Portrait of a Rebel*, p. 19.
30 See Luciano J. Iorizzo and Salvatore Mondello, *The Italian-Americans* (New York: Twayne Publishers, 1971), p. 88.
31 Pernicone, *Carlo Tresca: Portrait of a Rebel*, p. 105.
32 See ibid., p. 170.
33 Fraser M. Ottanelli, 'Anti-Fascism and the Shaping of National and Ethnic Identity: Italian American Vounteers in the Spanish Civil War', *Journal of American Ethnic History*, Vol. 27, No. 1, Fall 2007, pp. 9–31. Also see Fraser M. Ottanelli, '"If Fascism Comes to America We Will Push it Back into the Ocean": Italian American Antifascism in the 1920s and 1930s', in Donna R. Gabaccia & Fraser M. Ottanelli (eds), *Italian Workers of the World: Labour Migration and the Formation of Multiehtnic States* (Urbana, IL: University of Illinois Press, 2001).
34 Philip V. Cannistraro, *Blackshirts in Little Italy: Italian Americans and Fascism 1921–1929* (West Lafayette, IN: Bordighera Press, 1999), p. 37.
35 Pernicone, *Carlo Tresca: Portrait of a Rebel*, p. 134.
36 Ibid., p. 140.
37 See *New York Times*, 11 April 1923.
38 Nazzaro, *Fascist and Anti-Fascist Propaganda*, p. 107.
39 Nazzaro, 'Manifesto of the North American Anti-Fascist Alliance', p. 425.
40 Cannistraro, *Blackshirts*, p. 38.
41 Nazzaro, *Fascist and Anti-Fascist Propaganda*, p. 175.
42 Nazzaro, 'Manifesto of the North American Anti-Fascist Alliance', p. 419.
43 Nazzaro, *Fascist and Anti-Fascist Propaganda*, p. 119.
44 Nazzaro, 'Manifesto of the North American Anti-Fascist Alliance', p. 419.
45 See Nigel Copsey, 'Towards a New Anti-Fascist "Minimum"', in Nigel Copsey and Andrzej Olechnowicz (eds), *Varieties of Anti-Fascism: Britain in the Inter-War Period* (Basingstoke: Palgrave Macmillan, 2010), p. xviii.
46 Gabaccia, *Italy's Many Diasporas*, p. 152.
47 Travis Tomchuk, *Transnational Radicals: Italian Anarchist Newtorks in Southern Ontario and the Northeastern United States, 1915–40,* Queen's University, Kingston, Ontario, PhD thesis, 2010, p. 166.
48 Nazzaro, 'Manifesto of the North American Anti-Fascist Alliance', p. 425.
49 Iorizzo and Mondello, *The Italian-Americans*, p. 200.
50 Tom De Fazio, 'Fascist Terror in Italy', *Labor Defender*, June 1929.
51 Madeline J. Goodman, 'The evolution of ethnicity: Fascism and anti-fascism in the Italian-American community, 1914–1945', Canergie Mellon University, PhD thesis, 1993, p. 215.
52 Nazzaro, 'Manifesto of the North American Anti-Fascist Alliance', p. 418.
53 John P. Diggins, *Mussolini and Fascism: The View from America* (Princeton, NJ: Princeton University Press, 1972), p. 128.
54 Tomchuk, *Transnational Radicals*, p. 235.
55 Gallagher, *All the Right Enemies*, p. 129.
56 See Pernicone, *Carlo Tresca: Portrait of a Rebel*, pp. 185–186.
57 Gallagher, *All the Right Enemies*, p. 129.
58 Ibid., p. 109.

59 See Writers' Project, *The Italians in New York* (New York: Arno Press and NYT, 1969).
60 Nunzio Pernicone's entry on Carlo Tresca in Mari Jo Buhle, Paul Buhle and Dan Georgakas (eds), *Encyclopedia of the of the American Left* (Urban, IL: University of Illinois Press, 1992), p. 781.
61 Pernicone, *Carlo Tresca: Portrait of a Rebel*, p. 194.
62 Ibid., p. 222.
63 For more on the American League Against War and Fascism, see Nigel Copsey, 'Communists and the Inter-War Anti-Fascist Struggle in the United States and Britain', *Labour History Review*, Vol. 76, No. 3, 2011, pp.184–206. On Untermeyer and the Non-Sectarian Anti-Nazi League, see Richard A. Hawkins, 'The internal politics of the Non-Sectarian Anti-Nazi League to Champion Human Rights, 1933–1939', *Management and Organizational History*, Vol. 5, No. 2, 2010, pp. 251–278.
64 See Angelo Principe, *The Darkest Side of the Fascist Years: The Italian-Canadian Press, 1920–1942* (Toronto: Guernica, 1999), p. 38.
65 See ibid., p. 41.
66 Luigi G. Pennacchio, 'Exporting Fascism to Canada: Toronto's Little Italy', in Franca Iacovetta, Roberto Perin, & Angelo Principe (eds), *Enemies Within: Italian and Other Internees in Canada and Abroad* (Toronto: University of Toronto Press, 2000), p. 52.
67 See Franca Iacovetta and Roberto Ventresca, 'Italian Radicals in Canada: A Note on Sources in Italy', *Labour/Le Travail*, Vol. 37, Spring 1996, pp. 205–220.
68 See Bertonha, 'Fascism and the Italian Immigrant Experience in Brazil and Canada'.
69 Paul Avrich, *Anarchist Voices* (Edinburgh: AK Press, 2005), p. 180.
70 Years later, in 1940, when Bortolotti was facing potential deportation, Tresca, who had been approached for help, refused to offer his assistance, citing the 'very bad ingratitude' of *L'Adunata*.
71 Attilio Bortolotti and Rossella Di Leo, 'Between Canada and the USA: A tale of immigrants and anarchists', online at www.katesharpleylibrary.net/8pk1h4 (accessed 20 June 2019).
72 Ibid.
73 See Filippo Salvatore, *Fascism and the Italians of Montreal: An Oral History, 1922–1945* (Toronto: Guenica, 1998), pp. 40–41.
74 See *The Windsor Star*, 23 September 1929.
75 Salvatore, *Fascism and the Italians of Montreal*, p. 107.
76 Pennacchio, 'Exporting Fascism to Canada', p. 59.
77 Lita-Rose Betcherman, *The Swastika and the Maple Leaf: Fascist Movements in Canada in the Thirties* (Toronto: Fitzhenry & Whiteside, 1975), p. 7.
78 Pennacchio, 'Exporting Fascism to Canada', p. 60.
79 Kenyon Zimmer, *The Whole World is our Country: Immigration and Anarchism in the United States, 1885–1940*, University of Pittsburgh, PhD thesis, 2010, p. 376.
80 See Alfio Bernabei, *Esuli Ed Emigrati Italiani Nel Regno Unito,* 1920–1940 (Milan: Mursia, 1997), pp. 67–68.
81 On Emidio Recchioni, see Alfio Bernabei, 'The London Plot to Kill Mussolini', *History Today*, Vol. 49, No. 4, April 1999, pp. 2–3.
82 Diggins, *Mussolini and Fascism*, p. 127.
83 Judith R. Walkowitz, *Nights Out: Life in Cosmopolitan London* (New Haven, CT: Yale University Press, 2012), p. 143.
84 See *New York Times*, 9 December 1922.
85 Claudio Baldoli, *Exporting Fascism: Italian Fascists and Britain's Italians in the 1930s* (Oxford: Berg, 2003), p. 10.
86 See Stefania Rampello, 'Italian anti-Fascism in London, 1922–1934', *Modern Italy*, Vol. 20, No. 4, 2015, pp. 351–363 (quote at 358).
87 Richard Wright, *Italian Fascism and the British–Italian Community, 1928–43: Experience and Memory*, University of Manchester, PhD thesis, 2005, p. 151.
88 Walkowitz, *Nights Out*, p. 123.

89 Cresciani, *Fascism, Anti-Fascism and Italians in Australia*, p. 97.
90 See Gianfranco Cresciani, 'Refractory Migrants: Fascist Surveillance on Italians in Australia, 1922–1943', *Italian Historical Society Journal*, Vol. 15, 2007, pp. 9–58.
91 Gianfranco Cresciani, 'The Proletarian migrants. Fascism and Italian Anarchists in Australia', *The Australian Quarterly*, Vol. 51, No. 1, March 1979, pp. 4–19 (quote at 4).
92 David Brown, *'Before Everything, Remain Italian': Fascism and the Italian Population of Queensland 1910–1945*, University of Queensland, PhD Thesis, 2008, p. 65.
93 See ibid., pp. 64–65.
94 Cresciani, 'Refractory Migrants', p. 19.
95 Cresciani, 'The Proleterian migrants', p. 8.
96 Cresciani, *Fascism, Anti-Fascism and Italians in Australia*, p. 106.
97 Ibid., p. 108.
98 James Griffin, 'Schiassi, Omero (1877–1956)', *Australian Dictionary of Biography*, Vol. 11 (Melbourne: Melbourne University, 1988), online at http://adb.anu.edu.au/ (accessed 21 August 2019).
99 Cresciani, 'Fascism, Anti-Fascism and Italians', p. 10.
100 Cresciani, 'The Proletarian migrants', p. 13.
101 Gabaccia, *Italy's Many Diasporas*, p. 151.
102 See Nigel Copsey, *Anti-Fascism in Britain* (Abingdon: Routledge, 2017).
103 Rampello, 'Italian anti-Fascism in London', p. 354.
104 This may have been the case in Manchester in the 1930s, see Wright, *Italian Fascism and the British–Italian Community, 1928–43,* p. 151.
105 Cerulli, 'In Memory of Carlo Tresca, The Italian Vanguard of Anti-Fascism in New York'.

2

ANTI-FASCISM IN BRAZIL DURING THE INTERWAR PERIOD

International repercussions, national expressions and transnational networks between Europe and the Americas

João Fábio Bertonha

Introduction

If sectors of the Catholic Church expressed discomfort with some fascist practices (and especially Nazi ones) and liberal politicians did the same, the struggle against fascism in Brazil was, at its core, a struggle of the political left. During the late 1930s, the Brazilian government launched measures against Italian fascist and Nazi activities in the country and against Brazilian fascism – named Integralism – as well, but they were motivated more by foreign or internal problems, not by some fundamental ideological aversion to fascism. Being an anti-fascist in Brazil between the two world wars was practically synonymous with participation in parties, unions or other groups on the *left*, whether communist, socialist, anarchist or progressive.

The Brazilian Communist Party had been founded in 1922 (clandestine most of the time). Anarchist groups were active – largely but not only due to the influence of Italian, Spanish and Portuguese anarchist immigrants. There were anticlerical groups, Freemasons and other leftist tendencies. Socialists were never very strong in Brazil for various reasons, but groups, schools and socialist organisations did exist, both nationally and within European migrant communities. Trade unions and workers' movements, although heavily repressed by the state, were also growing, especially within industrialising areas such as Rio de Janeiro and Sao Paulo. This would be the core constituency for the future anti-fascist movement.

As we shall see, anti-fascism had several facets and moments. In the 1920s, fascism was viewed as something singularly Italian, restricted to Italy and Mussolini. Following this reasoning, Brazilian leftist forces tended to see the anti-fascist struggle in terms of an act of solidarity with Italian anti-fascists exiled in Brazil and not a pressing concern. International solidarity from the Brazilian left-wing towards anti-fascist exiles would continue, especially after anti-fascism took root in the German, Portuguese and Spanish communities. With Hitler's rise in Germany, the expansion of international fascism, and the founding of the largest fascist party outside Europe – Brazilian Integralist Action (AIB) – in 1932, the priorities of the Brazilian left changed and fighting fascism became a key part of its struggle.

Fighting fascism meant opposition to the AIB, of course, especially between 1932 and 1938, but it also meant fighting the Estado Novo of Getúlio Vargas (1937–1945), considered by many anti-fascists to be an offspring of fascism and integralism or, at the very least, a close ally of it. The problem is that, in historical and conceptual terms, the Estado Novo was not a manifestation of fascism, but a right-wing authoritarian regime. Besides, it was Vargas himself who outlawed integralism and the activities of Italian and German fascist parties in Brazilian territory after 1938. Vargas, however, was also the one who repressed the left and anti-fascism in the 1930s, especially after 1935.

This situation, especially after 1938, created ambiguities and contradictions among anti-fascists, who saw the Vargas regime fighting fascism, but, at the same time, denying space to anti-fascism. The struggle against Integralist Action was less ambiguous and contradictory and so the 'golden age' of anti-fascism in Brazil was in those years (1932–1935) when integralism was on the rise and in which the Brazilian State was not yet openly repressing anti-fascism and the left.

In the course of this chapter, I will follow the general trajectory of Brazilian anti-fascism, focusing especially on the period 1932–1935. At the same time, I will follow the specific anti-fascisms of the numerous European communities within Brazil during these years and discuss how this migrant anti-fascism related to both national and international forms.

Anti-fascism in Brazil

In the 1920s, anti-fascism was a manifestation of Italian migrants, as we will see in more detail below. Fascism, in this period, was seen by Brazilians as an Italian issue, to be discussed and dealt with by Italians. Of course, sympathy for the anti-fascist cause was present among intellectuals, unions and Brazilian left-wing parties and movements, who expressed their support for Italian anti-fascism and against Mussolini where necessary. The topic, however, was not regarded a priority, and Italian anti-fascists living in Brazil complained about the lack of interest from Brazilians who tended to view fascism as something circumscribed and distant.[1]

In the 1930s and especially post-1932, however, everything changed. Hitler's rise to power made it clear that fascism was an international and transnational issue and, in that same year, integralism was founded. This forced the left to re-evaluate the issue and the fight against fascism became a top priority.

The rise of integralism from 1932 was really a milestone in redefining the priorities of the left. Led by Plínio Salgado, Brazilian Integralist Action grew exponentially, amassing hundreds of thousands of followers in a few years. Integralist newspapers and rallies spread throughout the country and their links with international fascism were so evident (in symbolism and in open solidarity with international fascism) that anti-fascism was forced to reassess its priorities and organise itself to fight an ideology that came from outside but also took native form within Brazil.

As early as 1932, spontaneous anti-fascist groups – such as the *Comitê Anti-guerreiro e Antifascista* – emerged with the support of trade unions and other leftist forces. In 1933, a proposal for greater collaboration of anti-fascist forces began to take shape, initially under the initiative of Trotskyist groups. The practical result of this was the *Frente Única Antifascista* (FUA). This organisation brought together socialists, anarchists, communists (especially Trotskyists) and other leftist groups and was active between 1933 and 1934, especially in Sao Paulo. It fought the Integralists in the press, in cultural associations and trade unions, and on the streets, in armed clashes. Its highpoint was the famous 'Batalha da Praça da Sé' in Sao Paulo on 7 October 1934, when, in a violent struggle, it managed to disperse a major Integralist demonstration.

The 'Batalha da Praça da Sé' was effectively the most important landmark in the history of Brazilian anti-fascism. Street conflicts between integralists and anti-fascists, including dead and wounded, had been taking place in Brazil since 1932, but the conflict on 7 October 1934 was by far the most important and symbolic. Thousands of Integralists attempted to hold a demonstration in one of the main public spaces in Sao Paulo, but they were met by a counter-demonstration of anti-fascists of all political tendencies (anarchists, socialists, communists and others); by Italians, Brazilians and other foreigners, as well as members of unions and workers from various sectors. Seven people were left dead, and numerous especially among the fascists, were left wounded. The 'Batalha da Praça da Sé' was a landmark in the history of Brazilian anti-fascism, for it demonstrated the value of popular anti-fascist unity.

The FUA had a central nucleus, formed by the Communist League (Trotskyist) and by the Brazilian Socialist Party. Around this nucleus gravitated anarchists, independent anti-fascists and other leftist groups, in addition to the sporadic participation of the Brazilian Communist Party. However, the Frente Única Antifascista soon collapsed, due to its internal contradictions (not helped by the position of the Brazilian Communist Party). The Communist Party had launched several initiatives against fascism, but, reflecting the Comintern's 'social fascism' policy, it hesitated to associate openly with other leftist forces. This explains its ambiguity vis-a-vis the FUA (oscillating between approach and detachment), which contributed to its dissolution.[2]

Shortly afterwards, in March 1935, the main Brazilian anti-fascist organisation, *Aliança Nacional Libertadora* (ANL), was founded.[3] The ANL included in its program points such as the cancellation of all debts to foreign nations, the nationalisation of foreign companies, the guarantee of public freedoms, the distribution of plantation lands among peasants and the protection of small and medium-sized business. With sections in various cities across the country, the ANL expanded and quickly became a mass movement.

The *Aliança Nacional Libertadora* claimed to have founded, in its just three and a half months of legal existence, 1,600 nuclei throughout the national territory, with the number of militants being calculated at between 70 and 100,000. It is difficult to confirm these numbers, provided mainly by the leadership of the movement.[4] There is no doubt, however, that it was an essentially urban movement with participation drawn mainly from the lower-middle class and the working-class.

The forces that commanded the alliance were undoubtedly the 'lieutenants' (low-ranking military officers who wanted reforms in Brazil since the 1920s) and the Communists, even though the organisation brought together representatives of different political currents, such as socialists and some progressives and Catholics. It also had support from civil society, such as trade unions, professional associations and cultural entities. The communist presence, however, was real. One indication of that is that its honorary president was the head of the Brazilian Communist Party, Luís Carlos Prestes.

There is a great debate among Brazilian historians about the degree of control that the Brazilian Communist Party had over the ANL, which we do not need to address here.[5] In any case, the ANL was a derivation, adapted to the national context by the decisions of the Seventh Congress of the Comintern and its policy of forming popular fronts against fascism. A derivation perhaps, but it was not merely an involuntary imposition from abroad. If the Comintern itself changed its position regarding fascism in response to the pressure of militants, especially in France,[6] in Brazil we can see the same: left-wing militants were moving towards unity against fascism, which the new Comintern posture only consolidated.

The ANL coordinated, in its short period of legality (March to July 1935), a large part of the Brazilian anti-fascist activity in the period. However, in July 1935, the Vargas government declared the ANL illegal and in November, state repression became even stronger following an attempt at communist insurrection.

From that moment on, and especially from 1937, when Vargas became dictator and outlawed left-wing parties, unions, and associations, the space for anti-fascism sharply reduced. Isolated individuals and groups continued to speak out against integralism and international fascism. Some literary and cultural journals (such as *Revista Acadêmica, Diretrizes, Cultura* and others) managed to maintain a free space for discussion of progressive ideas and programs, but anti-fascism as an organised force practically disappeared. It was only after 1942 that anti-fascism had a new moment of activity, guided especially by moderate socialists and liberals, thanks to the association between anti-fascism, democracy and Pan-Americanism.

The period of the Second World War is, in fact, exemplary of the contradictions of Brazilian anti-fascism. The Vargas government aligned itself with the United States from the late 1930s and, in 1942, declared war on the Axis. Two years later, a division of 25,000 Brazilian soldiers was fighting in Italy against fascism, within the US Fifth Army and in alliance with the Soviet Union. Brazil, therefore, joined the great anti-fascist coalition.

This support for the anti-fascist coalition exposed contradictions within the Vargas regime. The Vargas government was not fascist, and its sympathy for Axis governments was not based on any solid ideological basis. That is why strategic and economic considerations easily surpassed ideological ones: the advantages of an alliance with the United States were so great that the Vargas regime's relative sympathy for Germany and Italy was quickly forgotten. Even so, it was a fact that during the previous five years the Brazilian government had defended the legitimacy of the dictatorship from an anti-communist perspective, which included the elimination of anti-fascism. From 1942 on, a dictatorial and anti-communist government was sending soldiers to Europe in defence of democracy and against fascism. This contradiction was so obvious that there was a need to open some space for the democratic and anti-fascist forces. The banner of anti-fascism was now turned into a defence of democracy, and this new approach gave new life to anti-fascism, especially the more moderate, liberal-democratic forms.

Vargas, however, was able to justify Brazil's entry into Second World War without appealing openly to anti-fascism, and much less to a left-wing anti-fascism like the one professed by the communists. The Allied powers themselves, to the disappointment of the remaining anti-fascists, saw no problem in supporting the Vargas dictatorship, provided that the country kept up its contribution to victory against the Axis. Left-wing forces such as the Socialist Party and the Communist Party would remain illegal until the end of the dictatorship in 1945.

The central contradiction of the period 1942–1945 – a dictatorship that had been sympathetic to fascism struggling against fascist dictatorships – was nonetheless a factor in the fall of Vargas in 1945. Forced to open the regime and give some space to the opposition to justify Brazilian participation in the Allied camp, Vargas was forced to give more and more space to progressive and democratic forces until the regime's final collapse. Without the anti-fascist struggle, perhaps the dictatorship of Vargas would have lasted longer. This indicates how Brazilian anti-fascism, despite its defeats in the 1930s, played an important role in the history of Brazilian democracy in that period.

Anti-fascism in Brazil, however, was not exclusive to Brazilians; it was present also in the migrant communities living in the country during these years. Due to the importance of these communities for the internationalisation of Brazilian anti-fascism, it is worthwhile to look at their experiences on Brazilian soil. The Portuguese, Spanish, German and especially Italian cases must be studied in order to properly understand the international connections of Brazilian anti-fascism.

Portuguese anti-fascism

Brazil has always been, given the communion of language and culture, a privileged place for Portuguese political exiles. The case of the anti-fascists or the opponents of the Salazar regime (not conceptually fascist but seen as such by many of the protagonists) was no exception and many Portuguese refugees began arriving in Brazil as early as the 1930s. The exiled opposition to Salazarism, in fact, lasted for many decades and only ended with the fall of the regime in 1974 and it was, probably more intense in the post-Second World War period than before.[7] Even so, in the 1930s, there were nuclei of opposition to Salazarism in Brazil.

The tension between people for and against Salazar in Brazil was fuelled by Portuguese news and events and became even more intense with Salazar propaganda aimed at Portuguese emigrants. Most of the community was seduced by Lisbon and, especially during the Spanish Civil War, there was direct involvement of the Portuguese community in Brazil in defence of Salazar.[8] Nonetheless, an element, at least, of the local Portuguese remained averse to Salazar and his regime, but their activities were curtailed by both the Brazilian government and Portuguese diplomatic authorities. Even so, Portuguese opponents did manage to garner resources to support Portuguese volunteers in the International Brigades during the Spanish Civil War and to carry on some activities – mainly cultural and in the press – against Salazarism.[9]

Spanish anti-fascism and the Spanish Civil War

Much has already been written about the effects of the Spanish Civil War in Latin America. We are now able to identify the positions of the various governments, and of Latin American societies. In general, the pattern does not vary much from country to country: right-wing groups (fascists, nationalists, Catholics, etc.) supported nationalist insurrection and left-wing groups (communists, socialists, anarchists, progressives in general) the Republic.[10]

In the Brazilian case, the Spanish Civil War was used by the Vargas government as a symbol of the international communist conspiracy that it tried to suppress in Brazil and most of the press opposed the Republic.[11] During the war years in Spain, the Brazilian government even censured the correspondence and the news that came from Spain, given the delicacy of the situation. The left-wing, or what remained of it, praised Spain as a symbol of resistance to fascism and social progress.

It is well known that the Spanish Civil War had a strong impact within the Spanish communities around the world, especially in Latin America. Brazil was no exception, split between Franco's sympathisers and enemies. Such a split survived until the 1970s and the arrival of Spanish refugees from the Civil War after 1939 only worked to maintain it.

The struggle between republicans and nationalists took place in many spaces, such as in the Spanish-language press published in Brazil. In Sao Paulo, for example, there was the newspaper *Gazeta Hispana*, founded in 1935. This opposed the papers that supported Franco, such as the *Nueva España*. Other Spanish-language newspapers either expressed their support for the Republic or against it, but the Francoist camp was able to secure its dominance. Other spaces of Spanish migrant culture, like the old associations, were also subject to challenge, and new associations – such as nuclei of Spanish *Falange Española*[12] and Republican support groups – were founded in Brazil.

In Sao Paulo, the heart of the Spanish community in Brazil, defence of the Republic was led by the *Centro Republicano Español*. Founded in 1918, it channelled, from 1936 on, the struggle against the Franco regime among Spaniards in Brazil, organising money subscriptions, public demonstrations and pronouncing itself in favour of the Republic on many occasions. The republican supporters, however, faced the hostility of Spanish elites in Brazil, as well as suspicion from the

Brazilian government, which, despite the protests of the Madrid government, considered them subversive and dangerous to the public order.[13]

Despite the importance of this Spanish anti-fascism, its effects on Brazilian anti-fascism were less than expected, simply because of the timing of events. When the Spanish conflict became more intense and direct, after 1936, Brazilian anti-fascism had already been heavily attacked by the State and it was unable, therefore, to help or be helped by its Spanish counterpart. In this way, any contribution coming from Spain to Brazil lost practical meaning. In symbolic terms, however, the Spanish question remained crucial to Brazilian anti-fascism.

German anti-fascism

Nazism would become a fundamental issue for Brazilian anti-fascism on two levels. First, the coming to power of Adolf Hitler made it clear that fascism was not an Italian phenomenon and could be replicated in other countries. This not only frightened national left-wing forces, but also stimulated the creation of Brazilian fascism, integralism. Second, Nazism was spreading party cells – as Italian fascism had already done – among the German communities in Southern Brazil and this movement was seen as a threat to Brazilian national independence. For the Brazilian left, fighting against German agents in Brazil meant taking a stand against an ideological and a national enemy.

Nazi activities stimulated resistance inside the German communities as well, generally by leftist Germans or Brazilians of German heritage, most of them active in the labour movement. These men had founded social-democratic or anarchist groups many years before Nazism and their struggle against Nazi activities started even before Hitler's rise to power. A case in point is that of the anarchist Friedrich Kniestedt. He had been engaged in workers' struggles in Porto Alegre since 1915 and became a very active anti-Nazi in the following decades, especially, but not only, through the German-language press.[14]

Beginning in 1933, anti-Nazi refugees started arriving in Brazil – especially intellectuals and Jews – and they created some German-speaking organisations to make a stand against Nazism. Most of them were socialists or social-democrats, but there were also a few liberal-bourgeois, conservative and Christian anti-Nazi refugees.

Apart from cases of intellectual and individual militancy against Nazism, anti-Nazi action in Brazil was centred on the publication of newspapers (especially in Sao Paulo and Porto Alegre) and also during the Second World War, on the organisation of groups named 'Free Germans' or 'Free Austrians'. Their purpose was to influence the Brazilian government and public opinion in favour of the German or Austrian peoples and to give, to German migrants in Brazil, an identity not related to Nazism.[15] German anti-fascists in Brazil were also part of transnational anti-Nazi efforts, such as the newspaper *Das Andere Deutschland*, published in Buenos Aires.

German anti-fascism, despite its importance, encountered some problems regarding contacts with their Brazilian counterparts, largely due to linguistic and cultural isolation. A different case was that of the Italians, the main protagonists of anti-fascism in Brazil in the 1920s and fundamental in the formation of Brazilian anti-fascism in the following decade.

Italian anti-fascism

Since 1919, left-wing newspapers linked to the Italian colony (such as the anarchist *Alba Rossa*) were publishing texts against fascism and Mussolini. The first systematic manifestation of Italian anti-fascism in Brazil was, however, the founding of the newspaper *La Difesa* in Sao Paulo in 1923, on the initiative of Antonio Piccarolo, a moderate Italian socialist who had been living in Brazil since 1908 and was very active in the life of the community.[16]

This newspaper housed various anti-fascist currents (such as the republicans, socialists and anti-fascists linked to the *Lega Italiana dei Diritti dell'Uomo* – LIDU) within it, and in 1925, the Italian anti-fascists gathered around it succeeded in creating the first official anti-fascist organisation in Brazil: the *Unione Democratica, La Difesa* being its official organ. In early 1926, an assembly of the *Unione Democratica* affiliated it to the LIDU, and in same year Piccarolo resigned from the newspaper's direction and, although he continued to work for it, he transferred the direction to Francesco Frola, a newcomer refugee from Europe.[17]

Frola introduced changes in the newspaper, opening it up to other Italian anti-fascists, such as anarchists, communists, and others. Due to this openness and other factors, Frola came into conflict with Piccarolo, wrangling with him over who should be the Brazilian representative of the *Concentrazione Antifascista* and over control of *La Difesa*. In the end, Piccarolo won his struggle with Frola in 1930 and transferred the direction of the newspaper to Nicola Cilla and Mario Mariani, anti-fascists who had recently arrived in Sao Paulo and who, together with Piccarolo, would lead the newspaper until its closure in 1934.

Even during *La Difesa's* existence, however, other groups and currents maintained their anti-fascist newspapers and anti-fascist organisations, such as the *Bolletino del Gruppo Socialista Giacomo Matteotti; Il Becco Giallo* by Nino Daniele, *I Quaderni della Libertà* by Alessandro Cerchiai, and others. The experience of *La Difesa* – conducted centrally by the Italian socialists and republicans – was, however, the most important in determining the trajectory of Italian anti-fascism in Brazil.

Between 1932 and 1935, Italian anti-fascism could count on the support of the Brazilian anti-fascists, which gave it new potency. After 1935, however, the scenario began to change, and Italian anti-fascism gradually disappeared. The end of the *La Difesa* newspaper in 1934 is evidence of its declining influence. There was an effort, by Italian anti-fascists, to agitate against Mussolini's regime during the invasion of Ethiopia in 1935 and to gather support for the republicans at the time of the Spanish Civil War, but intermittently and with few results. It was only in 1942, with Brazil's entry into the Second World War, that there was a space for a resurgence of Italian anti-fascism in this country, albeit restricted to democratic and socialist forms.

The international connections: European anti-fascisms in Brazilian anti-fascism

As stated before, there were two anti-fascisms in Brazil. The first one was Brazilian, focused essentially on the fight against integralism, Vargas's government and the cells of international fascism installed in the country. The second one was represented by the European migrant communities, with their national and specific struggles. They were not, however, self-contained units within Brazil, but chapters of the same book, with specific interests, but also general ideas and perspectives. The rise of integralism had the power of unifying them even more, since it provided a common, powerful and close enemy.

These anti-fascisms were indeed in full dialogue, especially when, in the 1930s, it became evident that fascism was an international phenomenon. This dialogue was partly journalistic, as when German anti-fascist intellectuals published articles against Nazism in the Brazilian anti-fascist press, or when FUA newspapers republished texts that had already appeared before in Italian anti-fascist newspapers in Sao Paulo.

There was also deep solidarity among the anti-fascists, with continuous efforts at mutual protection, especially against the pressures of the State and the integralists. Italian antifascists (such as Frola and Piccarolo) secured physical protection from Brazilian anti-fascists. Foreigners and Brazilians fought side-by-side in street conflicts in many places around the country and the 'Batalha da Praça da Sé', for instance, gathered together anti-fascists from Brazil, Italy, Spain and also from East European countries, all fighting the common enemy, integralism.

The dialogue was also symbolic, in the sense of giving Brazilian anti-fascism a sense of global struggle. The invasion of Ethiopia by Italy in 1935–1936 was an important moment in this direction. The Ethiopian war served to bring together different left-wing groups, since it represented the struggle against fascism, imperialism, militarism and racism, common flags of all of them. Italian anti-fascists and black activists from Sao Paulo, for instance, came together to try to reduce, albeit unsuccessfully, the strong support of the Italian community to Mussolini's efforts in Africa.[18]

The most important international event to bring together anti-fascists, however, was the Spanish Civil War. As in many countries, the war in Spain symbolised the struggle between reaction and progress and the anti-fascists of Brazil tried, as much as possible, to channel support for the Republic. They collected money, supported Spanish refugees, or simply defended the Republic in the press. In addition, forty-one Brazilians, mostly from ANL and PCB, joined the International Brigades in Spain, creating a physical connection between Brazilian and global anti-fascism. Incidentally, some Italian anti-fascists residing in Brazil, such as Libero Battistelli, also joined the Brigades. The number of Brazilians was small compared to about a thousand men who came from other countries in Latin America and it is almost nothing if one remembers that more than 40,000 men joined the Brigades.[19] Even so, it is indicative of how the appeal of Spain was strong even in a distant country such as Brazil.

The most relevant dialogue that was established, however, was intellectual, in the transfer of concepts, debates and ideas between Europe and Brazil. In this dialogue, the role of the Italian anti-fascists living in Brazil, and especially in the city of Sao Paulo, was crucial.

Brazilian anti-fascism, in fact, greatly benefited from the presence of so many Italian anti-fascists in Brazil, mostly in Sao Paulo. As already mentioned, these anti-fascists had difficulties in gaining support from the Brazilian left-wing in the 1920s, except in terms of mutual solidarity and sympathy. From 1932 on, however, the Italian anti-fascists began to receive unprecedented support from Brazilian anti-fascist forces, such as unions, parties, newspapers, particularly the Brazilian Socialist Party. At the same time, Italians gave their support to Brazilian anti-fascism, both practical and ideological.

A simple examination of the list of organisations and associations present in the FUA in 1933 can give us a measure of the Italian participation in this movement. Living and working side-by-side with the Brazilian anti-fascists, we could find the Brazilian section of the Italian Socialist Party, the *Socialismo* magazine (directed by Francesco Frola), the *Gruppo Socialista Giacomo Matteotti*, the *Italian Libera* group and others.

Even the idea of founding the *Frente Única Antifascista* owed much to an Italian anti-fascist living in Brazil, Goffredo Rosini. This Trotskyist, in Brazil since 1929 and who used to write in *La Difesa* during Frola's direction, was the author of the proposal to create the FUA. He also played a major role in encouraging the fight against integralism in several meetings, and it was also on his suggestion that FUA launched the newspaper *O Homem Livre*, to which Rosini also contributed. Oreste Ristori, another important Italian anti-fascist resident in Sao Paulo, also played a key role in the organisation of the FUA. Francesco Frola worked hard, writing in newspapers and as an orator, to alleviate the tensions and problems in such a way that Italian and Brazilian anti-fascists could find common ground to fight a mutual enemy.

Examples of the participation of Italian anti-fascists in the formation of the *Frente Única Antifascista* are numerous. It was on the suggestion of the *Gruppo Socialista Giacomo Matteotti*, that the Frente Única was publicly launched on 11 July 1933, the ninth anniversary of Matteotti's death. Besides, *Lega Lombarda* (an important Italian anti-fascist association in Sao Paulo) served as the gathering point for many meetings and celebrations organised by FUA. In the case of the *Frente Nacional Libertadora*, Italian participation was smaller, but, nevertheless, consistent. Several of the ANL meetings took place in the same *Lega Lombarda* and many Italian anti-fascists expressed their support for it.

We can see, therefore, how Italian participation was important for the diffusion of the concept of the 'united front against fascism' in Brazil. Of course, it is likely that this idea would have been introduced and discussed in Brazil also by other means, given its popularity in leftist circles around the world in the period. The fact, however, is that by maintaining an intellectual and political bridge with Europe, Italian anti-fascists collaborated in the introduction and application in the

Brazilian context of key concepts such as the 'single front against fascism', which was important for the Brazilian anti-fascism.

Of utmost importance, also, was the dialogue established in the daily fight against fascism. In demonstrations against integralism, it was common for Italian, Spanish, or German anti-fascists to join their Brazilian counterparts. Similarly, when threatened with expulsion, arrest, or physical violence, it was the Brazilians whom the foreign anti-fascists turned to for support. There was contact, collaboration, and mutual support, as far as possible.

Foreign anti-fascists based in Brazil were part of their own international communications networks[20] which facilitated dialogue not only between themselves, but also with their Brazilian allies and with the rest of the world. Brazilian anti-fascism itself also had, of course, its channels of communication with the world. The Comintern and its parallel associations allowed Brazilian and foreign communists living in Brazil to contact their counterparts outside the country. Socialists and anarchists had their own networks to connect with the rest of the world as well.

Brazilian anti-fascism was in contact with the discussions and debates that circulated among exiles coming from Italy, Germany, Spain and Portugal, as indicated above. It was also connected, moreover, with the heart of world anti-fascism in the 1920s and 1930s, namely, France. As indicated in the work of Ângela Meireles,[21] anti-fascist magazines throughout the Southern Cone were in permanent contact with their counterparts in France and, later, with the United States. Anti-fascist magazines from Argentina and Uruguay maintained a closer relationship with Paris, but even the Brazilian ones kept, for as long as possible, a dialogue with France. However, in relation to its Spanish-speaking neighbours, and reflecting Brazil's intellectual isolation in this period, contacts between Brazilian and other Latin American anti-fascists were relatively few. Even so, some Brazilian anti-fascists took refuge in Buenos Aires and Montevideo during the Vargas repression.

Regardless, the points of contact were obvious and even inevitable. If the struggle against fascism was the element that unified the left-wing in the Western world during the 1930s, in each national context and internationally, there would be no reason why Brazil, an integral part of the Euro-American universe, would not share in this transnational reality.

Conclusions

For some time, fascist and anti-fascist expressions in Latin America were seen as mere copies of European originals. Brazilian or Argentine fascism would be mere caricatures of Italian or German models, and anti-fascism would represent a copy, artificially imposed by the Comintern, or else the fruit of the imagination of leftist intellectuals.

Recent historical research has indicated how this interpretation is not correct. Latin American fascisms, and the Brazilian one in particular, could only grow and develop because they had a basis in the national political culture and because they made sense in the reality of each country.[22]

This national reality was associated, of course, with an internationalist appeal, a feeling that the national struggle only made sense within a larger, global or, at least, Western context. The presence of cells of European fascist parties in Brazil also supported and fostered this sentiment of a global fascism, helping to make Brazilian fascism a strong political actor in the 1930s.[23]

Anti-fascism, likewise, had global appeal and an internationalist essence, based on the observation of what was going on in Europe and the Americas. But it could only develop when there was also a national reality in which it made sense. Unlike the idea expressed by Andrés Bisso,[24] who saw Latin American anti-fascism as a political discourse imported from Europe by local political motivations, I consider the national/international relationship much more dynamic and self-nourishing.

The work of Ângela Meireles, quoted, indicates this with clarity. In the South America, the struggle against fascism was also a struggle against the authoritarian regimes that were settling in the region at that time, against the fascist parties and movements that were being created there, and against the expansion efforts of the European fascist or authoritarian regimes (especially Italy, Germany and Spain) in the region. National and international were perfectly connected and this connection gave a transnational character to the anti-fascist struggle.

The result of the struggle between fascism and anti-fascism in each national context was influenced by both the national and the international context. In the study by Ângela Meireles, quoted above, on the anti-fascist movements of the Southern Cone (Brazil, Argentina and Uruguay) and in my own research on Italian anti-fascism,[25] it is evident how the durability of the democratic system and the presence of a progressive political culture were fundamental for the existence of a strong anti-fascism. It is not surprising, then, that Brazilian anti-fascism was weaker than anti-fascism from Argentina and Uruguay, especially after the repressive wave post-1935.

Throughout the world, anti-fascism seemed defeated in 1939. It was only when the Allied powers gave the anti-Axis conflict an anti-fascist tone that anti-fascist movements could resurface and recover, though now centered in Moscow and Washington and no longer, as it had been until 1940, in France.

Now transmuted into the Resistance (especially but not only in countries such as France, Italy and Belgium) and with the support of the Soviet and Anglo-Saxon armies, anti-fascism was able to resurface. Its limits, however, are evident in the conservative restoration, for example, in Italy (which frustrated anti-fascists such as Francesco Frola) or the inability of anti-fascism to overthrow the Franco and Salazar governments. The anti-fascism of the 1920s and 1930s, however, provided a fundamental basis for the resurgence of democracy and left-wing thinking in the 1940s and beyond. In the Italian case, the reflections of exiled anti-fascists were fundamental in creating the intellectual base of the Italian Republic. In the case of Argentina and Uruguay, anti-fascism fostered the creation of an influential left-wing nationalism in later years.

Even in Brazil, where anti-fascism was aborted so early, anti-fascist reflections contributed to the later regeneration of left-wing thinking. Through an extensive dialogue with its allies and partners within Brazilian territory, in Latin America and in the world, Brazilian anti-fascists were a fundamental part of the country's history in the 1930s. Through these connections, they were able to bring reflections and practices that influenced Brazilian political history in the later period. As a political proposition, anti-fascism was defeated in the 1930s. Yet as a political practice and set of ideas, it left fundamental traits for the years and decades to follow.

Notes

1 For the following paragraphs, see João Fábio Bertonha, *Sob a Sombra de Mussolini: Os italianos de São Paulo e a luta contra o fascismo, 1919–1945* (São Paulo: Annablume, 1999); Ricardo Figueiredo de Castro, *Contra a Guerra ou contra o Fascismo: As Esquerdas Brasileiras e o Antifascismo (1933–1935)*, PhD thesis (history), Niterói, Universidade Federal Fluminense, 1999.

2 Fúlvio Abramo, 'Frente Única Anti-fascista, 1934–1938', *Cadernos CEMAP*, I, (1984); Fúlvio Abramo & Dennis Karepovs, *Na contracorrente da História: Documentos da Liga Comunista Internacionalista, 1930–1933* (São Paulo: Brasiliense, 1987); Ricardo Figueiredo de Castro, *A oposição da esquerda brasileira (1928–1934)*, Master's thesis, Niterói: Universidade Federal Fluminense, 1993; Eduardo Maffei, 'Gigi Damiani e outros', *Temas de Ciências Humanas*, 5, 1979, pp. 93–120; Eduardo Maffei, *A Batalha da Praça da Sé* (Rio de Janeiro: Philobiblion, 1984).

3 The bibliography on the ANL is immense. See, for example, in addition to what will be quoted below, Anita Leocádia Prestes, *Luiz Carlos Prestes e a Aliança Nacional Libertadora: Os caminhos da luta antifascista no Brasil (1934/35)* (Petrópolis: Vozes, 1997); Marly de Almeida Gomes Vianna, 'A ANL (Aliança Nacional Libertadora)', in Antonio Carlos Mazzeo (ed.) *Corações vermelhos: Os comunistas brasileiros no século XX* (São Paulo: Cortez, 2003) pp. 31–60; André Luiz Faria Couto, *ANL: Uma frente de esquerda nos anos 30*, Master's thesis, Niterói, Universidade Federal Fluminense, 1995.

4 Anita Leocádia Prestes, '70 anos da Aliança Nacional Libertadora (ANL)', *Estudos Ibero-Americanos*, Vol. 31, No. 1, 2005, pp. 101–120, here p. 107; Robert Levine, *O regime de Vargas – Os anos críticos, 1934–1938* (Rio de Janeiro: Nova Fronteira, 1978) p. 122.

5 See Valter de Almeida Freitas, *ANL e PCB: Mitos e realidade* (Santa Cruz do Sul: Edunisc, 1998); Wilson Montagna, *A Aliança Nacional Libertadora (ANL) e o Partido Comunista Brasileiro (1934–1935)*, Master's thesis, São Paulo, PUC, 1988.

6 Bruno Groppo, 'El anti-fascismo en la cultura política comunista', in Elvira Concheiro, Massimo Modonesi & Horacio Crespo (eds.) *El comunismo: Otras miradas desde América Latina* (Ciudad de México: ceich-unam, 2007) pp. 93–118, here p. 104.

7 Douglas Mansur da Silva, 'A oposição no exílio e a memória da "resistência" ao Estado Novo em São Paulo', *Migrações*, 5, 2009, pp. 239–254; Douglas Mansur da Silva, *A oposição ao Estado Novo no exílio brasileiro (1956–1975)* (Lisboa: Imprensa de Ciências Sociais, 2006).

8 Heloísa Paulo, *Aqui também é Portugal: A colônia portuguesa do Brasil e o salazarismo* (Coimbra: Quarteto, 2000).

9 See, among others, Heloísa Paulo, 'A colônia portuguesa no Brasil e a Guerra Civil Espanhola', in Alberto Pena-Rodriguez (ed.) *A Guerra da Propaganda: Portugal, Brasil e a Guerra Civil de Espanha: Imprensa, diplomacia e fascismo* (Porto Alegre: Edipucrs, 2014) pp. 311–330; Heloísa Paulo, 'Os «insubmissos da Colónia»: a recusa da imagem oficial do regime pela oposição no Brasil, 1928–1945', *Penélope*, No. 16, 2005, pp. 9–24.

10 Just to name a few classic works, see Mark Falcoff & Fredrik B. Pike (eds) *The Spanish Civil War 1936–39: American Hemispheric Perspectives* (Lincoln, NE: University of Nebraska Press, 1982); J. C. Sebe Bom Meihy, 'O Brasil no contexto da Guerra Civil Espanhola', *O Olho da História – Revista de História Contemporânea*, 2, 1996, pp. 117–124;

Victor Trifone & Gustavo Svarzman, *La repercusión de la guerra civil espanola en la Argentina (1936–1939)* (Buenos Aires: Centro Editor de América Latina, 1993); Mónica Quijada; Nuria Tabanera & José M. Azcona, 'Actitudes ante la Guerra Civil Española en las sociedades receptoras', in Pedro Vives (ed.) *Historia General de la Emigración española a Iberoamérica*, Vol. 1 (Madrid: Fundación Centro Español de Estudios de América Latina, 1992) pp. 461–556.

11 Maria Luisa Tucci Carneiro, 'A Guerra Civil Espanhola nos periódicos brasileiros: Mitos, imagens e imaginários' in Pena-Rodrigues (ed.) *A Guerra da Propaganda*, pp. 251–286.

12 See, for example, Eliane Venturine, 'A Falange Espanhola no Brasil', *Revista Ponto de Vista*, 3, 2007, pp. 55–62.

13 From the vast bibliography available, see Esther Gambi Giménez, 'El poder de la información: La Guerra Civil Espanola y la prensa in Brasil', in Pena-Rodriguez (ed.) *A Guerra da Propaganda*, pp. 287–309; Ismara Izepe de Souza, *A comunidade espanhola do Estado de São Paulo e a Polícia Política diante da Guerra Civil da Espanha (1936–1946)* (São Paulo: Humanitas, 2005).

14 René Gertz, *Memórias de um imigrante anarquista (Friedrich Kniestedt)* (Caxias do Sul: EST, 1989).

15 See, among others, Karl Eisterer, 'The Committee for the protection of Austrian interests in Brazil', in Klaus Eisterer, Gunter Bischof, *Transatlantic Relations: Austria and Latin America in the 19th and 20th centuries* (Vienna: Studien Verlag, 2006).

16 On Piccarolo, see João Fábio Bertonha, 'O fascismo na visão de Antonio Piccarolo: Anti-fascismo e reformismo no Brasil dos anos 20', *História e Perspectivas*, No. 11, 1994, pp. 233–269; Alexandre Hecker, *Um socialismo possível – A atuação de Antonio Piccarolo em São Paulo* (São Paulo: T. A. Queiroz, 1988). For a general view on Italian anti-fascism in Brazil, see Bertonha, *Sob a Sombra de Mussolini*.

17 On Frola, see João Fábio Bertonha, 'Um anti-fascista controvertido: Francesco Frola', *História Social*, No. 7, 2000, pp. 213–239; João Fábio Bertonha, 'Un anti-fascista controverso: Francesco Frola', *Mezzosecolo – Materiali di ricerca storica*, No. 13, 2003, pp. 217–232. Another important text on Italian anti-fascism in Brazil that has not yet been mentioned is Angelo Trento, 'L'anti-fascismo italiano in Brasile', *Latinoamerica – Analisi, testi, dibattiti*, Vol. 9, No. 30–31, 1988, pp. 87–98. For a general survey of the bibliography available on Italian anti-fascism in Brazil, see João Fábio Bertonha, *Fascismo, anti-fascismo e gli italiani all'estero: Bibliografia orientativa (1922–2015)* (Viterbo: Sette Città, 2015) or João Fábio Bertonha, *Fascismo, Antifascismo e as comunidades italianas no exterior: Guia bibliográfico (1922–2015)* (Porto Alegre: Editora da PUCRS, 2017).

18 João Fábio Bertonha, O *fascismo e os imigrantes italianos no Brasil* (Porto Alegre: Editora da Pontifícia Universidade Católica do Rio Grande do Sul, 2001) (new edition, 2017); João Fábio Bertonha, *La Legione Parini, Gli italiani all'estero e la Guerra d'Etiopia (1935–1936)* (Milan: Unicopli, 2018); João Fábio Bertonha & Jaqueline Tondato Sentinelo, 'O conflito ítalo-etíope (1935–1936) no jornal A Offensiva: A solidariedade fascista, o valor dos "povos de cor" e a "civilização"', in Leandro Pereira Gonçalves & Renata Simões, *Entre tipos e recortes: Histórias da imprensa integralista* (Guaíba: Editora Sob Medida, 2011) pp. 87–107.

19 Paulo Roberto de Almeida, 'Brasileiros na Guerra Civil Espanhola: Combatentes na luta contra o fascismo', *Revista de Sociologia e Política*, 12, 1999, pp. 35–66; Thaís Battibugli, *A solidariedade anti-fascista: Brasileiros na Guerra Civil Espanhola (1936–1939)* (Sâo Paulo: Autores Associados e Edusp, 2004).

20 In the case of the Italian anarchists, see João Fábio Bertonha, 'Anarquistas italianos nas Américas: A luta contra o fascismo entre o Velho e o Novo Mundo (1922–1945)', *História Social*, 22/23, 2012, pp. 269–293.

21 Ângela Meirelles de Oliveira, *Palavras como Balas: Imprensa e intelectuais anti-fascistas no Cone Sul* (São Paulo: Editora Alameda, 2015).

22 See, among others, João Fábio Bertonha, 'Los fascismos em América Latina: Ecos europeos y valores nacionales em uma perspectiva comparada', in João Fábio Bertonha & Franco Savarino, *El fascismo em Brasil y América Latina: Ecos europeos y desarrollos autóctonos*

(México (DF): Instituto Nacional de Antropologia e História, 2013) pp. 31–66; Plínio Salgado, *Biografia política (1895–1975)* (São Paulo: Edusp, 2018) and João Fábio Bertonha, 'Salgado, Reale e Barroso: Políticos e intelectuais em circulação entre o Brasil, a Itália, a Alemanha, a França e Portugal', *Revista Perseu*, Vol. 12, No. 16, 2018, pp. 11–37.

23 João Fábio Bertonha, 'A Segretaria Nazionale dei fasci all'estero, a NSDAP-Auslandsorganisation, o Servicio Exterior de la falange e as políticas externas dos partidos fascistas no entreguerras: O caso latino-americano', *Nuevo Mundo Mundos Nuevos*, 6 June 2017, online at http://nuevomundo.revues.org/70513 (accessed 10 June 2017).

24 Andrés Bisso, *El anti-fascismo argentino: Selección documental y estudio preliminar* (Buenos Aires: CeDInCI Editores/Buenos Libros, 2007).

25 See, among others, João Fábio Bertonha, 'Fascismo, antifascismo y las comunidades italianas en Brasil, Argentina y Uruguay: una perspectiva comparada', *Estudios Migratorios Latinoamericanos*, Vol. 14, No. 42, 1999, pp. 111–133; João Fábio Bertonha, 'O antifascismo italiano no Brasil: Comparações internacionais e vivências transnacionais', *Anuario del Istituto de Estudios Historicos Sociales* 19, 2004, pp. 63–78. They are all reprinted in *Sobre a direita: Estudos sobre o fascismo, o nazismo e o integralismo* (Maringá: Eduem, 2008).

3

'CON SALUDOS COMUNISTAS'

The Caribbean Bureau of the Comintern, Anti-Imperialist Radical Networks, and the Foundations for an Anti-fascist Culture in the Caribbean Basin, 1927–1935

Sandra Pujals

Introduction

Between 1930 and 1935, the Caribbean Bureau of the Communist International (Comintern), the intermediary agency for communist internationalism in the Caribbean Basin, outlined a new political and cultural framework for radical activity in the region. The Bureau, consort to the USA communist party's Colonial Department, incorporated projects and agents involved in earlier regional ventures. Within this structure, anti-imperialism stood out as a major unifying agent and discursive vehicle in relation to capitalist exploitation and the evils connected to it, from dictatorship to racial abuse. By the early 1930s, as the rise of fascism increasingly became a central focus of the Comintern's European agenda, the Caribbean Bureau systematically mapped an organisational course in which the interpretation of the international scene, including the fascist threat to European peace and stability, was intertwined with images of the local reality. Fascism was to Europe what Imperialism was to Latin America and the Caribbean: militarism, ruthless repression, and dictatorship. This subliminal mental formula related to iniquity at both sides of the Atlantic provided an infrastructure for future united-front, anti-fascist initiatives in the hemisphere, such as the International Brigades in the Spanish Civil War, and Mexico's support of the Allies after 1941. It also created methodological foundations for the ideologically eclectic, international anti-fascist campaigns that were, nevertheless, sometimes formatted according to the communists' former experience in Latin America since the late 1920s.

Most scholars seem to agree that anti-fascist efforts in Latin America and the Caribbean since the outbreak of the Spanish Civil War included both communist and non-communist organisations with very diverse ideological and political backgrounds. They also point out that local political and social experiences allowed populations to interpret, understand, and sympathise with anti-fascism in Europe as a common struggle similar to their own. As in the case of most of the historiography for anti-fascism throughout the globe, the dominant role of communists and international communism in anti-fascist activity in Latin America and the Caribbean is brought into question in view of a supposedly autonomous organisational network united by the universality of an agenda that steered away from ideological vestiges.

However, the archival records for the Caribbean Bureau of the Comintern confirm the development of a structural scaffold that fused ideologically generic anti-imperialist postulates with distinctly class-infused anti-war propaganda long before anti-fascism became a Comintern policy priority in Europe. The Bureau's representative discourse, for example, underscored imperialism's effects in the region as autochthonous manifestations of international fascism even before Hitler's ascent to power. Within the Latin American and Caribbean context, 'fascism' stood as synonym for 'imperialism'. After all, expansionism, militarism, racism, and the exploitation of native populations, along with the imperial powers' support of dictatorships in the zone had been everyday malaises in the colonial periphery decades before becoming part of the European reality. The term 'fascism' itself as modifier, trope, and keyword for local politicians' dictatorial demeanour promoted a mental framework that informed populations' understanding of fascism as a recognisable icon related to evil. Its semiotic quality also fostered a didactic method for the development of an anti-fascist culture with a long-term effect and transcendence.

Comintern archival documentation for radical activity in the Caribbean Basin indicates that, although suggested as a strategic priority during the VII Comintern Congress in 1935, the fusion of anti-imperialism into the anti-fascist agenda and the articulation of fascist tropes by means of imperialist imagery and discourse were not a novel approach.[1] This subliminal interconnection of concepts and interpretative strategies merging the international and the local, as well as the definition of fascism in a local and regional context had been already implemented in the American hemisphere several years before the conflict in Spain opened the way to an active anti-fascist movement in the area. The messages were easy to read beyond communism's ideological constraints precisely because they had been initially formulated for a politically eclectic array of intellectuals, radical leaders, and organisations that were mostly nationalist rather than communist and, hence, staunchly anti-imperialist. The foreboding yet farfetched warning of impending war during a period of peace may have also added an almost prophetic aura to communist propaganda once the possibility of a European conflict materialised several years later.

This chapter examines the evolution of the Caribbean Bureau's anti-war effort in the Caribbean Basin, and identifies several elements that distinguished its activity throughout the first half of the 1930s. The study also traces the origins of its regional anti-fascist agenda as far back as 1927, when a dynamic communist enclave in Mexico first merged their anti-imperialist platform to international communism's still elementary anti-fascist venture. The discussion underscores the role of Comintern-supported, anti-imperialist initiatives in Latin America and the Caribbean before 1935 as an inadvertent testing ground for future anti-fascist propaganda campaigns at both sides of the Atlantic. It also focuses on the development of a mental conveyer belt for ideas that subliminally equated the heinous nature of imperialism to that of fascism. Organised as a culturally recognisable set of icons related to injustice and violence, the formula contributed to the local populations' understanding of fascism as evil, and promoted the public's support for future anti-fascist campaigns beyond ideological lines.

Although scholars insist in the generic diversity of the anti-fascist network in the region, many if not all of the organisations involved had a direct or indirect relationship, past or present, with Comintern-supported networks, either through the Caribbean Bureau or regional and international Comintern front agencies. Such entities included the main regional network, the Anti-imperialist League of the Americas (LADLA), and international conglomerates such as the International Red Aid or Willi Münzenberg's anti-colonial and anti-war domain between 1927 and 1933. Intellectual contacts and groups since the early 1920s also paved the way for consolidated movements later on. For example, Henri Barbusse's international literary enterprises *Clarté* and *Monde* promoted the establishment of an early network with indirect ties to the Comintern at both sides of the Atlantic. Composed mostly of politically committed radical writers and communist fellow travellers, Barbusse's 'International of the Mind' also created a line of communication and solidarity between left-wing Latin American intellectuals and the European Comintern milieu. The group also served as a long-term organisational platform for regional participation in future internationalist projects, such as Münzenberg's 'world' congresses.[2]

Rather than engaging in the debate concerning international communism's hegemonic role in the global anti-fascist movement, the chapter sheds light on the grey areas overlooked as a result of the past century's polarisation. The work argues in favour of understanding the pre-history of anti-fascism within the context of the Comintern's pre-Stalinist, eclectic periphery, as an offspring of the 'united front' organisational networks later rekindled as a platform for the international movement. In this sense, it confirms anti-fascism's non-communist, heterogeneous ideological character as a rather natural by-product of communist internationalism's 'yesteryears'.

On the other hand, the discussion highlights the impact of the region's experience with imperialism in relation to the articulation of a unified agenda for a future anti-fascist movement, particularly against Franco's dictatorship in Spain, and German military expansionism, racism, and repression. It also points to the ideological exchange between communist internationalism and the anti-imperialist radical community in the region between 1925 and the early 1930s as a foundation for the homogeneous, ethical standards that represented global anti-fascism after 1933. This chapter, thus, underscores the role of local and regional activity, organisational interaction, and individuals related to communist internationalism in Latin America and the Caribbean prior to 1935 as groundwork for anti-fascist initiatives of later years. The term 'regional' refers mostly to the territories in the Caribbean Basin that comprised the anti-imperialist radical networks organised along the second half of the 1920s including most of Central America, the costal countries in the Southern continent, and Puerto Rico.

Along with the anti-imperialist tactical design, regional communists also set up an organisational infrastructure of ideologically diverse radical networks, particularly through the Anti-imperialist League in Mexico, which would later serve as launching-pad for anti-fascist activity. Within this structure, the chief Comintern manager for the Caribbean Bureau, the Italo-Argentinian Vittorio Codovilla, coordinated regional operations from Madrid during the Spanish republican era. Two outstanding participants in the early anti-imperialist campaigns in Latin America, the Italians Vittorio Vidali and Tina Modotti would also play a part in the Spanish Republic's propaganda campaigns and in Mexican anti-fascist initiatives later on. Until his death in 1934, one of Cuba's principal communist leaders in exile, Ruben Martínez Villena, would also be instrumental in the development of the discursive scaffold for the anti-imperialist/anti-fascist formula, as head of the regional *Socorro Rojo International* (International Red Aid) radical network. Their presence, thus, suggests Comintern participation in setting up a regional preliminary organisational infrastructure and a communication network that later served as platform for anti-fascism beyond its limited ideological framework. It also points to an international application of strategies previously developed for Latin American anti-imperialist regional campaigns thanks to some communist leaders' prior experience and transnational connections.

The present work contributes to the understanding of anti-fascism's labyrinthine complexities beyond the traditional ideological divide. It also provides an example of the unexpected geographical dimensions of the so-called 'transnational world' of communist internationalism and its intricate interpersonal networks. After several decades of globalised historiographical discussions, and in particular, an impressive amount of research on the Comintern, simplistic approaches on this agency's worldwide context persist. Even today, Eurocentrism still seems to represent, if not the standard, at least an acceptable 'international' perspective; one in which the 'world' still refers mostly to Europe.[3] Within these supposedly 'global' landscapes, Latin America and the Caribbean rarely figure as a historical agent, although the large number of self-denominated 'Marxist' revolutions have taken place in its territory. Aside from this somewhat chauvinistic optic, other drawbacks such as lack of reliable sources, limited access to local research and academic journals, and the language barrier also hindered a wide-angle approach to this history. Latin Americans' own sort of self-centred, nationalist insolence has also limited the scope of a historiography in which the Southern Cone countries or Mexico sometimes represent 'Latin America' as a unit, and the Caribbean remains an isolated factor with an inconsequential role or impact.

Recent works underscoring the magnitude, vitality, and ideological diversity of communist internationalism's transnational network in Latin America and the Caribbean, however, confirm the global significance of the regional radical experience.[4] The merging of the two hemispheric histories becomes, therefore, imperative in order to offer an authentically 'world' perspective. In the particular case of anti-fascism, except for very specific issues, the relationship between the international and the regional Comintern transmission belt has yet to be explored. As the first wide-angle, systematic appraisal of the anti-imperialist roots for a globalised culture of anti-fascism after 1935, this chapter aims at contributing to an expanded perspective that integrates the Comintern's regional organisational experience as point of departure for future anti-fascist international initiatives outside ideological boundaries.

Fascism and anti-fascism in Latin American and Caribbean historiography

Until recently, fascism and anti-fascism in Latin America and the Caribbean were two of the most disregarded, if not snubbed, subjects in the region's history. In general, the topics were traditionally understood as elements pertaining to another geographical area, particularly related to European events such as the Spanish Civil War or the Second World War. Many countries' national histories probably ignored these questions in view of their apparently 'foreign' nature. Elements such as the Jewish component or anti-fascism's assumed allegiance to communist ideology most likely sanctioned these phenomena's exclusion from discussions. Apart from Argentina, for example, where large Jewish and Italian populations are still a demographic factor, the issue of regional participation on the global anti-fascism movement rarely has a space in historical narratives. In the Spanish Caribbean, where anti-fascism is mostly understood within the context of the Spanish Civil War, recent research and solid archival sources have contributed to recovering global aspects for this local history.[5] Fascism in the region, on the other hand, has mostly been treated as a theoretical problem within a debate concerning its unique autochthonous character unrelated to the European counterpart or as a multifaceted, plural category '*fascismos*' based on national peculiarities.[6]

The focus on the significance of fascism and anti-fascism in the area as a theoretical rather than historical issue has, unfortunately, served as a convenient distraction to conceal perhaps one of the region's best kept secrets: local regimes' support of fascism and its military expansion beyond Europe. Some governments even imitated Nazi practices, and created their own versions of fascist policies. For example, Honduras's immigration laws between 1929 and 1934 prohibited 'the entry of Negroes, coolies, gypsies, and Chinese into the territory of the Republic', although the mestizo was recognised as an iconic identity for the country's population.[7] In Mexico, central authorities created lists specifying 'unrestricted' immigration controls for numerous nationalities, arguing that their 'mixed blood, cultural level, habits, [and] customs, make them exotic to our psychology'.[8]

However, despite the establishment of groups in several countries as early as 1923, European fascism's presence in the region is rarely addressed as a historical issue. As one historian has commented concerning the Argentinian case, the topic is rather a 'non-event' of very little concern to scholars.[9] In addition, except for John Guther's 1941 well-informed work, *Inside Latin America*, which included detailed discussions of 'fifth-column' activity as the United States prepared for war, European fascism's infiltration in the region rarely appears in the period's accounts.[10]

Although not as significant as in Europe, German and Italian fascism did have a presence in Latin America and the Caribbean thanks to the support of immigrant communities already established in the territories. In Argentina, Italian migrants established the Fascist National Party in 1923, and the Argentine Fascist Party in 1932. Chile had a German-inspired National Socialist Movement, that by 1938 unexpectedly shifted left in support of the popular front initiative. During the early 1930s, the country's paramilitary force, the *Carabineros*, had a German instructor, Otto von Zipellius, who, according to a 1941 article in *The New York Times,* signed his correspondence to Berlin as 'chief of the district leaders of the German Nazi Party in Chile'.[11] In Brazil, the so-called 'integralist' party *Ação Integralista Brasileira*, founded in 1932 and liquidated in 1937, is recognised as one of the only authentic 'fascist' movements in the region.[12] Even in Puerto Rico, where a small Corsican immigrant community controlled a significant portion of the island's coffee production, Italian fascism enjoyed a fleeting moment of fame after the formation of the 'Italian *Fascio* of Puerto Rico' in 1927.[13] The movement probably quickly fizzled after several articles on 'twenty-four hours a day with Mussolini' in one of the island's main newspapers.[14] Prominent Spanish-born merchants also formed an anti-republican network with strong ties with the *Falange* and Franco's faction during the civil war.[15]

In Central America, several countries had small fascist enclaves, out of which Costa Rica's Nazi Party is perhaps the most outstanding. Founded in 1931 within the well-established and economically affluent German community's *Club Alemán*, the party's leadership included Max Effinger, in charge of immigration affairs under President León Cortés (1936–1940) during the period when Jewish migration was practically suspended and public humiliation of local Jews replicated German conduct in the Aryan homeland.[16] In 1941, the new president, Rafael Calderón Guardia, proclaimed the country's allegiance to the Allied cause. A 1943 government pamphlet insisted in the nation's 'commitment to peace' and its support of a unified 'American' policy since the previous decade, even describing the ongoing European war as an attack of 'the aggressor's troglodyte force', without ever referring to the enemy by name.[17] The publication attempted to erase Costa Rica's dubious past relationship with fascism, particularly as sanctuary for supporters of National Socialism. However, a ceremonial field recently discovered in a remote rural area, with a staircase leading to a pedestal with a Nazi eagle set on a swastika documents the magnitude of that ideology's cultural impact for the local German population thousands of miles away from the European mainland.[18]

Venezuela and Mexico also became fascist bastions due to their immigrant populations and a strategic significance related to oil.[19] According to Dutch diplomatic intelligence, some 600 Germans entered Venezuela between 1938 and 1940 thanks to several naturalised individuals working inside the Ministry of Foreign Affairs.[20] One of the directors of the Bayer & Westcott Chemical Company's subsidiary in Venezuela, Arnold Margerie, was also identified as the chief Nazi representative in the country.[21] By 1942, the country had a Nazi party in which 99% of the non-Jewish Germans in the territory were allegedly members. Mexico's 'neutrality' and its government's lenient stance on the Nazis also remain ignored subjects of inquiry in view of the controversial issues involved.[22] While some historians underscore the country's role in regional anti-fascism,[23] others insist on the impact of elements such as anti-Semitism as policy guidelines.[24] For one, Lázaro Cárdenas's decision to nationalise British and US oil companies in 1938 opened the way for a profitable oil sale to Germany, although some historians claim the deal served as a bargaining chip to rescue Spanish civil war refugees from Vichy France.[25] The power of its affluent German community, and traditional 'anti-gringo' sentiments also account as strong defining factors for the regime's stance until the declaration of war in 1942.[26]

Anti-fascism in Latin America and the Caribbean, in turn, is a relatively recent historical discussion. Perspectives on the subject generally follow a stance already delineated in European anti-fascism historiography.[27] Distinctive features of the contemporary European debate include a focus on the role of an autonomous network of organisations and individuals, and the intellectual or experiential aspects as unifying force rather than ideologically defined political connections. These innovative perspectives have expanded the geographical boundaries and even the chronological scope as far back as the early 1920s.[28] They have also begun to question the role of both communists and the Comintern in local and international anti-fascist ventures, while underscoring the transnational and global character of movements.[29]

Replicating recent trends in Europe, several new works on Latin American anti-fascism have contributed to a revision of traditional outlooks. Historians now highlight its significance as a local, regional, and transatlantic issue beyond its ethnic or ideological specificity, focusing on the organisation of intellectual networks. The Spanish Civil War, they argue, turned a distant international event into an issue closely related to Latin American and Caribbean populations in view of their common cultural kinship.[30] Spain's experience not only resonated with the Mexican and Cuban revolutionary tradition, but also fostered numerous associations of prominent social and cultural figures beyond rigid ideological boundaries.[31] Not a theoretical dogma but a common experience of repression, militarism, and imperialism made populations gravitate towards the anti-fascist stance. The novel viewpoint insists that, far from a communist monopoly, anti-fascism became a generic frame of reference for intellectuals and politicians of the region, a common denominator for diverse political sensibilities, and even a discursive foundation through which to express local grievances in a universally understood context.[32]

In addition, the disparate nature of organisational networks related to anti-fascist culture seems to confirm the ideological eclecticism that distinguished this global, transnational phenomenon.[33]

When it comes to anti-fascism's international scope, however, heterogeneous intellectual networks and organisational infrastructures are but the tip of the iceberg. Although not directly related to the subject of the present chapter, several points regarding the future of anti-fascist historiography seem fit. While in Latin America and the Caribbean, the Spanish Civil War brought fascism closer to home, and the imperialist prism injected an anti-fascist spirit into the local social and political environment during the period of the Second World War, certain practical aspects of this process still pose challenging queries. For one, the issue of logistics brings into question the capability of an eclectic, decentralised infrastructure to efficiently hold together an enterprise of that magnitude. During the Spanish Civil War, for example, ships were chartered to send brigades overseas, and food, goods, and supplies were stored and dispatched from the American hemisphere in bulk. However, discussions seldom address the internal dynamic and complex configuration of the venture in panoramic terms, bringing together the numerous hubs and activists at both sides of the Atlantic as an interactive organism.

Another consideration rarely examined is the financial burden of cooperating in anti-fascist global initiatives, such as lodging and office space rental, publishing and distribution of propaganda materials, and individuals' travelling expenses for train or ship journeys. While renowned intellectual figures may have been instrumental in rallying support for this just cause, and perhaps even negotiating some of the financial assistance needed, the enterprise's practical complexities required a very specific sort of team work, experience and operational set-up. For example, given the political climate, crossing borders, in both Europe and Latin America, could also require practice with a clandestine alternative identity, along with a costly fake passport, and perhaps even a revolver for self-defence in extreme cases. A safe-house system and trusted individuals in charge of this kind of underground railroad added to the complexity of transnational operations. In view of the Comintern networks' past experience with this sort of covert operations, its role as mediator between idealism and practicality must also be considered in this case. These questions represent new lines of inquiry that may contribute to a deeper understanding not only of Latin American and Caribbean anti-fascism, but of its broader, global context as well.

Anti-imperialist radical networks, and the origins of a regional anti-fascist initiative

While European fascism's organisational life in Latin America and the Caribbean can be traced back to the early 1920s, anti-fascist groups in the region sprung up much later, around 1927. The earliest, or at least the most active seem to have been the Argentine *Alianza Antifascista*, and the Mexican *Liga Pro-luchadores Perseguidos* (League for Persecuted Fighters) that joined the Anti-imperialist League of the Americas (LADLA) in a 'wide front' in support of the Sacco and Vanzetti campaign led by US communists.[34] In late 1927, Vittorio Vidali *aka* Enea Sormeti, an obscure Italian communist agent, arrived in Mexico from Moscow to coordinate an anti-fascist initiative sponsored by the Comintern front organisation, *Socorro Rojo Internacional* or International Red Aid (IRA).[35] In view of his relationship with the Workers' Party enclave in Chicago,[36] Vidali's trip could have also been one last attempt by the Chicago communists to expand their scope of activity through their connection with the Mexican CP and the Anti-imperialist League, after their leader's, Charles Ruthenberg's, death earlier that year.

Until the establishment of the Caribbean Bureau of the Comintern as a centralised office for regional communist activity in 1930, most of the internationalist radical ventures in the area had been managed by the Mexican Communist Party and the Anti-imperialist League of the Americas (LADLA) located in the Mexican capital. In view of the difficulties involved, the radius of operations was limited to several territories in Central America, mostly Honduras, Guatemala, and El Salvador. The scope and magnitude of the enterprise was miniscule, and depended on the personal efforts of a very small group of committed individuals and their travelling schedules. In real terms, the Comintern's presence in the region throughout the 1920s was mostly a mirage that not only served to certify the supposedly 'international' character of these haphazard, autonomous undertakings, but also boosted the credentials of the alleged 'Comintern emissaries'. By 1925, the LADLA was taken over by a dynamic team of Venezuelan and Cuban communists exiled in Mexico, who expanded the League's agenda and scope of activity. Until 1929, the troupe organised a network of radical leaders in other areas of the Caribbean Basin, including Colombia, Venezuela, and Puerto Rico. They also set up the organisation's most successful venture, the *Manos Fuera de Nicaragua* enterprise in support of Augusto César Sandino's military campaign against the US invasion of Nicaragua.[37]

When Vittorio Vidali arrived in Mexico in 1927 to establish his anti-fascist post, the LADLA had already become a central figure in the Comintern's efforts to revamp a regional, ideologically generic platform to assure a stronger presence in the area.[38] With the help of another Italian émigré, photographer Tina Modotti, Vidali focused on organising several entities: *Liga Internacional Antifascista, Comité en Defensa de las Víctimas del Fascismo,* and the *Patronato Italiano Mexico-California*. The miniscule groups soon merged with the Anti-imperialist League, whose main leader, the charismatic Cuban communist Julio Antonio Mella, also became Tina Modotti's lover until his death in 1929.

The fusion of the regional anti-fascist and anti-imperialist agendas may have been actually an indigenous proposal rather than an organisational strategy promoted by Comintern central organs in the late 1920s. In 1924, fascism's presence began to be felt in the American hemisphere, as the Italian government initiated its peaceful, cultural expansionist project in Latin America, which included the principal territories in the Southern continent, Cuba, Haiti, and Mexico.[39] In September of 1924, the ship *Italia* set its course towards Latin American ports, carrying an eclectic, floating display of achievements from the homeland of *Latinità*: First World War memorabilia, a Cristopher Columbus exhibit, objects of art, architectural models, and products 'made in Italy'.[40] Thousands of eager visitors enjoyed the ship's interesting cargo in Brazil, Argentina, Uruguay, and Peru, while the local elites and government officials and diplomats welcomed their Italian guests with flamboyant parties, celebrations, and lofty speeches. In several cities, ceremonies and rituals, such as a parade of Black shirts carrying urns with Italian revered soil in Buenos Aires, captivated the crowds who, for the most, seemed oblivious to the fascist elements and the political significance of the *Italia*'s covert mission of 'cultural colonisation'.[41]

The ship's reception in Mexico, however, was far from cordial. Even before the *Italia* approached Mexican shores, *El Machete* had already initiated a ferocious campaign against the ship as showcase for fascism and Mussolini's ruthless regime.[42] The attacks were complemented by articles narrating the details regarding Giacomo Matteotti, an Italian Socialist Senator and Mussolini's fierce nemesis who had been brutally murdered several months before. *El Machete's* rustic woodcuts by Diego Rivera, with hordes of Blackshirts with skulls painted on their chests, added a dramatic visual effect that Mexicans could immediately connect with death. In the port city of Veracruz, protesters pledged to burn the ship down. The government finally refused to allow disembarking, particularly after the travelling *fascio* rejected the Mexicans' request that black shirts not be worn outside of the ship's premises.

Thanks to a centuries old, maritime route of the Indies and a radical network of shipyard workers and sailors, news in *El Machete* travelled to Cuba, where demonstrations soon surged. The most vocal protests came from the organisation of university students led by Julio Antonio Mella, who published a declaration where Italian fascism's connection to criminal activity and bloody deeds was reviewed. 'If the Cuban people do not protest', Mella warned, 'they will be condoning the crimes exposed above … If those unscrupulous opportunists celebrate and join in solidarity with tyrants and assassins, the free people must protest.'[43] Several days later, the publication of his personal letter to the Italian ambassador in Cuba, 'To the official representative of Mussolini's tyranny in Cuba', landed Mella in prison,[44] but did very little to impede a lavish week of celebrations in which the ship's passengers were even praised as 'messengers of peace'.[45]

Mella soon began constructing discursive parallelisms in which Italy's fascist experience served as keyword for the local political reality, especially after Gerardo Machado's ascent to the Cuban presidency in May of 1925. In early 1925, the journal for the university student association Mella presided, *Juventud*, published his article 'Machado, Tropical Mussolini', where he mocked Machado's 'evolution towards the fascist school'.[46] According to a Cuban source, in his letter to the president of the University of Havana protesting against his ousting after a student strike, Mella described the situation as another example of the 'era of tropical fascism' that represented the country's present political state.[47] Soon after, he escaped to Mexico, where he led the Anti-imperialist League's numerous rallies and campaigns.

Despite his focus on Caribbean, and particularly Cuban, issues throughout his most intense political activity between 1927 and 1928,[48] Mella's semiotic fusion of European fascism and its local manifestations still sometimes served as discursive strategy. In view of his experience as the League's most public figure, the role of imperialism in fostering and supporting wannabe fascist regimes in the region represented another powerful element in his formula. In 1928, for example, after Machado's attempt to extend his presidency despite constitutional limitations, Mella returned to his iconic trope in an article for *Cuba Libre*: 'In view of the electoral travesty, our opposition to the attempt to legalise the fascist coup.'[49] 'Once the Presidency was obtained', he pointed out, '[Machado] carried out an authentic coup and established a regime of tropical fascism'. Shunning the value of the Cuban dictator's political creed, Mella insisted on the opportunist nature of the latter's ideological postulates: 'Machado's nationalism is the classic nationalism of European fascists and of the agents of America's imperialist [financial] capital'.[50]

Mella's optic also inspired close friend and Cuban communist party boss, Rubén Martínez Villena, who echoed Mella's metaphor in one of his own articles in 1927: '*Machado: el fascismo tropical*'.[51] In Menotti's case, her personal relationship and close collaboration with Mella seems to have expanded her ideological understanding of fascism as a transnational phenomenon. After working as secretary in Vidali's rudimentary anti-fascist enterprises, she probably also developed valuable experience for later radical undertakings. As communist envoys in the Spanish Republic between 1934 and 1939, Vidali's and Modotti's work in Mexico may have also contributed to the anti-imperialist tone of republican anti-fascist propaganda that characterised the Republic as a 'homeland' under siege by a foreign enemy.[52]

The conclusion of the Mella-Modotti-Vidali story beyond its ideological significance, however, adds a sort of Mexican soap-opera aura to these characters' brief interaction. One year after Mella's assassination in 1929, Modotti and Vidali reunited in Moscow and began a love affair, before embarking on an International Red Aid mission to Spain in 1934.[53] In 1939, Vidali facilitated Modotti's return to Mexico, where she worked in the anti-fascist group 'Garibaldi', managed by Mario Montagnana, brother-in-law of the Italian communist party chief, Palmiro Togliatti.[54] In view of the couple's relationship, Cuban dissidents' speculation regarding a love triangle and Vidali's involvement in Mella's death has recently brought into question the official version of a Machado plot.[55] A few months before her mysterious death in 1942, Modotti apparently confessed her feelings to Jesús Hernández, friend and former minister in the Spanish Republic: 'He [Vidali] is nothing but an assassin, and he dragged me to a monstrous crime. I hate him with all my soul.'[56]

After Mella's death, regional anti-imperialist activity practically ceased altogether. By 1930, Mexico's political climate also began to change. The government became increasingly intolerant of foreign radicals, particularly communists, forcing many to emigrate. As a result, the former anti-imperialist leadership regrouped in New

York. By then, US communist leaders in Chicago had also moved to the Big Apple, and two consecutive purges between 1928 and 1929 brought a new, militant clique to power within a consolidated Communist Party of the United States. However, communist internationalism would soon recover some of its influence in the region, as the Italian-Argentinian communist Vittorio Codovilla joined the troika of the Latin American Secretariat by 1930, after the ousting of his boss and Swiss party leader, Jules Humbert-Droz. One year later, the Caribbean Bureau of the Comintern initiated operations as wingman to the CPUSA's Colonial Department. Between 1931 and 1935, the Bureau's propaganda strategies, activities and personnel, along with a revamped anti-imperialist network, would become an infrastructure, both cultural and organisational, for the region's response to European events, particularly between 1936 and 1945.[57]

The Caribbean Bureau and the foundations of a regional anti-fascist infrastructure

In 1931, the establishment of the Caribbean Bureau of the Comintern in New York coincided with a reorganisation of communist internationalism's enterprise in Latin America and the Caribbean Basin, the restructuring of its line of command, and the remapping of its field of action. As a consolidated agency for the Comintern in the Caribbean Basin, the Bureau merged activity, leadership, networks and groups that had worked together only sporadically, such as a Profintern-organised union network, Mexican regional operations for the Anti-imperialist League and the International Red Aid, local communist groups or parties, and the US communist ventures against racial segregation. In organisational terms, the new structure expanded the geographical extent of the traditional anti-imperialist configuration, by adding new radical enclaves in the British and French West Indies led by native communists then residing in New York. As appendage of the CPUSA's Colonial Department, it also integrated some elements of the US communist local agenda, such as the race issue, and some of its members as leaders.

Although fascism had all but disappeared from the regional radical agenda as anti-imperialist operations in Mexico reached a standstill, the Bureau instructions introduced the topic in connection to regional regimes' repressive stance soon after its establishment. Rather than a foreign issue, fascism was staged as a regional and local threat. The Mexican government was particularly targeted, and accused of employing different 'forms of fascist terror' and a 'fascist labour code', which probably referred to military action against workers on strike.[58] Most likely connected to some of the Bureau leaders' own recent experience with the Cárdenas regime, the attack evoked Mella's past indictment: 'In Mexico, if the middle class continues in its present path to attempt a stabilisation of its [position of] power … [by] destroying the proletariat, it only has one way to go, organize the *fascios*'.[59] Instructions for the First of May agitation also called for a special focus on the 'fascist terror' of '*yanqui*' imperialism's local 'footmen'.[60] The fact that Mella's friends, Rúben Martínez Villena, Jorge Vivó and Frank Ibañez, were closely involved in the Bureau's early activity could perhaps help explain the application of the 'fascist' trope to local issues.

In August 1932, the International Congress Against War and Imperialism organised by Willi Münzenberg in Amsterdam galvanised an anti-fascist international movement and revamped the inactive network of anti-imperialist organisations worldwide.[61] It also became a 'prologue' to the end of the anti-imperialist international enterprise Münzenberg had led since the mid-1920s.[62] Endorsed by revered writers Henri Barbusse and Romain Rolland, traditional icons of anti-imperialist radicalism, the event signalled a *detente* between the communist and socialist camps in the wake of degenerating political conditions in Europe and the threat of war.[63] Its promotion of unity, however, clashed with the Comintern's Third Period 'class against class' policy that included an attack against socialists and other non-communist radicals as 'social fascists'. Hitler's ascent to power several months later would solve the standoff between Comintern hardliners and the more moderate proponents of socialist unity.

The congress seems to have had particular repercussion for the Caribbean Basin communist organisations, particularly in Cuba, where a new anti-imperialist league began operating as a meeting point between the international and the regional networks.[64] However, the events in Germany and in Austria shortly after, no doubt, served as catalyst for the changes in the Bureau's discourse and focus. In 1933, documents evince an intensification of messages connecting fascism in Europe with the local political environment. For example, directives underscored the importance of promoting the establishment of a 'united anti-fascist front, whose objectives seemed similar to those of anti-imperialism, such as the struggle against exploitation, oppression, fascism, and the war'.[65] They also subliminally downplayed the distance between European events and the Caribbean region by stressing the consequences of fascist violence and developments in Europe for the local populations:

> Hitler's take-over of power in Germany, the imprisonment and murder of hundreds and thousands of workers, the attack against the Communist Party and revolutionary unions, and the attack against the working class foretell an intensification of fascist methods in all of the countries and especially in colonial and semi-colonial countries.[66]

Within the Bureau's domain, the international political environment had yet another use in the local ideological terrain. Between 1931 and 1934, fascism sometimes became a vehicle for an iconic, subliminal representation of a proletarian threat during a purging season in some of the local communist hubs then experiencing a factional conflict, such as those in Cuba and Colombia. 'Social-fascists' was the label for nationalists and socialists, as well as moderate communists who favoured a united front approach to radical activity.[67] The group, particularly identified with Trotskyism, represented a direct threat to the proletariat and an obstacle, since they were 'trying to prevent workers [in the forces] of social democracy to cross to the communist camp'.[68] Once defined as a 'social fascist' stance in holographic terms, the category could most likely serve as justification for suspension or expulsion of targeted party members. Instructions also merged the international and the local in attacks against the 'fascist decrees and methods' of the newly established Mendieta regime in Cuba, following an intense revolutionary period and the end of the Gerardo Machado dictatorship.[69] In view of the disarray inside the Cuban communist camp at the time, and an internal dispute concerning collaboration with other revolutionary groups, it is possible that the term could have also been used to classify opposition to centralised policy as another form of fascist conduct.[70]

As the Bureau prepared for the Comintern's historic VII Congress in 1935, a report on the 'possibility of fascism in the Caribbean' alerted its sections regarding the contemporary climate in the region. The increasingly fascist attitudes of the region's governments, and the presence of 'fascist bands and organisations', particularly the 'golden shirts' in Mexico, groups in Costa Rica, and the ABC (urban terrorist cell) in Cuba, were specifically underscored. In addition, the directives noted the difference between fascism in the 'semi-colonial countries' and that of 'the capitalist countries (Germany and Italy)', and the fact that fascism was much more 'closely linked to imperialism'. The discussion also highlighted the need to accommodate the struggle against fascism to the actual conditions of each territory when creating 'a mass, ample anti-fascist united front'.[71]

Several months after the report, the Caribbean Bureau apparently ceased to exist, at least officially. One year later, the outbreak of the Spanish Civil War initiated a reorganisation of regional radical forces and yet another revamping of anti-imperialist networks for a new mission. The 'front rhetoric and policies' that had characterised the Latin American anti-imperialist movement since its origins were replaced by a Comintern-enforced anti-fascist agenda.[72] However, the organisation of Cuban and Puerto Rican contingents as part of the Lincoln Brigade, the establishment of Spanish refugee hubs in New York, Puerto Rico and Mexico, and the propaganda campaign in support of the Allies in Mexico point to the resilience and lasting effect of regional anti-fascist cultural foundations constructed a decade before.

Concluding remarks

Anti-fascism in Latin America and the Caribbean adds a new dimension to the debate regarding international communism's role in the organisation of a worldwide movement. While the global anti-fascist network undoubtedly represented an eclectic group of organisations and individuals, the experience in the Latin American region points to communist agency in the construction of an anti-fascist culture beyond ideology long before the consolidation of an anti-fascist initiative in Europe. By 1926, the Anti-imperialist League of the Americas was already organising a metaphoric formula for fascism as a mirror image for events closer to home. Although superficially apolitical in character, the LADLA congregated an anti-imperialist dream team of communist leaders with a somewhat lukewarm relationship to the Comintern. Among them, the Cuban Julio Antonio Mella would be instrumental in the development of a powerful semiotic, discursive system, that may have also reached Europe through a variety of entities and channels, including Henri Barbusse's and Romain Rolland's intellectual network and Willy Münzenberg's Anti-colonial congresses.[73]

It would take Europeans almost a decade to understand fascism as an invading force of a self-proclaimed racially superior civilisation. In Latin America, however, the long history of European and US imperialism made fascism easy to identify and classify. Some of its representative characteristics, such as militarism, dictatorship, and racial discourse made it a malevolent European analogy to imperialism. Most probably, however, violence was perhaps the ultimate common denominator. As Mella's commanding formulas evince, the term first served as keyword to represent all sorts of evils as a didactic strategy that could help local populations to understand both as an enemy. When the Caribbean Bureau of the Comintern became the regional middleman for Comintern-related activities by the early 1930s, vestiges of Mella's discursive formulas contributed an organisational framework for propaganda related to the fascist war threat against the Soviet Union and the US communist party campaigns against racial segregation and abuse. In addition, the Bureau's New York headquarters provided a stronghold for organisation among Latin American and Caribbean immigrants in the city, as well as a demographic base for the Lincoln Brigade recruitment later on.

With the upsurge of the Spanish civil war in 1936, communist internationalism and its radical networks became a conveyer belt for the anti-fascist/anti-imperialist culture developed a decade before during the LADLA's golden epoch. In terms of its contribution to a global anti-fascist movement, the events in Spain served as a bridge connecting the two sides of the Atlantic. For example, the role played by several individuals in communist activity in Mexico, the Caribbean Bureau of the Comintern, and later on in Spain, such as Vittorio Codovilla, Vittorio Vidali, and Tina Modotti, suggests a direct link between communist internationalism's Latin American radical network and the development of the anti-fascist culture that represented the Spanish republican cause. Modotti's and Vidali's direct relationship to Mella's anti-imperialist work point to the significance of the Latin American and Caribbean communist experience to later European developments related to anti-fascism as well. As Hitler's fascist offensive led Europe to war, an expanded anti-fascist, ideologically heterogeneous grid was set in motion. But the organisational base and cultural paradigms that brought the movement together had long since been established, perhaps thousands of miles away.

Notes

1 While anti-imperialism as an ideological concept was not mentioned directly as part of the Comintern agenda in the VII Congress, the idea of fascism as the instigator of an upcoming imperialist war delineated the fundamental policy objectives. See, for example: Georgi Dimitrov, 'The Fascist Offensive and the Tasks of the Communist International in the Struggle of the Working Class against Fascism, Main Report to the Seventh

World Congress of the Communist International', *Georgi Dimitrov, Selected Works*, Vol. 2 (Sofia: Sofia Press, 1972), online at www.marxists.org/reference/archive/dimitrov/works/1935/08_02.htm; Georgi Dimitrov, 'Unity of the Working Class against Fascism, Concluding speech before the Seventh World Congress of the Communist International', Dimitrov, *Selected Works*, Vol. 2, pp. 86–119, online at www.marxists.org/reference/archive/dimitrov/works/1935/unity.htm.

2 Rogelio de la Mora Valencia, 'Henry Barbusse en América Latina: De la Liga de Solidaridad Intelectual a *Monde*, 1919–1934', *ULÚA, Revista de Historia, Sociedad y Cultura de la Universidad Veracruzana*, Vol. 15, January–June 2010, pp. 97–126; Ricardo Melgar Bao, 'Cominternismo intelectual: Representaciones, redes y prácticas político-culturales en América Central, 1921–1933', *Revista Complutense de Historia de América*, Vol. 35, 2009, pp. 135–159.

3 Silvio Pons, *The Global Revolution: A History of International Communism, 1917–1991* (Oxford: Oxford University Press, 2014); Brigitte Studer, *The Transnational World of the Cominternians* (New York: Palgrave Macmillan, 2015); Kevin Morgan, Gidon Cohen & Andrew Flinn (eds), *Agents of the Revolution: New Biographical Approaches to the History of International Communism in the Age of Lenin and Stalin* (Bern: Peter Lang, 2005).

4 Lazar Jeifets & Victor Jeifets, 'Formirovanie i razvitie Latinoamerikanskogo levogo dvizheniia', Sankt Peterburg, Institut *Latinskoi Ameriki*, 2012; 'Jaime Nevarez y la fundación del movimiento comunista y anti-imperialista en Puerto Rico', *Pacarina del sur* [online], Vol. 5, No. 21 (October–December); *La Internacional Comunista y América Latina, 1919–1943: Diccionario bibliográfico* (Santiago de Chile: Ariadna Ediciones, 2015).

5 Nial Binns, Jesús Cano Reyes & Ana Casado Fernández (eds), *Cuba y la guerra civil española: La voz de los intelectuales* (Madrid: Calambur, 2015); Ariel Lambe, *Cuban Antifascism and the Spanish Civil War: Transnational Activism, Networks, and Solidarity in the 1930s*, doctoral thesis, Columbia University, 2014; José Alejandro Ortíz Carrión & Teresita Torres Rivera (eds), *Voluntarios de la libertad: Puertorriqueños en defensa de la república española* (San Juan: Ediciones Callejón, 2015).

6 Helgio Trindade, 'La cuestión del fascismo en América Latina', *Desarrollo Económico*, Vol. 23, No. 91, October–December 1983, pp. 429–447; Franco Savarino, 'Juego de ilusiones: Brasil, México y los 'fascismos' latinoamericanos frente al fascismo italiano', *Historia Crítica*, No. 37, January–April, 2009, pp. 120–147; Franco Savarino, 'Fascismo en América Latina: La perspectiva italiana (1922–1943)', *Diálogos, Revista do Departamento de História e do Programa de Pós-Graduação em História*, Vol. 14, No. 1, 2010, pp. 39–81.

7 Dario Euraque, 'The Banana Enclave, Nationalism, and Mestizaje in Honduras, 1910s–1930s', in Aviva Chomsky & Aldo Lauria-Santiago (eds), *Identity and Struggle in the Margins of the Nation-State: The Labouring Peoples of Central America and Hispanic Caribbean* (Durham, NC: Duke University Press, 1998), p. 152.

8 Manuel Alejandro Hernández Ponce, 'México ante la crisis económica y la amenaza de la Segunda Guerra Mundial: La controversia racial y de ciudadanía, 1930–1942', *Revista del Colegio San Luis*, Vol. 5, No. 10, July–December 2015, p. 15.

9 Ricardo Pasolini, 'Intelectuales antifascistas y comunismo durante la década de 1930, un recorrido posible: Entre Buenos Aires y Tandil', *Estudios Sociales, Revista Universitaria Semestral*, 2004, pp. 81–116, online at http://historiapolitica.com/datos/biblioteca/Pasolini%201.pdf.

10 John Guther, *Inside Latin America* (New York: Harper & Bros., 1941); Von Hans-Jurgen Schröder, 'Die neue deutsche Südamerika-Politik: Dokumente zur nationalsozialistischen Wirtschaftspolitik in Lateinamerika von 1934–1936', *Jahrbuch für Geschichte von Staat, Wirtschaft und Gesellschaft Lateinamerikas*, Vol. 6, 1969, pp. 337–346; Brigida von Mentz, Ricardo Pérez Montfort & Verena Radkau (eds), *Fascismo y antifascismo en América Latina y México: Apuntes históricos* (México D.F: CIESAS, 1984).

11 Sami Rozenbaum, 'El nazismo y su acción en América Latina', Enlace Judío (México), 7 September 2018, online at www.enlacejudio.com/2018/09/07/el-nazismo-y-su-accion-en-america-latina.

12 Trindade, 'La cuestión del fascismo en América Latina'.

13 *El Mundo*, 17 February 1927, p. 3.
14 'Ha quedado constituido el 'Fascio Italiano de Puerto Rico'', *El Mundo*, 17 February 1927, 'Veinticuatro horas al día con Benito Mussolini', *El Mundo*, 14 January and 18 January 1927, p. 3; 'Definición del fascismo hecha por Mussolini', *La Democracia*, 24 February 1927. I am indebted to Carmen Orive, Ph. D. student and research assistant for the bibliographical data on fascism in Puerto Rico.
15 Luis Ferrao, *Puertorriqueños en la Guerra Civil Española* (Río Piedras: Editorial de la Universidad de Puerto Rico, 2009).
16 Christiane Berth, 'La inmigración alemana en Costa Rica, migración, crisis y cambio entre 1920 y 1950: Entrevistas con descendientes', *Revista de Historia de América*, No. 137, 2006, pp. 9–31; Jacobo Schifter, Lowell Gudmundson & Mario Solera Castro, *El judío en Costa Rica* (San José, Costa Rica: Editorial Universidad Estatal a Distancia, 1979).
17 Juan Francisco Rojas Suárez (ed.), *Costa Rica en la Segunda Guerra Mundial* (San José, Costa Rica: Imprenta Nacional, 1943), online at www.asamblea.go.cr/sd/Otras_publicaciones/Costa%20Rica%20en%20la%20segunda%20guerra%20mundial%207%20de%20diciembre%20de%201941-7%20de%20diciembre%20de%201943.pdf.
18 'Descubierto en Costa Rica posible monumento Nazi de 1931', Redpress.com, 2 June 2010, online at www.redpres.com/t102-descubierto-en-costa-rica-posible-monumento-nazi-de-1931#sthash.BIxl5bqT.dpbs.
19 Friedrich E. Schuler, *Mexico Between Hitler and Roosevelt: Mexican Foreign Relations in the Age of Lázaro Cardenas, 1934–1940* (Albuquerque, NM: University of New Mexico Press, 1998); Steve Ellner, 'The Venezuela Left in the Era of the Popular Front', *Journal of Latin American Studies*, Vol. 11, No. 1, May 1979, p. 172.
20 Rozenbaum, 'El nazismo y su acción en América Latina'.
21 Ibid.
22 Friedrich Katz, *The Secret War in Mexico: Europe, the United States, and the Mexican Revolution* (Chicago, IL: University of Chicago Press, 1981); Ponce, 'México ante la crisis económica y la amenaza de la Segunda Guerra Mundial'. The author would like to thank her former student Ángel Villegas Cruz for this bibliographical data.
23 Andrea Acle-Kreysing, 'Antifascismo, un espacio de encuentro entre el exilio y la política nacional: El caso de Vicente Lombardo Toledano en México, 1936–1945', *Revista de Indias*, Vol. 76, No. 267, 2016, pp. 573–609.
24 von Mentz, Pérez Monfort & Radkau (eds), *Fascismo y antifascismo en América Latina*; Bokser Liwerant, 'El México de los años treinta: Cardenismo, inmigración judía y antisemitismo', in Delia Salazar Anaya (ed.), *Xenofobia y xenofilia en la historia de México, Siglos XIX y XX: Homenaje a Moisés González Navarro* (México: SEGOB-INAH-DGE Ediciones, 2006), pp. 379–416; Nicolás Cárdenas & Mauricio Tenorio, 'Mexico 1920's–1940's: Revolutionary Government, Reactionary Politics', in Stein Ugelvik Larsen (ed.), *Fascism Outside Europe: The European Impulse against Domestic Conditions in the Diffusion of Global Fascism* (New York: University of Columbia Press, 2011), pp. 593–627.
25 Friedich Katz, 'Mexico, Gilberto Bosques and the Refugees', *The Americas*, Vol. 57, No. 1, 2000, pp. 1–12.
26 Schuler, *Mexico Between Hitler and Roosevelt*; Jürgen Buchenau, 'The German Colony in Mexico City, 1821-present', *Jahrbuch für Geschichte Lateinamerikas*, Vol. 39, 2002, pp. 275–297.
27 Hugo García, Mercedes Yusta, Xavier Tabet & Cristina Clímaco (eds), *Rethinking Fascism: History, Memory and Politics, 1922 to the Present* (New York: Berghahn Books, 2018), pp. 1–19.
28 Kasper Braskén, 'Making Anti-Fascism Transnational: The Origins of Communist and Socialist Articulations of Resistance in Europe, 1923–1924', *Contemporary European History*, Vol. 25, No. 4, 2016, pp. 573–596.
29 Michael Siedman, *Transatlantic Antifascisms: From the Spanish Civil War to the End of World War II* (Cambridge: Cambridge University Press, 2017); José M. Faraldo, 'Resistance Against Fascism and Communism in Europe: Towards a Model of Analysis', *Annals of the University of Bucharest/Political Science Series*, Vol. 16, No. 2, 2014, pp. 23–38.

30 Gino Baumann, *Los voluntarios latinoamericanos en la guerra civil española: En las brigadas internacionales, las milicias, la retaguardia y el Ejército Popular* (San José, Costa Rica: Guayacán, 1997).
31 Acle-Kreysing, 'Antifascismo'; Lambe, *Cuban Antifascism*.
32 Ricardo Pasolini, 'El nacimiento de una sensibilidad política: Cultura antifascista, comunismo y nación en la Argentina: de la AIAPE al Congreso Argentino de la Cultura, 1935–1955', *Desarrollo Económico*, Vol. 45, 2006, pp. 403–433; *Los marxistas liberales: Antifascismo y cultura comunista en la Argentina del Siglo XX* (Buenos Aires: Sudamericana, 2013).
33 Adrián Celentano, 'Ideas e intelectuales en la formación de una red sudamericana antifascista', *Literatura y Lingüística*, No. 17, 2006, pp. 195–218.
34 Daniel Kersffeld, *Contra el imperio: Historia de la Liga Antiimperialista de la Américas* (México: Siglo XXI Editores, 2012), pp. 119–123.
35 Mario Passi, *Vittorio Vidali* (Rome: Edizione Studio Tesi, 1991).
36 Randi Storch, *Red Chicago: American Communism at Its Grassroots, 1928–1935* (Urbana, IL: University of Chicago Press, 2009).
37 Kersffeld, *Contra el imperio*.
38 Ibid., p. 120.
39 According to Italian archival documents, Mussolini's government focused on strengthening commercial relations with Cuba and a fascist propaganda hub in Mexico as part of a strategy to reinforce Italian fascism's political presence in the region. See: Adys Cupul & Froilán González (eds), *Julio Antonio Mella y Tina Modotti contra el fascismo* (La Habana: Casa Editora April 2005), pp. 65–67. I would like to express my appreciation to Fernando Norat, PhD student at Brown University, for making this rare book available to me.
40 Laura Moure Cecchini, 'The *Nave Italia* and the Politics of Latinità: Art, Commerce, and Cultural Colonization in the Early Days of Fascism', *Italian Studies*, Vol. 71, No. 4, 2016, pp. 1–30.
41 Ibid., p. 19.
42 Ibid., pp. 23–29.
43 Cupul & González, *Julio Antonio Mella y Tina Modotti*, pp. 13–14.
44 Ibid., p. 39.
45 Ibid., p. 35.
46 Cupul & González, *Julio Antonio Mella y Tina Modotti*, p. 46. The original article in *Juventud*, 'Machado, Mussolini tropical', was published on 25 March 1925.
47 '18 de enero de 1926, Carta de Mella al Rector de la Universidad de La Habana', blog for *Radio Cadena Agramonte, Camaguey*, online at www.cadenagramonte.cu/efemerides/ver/carta-mella-rector-universidad-habana.
48 Caridad Massón Sena, 'Mella y el movimiento obrero mexicano', unpublished paper for the *Instituto Cubano de Investigación Cultural Juan Marinello* (2004), available at the digital libraries network of the CLACSO (Argentina): http://biblioteca.clacso.edu.ar/Cuba/cidcc/20120828014558/mella.pdf. The author would like to express her appreciation to Dr Massón Sena for sharing her work and Julio César Guanche's *Julio Antonio Mella* (Melbourne: Ocean Press, 2010).
49 Cupul & González, *Julio Antonio Mella y Tina Modotti*, p. 133. The original article was published on 28 November 1928. *Cuba Libre* was the journal for the ANERC, the organisation of Cuban exiles in Mexico that Mella presided.
50 Ibid., p. 133.
51 Olivia Miranda (ed.), *Rubén Martínez Villena: Ideario Político* (La Habana: Sociedad Económica de Amigos del País, 2003), pp. 134–143.
52 José M. Faraldo & Xosé Manoel Nuñez Seixas, 'The First Great Patriotic War: Spanish Communists and Nationalism, 1936–1939', *Nationalities Papers*, Vol. 37, No. 4, 2009, pp. 401–424.
53 Passi, *Vittorio Vidali*, pp. 17–20.
54 Pietro Rinaldo Fanesi, 'El exilio antifascista en América Latina: El caso mexicano: Mario Matagnana y la 'Garibaldi' (1941–1945)', *Estudios Interdisciplinarios de América Latina y el Caribe*, Vol. 3, No. 2, 1992, pp. 39–57.

55 Guanche, *Julio Antonio Mella*, p. 3; Oscar Montilla, 'Notas sobre la muerte de Julio Antonio Mella', *Gramacimanía*, 8 May 2009, online at www.gramscimania.info.ve/2009/08/notas-sobre-la-muerte-de-julio-antonio.html; Pino Cacucci, 'La otra cara de la historia: El asesinato de Mella', *El Nuevo Acción*, 13 August 2015, online at http://nuevoaccion.com/noticias/la-otra-cara-de-la-historia-el-asesinato-de-mella-los-motivos-que-llevaron-a-la-decision-de-liquidar-a-julio-antonio-mella-un-complot-internacional-de-mentirosos.
56 Gloria Crespo-MacCleenan, 'Tina Modotti, un puñado de niebla', *Revista Contexto*, No 25, 8 July 2015, online at https://ctxt.es/es/20150708/culturas/1659/Fotograf%C3%ADa-méxico-guerra-civil-española-Vitoria-Vidali-Diego-Rivera-Edward-Weston.htm. Modotti might have referred to the Trotsky assassination, since Vidali's involvement in this crime has also been the subject of some speculation.
57 Kersffeld, *Contra el imperio*, p. 441.
58 'Resolución del Buró del Caribe de la IC sobre el trabajo de la Sección Mexicana del SRI', 29 April 1931, RGASPI, *fond* 500, *opis* 1, *delo* 3, *list* 3 (hereafter RGASPI, fond/opis/delo, p.); 'Actas de la reunión del Buró', 27 August 1931, RGASPI, 500/1/3, p. 36.
59 Guanche, *Julio Antonio Mella*, p. 378.
60 'Carta de instrucciones del 1ero de mayo', 27 March 1931, RGASPI, 500/1/4, pp. 3–7. Other inclusions of 'fascism' as a local representation in Bureau discussions in 1931 include: 'Resolución del Buró del Caribe de la IC sobre el trabajo de la sección colombiana del SRI', 29 April 1931, RGASPI, 500/1/3, p. 12; 'Acta de la reunión del Buro', 27 August 1931, RGASPI, 500/1/3, p. 36.
61 Kersffeld, *Contra el imperio*, p. 441.
62 Fredrik Petersson, *We are Neither Visionaries, nor Utopian Dreamers: Willi Münzenberg, The League Against Imperialism and the Comintern, 1925–1933*, PhD dissertation, Abo Akademi University, Turku, 2013, p. 469.
63 Fredrik Petersson, 'Hub of the Anti-imperialist Movement: The League Against Imperialism and Berlin, 1927–1933', *International Journal of Postcolonial Studies*, Vol. 16, No. 1, 2014, pp. 49–71.
64 Kersffeld, *Contra el imperio*.
65 'Los CC de los Partidos Comunistas del Caribe', 18 April 1933, RGASPI, 500/1/13, p. 8.
66 Ibid.
67 'Directivas para la popularización del marxismo-leninismo en relación con la campaña de conmemoración de la muerte de Carlos Marx', 6 February 1933, RGASPI, 500/1/12, pp. 1–2.
68 'A los CC de los PC del Caribe', 30 January 1934, RGASPI, 500/1/16, p. 5.
69 'A los CC de los PC del Caribe', 16 March 1934, RGASPI, 500/1/16, p. 29.
70 During the 1933–1934 revolutionary period in Cuba, two communist groups struggled for control of the party: A 'native' group inside Cuba and the exile camp abroad, whose attempts to negotiate with bourgeois nationalist forces during the revolution had been strongly opposed by the new generation of militant communists who had stayed behind. The death of Mella's close associate and International Red Aid regional rep, Rúben Martínez Villena, in early 1934, opened the way for a militant, pro-Stalinist takeover.
71 'Esquema sobre algunos problemas del movimiento revolucionario del Caribe relacionado con la discusión para el séptimo congreso de la IC', 27 February 1935, RGASPI, 500/1/18, p. 6.
72 Kersffeld, *Contra el imperio*, p. 278.
73 Fabio Moraga Valle, 'El resplandor en el abismo: El movimiento Clarté y el pacifismo en América Latina (1918–1941)', *Anuario Colombiano de Historia Social y de la Cultura*, Vol. 42, No. 2, 2015, pp. 127–159; Peter J. Gold, 'The Influence of Henri Barbusse in Bolivia', *Bulletin of Latin American Research*, Vol. 2, No. 2, 1983, pp. 117–122; Florencia Ferreira de Cassone, *Claridad y el internacionalismo americano* (Buenos Aires: Editorial Claridad, 1998).

4

ANTI-FASCISM IN SOUTH AFRICA 1933–1945, AND ITS LEGACIES

Jonathan Hyslop

Between the 1970s and the early 1990s, quite a number of young men and women from the global north – especially from the Netherlands, Britain and Canada – travelled to South Africa to work underground for *Umkhonto we Sizwe*, the armed wing of the African National Congress (ANC). A strikingly common feature of this cohort was the way in which they saw their actions as connecting to the struggles against Franco and Hitler which had been the defining experience of their parents' generation. Sean Hosey, from north London, who served a five year prison sentence in Pretoria in the 1970s, said in retrospect: 'There was a thread that ran through my upbringing, Spain, the Second World War, American Civil Rights, Vietnam and of course South Africa.'[1] The actions of this group were perhaps the most dramatic manifestation of the way in which international opinion identified the apartheid regime as a continuation of pre-1945 fascism, and their opposition to it as taking forward an old struggle. Much of the power of the international anti-apartheid movement came from this perception. And to a large extent the liberation movements themselves shared the characterisation of apartheid as fascist; a widely circulated paperback of the 1960s, written by ANC political exile Brian Bunting recounted *The Rise of the South African Reich*.[2] There was indeed a relationship between the struggle against apartheid and the worldwide traditions of anti-fascism. But it was far more complex than a simple equation of apartheid and fascism would allow for. This chapter explores in some detail the South African fascisms and anti-fascisms of the 1930s and 1940s, and then points briefly toward some of the consequences of that historical experience for the country's later politics.

Until relatively recently, there has been a strong strain of 'methodological nationalism' in South African historiography, with the contours of the nation's history described and explained in rather inward-looking terms. But South African history is currently being re-thought in a global framework,[3] and this more expansive view is especially germane to our understanding of the politics of fascism and anti-fascism from 1933 to 1945. South African political actors were acutely aware of the transnational political struggles to which they were connected. There was a strong overtly fascist strand in South African politics, mainly within Afrikaner nationalism, and there was a range of political forces that identified with anti-fascism. Transnational imaginaries of fascism and anti-fascism, and real links to international movements and their political sponsors, were crucial to the whole spectrum of South African politics. Opposition to fascism was particularly shaped by the linkages of the South Africa to the United Kingdom, especially through the influence of the Communist Party of South Africa (CPSA), which was to some extent guided by the Communist Party of Great Britain, and the South African Labour Party (SALP) and its affiliated trade unions, which had connections to the British Labour Party and Trade Union Congress. Moreover, given the key role which South African Jewish communities were to play in anti-fascism, the networks between them and British Jewish organisations were important. Many of the European Jews who emigrated to South Africa at the turn of the century had come via England rather than directly from Eastern Europe, and there were a myriad of connections, personified in the Chief Rabbi of the British Empire from 1913 to 1946, Joseph Hertz, who had previously spent years in South Africa. As in the UK, the 1930s saw a running battle between fascists and anti-fascists, utilising a similar political vocabulary. But there were also important differences. As in the UK, in South Africa, during the war years overt fascists were interned, but this policy was not carried out on the same scale. There was a much broader support base for fascism in South Africa than in Britain, located in the ranks of radical Afrikaner nationalism. Unlike in Britain, a substantial fascist movement survived the outbreak of war, there was an active sabotage campaign by Nazi sympathisers, and street fighting between fascists and anti-fascists continued well into the 1940s.

South African anti-fascism also differed from that of Britain in that it was fundamentally shaped by the country's profound racial cleavage in access to political power. Recent international scholarship has rightly questioned crude assumptions that anti-fascism was a unitary phenomenon based on the manipulations of the Comintern. It has revealed a wide range of anti-fascisms, cross-cutting with liberalism, nationalism and Social Democracy as well as Communism.[4] This was certainly the case in South Africa. But in addition, in a segregationist social order, anti-fascism was critically segmented along racial lines. The chapter will show that though there were some points – in the small but hyper-active CPSA, some small liberal circles and broader united front movements – at which people of different races came together, to a large extent there were *different* black and white anti-fascisms.

1930s and 1940s fascism and anti-fascism was to shape South Africa's post-war history. There was a definite fascist ideological influence on the Afrikaner-dominated apartheid state established in 1948, and many of its early key personnel had fascist histories. Yet it differed significantly from classical fascism; the dominant strand of Afrikaner nationalism was populist rather than fascist. Despite the violent repressiveness and brutality of the state, there was a bigger element of surviving civil society and a greater element of legalism than was typical of fascist regimes. To put it provocatively, the apartheid state was a state with many fascist-inclined personnel, but it was not a fascist state.

Yet a number of important political activists in the country saw the struggle against apartheid through the lens of the fight against Nazism, and especially of the Second World War. This view became a key part of the ANC's political vision during the movement's turn to armed struggle under the leadership of Nelson Mandela and a mainly Communist leadership group in 1960–1961. Their tendency to characterise the regime as fascist was highly understandable. But it did not recognise the small but important remaining space for the emergence of above ground political movements. A militarisation of politics occurred in the liberation movement which was partly a legacy of the anti-fascism of the Second World War.

Pre-war white politics and the fascist powers

There was surprisingly strong resistance by the South African state to the claims of Mussolini and Hitler in the 1930s, primarily based in contingent geopolitical interests. But it nevertheless established a distance between the South African state and the dictators. On the other hand, the radical rightist political opposition who saw the state as failing adequately to assert Afrikaner racial and ethnic interests, were drawn to the German example.

The Great Depression had a disastrous impact on South Africa, sparking a major crisis in the white-dominated political and social order. In a major realignment in 1933 the supporters of Prime Minister J. B. M. Hertzog, the historic leader of Afrikaner Nationalism, and those of the opposition leader Jan Smuts, representing the forces of British Empire loyalism, came together to create a coalition government. Hertzog remained as Prime Minister, with Smuts as his deputy. The instinctive responses of the two key figures in the government to the rise to power of Hitler were very different. Hertzog's reflected a strong strand of Germanophilia in Afrikaner nationalist politics, which went back to German support for their cause in the Boer War: he told the German Consul-General Wiehl of his admiration for the 'new Germany'. Smuts on the other hand, racial paternalist and elitist as he was, was consistently hostile to the Nazis. He conceived of freedom as a matter of individual self-realisation within a legal order, was suspicious of popular politics, unattracted by biological racism and saw the British Empire as the crucial historical vehicle for the gradual extension of freedom. He was thus appalled by Nazism's disregard for law, its collectivism, its racial ideology and its threat to the British imperial order. Wiehl called him 'the Jew-protector'. Smuts was staunch in his hostility to the fascist powers through the pre-war period and later as leader of South Africa's war effort in the British cause.[5]

Despite Hertzog's sympathetic predisposition toward Germany, geopolitical factors quickly made him suspicious of German intentions. The Nazis made it clear that one of their key foreign policy aims was the return of Germany's African colonies. Hertzog had no intention of giving up South West Africa (now Namibia), which had been conquered by the South Africans in 1915 and then allocated to South Africa to rule as a League of Nations mandate territory, under the Treaty of Versailles. There had been considerable settlement of Afrikaners as farmers in the territory since the war. The small but cohesive South West African German settler community though still dominated the economy and were to prove extremely receptive to the appeals of National Socialism. There was a full-blown Nazi movement throughout South West under the auspices of the party's Berlin-based *Auslands-Organisation* (*A-O*: Foreign Organisation). There were also Nazi party branches among the small but influential German community in South Africa. Hertzog took measures to constrain the Nazi Party in South Africa and the mandate territory, but the *A-O* always found ways to continue their activities. In 1937 Smuts, with Hertzog's support, sent a large contingent of police to South West Africa in order to crack down on Nazi agitation.[6] Geopolitics also led the government to take a strong stand against Mussolini's invasion of Ethiopia in 1935. Both Hertzog and Smuts strongly condemned Mussolini, with Hertzog calling for a tougher line by the League of Nations against Italy. They were apprehensive both of Mussolini's further ambitions on the African continent, and that the disruption of the status quo in Africa would lead to concessions by the great powers to Hitler's colonial claims.[7]

But there was a level of Nazi sympathy within the Hertzog government, which did affect its policy in a more pro-Hitler direction. Hertzog restricted Jewish immigration, mainly in order to stave off the pressure on his right flank. The main figure in this ultra-rightist configuration was Oswald Pirow, a senior cabinet minister. The son of a German immigrant family, Pirow became rabidly pro-Nazi. He visited Germany in 1933 and again in 1938, and was received by the Führer on both occasions.[8]

The origins of South African anti-fascism

The Smuts–Hertzog rapprochement led to breakaway movement by more hard-core Afrikaner nationalists to form a 'Purified' National Party, under the leadership of D. F. Malan. Accusing Hertzog of having sold out to pro-British stooges, they launched a populist movement aiming to mobilise all sectors of Afrikaner society. The 'Purified' party envisaged a united Afrikaner people in which class divisions would be overcome. They sought to mobilise the savings of Afrikaners in order to build independent businesses, which, it was promised, unlike British enterprises would not exploit the workers. The central aims were to displace the social domination of the Anglophones, to make a republican break with the British Empire and to establish a far a more rigid form of racial segregation, which they named as 'apartheid' (separateness). A key role was played by the *Broederbond* (Brother's League), a secretive fraternity which sought to coordinate every aspect of Afrikaner social and political activity. A vast array of social organisations – women, youth, charitable and so on – were organised or taken over.[9]

Hendrik Verwoerd, the Malanite party's leading intellectual, made his career as an expert on the 'problem' of the poor whites, and the project of 'upfliting' them socially and economically in order to save them from racial mixing.[10] The demoralising effects of urban life and the need to destroy the hold on Afrikaner workers of the existing, often leftist, British and East European Jewish leadership of the trade unions became a central part of Malanite ideology. The Malanites were brilliant cultural entrepreneurs: a major coup for them was their successful take-over of the spectacular 1938 centenary commemoration of the Great Trek.

There were clear resonances with Nazism in Malanite ideology, although whether this came from shared intellectual roots or from common social dynamics of the movement is perhaps debatable.[11] The direct ideological influence of the Nazis on the Malanites via intellectuals who studied in Europe in the 1920s and 1930s has probably been overstated. But certainly, there were similarities in ideological terms – the need for *volk* unity, negation of class division within the nation, mystical nationalism – and in mobilisational techniques, such as spectacular rallies. There was, too a strong streak of anti-Semitism in their world view. Arguably, anti-Semitism in Afrikaner culture in the nineteenth and early twentieth century was relatively weak – British-origin South Africans were probably much more guilty of it. But anti-Semitism began to creep into the nationalist movement in the 1910s, with a tendency to conflate Rand mining magnates and Jews, and greatly intensified in the 1930s, propagated in Malan's speeches. Verwoerd again played a crucial part, leading to a 1936 protest campaign against the arrival in Cape Town of the ship *Stuttgart*, carrying Jewish refugees from Germany. The Johannesburg mass circulation newspaper which he edited from 1937, *Die Transvaler,* had a strongly anti-Semitic tone: the city was portrayed in its columns as the 'cosmopolitan' den of vice which was destroying the Afrikaner character. There were also some direct links between the Malanites and the Nazis, who seem to have considered them as potential future allies. There were a series of student trips to Hitler's Germany organised by the Afrikaner *Studentebond* (Student League), which impressed the visitors with the regime's 'achievements'. Piet Meyer, a future head of the *Broederbond*, led a student delegation to Germany in 1933 and was actually invited along on a skiing holiday by Rudolf Hess.[12]

The Malanites cannot strictly be considered a fascist organisation as such, in that they broadly accepted a framework of legality and change through the parliamentary mechanisms. Aside from occasional punch-ups at political meetings, they did not by and large, actually advocate physical violence. There was a great deal of informal individual racial violence in South African workplaces and farms, and Malan supporters were certainly involved in violent incidents against Indian shopkeepers which characterised the upsurge of nationalist sentiment in 1938. But killings, lynchings or political assassinations were not a significant feature of the movement. This is perhaps attributable to the sense that whites could rely on the state to do their repression for them, but it also reflects a certain legalist ideology. The Malanites are better understood as authoritarian racial populists than fascists as such.

Outside the 'Purified' ranks a sprinkling of overtly fascist organisations grew up. The most effective of these was the movement known as the 'Greyshirts'. Modelling themselves on the Nazis, they were founded in 1933 by a hairdresser, Louis Weichardt. They published a bilingual newspaper *Die Waarheid/The Truth*, putting forward the conventional Nazi equation of Communism with a Jewish conspiracy. The Greyshirts were responsible for a great deal of harassment of Jewish communities. They had support among white workers and also among a few intellectuals. From 1934, there were regular gatherings in Johannesburg and Cape Town by the Greyshirts. They also were to the fore of the campaign against Jewish immigration. But they never became a real mass movement – the Malanites occupying most of the available political space on the right until 1939.[13]

From 1933 on, a wave of anti-fascist sentiment started to surge among white political liberals and leftists. This was remarkable given the weakness of white liberal and left politics. An earlier strand of white radicalism, the syndicalism of the 1910s and early 1920s, had largely disappeared. The main party of white workers, the SALP, pursued a white labour protectionist agenda. The CPSA, a movement that initially came out of a fusion of small groups of British trade unionists and Jewish Bund socialists, had been quite disproportionately effective in the 1920s. But it almost destroyed itself through purges and infighting in the early 1930s and collapsed into a rump sect. And many liberals had been sucked into the stifling hegemony of the Smuts–Hertzog alliance.

The first public manifestation of opposition to the Nazis came, almost immediately after the *Machtegreifung*, from the Jewish communities of the country. These communities included a highly successful business sector in the major cities, a significant number of traders in small towns, and a working class component, especially in Cape Town and Johannesburg. Many Jews had family connections in Eastern Europe and thus they were acutely aware of the rise of Hitler.[14] There was a high level of political engagement with the threat to the Jews in Germany, from establishment community organisations led by the Jewish Board of Deputies, from Zionist groups and from the Jewish leftists. The first Jewish community protest meetings in Johannesburg in 1933 also had strong support from the Anglo-South African establishment, including senior Anglican clerics, and leading lawyers, educationists, and journalists. The Communist-orientated Johannesburg Jewish Workers Club was to be relentlessly active in anti-fascist causes for the next decade. A boycott of German businesses was launched by the Jewish community organisations, and seems to have been rather strong – by 1934, the German Consul-General complained that though boycotts in other countries were fading, that in South Africa continued to be effective.[15]

The Greyshirts became a focus of anti-fascist activity, in a sense providing a target that could dramatise the fascist threat. A number of Jewish groups, including the Board of Deputies, produced publications attacking the Greyshirts. In a celebrated 1934 libel case in the Eastern Cape, Rabbi Abraham Levy successfully sued three Greyshirt leaders over their claim that there was a Jewish plot to take over South Africa, inflicting serious damage on the organisation.[16] However, there were divisions in the South African Jewish world over how to respond to the fascist groups. The Jewish Workers Club were committed to physical confrontation whereas the Board of Deputies were anxious to avoid violence.[17] There were regular physical clashes between the Greyshirts and leftists in Johannesburg and Cape Town. In April 1936 there was a major confrontation between leftist and Jewish demonstrators and the Greyshirts when Weichardt spoke on the Grand Parade in central Cape Town.[18] Around the Johannesburg area in 1938, a considerable amount of mayhem arose from the activities of a small but virulent fascist movement known as the Blackshirts. In May, in the nearby mining town of Benoni, there was a vicious battle in which two hundred people stormed a Blackshirt meeting. This was followed by an attempted bombing of the Benoni synagogue by the Blackshirts. On 27 November 1938, the clashes between fascist groups and leftist and Jewish organisations culminated with violent fights in central Johannesburg between Blackshirts and anti-fascists. This was said to have been the biggest disturbance in the city since the insurrectionary white workers' rebellion of 1922. These events led to a temporary government ban on Fascist and anti-Fascist meetings in the Cape and the Transvaal.[19] It is perhaps important to emphasise that Jewish communities were by no means isolated in these confrontations with the 'shirt' movements. In the 1936 Cape Town protest, Jewish protesters were joined by 'Coloured' political militants from the National Liberation League led by then-Communist Cissie Gool.[20] Even in the small Cape town of Oudtshoorn, when the Greyshirts arrived to intimidate the local Jewish community in 1934, the Afrikaner town councillors opposed their activities and the demonstration fizzled out.[21]

The Spanish Civil War captured the imagination of young white radicals for the anti-Fascist cause. Uys Krige, a glamorous young Afrikaner who had travelled widely in France and Spain, wrote '*Die Lied van die Fascistiese bomwerpers*' (Song of the Fascist Bombers) a savage attack on Franco which remains among the best known poems in Afrikaans literature.[22] A handful of South Africans fought on the Republican side in Spain including Buck Parker in the British Independent Labour Party contingent and Jack Flior, a member of the Johannesburg Jewish Workers Club in the International Brigades.[23] South African-raised Jason Gurney was to write one of the most notable memoirs of the International Brigades and South African photographer Vera Elkan created the outstanding photographic record of the Brigades.[24] Journalist George Steer, who had formerly worked on the *Cape Argus*, had gone to the Horn of Africa to cover the invasion for the London *Times*. Dismissed by his arch-reactionary colleague Evelyn Waugh as a 'zealous young colonial reporter', he sympathised with the Ethiopian cause and was befriended by Haile Selassie. In Spain, Steer broke the story of the bombing of Guernica in *The Times:* it was his report that inspired Picasso's famous painting.[25] There was a spread of political activity inspired by the events in Europe. For instance, in Johannesburg a student, Rusty Bernstein, a future stalwart of the anti-apartheid struggle, got involved in politics through raising money for medical aid for Spain. This led him into Labour League of Youth – the youth wing of the SALP – and into the discussion group of the local branch of the Left Book Club.[26] The

Club – created by the London-based Victor Gollancz publishing house – had a following in South Africa and even in Southern Rhodesia, with its titles largely focused on the battle against fascism in Europe. A discernible left emerged in the SALP, sympathetic to anti-fascism and as a consequence more progressive than the old trade unionist party leadership. The Labour League of Youth became critical of their party, demanding that the SALP started admitting black members and develop a more egalitarian racial policy. A Friends of the Spanish Republic group was set up in Johannesburg, which sought to raise money to send a 'food ship' to Spain.[27] An Anti-Fascist League emerged, operating in Cape Town, Johannesburg and Durban, and frequently coming to blows with the Greyshirts. It was a CPSA initiative, but seems to have escaped control and to have been seen by the party – reflecting its paranoid mood – as something of a redoubt of expelled oppositionists and maverick leftists.[28] In Johannesburg, a leading part in the League was played by recent British immigrant, SALP member and trade union organiser, E. J. Burford. Burford had been on holiday in Madrid when the Spanish Civil war had broken out and had got involved in driving Republican soldiers to the front and broadcasting on Radio Barcelona. In Johannesburg he organised guards for left meetings and distributed anti-Hitler propaganda.[29] At the time of the Munich crisis there was a protest meeting and demonstration against Hitler organised by University of the Witwatersrand students who clashed with members of the German Club in central Johannesburg.[30] These developments largely took place in a white political world: but they also portended a potential shift in the politics of race.

African nationalist politics and anti-fascism

The 1930s was a decade of relatively weak black political opposition in the country. The ANC, although generally recognised as the main political organisation of the black elite, was small, gradualist, and rather ineffective. The great mass movement of 1920s, the ICU (Industrial and Commercial Workers Union) had collapsed. The CPSA, which in the late 1920s recruited some leading young black labour and political activists, was now lacking in mass influence. There was considerable small radical group activity in Cape Town, but only at the end of the decade were local leaders like Cissie Gool able to start big political mobilisations based in the 'Coloured' community. Black activists were to respond to the challenge of fascism, but by and large in different ways from whites. Black anti-fascism foregrounded questions of racial inequality and colonial rule, and implicitly or explicitly mounted a critique of white leftists' blindness to these questions, or of their willingness to subordinate anti-colonialism to defeating fascism.

The Italian invasion of Ethiopia in 1935 aroused fury among African nationalists. The symbolic importance of an imperialist attack on one of the two self-ruled African states of the continent was vast. The most dramatic expression of this was the solidarity strikes that took place among dockworkers, in Durban, Cape Town and South West African Lüderitz. In all three ports, dockers refused to work on vessels carrying cargos to the Italian Army in the Horn of Africa.[31] The strong influence of Pan-Africanist ideas in these harbours was important here. In the 1920s, African American, West Indian and West African sailors and labourers had been highly active in bringing the doctrines of Marcus Garvey's Universal Negro Improvement Association to southern African Ports. Arturo Emile Wattlington, from St Thomas in the Virgin Islands was to the fore of the 'Hands off Ethiopia' campaign in Cape Town, and a number of South African Garveyites such as Zach Masopha and A. J. Maphike also participated.[32] Former Garveyites such as Bennett Ncwana and Joel Bulana spoke out against the invasion. In Cape Town, the various small leftist groups agitated around the war and a Communist front organisation, the League against Fascism and War, held mass meetings in support of Ethiopia, attended by large, predominantly black, crowds. There were even discussions among black activists of whether it was possible to join Haile Selassie's forces.[33]

At the start of the Second World War, the ANC had taken up a position in support of the British and South African war effort. In a sense this was a repeat of the approach its predecessor, the South African Native National Congress had taken in 1914, in the anticipation that a grateful British Empire would intervene with the white South African authorities to bring about egalitarian reforms in the country – a hope that was completely and bitterly disappointed. However, American-educated Dr A. B. Xuma brought an astute understanding of the global politics of the war to his position when he became Secretary General of the ANC in 1939. He was assisted in his new political project by Z.K. Matthews of Fort Hare University, a former student of Malinowski at the LSE, who also had a shrewd sense of the international political potentialities of the war. The Xuma leadership seized on the ambiguities in the 1941 Atlantic Charter issued by Britain and the US. With the entry of the US into the war as Britain's senior partner, the ANC understood that there was a political space to exploit American hostility to British territorial empire and the Allies' desire to cast the war as a fight for democracy. The 1943 conference of the ANC produced a document entitled 'The Atlantic Charter and the Africans', adopting a Rooseveltian rhetoric, and positioning African nationalists within the war against fascism.[34] While maintaining full support for the war, the Xuma–Matthews approach was to try to leverage the British – American split over the issue of European empires, in the hope that the US, as the new factor in the equation, would lean on Britain, and thus on South Africa, for change. The language of American liberal anti-fascism – Roosevelt's 'Four Freedoms' – was specifically invoked by Xuma against the recalcitrant British government.[35]

A very different political response to the war against fascism emerged in the Western Cape. In 1943, a group called the Non-European Unity Movement (NEUM) was founded in Cape Town. It elaborated its own political positions, emerging from Trotskyism, but developing into a more broad internationalist anticolonial nationalism. It gained a strong hold among the 'Coloured' and African intelligentsia in the Cape, and especially among teachers. The NEUM straightforwardly characterised the Smuts government as *itself* Fascist. They recast the struggle in South Africa in rhetorical terms derived from the conflict in Europe. The dominant whites were sarcastically referred to as the *Herrenvolk*, thus appropriating the Nazi term for the dominant 'race'. Black people who worked with the government were referred to as 'Quislings' in reference to Vidkun Quisling, the pro-Nazi Norwegian traitor.[36] The NEUM used the power of European anti-Fascist resistance language for anti-colonial purposes. They placed an overwhelming emphasis on refusal to 'collaborate' with the state, stressing the need to boycott government institutions, thus invoking the European resistance model of rejecting and targeting those who had sold out.

However, the three key emerging young African Nationalist leaders – Mandela, Oliver Tambo and Walter Sisulu, worked within the ANC. But they were not now convinced by ANC's pro-war position. When this youth circle formed the ANC Youth League in 1944, the importance of the war for Africans was largely denied. Whereas the ANC leadership (and the small but influential number of CPSA activists) continued to stress the importance of choosing the side of the Allies, the ANCYL made only a nod to the notion of the war as a fight for freedom, essentially treating it as irrelevant to African interests. The ANCYL insisted that no outside force could accomplish anything for African people. The enemy was at home and had to be tackled head on, in a spirit of self-reliance. The ANCYL document pursued a shrewd rhetorical strategy, ventilating some of the NEUM-style criticisms of the ANC leadership, but attributing them to outsiders, and assuring their own loyalty to the ANC.[37] Their approach was to lay the groundwork for a gradual takeover of the ANC by the advocates of a more militant strategy and for the campaign of mass disobedience which the ANC would launch in the 1950s.

White anti-fascism in wartime

In 1939, a new political movement arose, merging Afrikaner nationalism with overt fascism. It was called the *Ossewabrandwag* (OB) – the 'Ox-wagon Sentinels', evoking the symbolism of the previous year's Great Trek commemoration. Although it initially posed itself as complementary to other Afrikaner organisations, the OB was clearly a challenge to Malan's dominance in the political realm. The message – although initially not always explicitly stated – was that it was not Malan's parliamentarianism, but insurrectionary nationalism that would bring the desired republic. A complex struggle for the political soul of Afrikanerdom between Malan and the OB unfolded. The OB proved particularly adept at winning over white workers in the industrial towns and cities. It established a paramilitary wing, the *Stormjaers* (Stormtoopers), created a cult around its leader, Hans van Rensburg, and devised its own uniforms and salute (right hand raised horizontally across the chest).[38] Unlike the Greyshirts, the OB became a real mass movement.

When war broke out the SALP heartily supported the war, although at the cost of losing some of its Afrikaner support. The Communists had been thrown into confusion immediately before the outbreak by the Hitler–Stalin Pact, and even more by the Comintern's deposing of the British Communist leader Harry Pollitt, who was admired in the South African party, over his initial support for the declaration of war. But the CPSA ultimately accepted the line of the new CPGB Secretary, R. Palme Dutt, that the war was an 'imperialist' one.[39] The CPSA began to recover from the disaster of the 1930s, starting to make connections to the growing discontent in black townships through trade unions and local protests.[40] The anti-war position was also popular with the Indian community because it corresponded to that of the anti-colonial movement in India itself. Given the party line, anti-fascism was somewhat put on the back burner as a political project. But the party's public meetings – for instance those held on the steps of the Johannesburg City Hall every Saturday night – involved frequent clashes with the OB and other Fascists.

As the United Kingdom went to war, Smuts advocating support for the British cause, and Hertzog, calling for neutrality, clashed. Smuts won a majority in parliament and led the country into the conflict on Britain's side. He set about building the armed forces and war industries and achieved considerable success in doing so. Because of Afrikaner resistance to participation, Smuts called for volunteers rather than using conscription. The army was to be segregated, with only whites as combat troops and blacks confined to support roles. Over the course of the war, over 200,000 white and 100,000 black troops, and 100,000 white women auxiliaries were mobilised. South Africans were to fight in the Horn of Africa, in the Western Desert and in Italy. A sizeable Air Force was created which was to play a significant role in the Mediterranean theatre. Industrial production was reorganised and produced significant amounts of military equipment for the British as well as the South African forces. Coastal defences were strengthened and South African ports serviced huge British convoys to North Africa and the Far East. Though Smuts was himself notoriously conservative on racial issues, the departure of the Hertzogites produced a significant liberalisation of the political administration. Some white liberals and social democrats, with broadly anti-fascist positions, gained influential positions in the civil service. This was to create political space for both liberals and the left which had not existed before, with, some important consequences for anti-fascist projects.[41]

In the years between 1939 and 1942, when there appeared to be a possibility that Hitler would win the war, Malan hedged his bets. Although he certainly did not want to be subordinated to Germany, he hoped that a victorious Hitler might place control of the country in Afrikaner hands. He held clandestine talks with Nazi emissaries. On the other hand he did not depart from his basically parliamentary politics, giving him another option if Hitler did not prevail. Pirow, who had left the government with Hertzog, intensified Malan's problems by establishing another overtly fascist group the *Nieuwe Orde* (New Order), which initially had some following among disaffected nationalists in parliament – but quickly faded. The OB by contrast, thrived, attracting powerful support from radicalised Afrikaners. The *Stormjaers* began engaging in sabotage and working toward a future insurrection. They also connected up with Axis intelligence networks operating out of Portuguese East Africa, which were particularly dangerous because they were passing information on British convoys to the German navy, which was mounting a serious submarine campaign on the African coast. A spectacular role was played by one Robey Leibbrandt. Leibbrandt had represented South Africa in Boxing at the 1936 Olympic games and been dazzled by Nazi showmanship. He returned to Germany and after the outbreak of war was trained as an agent by the *Abwehr*. He was landed on the South African coast from a yacht, with the mission of building an underground network, carrying out sabotage, and, allegedly, assassinating Smuts. It took a long time for the police to catch Leibbrandt, and he attained a legendary status in South African political mythology.[42] Smuts interned a considerable number of OB members and other fascists and German nationals, but the underground enemy proved difficult to subdue.

Malan knew how to bide his time, and was an extremely canny political operator. When it became clear in early 1943 that the Nazis would lose the war, the steam started to go out of the OB. Malan was able gradually to roll up most of the OB and the Pirow faction, incorporating them into his party, and benefiting from the organised base that the OB had built in the urban working class. What he also inherited though was a number of individuals whose thinking came out of the mainstream of the fascism of the 1930s and 1940s. Some would become politically important after Malan came to power on his platform of 'apartheid' in 1948. But they were subordinated to Malan and Verwoerd's leadership.[43]

When the Soviet Union was invaded in June 1941, the CPSA turned to the policy of supporting the war effort. They also saw – by no means mistakenly – the opportunity to draw some of the South African military forces toward the left. After some initial meetings in the second half of 1941, the Communists played the key role in founding an organisation called the Springbok Legion (SL), aimed at organising servicemen. This movement was very broadly socially based, but it was led by the Communist network in the Union Defence Force. The Legion was conceived as a soldiers' trade union, addressing issues of pay, conditions, and post-war social reintegration. It also sought to use the uniting theme of anti-fascism as a vehicle for drawing white soldiers towards a more egalitarian politics. This was by no means a hopeless task – hatred of the OB and Malan nationalists, who were seen as traitors, was intense among the troops, and servicemen on leave on the Rand and in Cape Town were frequently involved in physical fights with them. Soldiers had many practical grievances and consequently, a sense of injustice. White servicemen were impressed with Soviet resistance to Hitler. And they were resentful of the British Army's patronising attitude to 'colonials'. One sergeant in the Western Desert campaign summarised his men's attitudes as 'admiration for Uncle Joe, fury and impatience with Britain's ineptitude and constant disasters', and disillusion with Smuts ('a bloody platitude factory').[44] The SL was also influenced in Egypt by the radicalisation underway in the British forces, and especially its expression in the 'Soldier's Parliament' which included in its leadership such notable figures as the Communist Party theorist James Klugman, the future Labour MP Leo Abse, and the future historian of African nationalism, Basil Davidson.[45]

Soldiers of colour were included in the movement, and there is certainly some anecdotal evidence that the rigidity of racial boundaries weakened at times in the

North African campaign – but the SL's intended audience was clearly mainly white (and male). The organisation was astonishingly successful, peaking in 1944 at 50,000 to 60,000 members, a number equivalent to about quarter of all the white troops who volunteered for the war, and a much bigger proportion of the men actually serving at that time. It also created the Home Front League (HFL) organising women and male civilians. An SL–HFL protest campaign about soldier's pay and widow's pensions in 1943 succeeded in winning a meeting between the Legion leadership and the government, which resulted in modest improvements. The combination of championing material grievances and street-level anti-fascism provided a basis for the SL. But it also tried to change the social and racial attitudes of white soldiers, emphasising wartime comradeship across the colour line and advocating progressive social policy. SL activists believed that white working class soldiers, once removed from the direct influence of the Afrikaner nationalists and British chauvinists, were remarkably open to entertaining ideas about egalitarian post-war social reforms and about improving the social conditions of African workers. The SL was genuinely keen to support the war effort. In mid-1942, at a time when the British position in North African was threatened, it energetically supported the recruitment campaign for a new South African Division. In the 1943 election it put its now considerable organisational resources behind securing a Smuts victory, subordinating its critique of the government to the need to keep the anti-war Afrikaner nationalists from power. However the Legion also advocated policies which went against the government line in many respects. It called for conscription for whites, which Smuts resisted on the grounds that it would antagonise many Afrikaners. And on both egalitarian and military grounds, the SL demanded the arming of black soldiers, which the government was opposed to both for racist reasons and because of fear of white public opinion.[46]

A key figure in the Springbok Legion was its Secretary, Jack Hodgson. Jack was the son of an English immigrant who had been killed in a mining accident. He grew up in extreme poverty, spending some time in an orphanage. Becoming a miner, Jack went to work on the Northern Rhodesia Copperbelt. There he participated in leading a major strike of the white workforce, and was won over to Communism by the strike's main activist, an Australian called Frank Maybank. Hodgson served in the army in North Africa, carrying out dangerous missions in a mobile unit which operated behind enemy lines. After he was invalided out, he set up and operated the Springbok Legion's central office in Johannesburg. He then met Rica Gampel, a middle class Jewish woman then in the Air Force, who was in a mainly Coloured branch of the Legion.[47] Rica became the Legion's highly effective fund raiser; they married and were later to play a key role later in the liberation movement's turn to armed struggle.

Developments within the Communist-led SL also interacted with a broader swing to the left in state policy and white public opinion. The left in the SALP strengthened its position, with figures like the leftist Johannesburg SALP City Councillor, Jessie McPherson, advocating egalitarian post-war social and racial political reforms. The CPSA-steered South African Friends of the Soviet Union and Medical Aid for Russia became influential: for example a 1944 Cape Town event under the slogan of '3 Years Fighting Alliance with Russia', was addressed by an Anglican Church Bishop and by McPherson.[48] The SL joined in these campaigns, which also echoed the British left's demand for a 'second front' in Europe. The CPSA even won a handful of municipal council seats in white areas in Johannesburg, Cape Town and East London. Smuts's director of intelligence, E. G. Malherbe, created an Army Educational Scheme (AES) which was aimed to help inoculate the troops against the ideas of the pro-Nazi political forces in South Africa. Under the leadership of a very able liberal, Leo Marquard, it not only performed this task but also sought to make the troops more sympathetic to the idea of social and racial reform in the future. Many of the lecturer posts in the AES were taken by advanced liberals, social democrats and communists, who initiated wide-ranging discussions in the camps in Egypt and later in Italy, and who took the opportunity to advance their anti-fascist ideas.[49] Guy Butler, later to become a leading intellectual figure in South African liberalism, was as an AES officer and was extremely sympathetic to the Soviet Union at this time. He described himself and his colleagues as 'social democrats' and as hoping that the post war period would see the end of the 'industrial colour bar' (which prevented Africans from taking most skilled jobs) and a (gradualist) extension of the franchise.[50] The war ended on a note of anti-fascist euphoria for the activists. Rusty Bernstein, now an SL activist with the troops in Northern Italy, recalled fraternising with partisans and making friends with a journalist on the Italian Communist Party's paper *L'Unità*. He experienced the celebration of victory in Milan as the most glorious of his life, next to South Africa's 1994 democratic election.[51]

But the SL's mass support did not long survive the war, perhaps primarily because of the underlying racial politics. The racism of the South African troops was hard to shake, and it was often tied to a suspicion of egalitarianism. Guy Butler eventually despaired of winning over the men to a social democratic or non-racial perspective.[52] Moreover, the immediate aftermath of the war had a hugely demoralising effect on the South African troops abroad. Bernstein recalled how the extreme delays in repatriation from Italy caused the troops to sink into political lethargy, psychological depression and epidemic black marketeering.[53] At a transit camp in Helwan, Egypt, a major riot by frustrated soldiers took place in which the entire facility was burned to the ground – but it was perhaps as much a sign of despair as of politicisation.[54] By 1946, the SL's membership had completely collapsed; it struggled on until 1953, but essentially reduced to a tiny core of Communist-aligned activists. Government mismanagement of demobilisation, including a desperate housing shortage for veterans, may well have tipped a number of Afrikaner former soldiers toward voting for the Nationalists in 1948.

The afterlife of South African anti-fascism

The National Party came to power in 1948, and gradually created one of the most extensive and bureaucratically regulated systems of racial inequality in world history.

But though many of the officials of the new regime had genuinely fascist pasts in the OB or the Pirow faction, they were subordinated to the Malanite racial populists. And the latter too sought to cover the tracks of their anti-Semitism and ambiguous relation to the Nazis.

Wartime anti-fascism had its own afterlife. This was most dramatically manifested in a brief revival of white soldier radicalisation. In 1951 the NP government sought to change the constitution in order to remove the franchise rights of 'Coloured' male voters in the Cape, which had survived until then. Protest over this led to the formation of a veteran's organisation called the Torch Commando (TC) which aimed to mobilise the ex-servicemen against the Afrikaner nationalists. The TC invoked the history of the war against Nazism, and sought to rekindle the brotherhood of the battlefield. Spectacular military-style parades and torchlight processions were held, and Group Captain A.G. 'Sailor' Malan, a South African who had been a fighter ace in the RAF during the Battle of Britain, emerged as a charismatic leader. The tone of the TC though was largely liberal, with a large presence of the white Anglophone establishment and influence from big business. Its policies were rhetorically constitutionalist and democratic, but vague, and its racial politics largely paternalist. The core of old SL Communist activists were involved, but they were not dominant, and were eventually pushed out of the movement. As the apartheid regime consolidated its control and ensured that it won the white elections through gerrymandering, the Commando gradually faded away.[55] White opponents of the NP continued to invoke the history of the OB and its wartime treachery in their polemics, but this was a last thin connection to an almost forgotten moment of radical anti-fascism.

As Neil Roos has shown, in the end both the Springbok Legion and the Torch Commando foundered on the rocks of racial politics.[56] White soldiers and veterans were often genuine in their loathing of Nazism and its South African acolytes. They often felt sympathy for the sufferings of black South Africans, and were frequently persuadable that more egalitarian social policies and greater personal freedoms were desirable. Yet fundamentally, they did think of themselves as 'white' and thus as having a superior claim to power. They baulked at the possibility of a majority non-racial franchise. Anti-fascism did not trump racial identification.

But there was one other very important legacy of the Springbok Legion era. After the CPSA was banned in 1950, the Communists went underground. Around the same time, they developed a close alliance with the new ANC leadership group around Mandela and Tambo. Communists from a Springbok Legion background played a key part role in building this connection. These veterans tended to see Apartheid as another form of fascism, and the battle against it as a continuation of their participation in the war against Hitler. When in 1960, the state repressed oppositional movements, these white former soldiers were crucial in influencing the turn of the ANC and its allies toward armed struggle.[57] Jack Hodgson was an early and strong advocate of the military turn. His skills with explosives, acquired as a miner and in the army, came to the fore. The initial campaign planned the sabotaging of industrial and state infrastructure.[58] According to Nelson Mandela,

Hodgson became 'our first demolition expert', and Mandela was present when Hodgson set off the first trial explosive devices.[59] This interpretation of apartheid as a fascism which required a war to crush it was a highly understandable one given the experience of Hodgson's cohort. It was reinforced by the subsequent experience of the ANC's militants abroad. In the early 1960s, young black ANC members were sent to the Soviet Union for military training. There, they were taught by instructors who were veterans of the Great Patriotic War, and whose thinking was based on the experience of Soviet partisans from 1941 to 1945.[60] Thus the idea of the struggle as a war against fascism was further entrenched. Though the importance of political direction was often asserted, by the 1980s the ANC built up a considerable military apparatus, which was envisaged by at least some elements of the movements as eventually toppling the regime. Yet the ANC's armed struggle in the end remained symbolic; it never came remotely close to militarily threatening the regime.

By interpreting the regime as 'fascist', the ANC did not see the limited but important room for political manoeuvre that the nature of the state did give. Unlike in classical fascism, beleaguered but important civil society space did exist. It is not in fact clear that it would have been impossible in the early 1960s to continue with some form of mass political mobilisation.[61] When powerful independent black trade unions emerged in the 1970s, the ANC, on the assumption that real trade unions could not exist under fascism, denounced them as fake organisations. In fact, during the great political confrontations of the 1980s, these unions turned out to the bedrock of mass resistance.[62] While the regime was intensely repressive it did not ever fully close down civil society. Community organisations, civil rights groups, independent lawyers, a critical press, and critical intellectuals did continue to operate, albeit often under extreme harassment. Their work did open up space for challenges to the regime, which were crucial to the ultimately successful mass resistance of the 1980s. By construing the political terrain solely as one of war against fascism, the ANC prevented itself, until very late in the day, from seeing the importance of these social movements and institutional and cultural struggles. And because the regime was conceived as monolithic, proponents of a negotiated settlement within the ANC had to push back against militarist thinking in the organisation in order to achieve their eventually successful strategy. The mythology of the anti-fascist war militarised politics, in the end hindering more than helping the movement.

Conclusion

The global anti-fascism of the period 1933 to 1945 was central to modern South Africa's formation. In some respects the history of South African anti-fascism followed the pattern of anti-fascism in the United Kingdom, with the formation of a broadly based anti-fascist campaign in the mid-1930s and considerable enthusiasm for the Spanish Republican cause; a split between pro-war labourites and anti-war Communists between 1939 and 1941, and a return to left-liberal unity against the

Axis powers after the German invasion of the USSR. As in the UK, there was a political radicalisation among the armed forces that emerged from the politics of anti-fascism during the war years. There were, as in Britain, tensions during the 1930s between radical leftists on the one hand, and moderate labourites, liberals and Jewish establishment organisations on the other, as to whether to oppose local Fascists in a violent or a peaceful manner. But South African anti-fascism was also shaped by the country's specific social and political formation as a settler state with a majority, politically subordinate, indigenous population. It was fragmented along racial lines with the Garveyites, the opposing factions of the ANC, and the Unity Movement all conceptualising opposition to fascism in ways that differed both from each other, but also from the strategies and tactics advocated by white leftists. The very real politicisation of white troops in the Second World War could not overcome issues of race in the end. And, in a peculiar way, the wartime anti-fascism of white Communist soldiers returned in the early 1960s to help shape the African nationalists turn to the armed struggle.

The memory anti-fascism has had a remarkable persistence in the South African political imagination. From 1945 onward, across a broad political spectrum, there has been a tendency for all those who in any way identify with the cause of democracy, to cast themselves as continuators of anti-fascism and their enemies as the heirs of Mussolini and Hitler. At the time of writing both an Afrikaner organisation (*Afriforum*) and a black nationalist organisation (Economic Freedom Fighters) are daily accused of fascism in the South African press. Neither perhaps actually fully quite fits the bill: but it is no accident that political actors see the invocation of fascism as a crucial political resource. It is not only in Europe that politics cannot escape from the history of the anti-fascist struggle.

Notes

1 *Camden News Journal*, 31 May 2018.
2 Brian Bunting, *The Rise of the South African Reich* (Harmondsworth: Penguin, 1964).
3 Rob Skinner, *Modern South Africa in World History: Beyond Imperialism* (London: Bloomsbury, 2017), pp. 69–88.
4 Enzo Traverso, *Fire and Blood: The European Civil War 1914–1945* (London: Verso, 2016); Hugo Garcia, 'Transnational History: A New Paradigm for Anti-Fascist Studies?', *Contemporary European History*, Vol. 25, No. 4, 2016, pp. 563–572.
5 Robert Citino, *Germany and the Union of South Africa in the Nazi Period* (New York: Greenwood Press, 1991).
6 Ibid.
7 Tilman Dedering, 'South Africa and the Italo-Ethiopian War 1935–6', *The International History Review*, Vol. 35, No. 5, 2013, pp. 1009–1030.
8 Citino, *Germany and the Union*, pp. 185–189.
9 T. Dunbar Moodie, *The Rise of Afrikanerdom: Power, Apartheid and the Afrikaner Civil Religion* (Berkeley, CA: University of California Press, 1975); Dan O'Meara, *Forty Lost Years: The Apartheid State and the Politics of the National Party, 1948–1994* (Johannesburg: Ravan Press, 1996).
10 Alex Hepple, *Verwoerd* (Harmondsworth: Penguin, 1967).
11 Moodie, *Rise*; O'Meara, *Forty Lost Years*.

12 Patrick J. Furlong, *Between Crown and Swastika: The Impact of the Radical Right on the Afrikaner Nationalist Movement in the Fascist Era* (Hanover, NH: Wesleyan University Press, 1991), pp. 35–45.
13 Furlong, *Between Crown and Swastika*, p. 80.
14 Richard Mendelsohn & Milton Shain, *The Jews in South Africa* (Johannesburg: John Ball, 2008).
15 Citino, *Germany and the Union.*
16 Furlong, *Between Crown and Swastika.*
17 Taffy Adler, 'Lithuania's Diaspora: The Johannesburg Jewish Workers' Club, 1928–1948', *Journal of Southern African Studies*, Vol. 6, No. 1, 1979, pp. 70–92.
18 Rebecca Hodes, '"Free Fight on the Grand Parade": Resistance to the Greyshirts in 1930s South Africa', *The International Review of African Historical Studies*, Vol. 47, No. 2, 2014, pp. 185–208.
19 Atalia Ben-Meir, *The South African Jewish Board of Deputies*, PhD dissertation, University of Natal, Durban, 1995, pp. 64–65.
20 Hodes, 'Free Fight'.
21 Daniel Coetzee, 'Fires and Feathers, Acculturation, Arson and the Jewish Community in Oudtshoorn, South Africa, 1914–1948', *Jewish History*, Vol. 19, No. 2, 2003, pp. 143–187.
22 J. C. Kannemeyer, *Die Goue Seun: Die Lewe en Werk van Uys Krige* (Cape Town: Tafelberg, 2002).
23 George Orwell, *A Life in Letters*, edited by Peter Davison (New York: Norton, 2010), pp. 75–76; Adler, 'Lithuania's Diaspora', p. 85.
24 Jason Gurney, *Crusade in Spain* (London: Faber & Faber, 1974); IWM, 'Elkan, Vera Ines Morely', online at www.iwm.org.uk/collections/item/object/205004502 (accessed 27 April 2019).
25 Nicholas Rankin, *Telegram from Guernica: The Extraordinary Life of George Steer* (London: Faber & Faber, 2003).
26 Rusty Bernstein, *Memory Against Forgetting: Memoir of a Time in South African Politics 1938–1964* (Johannesburg: Wits University Press, 2017), pp. 5–6.
27 Adler, 'Lithuania's Diaspora', p. 83.
28 Apollon Davidson et al. (eds), *South Africa and the Communist International: A Documentary History*, vol. II (London: Frank Cass, 2003), pp. 128, 140, 144; Baruch Hirson, *A History of The Left in South Africa: Writings of Baruch Hirson* (London: I. B. Tauris, 2005), pp. 85–103.
29 Bernstein, *Memory Against Forgetting*, pp. 12–13; Peter Alexander, *Workers, War and the Origins of Apartheid: Labour and Politics in South Africa 1939–1948* (Oxford: James Currey, 2000), pp. 132–133.
30 Bernstein, *Memory Against Forgetting*, pp. 11–12.
31 Peter Cole, *Dockworker Power: Race and Activism in Durban and the San Francisco Bay Area* (Urbana, IL: University of Illinois Press, 2018), p. 191.
32 Robert Trent Vinson, *'The Americans Are Coming': Dreams of African American Liberation in Segregationist South Africa* (Athens, OH: Ohio University Press, 2012); Robert Trent Vinson, '"Sea Kaffirs", "American Negroes" and the Gospel of Garveyism in Twentieth Century Cape Town', *Journal of African History*, Vol. 47, No. 2, 2006, pp. 281–303.
33 Dedering, 'South Africa and the Italo-Ethiopian War 1935–6'.
34 A. B. Xuma, 'African Claims in South Africa 1943', *African History Online*, online at www.sahistory.org.za/archive/african-claims-south-africa-dr-xuma-anc-conference-1943 (accessed 23 March 2019).
35 Ibid.
36 Christopher Joon-Hai Lee, 'The Use of the Comparative Imagination: South African and World History in the Political Consciousness and Strategy of the South African Left, 1943–1959', *Radical History Review*, No. 92, 2005, pp. 31–61.
37 'ANC Youth League Manifesto 1944', *South African History Online*, online at www.sahistory.org.za/archive/anc-youth-league-manifesto-1944 (accessed 22 March 2019).
38 Christoph Marx, 'The Ossewabrandwag as a Mass Movement 1939–1941', *Journal of Southern African Studies*, Vol. 20, No. 2, 1994, pp. 195–219.

39 Bernstein, *Memory Against Forgetting*, p. 39.
40 Tom Lodge, *Black Politics in South Africa since 1945* (London: Longman, 1983).
41 Saul Dubow & Alan Jeeves (eds), *South Africa's 1940s: Worlds of Possibilities* (Johannesburg: Double Storey, 2005).
42 Furlong, *Between Crown and Swastika*, pp. 138–160.
43 Ibid.
44 James Ambrose Brown, *Retreat to Victory: A Springbok's Diary in North Africa: Gazala to El Alamein 1942* (Johannesburg: Ashanti, 1991), pp. 87–102.
45 Bernstein, *Memory Against Forgetting*, p. 56.
46 Neil Roos, *Ordinary Springboks: White Servicemen and Social Justice in South Africa, 1939–1961* (Aldershot: Ashgate, 2005), pp. 65–102.
47 Rica Hodgson, *Foot Soldier for Freedom* (Johannesburg: Picador Africa, 2010); Bernstein, *Memory Against Forgetting*, pp. 55–56.
48 Tangential Travel and Jewish Life, 'Harry's 16th Yahrzeit', online at https://elirab.me/tag/yahrzeit (accessed 15 March 2019).
49 Roos, *Ordinary Springboks*, pp. 45–63.
50 Guy Butler, *Bursting World: An Autobiography (1936–1945)* (Cape Town: David Philip, 1983), p. 113.
51 Bernstein, *Memory against Forgetting*, p. 67.
52 Butler, *Bursting World*, p. 278.
53 Bernstein, *Memory against Forgetting*, pp. 72–74.
54 Roos, *Ordinary Springboks*, pp. 94–102.
55 Ibid., pp. 129–157.
56 Ibid.
57 SL veterans who played an important part in the early years of armed struggle included the Hodgsons, Bernstein, Joe Slovo, Wolfie Kodesh, Cecil Williams, Brian Bunting, Ivan Schermbrucker and Fred Carneson.
58 Hodgson, *Foot Soldier*.
59 Nelson Mandela, *Long Walk to Freedom* (London: Abacus, 1994), pp. 325–339.
60 Ronnie Kasrils, *Armed and Dangerous: From Undercover Struggle to Freedom* (Johannesburg: Jonathan Ball, 1998), pp. 81–92.
61 Saul Dubow, 'Were There Political Alternatives in the Wake of the Sharpeville-Langa Violence in South Africa, 1960?', *Journal of African History*, Vol. 56, No. 1, 2015, pp. 119–142.
62 Martin Legassick, 'Debating the Revival of the Worker's Movement in the 1970s: The South African Democracy Education Trust and Post-Apartheid Patriotic History', *Kronos*, Vol. 34, No. 1, 2008, pp. 240–266.

5

'MAKE SCANDINAVIA A BULWARK AGAINST FASCISM!'

Hitler's seizure of power and the transnational anti-fascist movement in the Nordic countries

Kasper Braskén

On a global scale, Hitler's seizure of power on 30 January 1933 provided urgent impetus for transnational anti-fascist conferences and rallies. One of the first European, but almost completely overlooked major conferences was organised in Copenhagen in mid-April 1933 in the form of a Scandinavian Anti-Fascist Conference. This formed a transnational meeting point of European and especially Scandinavian workers and intellectuals that provided an important first response to developments in Germany. The chapter will use the Scandinavian conference as a prism to look back at anti-fascist activism in the Nordic countries during the preceding years, and to then follow its transformation after 1933. It will contribute to the global analysis of the transition period of communist-led anti-fascism from the sectarian class-against-class line to the inception of the popular front period in 1935.

What were these largely overlooked, first anti-fascist articulations in Europe, and how were they connected to the rising transnational and global anti-fascist mobilisation coordinated in Paris and London? As we shall see, on the one hand Hitler's seizure of power vitalised anti-fascism in Scandinavia but paradoxically, on the other, it further sharpened the communist critique of reformist social democracy and empowered social democratic anti-communism.

The Nazi seizure of power was not without its effects in the Nordic countries. It revealed several core dilemmas that most nations in the world were facing: to continue with, and develop foreign relations and trade irrespective of the new government, or be openly critical of internal German developments, perhaps even boycott Hitler's new regime. What space was there for anti-fascist activity in 1933 and what kind of restrictions and limitations did Nordic governments under pressure from the German foreign office impose on fighting fascism?

Between neutrality, appeasement and collaboration

Scandinavia might seem like an ideal location for anti-fascist exile. Fascist parties and movements in Denmark, Sweden and Norway remained extremely weak during the interwar period. No far-right party received more than two per cent of the electoral vote. Thanks to governmental crisis agreements that resulted in the formation of alliances between the social democrats and the peasants' parties in Denmark (1933), Sweden (1933), Norway (1935), Finland (1937) and Iceland (1937), Scandinavia remained 'free from fascism'. Finland was, for a moment, the exception as it headed towards serious political turmoil spearheaded by the far-right Lapua movement during the early 1930s. Although banned after a poorly staged coup attempt in February 1932, its leaders and many followers re-grouped in the fascist Patriotic People's Movement (*Isänmaallinen Kansanliike*, IKL).[1] Despite failures to form major political parties or membership organisations, fascism's indirect influences were significant. In Denmark, Norway and Sweden for example, the large conservative youth movements readily admired Hitler and were ready to implement Nazi ideology in their political programmes and propaganda.[2]

For sure, the social democratic turn from revolutionary socialism to wholesale reformism and broad peoples' parties played a significant role in isolating domestic fascisms. The wide social base of the so-called People's Home (*folkhemmet*), brought parliamentary stability through majority worker-peasant alliances, carried by strong populist rhetoric. This was especially so in Sweden and Norway. In this process, social democrats willingly detached themselves from Marxism in order to establish a stable centre-left alliance that was distinct from the left-alliances formed under the Popular Fronts in France and Spain.[3] The social democratic tactic in the Nordic countries was thus to pacify rather than to directly challenge the far right. As the major social democratic parties co-opted far-right tropes on the 'people' and 'nation' they argued that the far right would dissipate and wither away. Right-wing social democrats in Sweden such as Rickard Lindström[4] even described their political goal using the uncanny descriptor 'national socialism', irrefutably undercutting the far right's nationalist appeals and underlining how patriotic the social democrats were. But the crucial difference was that the social democrats positioned themselves as champions of a democratic society, fighting both fascist and communist dictatorships, and did not view liberalism or parliamentary democracy as anathema.[5] Nonetheless, as this chapter shows, the process of partly co-opting fascist themes resulted in a strong response from the far left that claimed that these parties were willingly or inadvertently pushing Scandinavia towards fascism, what we today might call 'mainstreaming' fascist ideas.

When analysing Nordic responses to Nazi Germany, it is important to keep the relatively strong position of Nordic social democracy in mind. Nordic communist parties were electorally small and always a part of the parliamentary opposition. Anti-communism was common long before the emergence of anti-fascism and, for example in Finland, the bitter and bloody civil war between the reds and the whites in 1918, and the long common border with the Soviet Union, made anti-communism a pivotal part of majority political culture, largely accepted by the social democrats as well as the far right. Finland was an 'anti-communist democracy'.[6] Even Finnish left-socialists who were pushing for a stronger social democratic anti-fascist position after 1933 were exposed to allegations by the social democratic party leadership of being 'communists', or sympathetic with the Russian Bolsheviks. This resulted in many being purged from the mother party.[7]

When the Nazis came to power, it quickly became apparent that the responsibilities connected to holding governmental office were difficult to reconcile with types of more militant anti-fascism as envisioned by the Social Democratic party's rank and file. This became acutely clear in the case of Denmark where the Social Democratic Youth (DSU) developed a militant, anti-fascist strand of social democracy. They were inspired by German and Austrian social democrats and formed militant defence units in the DSU. In the end, the Danish Social Democratic party put the lid on their most militant and confrontational anti-fascist activists. As a rule all DSU members who participated in united front demonstrations with the communists were threatened with exclusion.[8] During the Scandinavian anti-fascist conference in April 1933 the Danish communists acknowledged the important role of the DSU. According to the Chair of the DSU, Ivan Solgaard, it was apparent that there was a 'great will to fight' among the DSU members, although tragically the Social Democratic leadership was pressing the DSU not to engage in anti-fascism.[9]

When it came to it, the needs of governments overruled the needs of the social democratic movement; i.e. good foreign relations with Germany trumped efforts to form a strong anti-fascist position.[10] As a small neighbouring country, the Danes quickly succumbed to a path of appeasement in the name of neutrality. Germany was Denmark's second most important trade partner and the new German government was showing signs of being extremely sensitive to Danish criticism. Tellingly, on 1 March 1933, only one day after the cataclysmic German Reichstag fire, Thorvald Stauning, the leader of Danish social democracy and Prime Minister dictated a letter to H. P. Sørensen, the editor of the official organ of the Danish social democrats *Social-Demokraten*. Stauning insisted that *Social-Demokraten* should desist from attacking Hitler but blame the communists instead, because they had, according to Stauning, split the labour movement, empowered Hitler, and were essentially to blame for what was occurring now. The main attack was to be directed against communists not the new Nazi regime.[11] *Social-Demokraten* had initially strongly condemned Nazi Germany. Stauning now used his power as head of state and party leader to regulate its reporting. As a consequence, when reporting on events in Germany, it now did so with caution.[12] The German foreign office was also closely monitoring international press reaction. The head of the German legation in Denmark, Baron von Richthofen, approached the Danish foreign minister Peter Munch to protest against reports published in Denmark. On 2 March 1933, Munch urged the Danish press to remain neutral and to show moderation when choosing their headlines and caricatures. Moreover, they were instructed to desist from publishing interviews with people in Germany or anti-Nazi refugees.

Developments in Sweden followed a similar pattern. The Swedish social democratic foreign minister Rickard Sandler valued good trade relations with Germany above all else. This was a form of 'neutrality politics' that advocated negotiation with Germany. As the Swedish historian Klas Åmark notes, Sandler did not perceive the situation after 1933 as a fight between 'dictatorship or democracy' but as a more traditional conflict between the great powers, where also the small neutral states had to find their place. At the same time Sandler criticised those in the social democratic party who were possessed by a 'crusade mentality', meaning those pursuing a critical anti-fascist policy. As in Denmark, Sandler invited the chief editors of a number of Swedish newspapers to discuss what could be published about the German Nazis and Hitler. The new regime was irritated about 'pointed formulations' and satirical drawings, especially those published in the Swedish newspaper *Social-Demokraten*.[13] Even in Finland, Germans complained about the hostile tendency of parts of its press. The Swedish speaking left-wing press in Finland had been the most critical but the Finnish liberals (*Edistyspuolue*) and the social democratic press were also hostile to the new German government.[14]

How should we understand the restrictions made by democratic governments on the free press? The role of the press during the 1920s and 1930s – the golden age of newspapers and print media – cannot be underrated. The media formed the most significant platform for the formation of public opinion, and the censorship was clearly intended to appease Nazi Germany; it was the first, partly self-inflicted wound caused by neutrality.[15] Here, it is equally important to remember that the Nordic reactions were in no way unique. Most significantly, the actions of the Soviet Union reveal that anti-fascism as a Soviet State policy was also undesired. As Bernhard H. Bayerlein shows, the official Soviet position viewed the developments in Germany not solely in a negative light: the destruction of the German Social Democratic movement (i.e. the 'social fascists') was seen as an inherently positive development despite the parallel breakdown of German communism. Moreover, it was believed that Hitler's coming to power increased the conflict between the capitalist countries in the West, and therefore decreased the danger of an imperialist war against the Soviet Union. Already in 1933, the USSR's highest leadership perceived Hitler's domestic policy as an *internal* German development that the Soviet Union had no business to meddle with. Good foreign relations and the protection of mutual economic interests was more important, as the ratification of the Soviet-German trade agreement on 5 May 1933 perfectly illustrates.[16] If the Soviet Union itself was pursuing a line of 'neutrality' or 'non-intervention', what did it mean for transnational communist-led anti-fascism in the immediate post-1933 period?

Nordic communists and anti-fascism

Before further investigating the initiatives of 1933, we need to locate the longer trajectories of Nordic anti-fascism. The Comintern's sixth world congress in 1928 in Moscow had recommended that similar workers' defence organisations as the

German Red Front Fighters' League were to be established by all communist parties. The Swedish Red Front League (*Röda Front Förbundet*, RFF) was officially founded at a first, largely unknown 'Scandinavian antifascist conference' that was held in Stockholm in 1930. According to a Swedish governmental inquiry into the communist movement, the RFF's anti-fascism had arisen as a reaction to the radicalisation of the Finnish far-right Lapua movement. The goal of the RFF was to unite all 'real enemies of fascism, men and women' into a nation-wide anti-fascist fighting organisation. The official purpose of the RFF was to function as a workers' guard against fascism. Although it is very difficult to assess the success of the anti-fascist disturbances at Nazi meetings in Sweden, they should be historically acknowledged. The far right was not left unchallenged, as also highlighted in Helen Lööw's pivotal work on the history of the Nazis in Sweden.[17] The RFF had a separate youth section called the Anti-Fascist Youth Guards (*Anti-fascistiska unga gardena*, Antifa), which also closely collaborated with the Communist Youth Association (*Kommunistiska Ungdoms Förbundet*, KUF). According to the Stockholm police, the KUF had around 12,000 registered members in 1933. The youth Antifa was characterised in the government surveillance report as a reservoir for all working-class youths who were not prepared to directly join the KUF, but who wanted to be active in anti-fascist activities. Significantly, those involved in Antifa work were urged to fight against *both* their own social democratic leadership and the fascist menace.[18]

When the KUF organised a congress in 1931 in Stockholm its Central Committee member Nils Bengtsson urged all members of the KUF to visit the meetings organised by the Swedish National Socialists and to obstruct them from winning over any supporters. The methods to do this were, for example, singing or speaking at full volume and loud interruptions during speeches. If Birger Furugård – the leader of the Swedish National Socialist Party – was going to hold a public speech, Bengtsson advised KUF activists to take all their comrades along and attend the meeting. In a carefully organised and co-ordinated way they should form a circle around the podium and once Furugård had started speaking they would start singing, and irritate him and the crowd so that the speaker could not be heard. If this was unsuccessful, Bengtsson instructed, they should not hesitate to take the speaker by the collar. Bengtsson also warned the anti-fascists that the Nazis would be most likely armed with truncheons and they should prepare for things to get physical.[19]

In August 1932 a meeting near Copenhagen turned into a mass fight between uniformed members of the DSU and uniformed Danish SA members.[20] Later in April 1933, a newly founded 'Antifa-Committee' in Vesterbro, Copenhagen, described how, in its call for a powerful fighting front against fascism, comrades were becoming victims of Nazi violence. On 6 April 1933, merely two weeks before the Scandinavian Anti-Fascist Conference a 'young DSU comrade' who had been on his way from a meeting was suddenly seen stumbling into the premises of the Danish Communist Party in Vesterbro. When he entered the room, his entire body was shaking and he was about to collapse, but before passing out he uttered:

'It was the damn Nazis (*Det er de satans Nascister*).' The Antifa-Committee declared the young comrade a victim of the raw and ruthless 'Hitler murderbands' in Denmark. May it serve as an eye-opener to all workers, the committee declared in its bulletin, that in the current situation it is a necessity to form a strong united front against the 'fascist front of the upper classes'. Workers, working class women, social democrats, communists, and unorganised workers were urged to draw the proper conclusions from the attack: it showed what was waiting for them if they did not activate themselves.[21] Such confrontations were a vital part of the growing Scandinavian conflict between anti-fascism and fascism, and highlights the importance of analysing Nordic anti-fascism not only as a response to an external threat, but that it was inherently connected to domestic developments where especially the communist and socialist youth movements were heading the anti-fascist fight against local far-right enemies.[22]

Communist anti-fascism in Sweden drew from examples of social-democratic 'betrayal' starting with the German November Revolution of 1918, and the subsequent abandonment of socialist goals to preserve the capitalist Weimar Republic. The Swedish communists directly addressed claims in the social democratic press that the communists and fascists were comparable, and used the same methods in their struggle to create the 'bloody dictatorship of the few over the majority'. On the contrary the Swedish communist A. J. Smålan argued in 1933 that through debate and argument, they strove to win over the majority of the workers to the 'dictatorship of the proletariat' which, Smålan spelt out, meant real democracy as it represented the dictatorship of the great majority's over the bourgeois minority. Fascists, on the other hand, claimed that the masses had to be taught obedience and that a small group of 'expert' leaders would rule over the masses.[23] When the social democrats claimed that 'communism had been unable to hinder the fascist victory', Smålan retorted that the communists had never claimed to possess such a power. The communists were trying to turn the tables and blamed the social democrats for not using their power against the fascists, and for using it instead against the communists, against those who had been most eager to take up the anti-fascist fight. Perhaps the German communists could have gained the upper hand in 1933 in select cities, but what would have followed when the army, the SA squadrons and other fascist bands had attacked them? These uprisings would have drowned in blood and resulted in an unimaginable terror against the workers.[24] As long as the government tolerated developments on the far right and actively fought against the far left, the only remaining option was to form a united front of the workers from below. This was deemed both necessary and possible for it was only 25 years ago since they all had fought together as socialists, and it was the duty of the communists to remind social-democratic workers of these shared values and histories.[25]

In Sweden, Rickard Lindström declared that bolshevism had played an important role in paving the way for the far right. Communist 'atrocity propaganda' had resulted in its 'natural counterpart in the extreme parts of the bourgeoisie'. For Lindström, the main lesson from Germany in 1933 was that only a working-class movement that was 'totally free' from bolshevism could protect itself against fascism.[26] With such statements in mind, the idea of anti-fascist united or popular front alliances in Sweden could not be entertained. Arvid Wretling of the Swedish communists underlined that they did not want unity at any price, nor a platonic symbolic unity, but a 'fighting united front' of the working masses.[27]

In Sweden, like in the other Nordic countries, defence of democracy was one of the most crucial questions related to anti-fascism. Was it the duty of the workers to defend this flawed form of democracy? According to the communists, the current system labelled democracy was in fact a 'capitalist suppression technique'. Still it was of outmost importance that the workers defended elements in the system that were vital for them, such as the freedom of association, freedom of speech, a free press, the right to strike, and the freedom to assembly. These were the valuable results of decades of working-class struggle and had to be vigorously defended. Paradoxically, those 'screaming most loudly for the defence of democracy' were the ones limiting and circumscribing these very rights. 'In the name of freedom and democracy workers' freedoms are banned and restricted', Fritjof Lager complained as anti-fascist efforts were being suppressed by the government.[28] With the Swedish National Socialist parties becoming ever more marginal after 1933, the social democrats and the democratic bourgeoisie were congratulating themselves for overcoming the fascist threat in Sweden, and started presenting themselves as 'saviours' of Sweden's freedom.[29] However, as in Denmark, where the conservative youth movement had been sympathetic to fascist ideas and practices, the same was said to be happening in Sweden in the '*Nationella Ungdomsförbundet*' (National Youth Association). Moreover, the creation and strengthening of the police, the bourgeois parties' urge to put down the trade unions and crush the communist movement, were seen as further proof of a *fascistisation* of Swedish society. The communists therefore remarked that the major threat in Sweden was not 'open' fascism, but fascism in patent leather shoes and suits in the halls of government.[30]

Scandinavia and the European anti-fascist movement

After Hitler's rise to power, one of the first initiatives of the international communist trade union movement was to organise a 'European Workers' Congress against Fascism'. It was first planned to take place in Prague, but due to pressure from the Third Reich, the Czechoslovakian government banned the congress in early April 1933.[31] On an extremely short notice, and general confusion, it was first re-located to Copenhagen for 14–17 April 1933, before it was finally held in Paris on 5–6 June 1933. The confusion has even led historians to believe that no anti-fascist conference was held in Copenhagen, and completely overlooked the Scandinavian Anti-Fascist Conference. In spring 1933, Copenhagen had in fact become a new global centre of the Comintern's operations.[32]

Formerly top secret files in the Comintern archives reveal that the Comintern apparatus was initially uncomfortable with the realisation that the Scandinavian Anti-fascist Conference had a local Scandinavian origin. In March 1933 there were two competing communist-led initiatives: on the one hand, there was the

Amsterdam Anti-War movement which had been founded in August 1932. It had resulted in the creation of broadly based anti-war committees on a global scale, including the Scandinavian countries. These committees were set up under the global network of the World Committee against the Imperialist War (in autumn 1933 renamed the World Commitee Against War and Fascism). Meanwhile, a separate initiative for a *workers'* anti-fascist congress and a European *workers'* anti-fascist movement was being led by the leadership of the Profintern (The Red International of Labor Unions). Typically for the international communist movement, a kind of turf war erupted between these two initiatives as the anti-war committees started to engage in anti-fascism, whereas the anti-fascist initiative strived to keep them separate. This became explicitly clear in the case of the Scandinavian Anti-Fascist Conference. The Anti-War movement under Henri Barbusse and Willi Münzenberg's leadership was based in Paris, whereas the preparations for the European Anti-Fascist Congress were co-ordinated from Copenhagen. The central liaison person in Copenhagen was Richard Gyptner, who from 1929 to February 1933 had functioned as secretary of the Comintern's clandestine Western European Bureau (WEB) in Berlin. From February to August 1933 he functioned as the secretary of the 'Organising bureau of the European Anti-Fascist Congress'.[33]

These two communist-led initiatives were colliding as the anti-war committee in Copenhagen had been planning a broad anti-war conference for Easter 1933, but the Profintern's workers' anti-fascist conference was set for the same date in Prague.[34] In Gyptner's secret report to Willi Münzenberg, sent on 3 April 1933, he advised Münzenberg and the Paris anti-war committee to *stand down* in its efforts to broaden the anti-fascist movement through the anti-war movement. This was, according to Gyptner, totally contradictory to the line of the Comintern and inhibited the development of the anti-fascist movement. An 'Amsterdam type' of conference in Scandinavia was according to Gyptner out of the question. Events seem to have escaped Gyptner's hands as on 5 March 1933 the Norwegian anti-war committee had suddenly, and allegedly without consulting either Copenhagen or Stockholm, released an appeal for the organisation of a Scandinavian conference against *both* war and fascism. Gyptner explained that the comrades in Norway had misunderstood the Comintern's line and believed mistakenly that the anti-war committee would also take care of all anti-fascist work. However, the Norwegian anti-war committee did not correct its line, but pushed their interpretation that their 'Amsterdam Committee would hold an Antifa-Conference'. The result was major confusion in Scandinavia. Undoubtedly, this phase of disarray was not limited to the Scandinavian countries, but was more or less symptomatic for the global movement as well.[35] The Norwegian communists were reprimanded by the Comintern for pursuing a 'right-wing' deviation as it had taken the initiative too far when it on 11 March 1933 had reached out to the Norwegian social democratic party (DNA) to discuss the formation of a united front against fascism and capitalist reaction. Despite this admonition, the Norwegian Communist Party organised an anti-war meeting in Oslo on 12 March directed against fascism, which amplified the problem from the Comintern's perspective.[36] The situation would last until August 1933, when the Comintern finally notified Henri Barbusse that the anti-war and anti-fascist movements could be amalgamated. The Comintern realised that the rank-and-file did not understand why there needed to be two parallel organisations that separated the fight against fascism and war. Indeed, with slogans such as 'fascism means war' the dualism had become acute.[37]

Before this change of line, Alfred Kurella, who was the head of the Comintern's Agitprop department, had directly instructed the anti-war committee in Copenhagen to convince the anti-war committees in Stockholm and Oslo to change the Copenhagen meeting from an anti-fascist meeting into an anti-war conference. Kurella even travelled to Stockholm to set the line straight, but as he arrived the party newspapers had declared on their first pages that the Scandinavian conference was an anti-fascist conference.[38] As Barbusse was one the most prominent public figures of the Amsterdam anti-war movement, his personal attendance at the anti-fascist conference in Copenhagen thus signalled, some four months before the Comintern's revision of its position, that a merger of the anti-fascist movement and the international anti-war movement was occurring.[39]

Representatives of the Danish, Norwegian and Swedish CP Political Bureaus were called to Copenhagen on 31 March 1933. Among those present was the Norwegian representative Strand Johansen, the Secretary of the Norwegian Anti-War Committee.[40] He was singled out as the person responsible for starting the whole debacle over the Scandinavian conference. Strand Johansen had studied at the International Lenin School in Moscow from 1927 to 1930 and been thereafter elected to the NKP's central leadership. Later during the Nazi occupation of Norway he would be arrested by the Gestapo and deported with his Russian wife Helene Sterlina to the Sachsenhausen concentration camp. His wife was executed in Auschwitz while Strand Johansen himself survived and later became minister in the Norwegian government in 1945.[41]

As a result of the meeting in Copenhagen, an official call for a Scandinavian Anti-Fascist Conference was published. It was signed by the Copenhagen based 'Kampfronten mod Fascismen', the Stockholm-based 'Antifascistiska Enhetskomiten', the central leadership of the Revolutionary Trade Union Opposition (RGO) in Norway, and 'Finland's antifascists'. It was declared that Hitler's rise to power and the brown terror in Germany had empowered the fascist tendencies in the Nordic Countries. When explaining the urgency of the situation, the main focus was not on the open (and indeed minuscule) fascist movements, but on the dangers of *fascistisation*.[42]

The offensive of the Nordic fascists was to be met with a workers' counter-offensive. In stark contrast to the position of the social democratic mother party (to pacify rather than challenge), the far right was now confronted with a radical opponent ready to fight. Criticism was levelled at the Danish social democratic ministers and party leaders in particular, who were actively forbidding the social democratic workers from taking part in the anti-fascist movement and often disrupted conference preparations. This was not coming from the social democratic workers, the anti-fascists declared: they could feel 'the warm sympathy' for the anti-fascist cause that was emanating from working-class youths in Copenhagen and Oslo especially. They therefore called out to all social democratic, communist and unaffiliated workers, all working peasants and intellectuals to help 'make Scandinavia a bulwark against fascism'. Moreover, they urged all to organise meetings in trade unions, factories and mines, and all ships. The ongoing terror in Germany held an important position in the Nordic deliberations, as all were called to be active in solidarity campaigns with the German working class that was 'standing in the midst of a heroic fight against fascist barbarism'.[43]

The Scandinavian Anti-Fascist Conference, 14–17 April 1933

Until recently, sources shedding light on the Scandinavian Anti-Fascist Conference, organised over the Easter weekend, 14–17 April 1933, have been scarce. The following description is based on two new sources. The first is a 15-page surveillance report by the German police. The second is a Danish conference report with detailed transcripts of the event covering over 40 pages, held in the Comintern archives, and previously untapped. On the basis of these two major sources we can, for the first time, get an in-depth view of how fascism and anti-fascism were discussed in Scandinavia in the spring of 1933. How was the fascist threat defined and what were perceived as the most effective ways to mobilise workers, intellectuals, women and youths against fascist influences in Scandinavia?

According to the German police report, 348 men and 46 women participated in the conference. It turned out to be a truly transnational affair with representatives from ten countries, according to the following numbers: Denmark (218), Sweden (120), Norway (29), Germany (11), Britain (4), Finland (2), Iceland (2), France (2), Czechoslovakia (1), Indonesia (1), and 4 representatives from the 'European Committee' whose nationalities are not mentioned. Politically we know that the communists dominated with 228 delegates. They were followed by 139 persons without party affiliation, 16 social democrats, 6 from the Nordic Workers Party (Nord.Arb.Partei), 1 from the British Independent Labour Party (ILP), 1 from the German Socialist Workers' Party (SAP), 1 syndicalist, and 2 anarchists. The majority defined themselves as workers (345 of 394), but the number of intellectuals (41) was also significant.[44]

Aksel Larsen, the leader of the Danish CP and member of the Danish Parliament since 1932, marked in one of his speeches how the Danish press (from right to left) had sabotaged the conference by not printing a word about it. The entire press corps had been there to meet Barbusse at the airport, but no one mentioned that he was giving a speech in Copenhagen as a part of the Scandinavian Anti-fascist Conference. According to Larsen, the Scandinavian press was only printing Göring's official news bulletins, and ignoring the work of the anti-fascist committee. 'If we want to fight fascism,' Larsen elaborated, 'we cannot overlook how the social democratic leaders in Germany let Nazism grow strong.'[45] In *Antifaschistische Front*, that functioned as the European anti-fascist congress's newspaper, it was alleged that the Danish social democratic leadership had threatened anyone attending the conference with expulsion from the party. Moreover the Social Democratic Party leader and Danish Foreign Minister, Paul Munch, had allegedly dispatched letters to all newspapers in Copenhagen with a governmental directive banning them from publishing a single word about the fact that an anti-fascist conference was taking place in Copenhagen. According to the *Antifaschistische Front* these actions had confirmed and strengthened the conviction of those assembled that anti-fascism would only be realised if taken on by the workers themselves.[46]

Larsen underlined in his speech that it was not enough to sign protest resolutions against the terror in the Third Reich. They had to focus on the education of the workers. According to Larsen the workers in the Scandinavian countries were not yet conscious about the dangers of fascism. From Larsen's viewpoint, the current moment offered a unique chance to form the united front as the fight against fascism had become the most important mission of the working class. Thanks to close economic relations, geographic vicinity and similar languages (Swedish, Danish and Norwegian) it was presented as especially important to form a common anti-fascist centre in the Scandinavian countries. Moreover, the struggle was not supposed to be directed only against fascism, but anti working-class measures connected to fascism such as strike bans, demonstration bans, and all forms of capitalist exploitation. Fascism was growing in the Scandinavian countries and it was their duty to fight it. Larsen even envisioned that they could build Scandinavia into a pillar of the international workers' movement's fight against fascism.[47]

Larsen himself was becoming a major thorn in the side of the Danish social democratic coalition government that was trying to maintain a position of neutrality. One of Larsen's more spectacular moves was made in August 1933 when during a rally he symbolically tore a Nazi Swastika flag to pieces while declaring it to be a 'murder flag'. It caused a major uproar in the non-communist press and the German government demanded that Larsen be set on trial for offending the flag of a foreign nation. Larsen was eventually freed of all charges, but put under strict surveillance so that he would not cause another major international incident.[48]

When Henri Barbusse addressed the Scandinavian workers and intellectuals at the congress in Copenhagen, he stressed that the time of passing resolutions was over. Now was time for action. According to Barbusse, they needed to realise that the current situation was no longer about a general crisis, but the collapse of a whole system, and therefore he called for the united front of all workers, including social democrats, communists, anarchists, and syndicalists. Significantly, Barbusse explained to the Scandinavian public that they should not be misguided by the German fascist example. Fascism could take different forms in different countries, and for example in France, Barbusse claimed, fascism was taking on a more 'democratic mask'.[49] Larsen expressed in a similar vein that it was typical for international fascism to appear with distinct national peculiarities. In Scandinavia they were not going to get 'fascism with swastikas', just as in Italy, Germany and other fascist countries, fascism appeared in different guises.[50]

Among the Danish intellectuals at the conference was Professor Jørgen Jørgensen from the University of Copenhagen. He argued that although the working class formed the ultimate bulwark against fascism, the fight against fascism needed to embrace all 'freethinking people'. When looking at Nazi Germany, Jørgensen identified three issues that had to be condemned: Firstly, political violence against those of anti-Nazi political opinion; secondly, the persecution of other races, especially the Jews; and lastly, the nationalist delirium. Unlike many communist speakers, Jørgensen asserted that there was no need to waste time on discussing who was to blame for the rise of fascism. Nevertheless, he directed a warning to those democratic parties (i.e. the social democrats) that had abstained from participating as they should be ready to carry the responsibility for undermining the anti-fascist front. In his mind, all those absent could not be described as 'enablers' of fascism. It seemed instead as if they had been stricken with a blindness that hindered them from understanding the gravity of the situation. Jørgensen's appeal to broaden the working-class base of anti-fascism to include the 'intellectual workers' was echoed in several other speeches.[51]

The famous Danish author Andersen Nexø also attended the Scandinavian Anti-Fascist conference. He delivered a speech titled 'Antifascism is Socialism'. He had recently broken with the Social Democratic Party and wanted to show that he was not a man for compromise. Nexø declared that in its very nature, the bourgeois part of humanity was fascist. Fascism and the bourgeoisie were two descriptors for the same thing. The only difference was that the bourgeoisie was using liberalism and democracy as camouflage applied to its left side to fool the proletariat. Fascism was thus deemed a bourgeois worldview that in effect represented 'unmasked capitalism'. If you were against fascism, you needed to be against capitalism and, ultimately, in favour of communism, Nexø elaborated. Notably, both Jørgensen and Nexø belonged to the presidium of the Danish Anti-War Committee formed in 1932. This illustrates further the early conflation of the Scandinavian anti-war movement with the anti-fascist initiative.[52]

Among the international delegates attending the conference was the British representative William Payne of the Independent Labour Party (ILP). He assured the conference that despite the actions of the Labour Party against the united front, there was a growing mass movement from below in favour of the united front in Britain.[53] When returning to Britain, Payne penned the pamphlet *A London Busman Reports on the Fight against Fascism*, which was published by the 'British Delegation Committee of the European Workers' Anti-Fascist Congress'. Payne declared that 'the fascist danger is a menace to the whole European working class' and reproduced the fascism definition used by Aksel Larsen which identified fascism as the mobilisation of 'the most brutal and reactionary forces in capitalist society'. Interestingly, Payne tried to address the fact that although fascism was a brutal enemy operating 'in the interest of the big capital, the industrialists and the bankers' the fascists in Germany had been particularly successful in attracting working-class supporters (and therefore contrary to much Comintern dogma). Payne articulated a classic socialist belief in 'international working-class solidarity' and underlined that 'liberal protest and declarations about democracy' had no effect on stopping the fascist advance. The only thing that had enough power to hinder the fascists was the collective power of a united working class.[54]

Jeanette Olsen from Norway was another voice underlining the sorry state of the international working class. For her, the social democrats, and the reformists in the trade union movement, should be blamed. Olsen had been the secretary of the Norwegian Communist Party's women's section, but had broken with the party in 1928. She had since remained active in the openly left-wing *Clarté* movement and the revolutionary trade union organisations.[55] Refreshingly, she urged all those assembled in Copenhagen to reflect on their own part in the process. 'Each and every one of us has a larger or smaller responsibility for what was occurring'. They had all committed mistakes along the road. As a long-time activist for women's issues, Olsen offered interesting perspectives on how the far right was overpowering them through their focus on women and the youth. Hitler's victory was based on their own weaknesses and, according to Olsen, it was especially important for them to reflect on how they could win over women to the fight against fascism. Olsen believed that fascism had been victorious because it had been so successful in winning over working-class youth. She thus connected their poor work among women with the rise of fascist youth movements for Olsen was convinced that youths were being influenced by the women in their home environments. If the working-class women were separated from the anti-fascist movement, it would have devastating effects in their ability to reach the youth as well.[56] Marie Nielsen from Bergen, Norway, confirmed in her speech that they faced great challenges in their work among women. In Norway fascism was, in Nielsen's mind, using women through 'masked' women's associations, such as *Hjemmets Vel* (in 1933 re-named *Norges Husmorforbund*). Asmussen of the Copenhagen's Workers' Defence Units also regretted in his statement that not enough agitation had been made among women.[57] As the attendance numbers of the Scandinavian Conference illustrate, only 46 women were represented compared to 348 men. There was obviously much to be done in winning over women to anti-fascism not only in Scandinavia, but globally. Still, it must be highlighted that several speakers at the congress were women, and they effectively elaborated on the crucial nexus between fascism, the youth, women and the family.

Jeanette Olsen concluded that if they wanted to be successful in fighting fascism, they needed to attack social democracy. Olsen assumed that as the Nordic social democrats soon realised that the leaders of the German Social Democratic Party were also falling victim to persecution in Germany, they would join them in the anti-fascist fight. In the meantime Nordic social democrats might even join the fascist side and pave the way for a fascist rule in Scandinavia as well. Olsen concluded: 'Our mission is therefore to lead a ruthless fight against Social Democracy and the Trade Union Leadership.'[58]

Knut Senander, who led communists from the Gothenburg area of South Western Sweden, elaborated in his conference speech how Hitler had actively used anti-capitalist slogans to attract workers into the Nazi ranks.[59] Senander was the author of a booklet published in 1932 titled *Nationalsocialismen – arbetarklassens dödsfiende* (National Socialism: The mortal enemy of the working class). Here we can trace the intellectual basis of his anti-fascism. Senander argued that it was completely false to characterise fascism as a 'postwar phenomenon'. This was an all too easy and convenient explanation.[60] This was the standard explanation used on the social democratic side. In the major treatise on the dangers looming over democracy in interwar Europe, the chief ideologue of the Danish Social Democratic movement, Hartvig Frisch, in the monumental book *Pest over Europa: Bolschevisme – Fascisme – Nazisme*, clearly stated that fascist agitation in all fascist countries had originated from the fear of Bolshevism and from the real and presumed danger from the far left.[61] Senander connected fascism instead to the bourgeois practice of working-class oppression. In this respect, Mussolini had not created anything original, but was simply following the lead of the Russian Tsar Nicolai II and the 'black hundreds' that advocated reactionary, anti-revolutionary, and anti-Semitic violence in Russia during and after the Russian Revolution of 1905. In Senander's view, everywhere where class conflict had reached such a critical level that the ruling class felt threatened and insufficiently protected by conventional means, there was political space for fascism.[62]

When the Scandinavian Anti-Fascist Conference concluded, it passed a resolution to 'the working people of Scandinavia' and 'all Scandinavian anti-fascists'. It was the mission of the Scandinavian workers, just like it was the duty of the working masses of the entire world, to expose the lies of the Hitler regime. The unanimous conclusion of the conference was that the rise of fascism would never have been possible if the working class had remained united.[63]

For Nordic anti-fascists, it was clear that anti-Semitism was being used by Hitler as a tool to distract the workers from his attacks against the workers' movement. Nationalist furore was being used to divide the workers. Scandinavian anti-fascists thus called for an even stronger worker unity between all peoples, and to raise the proletarian banner of internationalism even higher. According to the resolution, 'Hitler wanted to transform Germany to a workers' penitentiary, to freedom's grave, to a fortress of murderous fascism.' Scandinavian workers were called upon to show their solidarity with their German 'class brothers', to strengthen their common struggle, and to help them overcome Nazism. But as the means to help those in Germany were limited, the focus was on Scandinavia and the slogan crystallised to 'Beat fascism, beat capitalism in your own country! Smother fascism in the Scandinavian countries!' Hitler's rise to power thus triggered a direct rise in anti-fascist activism in Scandinavia. Slogans were suggested for the upcoming May 1st demonstrations to be staged across Scandinavia: 'Down with murder-fascism!' but also 'Bring forth the workers and peasants' rule!' At the same time, the objective was already set for the next conference: a larger European Workers' Anti-Fascist Congress in Paris, and the sending of Scandinavian delegates.[64]

After the Paris congress, specific instructions guided anti-fascist work in Scandinavia. An important focus was the boycott campaign of the harbour workers and seamen directed against ships flying the swastika flag.[65] But the removal of the swastika was not limited to ships: anywhere, on buildings, posters, or newspapers, immediate action was required: 'No Swastika flag can be tolerated in Scandinavia (*Intet Hagekorsflag maa taales I Scandinavien*).' Taking inspiration from elsewhere, the recent example by British anti-fascists of chasing Hitler's foreign policy expert Alfred Rosenberg out of the country was to be followed with equal strength in Scandinavia.[66]

When studying calls to action, it is always important to remember that these were not automatically turned into actual practice. Anti-fascist responses in Scandinavia were not always occasions of supreme anti-fascist consciousness. For example, in the summer of 1933 members of the Swedish section of the International Workers' Relief and the International Red Aid received a strongly worded reprimand for their lack of action. A global solidarity week for the victims of Nazism had been announced for 17–25 June 1933 but apparently it had passed unnoticed in Sweden despite intensive propaganda efforts. Demonstrations had only taken place in Stockholm and Kiruna, but in all other places 'the class enemy and the fascist butchers had applauded in malicious pleasure'. Despite elaborate published reports on the crimes committed in Nazi Germany during 1933, a general 'ghetto effect' was becoming increasingly apparent. Nordic publications on the question of anti-fascism and the relation to refugees and exiles arriving from Nazi Germany were soon limited to left-wing audiences. The cultural battle in Denmark was directly influenced by the government that demanded publishers and newspapers to take into account the preservation of good relations to Germany. As Hans Hertel shows in an elaborate analysis of the Danish literary and cultural scene, the official meddling into the tone of the publications soon became redundant as authors, editors, publishers and theatre leaders started to implement self-censorship. As a result of the polarisation, anti-fascism was equated with 'cultural bolshevism'. Instead, in the name of good political and cultural relations to Germany, 'cultural neutralism' became the norm. This provided space for 'salon fascism' and the spread of apologetic and sympathetic views on Nazi Germany. If one wanted to read critical reports on fascism and Nazism one needed to read the communist press and small left-wing publishers, but as these publications were not accepted into general distribution channels, their readership remained limited to certain circles of society.[67]

In the final analysis, Norway stands out in relation to Sweden, Denmark and Finland. The initiative for the Scandinavian anti-fascist conference had originated from the Norwegians; the Norwegian labour movement was characterised by a stronger internationalism compared to the rest of Scandinavia.[68] Halvdan Koht of the Norwegian social democratic party (DNA) acted as Norwegian Foreign Minister from March 1935 onwards and took a firm stance against German efforts to hinder critical reporting in the Norwegian press. The German ambassador Heinrich Rohland was so unsuccessful in influencing the DNA's *Arbeiderbladet* that he was called back to Berlin in 1936. His successor, Heinrich Sahm, had the worst start imaginable as only two weeks after his arrival in Oslo, the Norwegian Nobel Committee announced that the 1936 Nobel Peace Prize was awarded to Carl von Ossietzky, the German socialist author and anti-fascist imprisoned in Nazi Germany. The German government perceived the nomination as a hostile action by the Norwegian government. The symbolical act of awarding the Peace Prize to Ossietzky marked the darkest moment in Norwegian-German relations that they would never recover from.[69] Ossietzky's Nobel Prize was perhaps one of the symbolically most powerful anti-fascist actions against Germany made in the Nordic Countries during the 1930s. Significantly, it was not hampered by the usual 'ghetto effect' but noted widely on a global scale. Certainly, neither Denmark, Sweden, Finland nor Iceland ever achieved such anti-fascist credentials. As the German anti-fascist exile Kurt Rosenfeld tellingly noted in the USA, what had particularly enraged Hitler and his followers was that this act of resistance had been realised by their supreme 'Aryan' blood brothers, the Nordic master race.[70]

Conclusions

This chapter has demonstrated that even before 1933, anti-fascism had been a vibrant part of the Scandinavian left, expressed in violent confrontations between fascists and anti-fascists. The events of 1933 then created a unique moment that invited engaging debate on the nature of democracy under pressure and the limits and possibilities of united anti-fascist action. The Scandinavian Anti-Fascist conference marked a historic highpoint in transnational anti-fascist activity within and beyond Scandinavia. It was organised at a crucial juncture in the development of the Comintern's global anti-fascist position, and played an important role in uniting the anti-war and anti-fascist causes. Anti-fascism invigorated transnational co-operation within the Nordic Countries and constituted an often overlooked radical, oppositional alternative to the hegemony of the centre-left alliances under social democratic leadership. It also led to bitter discussions on the origins of fascism and the role of communists and social democrats as enablers of fascism. Since the governments of Sweden and Denmark were strongly intertwined with social democracy in 1933, it quickly revealed the price of neutrality in historically uncomfortable acts of appeasement and collaboration especially in the field of anti-communism and 'anti-anti-fascism'. The communists tried to invite the broader civil society to think more openly about fascism as a political and societal phenomenon and warn against the *fascistisation* of society. If Scandinavia was to be made a bulwark against fascism, they needed to be vigilant and call out all fascist tendencies, sometimes at the cost of blurring the lines between fascism and capitalism.

The case of Scandinavia finally illustrates the power of the Nazi foreign office and how Nordic civil societies could be directly affected by Germany. Paradoxically, anti-fascists were charged at home with meddling in German internal affairs, while at the same time the German foreign office was permitted to interfere in the civil societies of the smaller nations. It shows how international diplomacy and transnational civil society activism were already deeply entwined, further blurring the lines between national and international history, or fascism as a domestic and international threat. In all too many cases the primacy of good foreign relations subdued the need to judge 'internal' German developments, and led to the suppression and limitation of anti-fascist activism in the North.

Notes

1 Oula Silvennoinen, 'Home, Religion, Fatherland: Movements of the Radical Right in Finland', *Fascism,* No. 4, 2015, pp. 134–154.

2 Knut Dørum, 'Conservative Fascist Sympathies and Anti-Fascism in 1930s Norway', in Kasper Braskén, Nigel Copsey & Johan A. Lundin (eds), *Anti-Fascism in the Nordic Countries: New Perspectives, Comparisons and Transnational Connections* (London: Routledge, 2019), pp. 82–85.
3 Donald Sassoon, *One Hundred Years of Socialism: The West European Left in the Twentieth Century* (New York: The New Press, 1996).
4 Rickard Lindström (1894–1950) was engaged in the Swedish social democratic movement from 1918 onwards. He was an advocated of revisionist socialism and polemicised strongly against 'vulgar Marxism' already during the 1920s. Later during the Second World War he became a controversial figure as he advanced a very appeasing and understanding position towards Nazi Germany's demands, especially 1940–1942, although he at the same time resisted Nazi influence in Sweden's domestic affairs. See further in Kent Zetterberg, 'K A Rickard Lindström', *Svenskt biografiskt lexikon,* online at https://sok.riksarkivet.se/Sbl/Mobil/Artikel/10703 (accessed on 10 January 2020).
5 Ulf Lindström, *Fascism in Scandinavia 1920–1940* (Stockholm: Almqvist & Wiksell International, 1985), p. 173; Sheri Berman, *The Primacy of Politics: Social Democracy and the Making of Europe's Twentieth Century* (Cambridge: Cambridge University Press, 2006), pp. 162–176, 204–205; Steiner Stjernø, *Solidarity in Europe: The History of an Idea* (Cambridge: Cambridge University Press, 2005), pp. 109–118.
6 Oula Silvennoinen, *Geheime Waffenbrüderschaft: Die sicherheitspolitische Zusammenarbeit zwischen Deutschland und Finnland, 1933–1944* (Darmstadt: WBG, 2010), pp. 32–39; Tauno Saarela, *Suomalainen kommunismi ja vallankumous 1923–1930* (Helsinki: Suomalaisen Kirjallisuuden Seura, 2008).
7 Tauno Saarela, 'Finnish Socialist Intellectuals on Fascism and Anti-Fascism in the 1930s', in Kasper Braskén, Nigel Copsey & Johan A. Lundin (eds), *Anti-Fascism in the Nordic Countries: New Perspectives, Comparisons and Transnational Connections* (London: Routledge, 2019), pp. 171–172.
8 Charlie Emil Krautwald, 'Three Arrows against the Swastika: Militant Social Democracy and the Radical Opposition to Fascism in Denmark, 1932–1934', in Kasper Braskén, Nigel Copsey & Johan A. Lundin (eds), *Anti-Fascism in the Nordic Countries: New Perspectives, Comparisons and Transnational Connections* (London: Routledge, 2019), pp. 104–106.
9 Bericht über Kongress in Kopenhagen (hereafter 'Bericht'), RGASPI 495/174/65, 42. On Sogaard and the DSU, see Jesper Jørgensen, 'Portræt af en ungkommunist. Ib Nørlund 1932–1940', Årbok, 2005, pp. 51–73.
10 Karl Christian Lammers, 'Faschismus-Interpretationen und Antifaschismus in den skandinavischen Arbeiterbewegungen', in Helga Grebing & Klaus Kinner (eds), *Arbeiterbewegung und Faschismus: Faschismus-Interpretationen in der europäischen Arbeiterbewegung* (Essen: Klartext-Verlag, 1990), pp. 227–229.
11 Henning Grelle, *Thorvald Stauning: Demokrati eller kaos* (Copenhagen: Jyllands-Postens Forlag, 2008), pp. 344–345.
12 Viggo Sjøqvist, *Danmarks Udenrigspolitik 1933–1940* (Copenhagen: Gyldendal, 1966), pp. 42–43.
13 Klas Åmark, *Att bo granne med ondskan: Sveriges förhållande till nazismen, Nazityskland och Förintelsen* (Stockholm: Albert Bonniers Förlag, 2016), pp. 69–70; Åke Thulstrup, *Med lock och pock: Tyska försök att påverka svensk opinion 1933–45* (Stockholm: Bonnier, 1962).
14 Risto Peltovuori, *Suomi saksalaisin silmin 1933–1939: Lehdistön ja diplomatian näkökulmia* (Helsinki: Suomalaisen kirjallisuuden seura, 2005), pp. 74–78.
15 Brian Klitgaard & Jens Melson, 'Die Flüchtlingspolitik als Bestandteil der dänischen Außenpolitik 1933–1940', in Hans Uwe Petersen (ed.), *Hitlerflüchtlinge im Norden: Asyl und politisches Exil 1933–1945* (Kiel: Neuer Malik Verlag, 1991), pp. 85–87.
16 Bernhard H. Bayerlein, 'Deutscher Kommunismus und transnationaler Stalinismus – Komintern, KPD und Sowjetunion 1929–1943', in Hermann Weber, Jakob Drabkin, Bernhard H. Bayerlein & Alexander Galkin (eds), *Deutschland, Russland, Komintern: Vol. I: Überblicke, Analysen, Diskussionen* (Berlin: De Gruyter, 2014), pp. 275–285.
17 Helene Lööw, *Nazismen i Sverige 1924–1979: Pionjärerna, partierna, propagandan* (Stockholm: Ordfront, 2016); Helene Lööw, *Nazismen i Sverige 2000–2014* (Stockholm: Ordfront, 2016).

18 Rapport över den kommunistiska verksamheten i Sverge [1933], Arbark, pp. 46–52, 238, 264–265.
19 Rapport över den kommunistiska verksamheten i Sverge [1933], Arbark, pp. 256–257.
20 Krautwald, 'Three Arrows against the Swastika', p. 99.
21 Antifa-Komiteen, Vesterbro; Copenhagen, April 1933, RGASPI 495/174/65, 3.
22 See also Johan A. Lundin, 'Social Democratic Youth and Anti-Fascism in Sweden, 1929–1939', in Kasper Braskén, Nigel Copsey & Johan A. Lundin (eds), *Anti-Fascism in the Nordic Countries: New Perspectives, Comparisons and Transnational Connections* (London: Routledge, 2019), pp. 111–123.
23 A. J. Smålan, *Fascismens banbrytare* (Stockholm: Förlagsaktiebolaget Arbetarkultur, 1933), pp. 1–6. Smålan was the alias of Johan Albert Johansson according to Yvonne Hirdman, *Den röda grevinnan: En europeisk historia* (Stockholm: Ordfront, 2010), p. 214.
24 Smålan, *Fascismens banbrytare*, p. 19.
25 Ibid., pp. 31–32.
26 Rickard Lindström, *Tyskland och socialdemokratin: Vad har vi att lära?* (Stockholm: Tidens Förlag, 1933), pp. 26–29.
27 Arvid Wretling, *Proletär enhetsfront mot fascismen* (Stockholm: Förlagsaktiebolaget Arbetarkultur, 1933), pp. 15–16.
28 Fritjof Lager, *Fascismen i knektstövlar och lackskor* (Stockholm: Förlagsaktiebolaget Arbetarkultur, 1934), pp. 15–16.
29 Ibid., pp. 3–4.
30 Ibid., pp. 4–9.
31 Organisationsbüro für die Vorbereitung des Antifaschistischen Arbeiterkongresses Europas; Copenhagen, 8 April 1933, RGASPI 495/174/65, 5.
32 Holger Weiss, 'Tallinn-Stockholm-Hamburg-Copenhagen-Oslo: The Northern Dimension of the Comintern's Global Network and Underground Activities, 1920–1940', in Mary Hilson, Silke Neunsinger & Iben Vyff (eds), *Labour, Unions and Politics under the North Star: The Nordic Countries, 1700–2000* (New York: Berghahn, 2017), pp. 290–292. Morten Møller, Niels Erik Rosenfeldt & Jesper Jørgensen, Den røde underverden: Hemmelig kommunistisk virksomhed i Skandinavien mellem to verdenskrige (Copenhagen: Gyldendal, 2019), pp. 122–126.
33 On Gyptner, see his autobiography (Lebenslauf) in SAPMO–BArch, RY 5/I 6/10/95, 83; 'Mg.' [Magnus alias Richard Gyptner] to 'Willi' [Münzenberg]; Berlin, 3 April 1933, RGASPI 495/60/242, 2–3.
34 Münzenberg to Piatnitzki; Paris, 22 March 1933, RGASPI 495/4/237, 14.
35 'Mg.' [Magnus alias Richard Gyptner] to 'Willi' [Münzenberg]; Berlin, 3 April 1933, RGASPI 495/60/242, 2–3.
36 Knut Dørum, 'De rødes kamp mot fascismen i Norge i 1930-årene', *Historisk Tidskrift för Finland,* Vol. 102, No. 1, 2017, p. 89.
37 Protokoll (B) Nr. 329 der aussenordentlichen Sitzung der Politkommission des Politsekretariats des EKKI, 9 August 1933, RGASPI 495/4/256, 4; 'Streng vertraulich: Resolution über die Vereinigung der Internationalen Antikriegsbewegung (Amsterdam) und der Europäischen Antifa-Bewegung', RGASPI 495/4/256, 12–14.
38 'Mg.' [Magnus alias Richard Gyptner] to 'Willi' [Münzenberg]; Berlin, 3 April 1933, RGASPI 495/60/242, 2–3.
39 "Mit voller Kraft Antifa-Kongress unterstützen!", *Antifa-Jungfront* [Nr. 1], April 1933.
40 'Mg.' [Magnus alias Richard Gyptner] to 'Willi' [Münzenberg]; Berlin, 3 April 1933, RGASPI 495/60/242, 2–3.
41 Ole Martin Rønning, *Stalins elever: Kominterns kaderskoler og Norges Kommunistiske Parti 1926–1949* (Oslo: Oslo Universitet, 2010).
42 Til alle Antifascister i Skandinavien! Til den arbejdende befolkningen i Norge, Sverige, Danmark, Finland och Island! (Copenhagen, 31 March 1933), RGASPI 495/174/65, 6–7.
43 Ibid.
44 Bericht über die in der Zeit vom 14. bis 17. April 33 stattgefunden Skandinavische Antifaschisten Kongress in Kopenhagen; Berlin, 20 April 1933, BArch, R 1501/20474, 109–109a.
45 Bericht, RGASPI 495/174/65, 20.

46 'Skandinavische Antifa-Konferenz: 400 Delegierte rufen zum Europakongress!', *Antifaschistische Front: Herausgegeben vom Organisationsbüro zur Einberufung des Antifaschistischen Arbeiterkongresses Europas,* Nr. 6, 20 April 1933.
47 Bericht, RGASPI 495/174/65, 24–26.
48 Kurt Jacobsen, *Aksel Larsen: En politisk biografi,* 2 ed. (Copenhagen: Vindrose, 1995), pp. 133–136.
49 Bericht, RGASPI 495/174/65, 39.
50 Ibid., 22–23.
51 Ibid., 21, 42.
52 Børge Houmann, *Kommunist under besættelsen,* 2 ed. (Copenhagen: Vindrose, 1994), pp. 28–30.
53 Bericht, RGASPI 495/174/65, 38.
54 William Payne, *A London Busman Reports on the Fight against Fascism* (London: European Workers' Anti-Fascist Congress, British Delegation Committee, 1933), pp. 35–41.
55 Per Maurseth, *Gjennom kriser til makt (1920–1935)* (Oslo: Tiden Norsk Forlag, 1987), p. 292.
56 Bericht, RGASPI 495/174/65, 36–37.
57 Ibid., p. 15.
58 Ibid., pp. 36–37.
59 Bericht, RGASPI 495/174/65, 18.
60 Knut Senander, *Nationalsocialismen – arbetarklassens dödsfiende* (Kristianstad: Västra Sverges distrikt av SKP (Sektion av Kommunistiska Internationalen), 1932), pp. 3–5.
61 Hartvig Frisch, *Pest over Europa: Bolschevisme – Fascisme – Nazisme* (Copenhagen: Henrik Koppels Forlag, 1933), p. 5.
62 Senander, *Nationalsocialismen*, p. 3–5.
63 Bericht, RGASPI 495/174/65, 43–44.
64 Ibid., 45–47.
65 Holger Weiss, '"Boycott the Nazi Flag": The Anti-Fascism of the International of Seamen and Harbour Workers', in Kasper Braskén, Nigel Copsey, & Johan A. Lundin (eds), *Anti-Fascism in the Nordic Countries: New Perspectives, Comparisons and Transnational Connections* (London: Routledge, 2019), pp. 132–137.
66 Retningslinjer og Anvisninger for den antifascistiske Bevægelses Arbejde i Skandinavien, [June 1933] RGASPI 495/174/61, 105.
67 Hans Hertel, 'Det belejrede og det besatte åndsliv: Kulturkampen omkring fascisme og nazisme i dansk litteratur, presse og kulturdebat 1920–45', in Henrik Dethlefsen & Henrik Lundbak (eds), *Fra mellemkrigstid til efterkrigstid: Festskrift til Hans Kirchhoff og Henrik S. Nissen på 65-årsdagen oktober 1998* (Copenhagen: Museum Tusculanums Forlag, 1998), pp. 34–48.
68 Edvard Bull (ed.), *Arbeiderbevegelsens historie i Norge*, Vol. 4: Klassen og nasjonen (1935–1946) (Oslo: Tiden Norsk Forlag, 1988).
69 Odd-Bjørn Fure, *Mellomkrigstid 1920–1940,* Norsk utenrikspolitikks historie, Vol. 3 (Oslo: Universitetsforlaget, 1996), pp. 277–280.
70 Kurt Rosenfeld Archiv 59, Akademie der Künste (Berlin), 1–4, here 2.

Acknowledgement

The research for this chapter was completed within the framework of Kasper Braskén's Academy of Finland research project 'Towards a Global History of Anti-Fascism: Transnational Civil Society Activism, International Organisations and Identity Politics Beyond Borders, 1922–1945'. I would like to thank Jesper Jørgensen at the Workers Museum in Copenhagen for commenting the article.

6

ANTI-FASCISM AND ANTI-IMPERIALISM BETWEEN THE WORLD WARS

The perspective from India

Michele L. Louro

On 25 February 1937, the foreign department of the Indian National Congress (INC) released a newsletter featuring a lengthy section on 'India and Spain'.[1] The newsletters provided information about Indian events and shared the opinions and policies of the INC, the mainstream nationalist organization under the leadership of Mohandas Gandhi. This particular newsletter featured the anti-fascist position of the INC and its president, Jawaharlal Nehru, in the case of the Spanish Civil War (1936–1939). Drawing upon one of Nehru's speeches, the newsletter argued that 'Fascism and Imperialism march hand in hand; they are blood brothers. The victory of either is the victory of both all over the world.'[2] The struggle in Spain, therefore, was not unlike India's anticolonial struggle for its 'own freedom'.[3]

The newsletter was not an anomaly, and rather it emblemised the INC's position on the question of fascism in the 1930s. As the world careened toward another world war, the INC articulated anti-fascism as the cornerstone of an emerging worldview and foreign relations initiative. Strongly influenced by Nehru, who served as INC president in 1936 and 1937, the Congress argued that anti-imperialism and anti-fascism were not mutually exclusive, and rather fascism and imperialism were manifestations of capitalist exploitation worldwide. India had a vital role to play in overturning the global forces of imperialism, fascism, and capitalism by upending British colonial rule and challenging one of the greatest empires of the day. Major cities across India hosted wide-scale demonstrations against fascist and imperialist aggression, while the Congress coordinated the shipment and supply of medical and food assistance to places like Spain and China. The Congress's moral and material commitment to anti-fascism demonstrated that the agenda and politics of India's independence struggle extended far beyond the colonial context and engaged the global struggle against fascism and imperialism in the 1930s.

This chapter offers a study of the significant role played by India in the global anti-fascist struggle, as well as a history of how the Congress leveraged international connections to anti-fascism and anti-imperialism to strengthen anticolonial resistance in India. The history of anti-fascism in interwar India has not received much scholarly attention. Instead, contemporaries and historians alike more readily note the fascist tendencies in colonial and postcolonial India. It is no secret that Hitler's *Mein Kampf* remains a bestseller in India today, while the subcontinent is home to the largest all-volunteer paramilitary organization, the Rashtriya Swayamsevak Sangh, which was established in 1925 and modelled after fascist groups in Europe.[4] Likewise, historians have been quick to point out other fascist inclinations and affinities of Indians in the colonial period. Perhaps the most significant case is that of Subhas Chandra Bose, who strategically aligned his politics with the Axis powers in the Second World War.[5] Other scholars have historicized the local and everyday articulations of fascism by less well-known historical figures based in interwar India.[6]

The emphasis on fascism in Indian historiography elides the stronger and more dominant trend toward anti-fascism, which was the first major foreign policy of the INC articulated by the Congress Foreign Department (CFD). Yet, even the history of the Congress and its commitment to anti-fascism have long been overshadowed by the INC's ultimate decision in 1939 to withdraw its support from Britain in the Second World War. This was not a decision based on indifference to fascism and the horrors wrought by Hitler, but rather it demonstrated the unwillingness of India to fight on the side of British imperialism unless the metropole promised unconditional independence for the crown colony once the war ended. The twinning of imperialism and fascism as 'blood brothers' before the war produced a dilemma that was not easily resolved within the INC in 1939. To support the allied powers against fascist regimes meant supporting British and French imperialism in another global military conflict, an unconscionable position for many anticolonial nationalists who remembered a similar set of circumstances in the First World War. At the same time, refusal to join the British war effort undermined the global resistance to fascism, which India had played an active role in mobilising before the onset of the Second World War. The Congress's ultimate decision to withhold support for Britain was not made without significant debate, and the final resolution provided a pretext for the colonial state to imprison Indian nationalists for the duration of the war.

This chapter recounts the oft-neglected story of the INC's commitment to anti-fascism in the 1930s as a cornerstone to the movement's burgeoning worldview. It focuses particularly on the work of the CFD, which disseminated Indian news for worldwide consumption and circulated world news within India. It also established a robust network of international correspondence with other anticolonial, anti-fascist, and anti-imperialist movements worldwide. The roots of the CFD can be traced back to 1927, when the Congress established the department, although it did little before 1936. Nehru was keen to renew the CFD activities in the turbulent milieu of world politics in 1936, and the Congress resolved to revitalise the department under his leadership. Nehru appointed Rammonhar Lohia as the CFD general secretary, a Congress leader who shared Nehru's desire to connect India to anti-imperialists abroad. Both Nehru and Lohia spent substantial time in continental Europe in the late 1920s and in Berlin especially where they worked closely with anti-imperialists within organisations like the League against Imperialism (LAI). By mid-1936, the CFD began producing biweekly newsletters that included more than four hundred recipients abroad.

On the ground in India, the CFD also boasted an impressive readership of Congress members who counted for nearly 4.5 million Indians by 1938–1939.[7] In the final years before the Second World War, Congress's appeal expanded beyond urban centres and into the rural countryside with the charismatic leadership of Gandhi and his attempts to appeal to the masses. The general election of 1937 extended franchise to nearly 39 million Indians, and Congress won by a landslide after an ambitious campaign by its leadership that further extended the INC's reach beyond a small urban elite. As Congress president, Nehru embarked on a campaign tour covering nearly all of British India and over the course of a year, from April 1936 to May 1937. A perusal of his speeches reveals the pre-eminence of the CFD's message about India's connections to global anti-imperialism and anti-fascism.[8] At the same time, CFD press releases were regularly published in leading Indian newspapers and circulated to the Congress provincial committees, appealing to a wide readership across the sub-continent and shaping the public discourse on India and its relationship to the wider world throughout the 1930s.

The focus on India and the CFD in this chapter also intervenes in histories of fascism and anti-fascism that concentrate on Europe. What has not been addressed is the importance of this global conflict to those in the colonies, who were inspired to act in solidarity with their counterparts abroad in places like Abyssinia, Spain, and China.[9] Anti-fascist solidarity formed a global imaginary in which anticolonial nationalists had a distinct and indeed critical role in the remaking of a world freed from fascism, imperialism and capitalist exploitation. At the same time, it is significant to recognise that peace and anti-fascist internationalism in the 1930s was not a European dominated affair. India assumed an active role in peace organisations internationally and sponsored aid programs for anti-fascism and anti-imperialism in Spain and China.[10] This chapter hopes to remedy this largely neglected story of anti-fascism by showcasing the agency of Indians in anti-fascist internationalism during the years leading to the Second World War.

At the same time, histories of colonial India, and anticolonial nationalism in particular, remain rather parochial by neglecting the important interplay between India and the interwar world. This is beginning to change as historians have uncovered new archives and broadened their questions beyond the local, national, and imperial frames to consider the global connections and conditions that Indians shaped and were shaped by.[11] Studies of the INC especially suffer from the narrow focus of colonial historiography on locality and nation.[12] While certain individuals within the INC have been rescued from the local and national framework and situated in the global politics of their times, a history of the INC movement that accounts for its commitments and interplay with the wider world remains to be written.[13] This chapter draws upon the untapped, yet substantial archival collection of the CFD papers to reveal the global dimensions of India's anticolonial nationalist movement with a special focus on its anti-fascism.

The story of India, the CFD, and anti-fascism is told in two parts. First, it argues that anti-fascism came to be a crucial element of the Congress political imaginary by conceptualising imperialism and fascism as 'blood brothers' produced by global capitalism. An analysis of the CFD literature, as well as the speeches and writing of INC president Jawaharlal Nehru, reveals the development of a worldview that cast fascism and imperialism as the dual outcomes of capitalism, and an articulation of India's need to struggle locally against British colonialism and globally against the dual forces of fascism and imperialism in order to topple the world system that oppresses workers and colonies. It also considers the CFD's contributions to the anti-fascist front in the 1930s, mainly by supplying both moral support and material aid to Abyssinia, Spain, and China. The second part argues that the war between imperialist Britain and fascist Germany and Italy provided a paradoxical dilemma for the INC and CFD. By twinning anti-fascism with anti-imperialism, the INC faced the choice of resisting British imperialism even in the context of war, or supporting the British and French empires against fascist aggression. Ultimately for the INC, anti-imperialist resistance to Britain trumped anti-fascist solidarity and support for the Second World War. This weakened and undermined anti-fascism within the Congress in the 1940s.

India and the anti-imperialist and anti-fascist world

Nehru's oft-cited trope, that imperialism and fascism were 'blood brothers', became a predominant theme in literature produced by the CFD in the period between 1936 and 1939. This twinning of anti-imperialism and anti-fascism served several purposes for the Congress. First, the CFD could cast the INC as a significant actor in a global drama unfolding in the 1930s by arguing that Indian political independence, under Congress leadership, was a vital precondition to the toppling of imperialist and fascist powers globally. It called upon the Congress, and the masses who supported it, to unite in the defeat of British colonialism not only for the benefit of the Indian nation, but also for those struggling in places as diverse as Abyssinia, Spain, China, and beyond. Secondly, the CFD galvanized political elites to recognize themselves as agents of the interwar world by contributing material support and leadership to anti-fascist and peace campaigns of the time. Anti-fascism called upon Indians to think and act globally. Finally, the twinning of imperialism and fascism enabled the Congress to strengthen its critique of the British as a threat that operated within and beyond the colonial context. By refusing to intervene on behalf of Abyssinia and Republican Spain, the CFD argued that Britain bolstered and empowered German and Italian fascism. Within India, the Congress began conceptualising colonial rule in India as a mode of fascism as well as imperialism. If the Congress fought for democracy within India and the British obstructed the power of elected Indian representatives to govern as they did in 1937, then colonial rule was not all that distinct from fascism as the antithesis of democracy in Europe.

The meaning of fascism and imperialism came to be informed by the critique of capitalism.[14] Writing his first major book between 1930 and 1933, *Glimpses of World History*, Nehru argued that 'capitalism led inevitably to a new imperialism, for everywhere there was a demand for raw materials for manufacture and markets to sell the manufactured goods'.[15] The 'easiest way' to meet this demand was to 'take possession' of other countries, and the power of Britain depended in particular on its possession of India. Likewise, Nehru argued that fascism was another manifestation of capitalism and emerged as the 'last desperate attempt' by the 'owning classes to crush the rising workers'.[16] Fascism swept Europe after the First World War as class conflict became 'acute' and the 'owning class' felt threatened by the working class.[17] According to Nehru, fascism used violence to crush workers, eliminate democracy, and impose a dictatorship in order to preserve the power of the capitalist classes.[18] Thus, the root cause of both imperialism and fascism was capitalism, and likewise the anti-imperialist and anti-fascist struggle required solidarity in order to weaken the power of capitalism globally. In other words, imperialism and fascism were not only 'blood brothers'. They were also the dual manifestations of world capitalism in the early 1930s.

This definition of fascism and imperialism was not unique in this period, and rather emblemised a widespread worldview held by many anti-imperialists and communists of the time. In particular, the League against Imperialism (LAI) was instrumental in propagating and amplifying the necessity for solidarity for those opposed to imperialism and fascism in the 1930s.[19] The INC had a longstanding connection with the LAI that dated back to 1927 when Nehru represented India at its inaugural conference, became a founding member of the organisation, and served on its executive council until 1930.[20] Lohia, the CFD general secretary, also had ties to the LAI and its personnel dating back to his residency in Berlin as a student in 1929. Although the INC formally split with the LAI in 1930 after tensions erupted between communists and non-communists, Nehru nevertheless maintained relationships with LAI members and promoted the anti-imperialist cause throughout the 1930s and beyond. Chief among the LAI's propaganda was the call for anti-imperialists to recognize fascism and imperialism were manifestations of capitalism and to unite against these global forces. Nehru attended LAI meetings in London in 1935 and 1936, where he met fellow anti-imperialists who encouraged him to revitalize the CFD and make a strong case for Indian support of Abyssinia and Republican Spain.[21]

The CFD calls for anti-fascist and anti-imperialist solidarity also echoed the policies of the Communist International (Comintern) in this period. Breaking from the class warfare tactics of the third period (1928–1934), the Comintern reengaged with former allies from the united front days in an effort to thwart the power of fascism in Europe. The popular front against fascism likewise called upon those struggling against capitalist exploitation and imperialism to unite in their resistance against the great powers asserting aggressions all over the world. Once an enemy of revolutionary communism in the third period, the INC and other bourgeois nationalist movements in the colonies were restored as potential allies for communists against fascism-imperialism and capitalism. Overall, the popular front articulated by the Comintern and practiced by the LAI appealed to Nehru and the CFD because it offered a framework that crystallised the relationship between Indian anticolonial resistance and the global events unfolding around the world.

The popular front was not the first communist policy to appeal to Nehru either. He visited Moscow in 1927 at the height of his work with the LAI, and Nehru came to admire international communism from afar since he never joined the party or identified as a communist. Still, the powerful ideas articulated in the Leninist moment, about the links between imperialism and capitalism and the necessity for solidarity between anticolonial nationalism in the colonies and the working classes worldwide, informed Nehru's politics and ideas throughout the interwar years and beyond.[22] The Comintern's return to solidarity-building across party lines after 1934 strongly appealed to Nehru once again, and his leadership of the CFD facilitated the INC's anti-fascist tilt. Thus, the anti-imperialist and communist movements came to inform the definition of imperialism and fascism as twin manifestations or 'blood brothers' that served capitalism.

The Italian invasion of Abyssinia underscored the urgency of the anti-fascist struggle in 1935. The League of Nations was rendered incapable of preventing a full-scale military invasion and occupation of Abyssinia by fascist Italy. Equally troubling was the indifference of Britain and France to Abyssinian sovereignty in the face of fascist occupation. The CFD's first anti-fascist campaign underscored the Abyssinian crisis and called upon Indian people to recognize their struggle as one and the same with their Ethiopian counterparts. The inaugural newsletter of the CFD in June 1936 featured the crisis and described India's 'Abyssinia Day', which included mass demonstrations organized by the Congress. Citing Nehru, the newsletter reminded readers that in the case of Abyssinia: 'whereever [*sic*] Imperialism appears in whatever guise it might be, it is the opponent of the forces struggling for freedom and we have to oppose it'.[23] Nehru also argued that the crisis in Abyssinia is 'not something distant or unrelated', but rather India must 'think of our own freedom struggle and see it in relation to the wider world struggle against fascist imperialism'.[24]

Beyond solidarity and sympathy, the Abyssinian crisis afforded new avenues for the Congress to condemn Britain. The third number of the newsletter characterised Britain's indifference to Abyssinian sovereignty as a 'great betrayal' and 'inexcusable desertion'.[25] The Congress was 'pained to see the brave nation conquered'.[26] Britain's neglect in intervening on the side of Abyssinia both as a nation and within the League of Nations was 'shameful'.[27] The newsletter also had harsh words for the League as an organisation 'too much dominated by imperialist influence and world [*sic*] powers to bring justice, much less equality, to weaker nations'.[28] It was the clear case of unchecked fascist aggression that made Abyssinia so troubling and also a cause for India to rally around. Yet, this critique also prompted a call for Indians to renew their anticolonial struggle with vigour because the 'united struggle of colonial countries may alone free the world from imperialist oppression'.[29]

The campaign for solidarity with Abyssinia offered only a preview of the CFD's anti-fascist commitments, which would intensify with the eruption of civil war in

Spain in July 1936. The war began as a military coup led by fascists under the direction of General Francisco Franco against the democratically elected Spanish Republic. The war immediately came to emblemise the struggle of the 1930s between the forces of fascism and democracy, and it captivated and inspired many across the world to contribute moral, financial, and military support on both sides of the divide. There is no dearth of scholarship on the contributions of Germany and Italy on the side of Franco, nor on the support of the Soviet Union for Republican Spain. What has been neglected almost entirely is the significance of the Spanish Civil War to the colonial world and India in particular.[30]

Anti-fascist solidarity with Spain became the dominant focus of the CFD and engendered unprecedented actions on the part of Congress leaders who extended their sympathy beyond sentiment and coordinated material support for republicans in the form of medical supplies and food aid. Immediately, the CFD recognised the Spanish Civil War as the 'struggle of our age' that 'cut across national barriers' and shaped the world and 'India's destiny' as well.[31] CFD literature celebrated Spanish republicanism as 'indomitable, invincible, a bright flame', that inspired the world even when 'ruins and death and starvation encompass it'.[32] Nehru actually travelled to Spain in 1938 and visited the battlefront near Barcelona where he briefly considered staying and fighting on the 'inhospitable looking hill-side which sheltered so much human courage, so much of what was worthwhile in life'.[33] Of course, he did not join the republican effort personally, but returned home to advocate for Indian support of the Spanish cause.

Like Abyssinia, the Spanish Civil War provided an arena for the CFD to condemn the British in a moment of global crisis. As Germany and Italy actively supported Franco's forces, the British once again retreated to a non-interventionist stance alongside France and the United States. The CFD argued that while British policies of non-interventions 'hindered and obstructed the Spanish in their fight for freedom', the world's 'lovers of freedom' have 'raised their voices in the defense of the Spanish people'.[34] Nehru further elaborated on Britain's role in Spain by arguing that 'imperialism comes to the aid of fascism and seeks to starve the people of Spain into submission'.[35] British imperialism, in this instance, remained the chief antagonist for Spain and India, while Indians ultimately must 'recognise that the trial of Spain is equally theirs'.[36]

The CFD also featured the voices of other prominent nationalist leaders, among them poetess and Congress leader, Sarojini Naidu. In a speech before the Indian League against Fascism and War in Calcutta, Naidu also made a case for India's engagement with the wider world:

> Unless we realize that we have to pass the narrow straits of Nationalism to emerge into the larger life of international destinies, we shall not be fit to be the legislators for the future in terms of liberty, in terms of democracy, because no democracy can truly be democracy in the widest sense of the word so long as its interest centres merely within its own geographical frontiers and ethnological barriers and does not transcend the limits of racial boundaries.[37]

Like Nehru, she argued that India must appreciate the Spanish struggle as one for the 'rights of democracy' worldwide, and that India 'dare not, for her own sake … refuse to take her share of the burden of sympathy, assistance, and decision'.[38]

The 'burden' of assistance became more than expressions of solidarity as the civil war progressed and the Congress began fundraising for the shipment of medical and food supplies to Spain. More is known about the stream of supplies and troops pouring into Spain from Germany, Italy and the Soviet Union. However, the Congress undertook an ambitious plan to send funds to London where the Spain-India Committee, under the stewardship of V. K. Krishna Menon, organised shipments to republicans and international brigadiers. Already by April 1937, the CFD boasted the success of the department in collecting 200 pounds sterling in only the first months of fundraising.[39]

The CFD also amplified the twinning of anti-imperialist and anti-fascist struggles in their press statements for the Indian public. In February 1938, a statement showcased the mass demonstration for India's independence in Trafalgar Square led by Krishna Menon's Indian League and Spain-India Committee. Although the emphasis was India's national liberation, the London demonstrators 'echo the sentiments of Nehru' that 'imperialism and fascism are blood-brothers', and recognise that the 'fight against imperialism in India, Burma, Ceylon, in Africa and in the rest of the Colonial Empire, is part of our common struggle for democracy and against fascism and war'.[40] Moreover, the demonstrators resolved on this day to pay 'tribute to the peoples of Ethiopia, China, and Spain, who though betrayed by powerful governments are fighting the battles of national independence against Fascist invaders and traitors and paying with their blood again and again for human liberty'.[41]

The moral and material support for Spain served many causes for India in the later 1930s. By conceptualising fascism and imperialism as mutually interdependent, the Congress made a stronger case for the significance of India beyond the colonial context. Overturning colonial power in India would weaken and possibly undermine British imperialism and its 'blood brother', fascism. In expressing solidarity and supplying material aid, Indians became agents on the world stage in ways that were distinct from non-interventionist Britain. The CFD capitalised on this new status by arguing that India's support for Republican Spain 'tears away from the moorings of British foreign policy and places our country on the international map as an entity separate from the British Empire'.[42] While the aims of British foreign policy remain the 'safeguarding of the Empire and the world capitalist order', India charted a new course that aligned not with great powers, but with those struggling against capitalist, imperialist, and fascist exploitation.

The Spanish Civil War dominated the CFD newsletters at the height of India's anti-fascist campaign, although Nazi Germany was not immune to Congress criticism. As Germany set its eyes on territorial expansion across Europe, the CFD characterized Nazism as the 'blood lust of fascism' that mobilised violence against democracy as its chief 'target'.[43] In the case of Hungary, Nazi fascism revealed a certain pattern that could also be discerned from the Spanish case. Nazis aimed to 'foment internal disorder', in smaller nations in order to 'overthrow popular government'. This political manoeuvring was the prelude for Nazis to facilitate the installation of 'military dictatorship of the fascist type' that aligns with Germany politically and ideologically. According to the CFD, the 'menace' of German fascism was no doubt the greatest spectre haunting Europe, India and the world.[44]

While the anti-fascist agenda, and its imagined ties to anti-imperialism mobilised Indians to act globally, it also informed a new conceptualisation of local politics in colonial India. British colonial policies and practices came to be represented by the CFD as a form of fascism particularly in the context of the new constitution introduced by the Government of India Act of 1935.[45] The new constitution offered provincial autonomy for democratically elected Indian officials, and a share of power for them at the all-India central legislature. However, at the provincial level, the British-appointed Governor retained overriding authority and emergency powers, and the British Parliament and Indian Viceroy continued to control defence, foreign affairs, and veto privileges.[46] British colonial power remained firmly intact, while provincial autonomy was curtailed at every level of the new constitutional government. Therein lies the rub; many Congress leaders believed that the new constitution did not go far enough in securing the primacy of democracy by delegating complete power to the provincial ministries and stripping emergency and veto powers from the colonial state. Democracy remained elusive for the Indian people in this moment.

The CFD covered in the newsletters the unfolding showdown between Congress and the Government of India over the new constitution. While Congress campaigned and won by a landslide in most provinces where over thirty million Indians voted, their election manifesto called for a repudiation of the new constitution and demand for parity of India's elected officials and their colonial counterparts including the viceroy and provincial governor. The first move on the part of Congress-run provincial ministries was a written request that governors publicly surrender their rights to dissolve or curtail the power of the democratically elected officials serving the provincial ministries. Unsurprisingly, the governors did not hand over their power and this opened an intense debate within the Congress over whether elected officials should take their seats in provincial ministries or boycott the constitution all together.

The CFD framed the struggle between the Congress and the British as one between democracy and fascism. In early newsletters during the campaign season, the CFD accused the British of interfering in provincial elections in favour of parties opposing Congress. Citing Nehru's speeches, the newsletter argued that within India, the 'true contest is between two forces – the Congress as representing the will to freedom of the nation, and the British Government in India and its supporters who oppose this urge and try to suppress it'.[47] In this situation, 'we find the world struggle represented in India, the struggle between progress and reaction, between fascism and anti-fascism, between imperialism and national freedom'.[48] To add fuel to the fire, government authorities censored this particular newsletter and launched a raid of the CFD headquarters on 26 September 1936. Colonial officials confiscated all CFD newsletters as 'unauthorized newssheets' under the Press Act, which monitored 'seditious ideas' in India.[49] In a circular to newsletter recipients, general secretary Lohia argued that government's move to curtail the freedom of press is perhaps an even 'more eloquent commentary on the state of civil liberties in India'.[50]

As the world situation came to be cast as the struggle between fascism and democracy, the Congress increasingly argued that the Government of India emblemised fascist oppression. In one provocative newsletter, the CFD announced that the 'Constitution is dead. It died before it started to function.'[51] By Britain's refusal to vest real power in the people and the democratic process, 'the real nature of the new Constitution was revealed'.[52] The elections offered a 'democratic veil' that disguised the authoritarianism of the new constitution. Drawing upon a speech by Nehru, the newsletter argued that the new constitution was 'essentially of the Fascist type concentrating power of the Governors and Governors-General; it is the culmination of the growth of the fascist spirit in the British Government in India'.[53]

The local and global anti-fascist struggle came to be deeply embedded in the CFD by 1938. In an article, 'India and the World', Lohia offered the INC's assessment of global and local conditions defining the history of the late 1930s.[54] His article cast the world as one divided by the forces of fascism and imperialism on one hand, and democracy and freedom on the other. It argued that the 'root disease' of the 'deplorable deterioration in international relations' was the imperialist world system, which gave rise to the conditions for fascism, the 'chief war-maker in the world'.[55] According to the article, the INC 'unreservedly' stood for 'national freedom against imperialist domination; democracy against fascism; and disarmament and collective security against war and brutal aggression'.[56] This global condition shaped both the Congress and the Government of India in the final months before world war. The CFD underscored the vital role of the Congress as it 'liberates' more than 350 million people in India from the 'pro-fascist policies of imperialist Britain'.[57] This conclusion signalled the height of Congress's amalgamation of British imperialism and fascism, which played out in the world and in colonial India. Accordingly, the Congress's duty to unify the masses in resistance to the Government of India was never more urgent locally and globally.

Not all Indians, even within the Congress, agreed with the anti-fascist position of the CFD, and no foreign policy initiative went without contestation. There remained many in India who formally and informally challenged this position by supporting fascist regimes over anti-fascist solidarity. Most prominent was Subhas Chandra Bose, a left-leaning Congressmen from Bengal who famously aligned with and raised an Indian army to support the Axis powers in the Second World War.[58] Well before the war and at the same time that the CFD championed the anti-fascist cause in Spain and Abyssinia, Bose argued in letters to Nehru that his foreign policy was 'nebulous' and filled with 'frothy sentiments and pious platitudes' that failed to prioritise the 'nation's self-interest'.[59] He appealed to Nehru to abandon 'lost causes' like Spain and instead leverage the international situation for

India's advantage by serving the British a strong ultimatum at a moment when their power in Europe is threatened.[60] He added that 'condemning countries like Germany and Italy', served no purpose for Indian nationalist goals.[61] The tension between Bose and Nehru reflected the overall conflict between many globally engaged leaders in India who weighed the possibilities of solidarity and collaboration with Britain's enemies abroad, although before the war it remained unclear which enemy challenged the empire more, fascists or communists. For Nehru and the CFD under his leadership, the conceptualisation of imperialism and fascism as manifestations of capitalism curtailed any possibility for him to imagine pragmatic alliances with Germany or Italy. This was less the case for leaders like Bose. Their conflict over Congress foreign policy also serves as a reminder that the INC never represented a homogeneous and monolithic nationalism, but rather it was heterogeneous and inclusive of disparate and contentious voices. Even so, the CFD went a long way in institutionalizing anti-fascism in the policies and practices of the Congress in the run-up to the Second World War even when some prominent voices raised concern and objection.

Ultimately, India came to shape and be shaped by the anti-fascist struggle in the years before the Second World War. Anti-fascism linked India to the world and encouraged the Congress to marshal moral and material support for their counterparts in Abyssinia and Spain. It was anti-fascism that prompted India's first departure from British foreign policy and unprecedented humanitarian effort to supply republicans in Spain with medical and food assistance. By 1938, the INC sent Indian representatives to international peace organisations and argued that no lasting peace could be built on the foundations of an imperialist world order. At the same time, the twinning of anti-fascism and anti-imperialism offered the CFD a chance to harden its critique of the British and their policies in the world and at home in India. If fascism was a recent manifestation of imperialism, which seeks to curtail democracy, then Britain represented 'fascist imperialism' in India and worldwide. Moreover, the Congress had an obligation and moral duty to contribute to the overturning of fascist-imperialism by leading the Indian masses to freedom and democracy for the nation and then the world.

Anti-imperialism over anti-fascism

Neville Chamberlain's declaration of war against Nazi Germany on 3 September 1939 brought the entire empire into the conflict as well. At this pivotal moment, Nehru was in the Chinese city of Chungking where the war had already arrived in 1937 with the Japanese full-scale invasion of mainland China. Nehru held talks with Chiang Kai-shek at his wartime base during the day and spent evenings in underground shelters under heavy Japanese bombardment. The announcement of war for Britain and the empire compelled Nehru to depart China early and return to India as intense debates over the Congress response to Chamberlain's declaration commenced. The war pitted German and Italian fascism against British and French imperialism, and this forced Nehru and the INC to uncouple anti-fascism and anti-imperialism. In doing so, the new geopolitical circumstances restrained India's anti-fascist campaign and forced the Congress to prioritise the struggle against imperialism over the struggle against fascism.

Already by 1937, the twinning of anti-fascism and anti-imperialism was challenged by circumstances in China. Although Britain and India were aligned in their sympathy for the Chinese, the question of dispatching Indian military support to British strongholds in Shanghai and Hong Kong provoked intense disagreement between the Congress and the Government of India. Provincial ministries in India were not consulted on the decision, and this engendered outrage. Without the consent of the Indian people, according to the CFD, Britain's deployment of Indian soldiers was an 'affront to India'.[62] Equally troubling, the Congress 'repeatedly declared' opposition to mobilising Indian troops and resources for Britain's defence of imperialist interests abroad. In fact, the Congress had already ratified anti-war resolutions at nearly all of their annual sessions since 1927. The dispatch of troops came to be seen as another attempt by Britain to protect its empire and imperialist interests with Indian manpower. In response to the situation in China, the CFD made clear that Indians would not become 'camp followers of imperialist Britain, being ordered about to fight her battles and preserve her interests'.[63]

Debates within the Congress commenced over how to support Chinese anti-imperialism against Japan and at the same time deny support for British imperialism in their East Asian holdings. In a circular prepared for the local and provincial Congress committees, the CFD articulated the INC position on China: 'Our sympathies inevitably be with the people of China and against the aggression of Japan.' At the same time, Congress declared that it 'must make it perfectly clear that if the situation develops towards world war, we will be no party to it.[64] Instead, the CFD organised several 'China Days' to demonstrate their solidarity with the Chinese and condemn Japanese aggression. In cities and towns across India, the 'China Day' demonstrations were accompanied by the reading of Congress resolutions on the crisis in East Asia. First, the Congress argued that the 'sympathy of the Indian people is entirely with the Chinese people'.[65] Second, the resolution situated the current crisis within a recent global history of fascism-imperialism that attacked the 'liberties of Ethiopia, Spain, and China'.[66] At the same time, Britain's deployment of Indian troops sought to preserve the fascist-imperialist system that made possible these global conflicts, and India must 'resist participation' in the case of war. This meant the immediate recall of India's 'sons' from China.[67]

The Congress encouraged other means to support the Chinese instead, ones that did not necessitate supporting British imperialism. An all-Indian boycott of Japanese goods began in late 1937, and the CFD encouraged Indians to obstruct where ever possible the shipment of war materials from India to Japan. In a more ambitious project, the Congress sponsored and facilitated the dispatch of an ambulance and medical team to China to assist in their resistance.[68] In doing so, the CFD circumvented British imperialism through alternative channels and means of assistance. At the same time, India's expressions of solidarity and medical support for China sat uncomfortably with the INC's refusal to support militarily their resistance to Japan because this would bolster the imperial power of Britain. These circumstances foreshadowed the conflict between the cause of anti-imperialism and anti-fascism that emerged when war against fascist Germany came to the British Empire and forced Congress to make decisive choices about their global commitments.

When war came to India, it was accompanied by repressive measures taken by the British Parliament and Government of India. Already in August 1939, Congress directed its members of the provincial government to boycott the Central Legislative Assembly in protest of Britain's ongoing deployment of India troops to conflict zones in Asia. On the same day as Britain's declaration of war, the British introduced the Defence of Indian Ordinance to limit civil liberties in colonial India during wartime. Also on that fateful day, the British Parliament amended the Government of India Act (1935) by concentrating more control in the Viceroy to nullify provincial autonomy and curtail the power of India's elected representatives. Thus, Congress anxieties about the 1935 constitution were indeed justified as Britain moved to exercise authoritarian power over the democratically elected provinces and to silence Indian dissent in the context of the war.

Still reeling from the dispatch of Indian soldiers to China without consulting provincial legislatures, the Congress developed a strong position on Britain's declaration of war and repression of democracy and provincial autonomy. Nehru, as the chief voice of the CFD, drafted the Congress resolution on the declaration of war. It argued that Congress 'repeatedly' condemned the 'ideology and practice of fascism and Nazism and their glorification of war and violence and suppression of the human spirit'.[69] It added that Congress has 'seen in fascism and Nazism the intensification of the principle of imperialism against which the Indian people have struggled for many years'.[70] Without hesitation, Congress denounced the recent Nazi aggression in Poland and sympathized with those who resisted it. Yet, if the war aimed to defend the 'status quo, imperialist possessions, colonies, vested interests, and privilege', then 'India can have nothing to do with it'.[71]

Congress called for cooperation and mutual consent between the Indian and British people in any wartime effort no matter how 'worthy' the cause.[72] While Britain and France made a case for a war to defend democracy against fascism, this appealed little to the Congress leadership who drew upon the recent history of the First World War when the Indian people supported the British war effort. According to the resolution, Britain and France 'broke their pledged word and imposed an imperialist peace on the defeated nations'. This recent history reveals 'how a seemingly fervent declaration of faith may be followed by an ignoble desertion'.[73] Since the Great War, Britain and France had done little to protect democracy and freedom in Manchuria, Spain, Czechoslovakia, and Abyssinia, and have actively stymied the power of the League of Nations to be effective in enforcing peace and ensuring sovereignty for smaller states. 'The true measure of democracy is the ending of imperialism and fascism alike and the aggression that accompanied them in the past and the present.'[74]

The resolution concluded by inviting the British Government to declare its aims for the war in relation to democracy and imperialism, and in particular how these aims will apply to India. Only with a pledge to end imperialism and introduce full democracy and national freedom for India will the Congress be induced to support the British war efforts regardless of its global causes. In its present state, British rule in India is 'the very negation of democracy and of the new world order for which Great Britain claims to be fighting in Europe'.[75] The Congress concluded unequivocally, 'India cannot associate herself in a war said to be for democratic freedom when that very freedom is denied to her.'[76]

Ultimately, the Second World War forced the Congress to prioritize anti-imperialism over anti-fascist struggle. Anti-fascism alone was not a powerful enough appeal for India and the Congress leadership once Britain faced off against fascism. Anti-fascism had served before the war as a powerful tool in galvanising Indians politically to unify in their struggle against the British by equating colonial rule to fascist policies set against democracy in India. Anti-fascism also provided a space for Indians to set an independent foreign policy agenda that differed substantially from Britain. By sending medical supplies and aid to Spain and China, the Congress established a set of policies for India that were distinct. While there is little doubt that Congress leaders like Nehru and Lohia were genuine in their anti-fascist sympathies with Spain, Abyssinia and China, the imperatives of anti-imperialist resistance trumped any other political possibilities for India by 1939 and in the context of another global military conflict that pitted fascism against imperialism. This weakened the possibility for the Congress to align India with anti-fascism when the chief advocates for the cause after 1939 would be British and French imperialists.

Conclusion

Most Congress leaders ultimately paid a heavy price for withdrawing their support for Britain in the Second World War. Several years after the 1939 resolution, the Congress launched its final campaign against the British. The Quit India movement in 1942 escalated the conflict between the INC and the Government of India, which was in no position to handle dissent or resistance in the context of another world war. Nearly all of the Congress leaders were rounded up and imprisoned for the duration of the war. When the dust settled and the peace agreements were signed, the Congress leadership emerged from prison as the chief negotiators for Indian independence, which came shortly after in 1947.

In the war's aftermath and the establishment of the independent Indian nation-state, however, the Congress never revisited their anti-fascist positions. By the conclusion of the war, the INC transitioned from an independence movement to a political party responsible for overseeing the ratification of independent India's first constitution and contesting elections in 1951–1952. Under the leadership of the INC and Prime Minister Nehru, leaders ratified a constitution that established a democracy with a parliamentary form of government. At the same time and paradoxically, the constitution borrowed heavily from colonial-era laws and particularly the Government of India Act of 1935.[77] Perhaps most controversial and directly relevant to this chapter was the decision by Indian leaders to retain the emergency powers of the central government, ones that the Congress argued were Britain's 'fascist' tools for undermining democracy and freedom in India. Ultimately, once empowered to determine their own constitution, Indian constitutional architects opted for a strong and centralised state capable of authoritarian power over the provinces and the people rather than the idealised democracy that they once advocated for in the 1930s under the banner of anti-fascism for India. The Internal Emergency clause under Article 352 of the constitution ultimately enabled Indira Gandhi to suspend the federal government, the fundamental rights of the people, and civil liberties nationwide for nearly two years from 1975 to 1977. Political opponents of Gandhi, calling for her resignation on the basis of corruption, were imprisoned and strict censorship of the press imposed in a fashion not all that distinct from British colonial tactics in the 1930s.

The history of anti-fascism in India and globally reveals the complicated world that existed in the interwar moment, one that afforded a more fluid transnationalism that linked a continuum of anti-capitalist, anti-imperialist, and anti-fascist politics and lives. Anti-fascism enabled India to envision their localised anticolonial struggle as interconnected with a wider world of resistance movements in the late 1930s. They expressed more than sympathy and solidarity by supplying material and humanitarian aid for places like Spain and China. At the same time, anti-fascism offered a way of strengthening resistance to British oppression and colonial rule in India.

The twining of fascism and imperialism, anti-fascism and anti-imperialism, were founded on flexible and ambiguous grounds as part of a larger critique of capitalism. This worldview rarely stood the test of the Second World War. From the vantage point of 1939, anti-imperialism and anti-fascism were not as compatible as they seemed in the late 1920s and earlier 1930s. This history affords us opportunities to reflect on the possibilities for solidarities in the context of events like the Spanish Civil War but were later challenged as the new world orders of the war and even the early Cold War radically shifted geopolitics. The postcolonial world and India after 1945, hardly resembled that which came before. Instead, the new nation-state founded on anti-imperialism chose to ignore the fascist tendencies of the colonial constitution of 1935 and instead borrow from it directly.

Notes

1 Congress Foreign Department Newsletter, No. 12, 25 February 1937, File FD-11 (Kw) (ii) 1936, All-India Congress Committee Papers (AICC), Nehru Memorial Museum and Library, New Delhi, India (hereafter AICC Papers).
2 Ibid.
3 Ibid.
4 On the popularity of Hitler in India, see for example Manimugdha S. Sharma, 'Why Hitler is Not a Dirty Word in India', *The Times of India*, 29 April 2018, online at https://timesofindia.indiatimes.com/india/why-hitler-is-not-a-dirty-word-in-india/articleshow/63955029.cms (accessed 7 February 2019).
5 See Sugata Bose, *His Majesty's Opponent: Subhas Chandra Bose and India's Struggle against Empire* (Cambridge, MA: Harvard University Press, 2011); and Leonard A. Gordon,

Brothers against the Raj: A Biography of Indian Nationalists Sarat Chandra Bose and Subhas Chandra Bose (Calcutta: Rupa Publications, 2008).

6 See for example the introduction and essays in the special issue on 'Global Fascisms and the Volk: The Framing of Narratives and the Crossing of Lines', *South Asia: Journal of South Asian Studies* Vol. 38, No. 4, 2015.

7 Data from Judith M. Brown, *Modern India: The Origins of an Asian Democracy* (Oxford: Oxford University Press, 1985), p. 294.

8 See *Selected Works of Jawaharlal Nehru*, edited by S. Gopal (New Delhi: Orient Longman, 1972) Vol. 7, pp. 211–406; Vol. 8, pp. 1–46. Citations are from the first series unless otherwise noted (hereafter *SWJN*).

9 Notable exceptions are Michele Louro, *Comrades against Imperialism: Nehru, India, and Interwar Internationalism* (Cambridge: Cambridge University Press, 2018), pp. 214–255; Maria Framke 'Political Humanitarianism in the 1930s: Indian Aid for Republican Spain', *European Review of History*, Vol. 23, No. 1–2, 2016, pp. 63–81; and Maria Framke, 'We Must Send a Gift Worthy of India and Congress!' War and Humanitarian in Late Colonial South Asia', *Modern Asian Studies* Vol. 51, No. 6, 2017, pp. 1969–1998.

10 For a history of the INC's involvement in the International Peace Campaign, see Louro, *Comrades against Imperialism*, pp. 218–235.

11 Interest in colonial South Asia and the wider world has grown with the publication of three seminal works: Mrinalini Sinha, *Specters of Mother India: The Global Restructuring of an Empire* (Durham, NC: Duke University Press, 2006); Sugata Bose, *A Hundred Horizons: The Indian Ocean in the Age of Global Empires* (Cambridge, MA: Harvard University Press, 2006); and Durba Ghosh & Dane Kennedy (eds), *Decentering Empire: Britain, India, and the Transcolonial World* (Hyderbad: Orient Longman, 2006). More recent contributions include among others, Sugata Bose and Kris Manjapra (eds), *Cosmopolitan Thought Zones: South Asia and the Global Circulation of Ideas* (Basingstoke: Palgrave Macmillan, 2010); Maia Ramnath, *Haj to Utopia: How the Ghadar Movement Charted Global Radicalism and Attempted to Overthrow the British Empire* (Berkeley, CA: University of California Press, 2011); Manu Goswami, 'Imaginary Futures and Colonial Internationalisms,' *American Historical Review Vol.* 117, No. 5, 2012; Ali Raza, Franziska Roy, & Benjamin Zachariah (eds), *The Internationalist Moment: South Asia, Worlds, and World Views, 1917–1939* (Los Angeles, CA: Sage, 2014); Kris Manjapra, *Age of Entanglements: German and Indian Intellectuals across Empire* (Cambridge, MA: Harvard University Press, 2014); Seema Alavi, *Muslim Cosmopolitanism in the Age of Empire* (Cambridge, MA: Harvard University Press, 2015); and Louro, *Comrades against Imperialism*.

12 Classic texts on the Indian National Congress include hagiographical accounts of its leaders in classic works like Bipan Chandra, *India's Struggle for Independence*, 1857–1947 (New Delhi: Penguin, 1989). More critical works are also framed within the nation. See, Sumit Sarkar, *Modern India, 1885–1947* (New York: St. Martin's Press, 1989); and Partha Chatterjee, *Nationalist Thought and the Colonial World: A Derivative Discourse?* (Minneapolis, MN: Minnesota University Press, 1986); and Partha Chatterjee, *The Nation and its Fragments: Colonial and Postcolonial Histories* (Princeton, NJ: Princeton University Press, 1993).

13 Notable exceptions include Gandhi's South African experiences, Subhas Chandra Bose's alignment with Axis powers, and Nehru's internationalism. The history of the Indian National Congress, as an institution, continues to be framed as a local or national history.

14 For a lengthier argument, see Louro, *Comrades against Imperialism*, pp. 214–255.

15 Nehru, *Glimpses of World History: Being Further Letters To His Daughter Written In Prison, And Containing a Rambling Account of History For Young People*, US edition (New York: The John Day Company, 1942), pp. 354–355.

16 Ibid., p. 687.

17 Ibid.

18 Ibid.

19 The history of the LAI is still developing. For recent works, see Michele Louro, Heather Streets-Salter, Carolien Stolte, & Sana Tannoury-Karam, *The League against Imperialism: Lives and Afterlives* (Leiden: Leiden University Press, forthcoming 2020); and various

articles written by Fredrik Petersson on the topic of his PhD thesis: Fredrik Petersson, *Willi Münzenberg, the League against Imperialism, and the Comintern, 1925–1933* (Lewiston, NY: Queenston Press, 2013).

20 For a history of Nehru and the LAI, see Louro, *Comrades against Imperialism*.

21 See also Mark Reeves's essay in *The League against Imperialism: Lives and Afterlives*, forthcoming 2020.

22 For a history of Nehru and the Comintern, see Louro, *Comrades against Imperialism*.

23 Congress Foreign Department Newsletter, No. 1, 4 June 1936, FD 11 kwi 1936, AICC Papers.

24 Nehru, Speech on Abyssinia Day, 9 May 1936, reprinted in the *Hindustan Times*, 11 May 1936, reprinted in SWJN, Vol. 7, p. 569.

25 CFD Newsletter, No. 3, 2 July 1936, FD 11 (kw) (i) 1936, AICC Papers.

26 Ibid.

27 Ibid.

28 Ibid.

29 Ibid.

30 Louro, *Comrades against Imperialism*, pp. 214–255; Maria Framke 'Political Humanitarianism in the 1930s', pp. 63–81; and Framke, 'We Must Send a Gift Worthy of India and Congress!', pp. 1969–1998.

31 CFD Newsletter, No. 7, 10 September 1936, FD 11 (kw) (ii) 1936, AICC Papers.

32 CFD Newsletter, No. 12, 25 February 1937, FD 11 kwii 1936, AICC Papers.

33 His memoirs of his journey were published in Nehru, *China, Spain, and the War: Essays and Writings* (Allahabad: Kitabistan, 1940), p. 77.

34 CFD Newsletter, No. 12, 25 February 1937, FD 11 kwii 1936, AICC Papers.

35 Nehru, Foreword to *Spain! Why?* (London: The India Committee for Food for Spain, undated), copy held at the International Institution of Social History (IISH), Amsterdam, Netherlands.

36 Ibid.

37 Reprint of Naidu's speech, CFD Newsletter, No. 14, 25 March 1937, FD 11 (kw) (ii) 1936, AICC Papers.

38 Ibid.

39 CFD Newsletter, No. 16, 22 April 1937, FD 11 (kw) (ii) 1936, AICC Papers. V.K. Krishna Menon was an Indian expatriate living in Britain and founder of the India League for Freedom (ILF), an organisation based in London that promoted Indian anticolonial nationalism and the INC platform. Menon later held various diplomatic posts for postcolonial India.

40 CFD Press Statement, 10 February 1938, FD 7 1936, AICC Papers.

41 Ibid.

42 CFD Newsletter, No. 17, 6 May 1937, FD 11 (kw) (ii) 1936, AICC Papers.

43 Lohia, 'Nazi Design on Hungary', 4 May 1937, FD 12 (i) 1936, AICC Papers.

44 Ibid.

45 The Government of India Act of 1935 restructured the governance of the colonial state. The Parliament and Viceroy continued to oversee governance and control defence, foreign affairs, and veto privileges. The provinces within India were comprised of an appointed governor and the provincial ministries, which would be elected in accordance to the new constitution by a limited electorate comprising of one-sixth of the colony's population. Elected provincial ministries would participate in a Central Assembly in New Delhi, which would set policy and govern. The power to dissolve the provincial ministries was bestowed on the provincial governor and the Viceroy.

46 For the mutually constitutive relationship between constitutional reforms and emergency legislation, see Durba Ghosh, *Gentlemanly Terrorists: Political Violence and the Colonial State in India, 1919–1947* (Cambridge: Cambridge University Press, 2017). Ghosh argues that progressive constitutional reforms in India were always accompanied by 'extraordinary' legal measures introduced by the British to ensure colonial power and to limit democracy and governance to certain Indian elites 'considered worthy of governing'.

47 CFD Newsletter, No. 8, 24 September 1936, FD 11 (kw) (i) 1936, AICC Papers.
48 Ibid.
49 Details of the raid are included in CFD circular No. 2, dated 1 October 1936, FD 11 (kw) (i) 1936, AICC Papers.
50 Ibid.
51 CFD Newsletter, No. 15, 8 April 1937, FD 11 (kw) (ii) 1936, AICC Papers.
52 Ibid.
53 CFD Newsletter, No. 15, 8 April 1937, FD 11 (kw) (ii) 1936, AICC Papers.
54 Lohia, 'Nazi Design on Hungary', handwritten, 4 May 1937, FD 12 (i) 1936, AICC Papers.
55 Ibid.
56 Ibid.
57 Ibid.
58 See Bose, *His Majesty's Opponent.*
59 Bose to Nehru, 28 March 1939, reprinted in Jawaharlal Nehru, *A Bunch of Old Letters* (London: Asia Publishing House, 1960), pp. 324–325.
60 Ibid.
61 Ibid.
62 CFD Newsletter, No. 24, 25 August 1937, FD 11 (kw) (ii) 1936, AICC Papers.
63 Ibid.
64 CFD Circular to Provincial Congress Committees signed by Nehru, 4 September 1937, FD 11 (kw) (ii) 1936, AICC Papers.
65 CFD Newsletter, No. 26, 30 September 1937, FD 11 (kw) (ii) 1936, AICC Papers.
66 Ibid.
67 Ibid.
68 For details on Chinese aid, see F 38–1937, AICC Papers.
69 'Congress Resolution on India and the War,' 14 September 1939, reprinted in *Selected Works of Jawaharlal Nehru*, Vol. 10, pp. 122–138.
70 Ibid.
71 Ibid.
72 Ibid.
73 Ibid.
74 Ibid.
75 Ibid.
76 Ibid., p. 126.
77 Ghosh argues that the postcolonial state adopted colonial-era legislation and surveillance mechanisms to target a variety of political dissidents. See Ghosh, *Gentlemanly Terrorists*, pp. 244–256.

7

NO PLACE FOR NEUTRALITY

The case for democracy and the League Against Nazism and Fascism in Syria and Lebanon

Sana Tannoury-Karam

On 6 and 7 May 1939, a group of activists, literati, intellectuals, and parliamentarians gathered in Beirut under the name the League Against Nazism and Fascism in Syria and Lebanon. The report of the organising committee of that League was presented by Ra'if Khoury, a Lebanese leftist intellectual, writer, and educator. Khoury described the danger of fascism engulfing the world and called for supporting the League in its fight against fascism and Nazism. He further added that 'neutrality is a joke in the struggle between democracy and fascism',[1] and that it was then more imminent than ever to take a stand. For the League and its supporters, the position to be taken was clear, 'we stand with the democratic front'.[2] Maqbula al-Shalaq, a Damascene writer and poet, declared in her speech at the conference, 'We are democratic Arab women, and we say proudly that we resent fascism [...] nothing will stop us from resisting it fiercely.'[3]

Ra'if Khoury, along with Maqbula al-Shalaq and other prominent Lebanese and Syrian intellectuals, founded the League Against Nazism and Fascism in Syria and Lebanon in 1939, the League's mouthpiece journal *al-Tariq* (the Path) in 1941, and the Friends of the Soviet Union organisation in 1942. During the war years, the League established branches across Lebanon, Syria, Iraq, and Palestine, and within these branches established women's sections. The League brought together a network of Arab communists, socialists, and liberal-progressives that had been advocating against fascism and Nazism since the early 1930s from across the political spectrum.[4]

During the interwar period, Arab nationalists and internationalists organised in various, often overlapping, circles on the local and the global realms. By the mid-1930s, the rise of fascism and schisms within the left created increasingly stricter demarcations of political and ideological lines in Europe and across the world. This in turn influenced the anticolonial structures built during the post-First World War period, particularly those functioning in European metropolises such as Berlin and

Paris. It divided activists and the movements they established across political lines.[5] However, a more complicated picture appears when we examine anticolonial leftists in Lebanon and Syria who opposed fascism by building spaces for a diverse group of activists from across the political spectrum. These spaces allowed for developing arguments and movements against fascism and Nazism, and for advocating for national independence from colonialism, democracy, progress, and women's rights.

This chapter brings to the fore the voices of Arab leftists who opposed Nazism and fascism and embraced democracy during the 1930s and 1940s. I examine how they organised against, debated, and rejected fascism, and how they framed and advocated for democratic principles. I address the foundation and development of the League Against Nazism and Fascism, and the significance of its journal *al-Tariq* in creating a platform for debates on the future of the region and the world.

The story of the Lebanese and Syrian left who stood against fascism is significant to tell because, first, the literature has predominantly emphasised Arab attraction to fascism and only recently have historians of the Middle East addressed Arab opposition to fascism.[6] Rather, historians have overwhelmingly examined the rise of pro-Nazi movements and forces in various Arab countries in the 1930s and 1940s and argued for their significance in the development of post-war Arab societies.[7] Yet, the failure of the Arab-Nazi project and the swift triumph of the Allies in the Middle East during the Second World War highlights the deficiency of this narrative and does not account for the rise of Arab anti-fascist movements. David Motadel has complicated the Arab attraction to fascism by showing Nazi efforts and propaganda directed towards Muslims to foster this attraction.[8] Motadel also argued for Nazi Germany's support for the development of an authoritarian anticolonial international in Berlin during the Second World War that attracted anticolonial nationalists, including Arab nationalists, to the Nazi project.[9] Yet, there has not been an examination of the way the anti-fascists organised under the umbrella of global anti-fascism despite lack of support from the Allies.

The significance of the history of the League also rests upon the realisation that this organisation developed beyond the parameters of a communist party and separate from Comintern directives, even when there was cooperation between the League and the party. Of the leftists who organised the League, some were members of the Communist Party of Syria and Lebanon, but the majority were fellow travellers. It was not therefore a direct outlet of the Communist Party despite the cooperation between the two.[10] Instead, the League, which brought together more than 200 representatives of 32 different organisations from Syria and Lebanon, represented a network that extended beyond the parameters of the party. This particular network was a product of the way the political left developed in Lebanon and Syria in the post-First World War period and therefore its history adds to our knowledge about the Arab left more broadly.

The late Ottoman period had witnessed a spread of socialist, anarchist, and radical leftist ideas in the Eastern Mediterranean, as Ilham Khuri-Makdisi has shown.[11] Although not all socialists and Marxists openly welcomed the Bolshevik Revolution, with the end of the First World War and the imposition of the Mandates on the former Arab provinces of the Ottoman Empire, the position of the Soviet Union within the post-war world order cast a favourable light on the Soviet project of communism. Moreover, the socioeconomic and political conditions created by a devastating war left a fertile ground for the spread of socialist ideas that would gravitate towards the Soviet model. A gathering of intellectuals and workers established the Communist Party in Mandate Lebanon in 1925.[12] The CP of Syria and Lebanon was admitted into the Comintern in 1928.[13] Shortly after, a series of coups ensued within the Party resulting in the purge of some of its founding members.[14] Some of those purged, along with fellow travellers – Marxist intellectuals and activists who were not officially members of the CP – continued to be active parallel to the party. They created a leftist milieu that overlapped with, but also functioned outside, the parameters of a communist party.[15] This milieu represented a heterogeneous left that would, in interwar and wartime Lebanon and Syria, mobilise against imperialism, capitalism, and fascism. It is from within this milieu that the anti-fascist movement, organised in the League, emerged.

Finally, and most importantly, the history of the League and Arab anti-fascism is a significant story to tell, not only because Arab leftists stood against fascism, but also because of the ways they chose to counter fascism. The arguments and debates that they invoked in their opposition to fascism indicate the issues salient for Arab intellectuals and activists in the building of their newly created states and evolving societies. Primarily, as this chapter argues, Arab leftists invoked democracy and its binary opposition to fascism, to push for independence from colonialism. They framed anti-fascism as an active form of the national liberation struggle and saw the opposition to fascism as a natural product of a long Arab tradition of freedom, and as a protector to that tradition from all kinds of oppression. Moreover, arguing for the need to 'take sides', leftists questioned what it meant to them and their countries to stand with the democratic front when democracy was being withheld from them by the very side they supported. Feminists declared their support for democracy in the face of oppressive fascism and argued for the incompleteness of democracy without political rights for women.

Despite the centrality of viewing opposition as a response to the rise of fascism and Nazism, it is important to understand and contextualise the actions of those speaking against fascism as more than reactive. Overall, anti-fascists in Lebanon and Syria did not encounter direct European fascism in their societies. Although there were parties founded in the interwar period in Lebanon and Syria that were inspired by fascist organisation and form, none were a mere imitation of European fascist parties and none adopted for instance racial theories.[16] Therefore, only by moving beyond the paradigm of response can we understand how discussions about fascism/Nazism created a space for larger discussions about anticolonialism, democracy, progress, and suffrage. These debates had roots in the history of Arab intellectual life during the late Ottoman and interwar periods.[17]

Anti-fascism and the struggle against colonialism

Leftists understood well that fascism was as much a product of capitalism as was imperialism. They continuously emphasised the intersectionality between fascism and imperialism and the interconnectivity of the struggle against both. As David Motadel has shown in his work, a number of anticolonial nationalist exiles during the Second World War, including several Arab nationalists residing in Berlin, embraced the fascist and Nazi projects in return for Axis support for their claims of national independence against Britain and France.[18] However, for Arab leftists organising in Lebanon and Syria during the Second World War, embracing fascism was not the solution to their colonial problems. Rather, leftists organised to simultaneously counter various structures of oppression, particularly colonialism and fascism, and their connection to Zionism.[19] They pushed for, first, prioritising the anti-fascism struggle during the war, and second, advocating for democracy as the solution to fascism, imperialism, and capitalism.

In its first public event organised in May 1939 in Beirut, the League addressed the suffering of those colonised by democratic imperial states; however, those gathered agreed that supporting fascism would not bolster the national liberation struggle. Arguing against the logic of 'the enemy of my enemy is my friend', leftists framed fascism as imperialistic in nature and antithetical to any liberation struggle. Ra'if Khoury identified fascism as the last breath of colonialism.[20] He argued that 'Fascism strongly believes in colonialism', even when it was at war with other colonisers, France and Britain.[21] Khoury warned against 'depending' on fascism to defeat colonialism, reminding Arab nationalists of their failed reliance on the British and French during the First World War to shed Ottoman rule.[22] Khaled Bakdash, the secretary general of the Communist Party of Syria and Lebanon, warned that the victory of fascism would bring an end to Arab national liberation movements. He cautioned against neutrality, explaining that a fascist victory will never differentiate between those who stood against it and those who remained neutral.[23] According to Bakdash, fascism, 'the dictatorship of the most brutal colonists', was seeking to take over the colonies of the rest of Europe and further subjugate the people of these colonies to oppression.[24] Antun Tabit, a Lebanese communist intellectual and president of the League Against Nazism and Fascism, framed the fight against fascism as a patriotic struggle, arguing that 'the fight to ally with democratic France, and the fight against the danger of fascism, is at the moment the greatest national liberation struggle'.[25]

Within the binary of coloniser and colonised, a sub-binary existed that divided the colonising nations between democratic and fascist. It was a priority to take the side of France and Britain in the struggle against fascism, without abandoning the anticolonial struggle against the French Mandate in Lebanon and Syria and the British Mandate in Palestine.

Just like fascism was not the solution to the colonial problem, it was also not the solution to Zionism. Leftists who organised against fascism framed the Palestine question and Zionism within the British colonial dilemma and not within anti-Semitic tropes. The League reiterated throughout the Second World War the need to resolve the Palestine question through the anticolonial struggle against British colonialism in Palestine. Ra'if Khoury, one of the main conveners of the League and leading anti-fascist leftist, wrote *Jihad Filastin* (The Struggle of Palestine) while teaching in Jerusalem in the Bishop Gobat School during the eruption of the Arab Revolt.[26] He blamed Zionism for dispossession of Arab land and the displacement of Arab peasants and workers in the Palestinian economy, and he identified the liberation movement as first and foremost against British colonialism.[27] He acknowledged that Zionists were acquiring weapons and forming militias with the knowledge and sometimes support of the British colonisers, arguing that a Jewish state in Palestine was strategically important and desirable for the project of British colonialism across the world.[28] Writing in 1936 about the relationship between fascism and Zionism, Khoury proclaimed Zionists as fascist colonists and refuted their claims of socialism. He explained that Zionist socialism 'is working towards invading a country, displacing its peasants, impoverishing its workers, and destroying its people completely'.[29] According to Khoury, fascism and Zionism were not enemies, but rather it was in Zionism's interest that the Jews be persecuted in order to justify its 'tyrannical immigration' as a humanitarian vindication of their persecution. Thus, any lauding of fascism as seen in Arab and Palestinian newspapers 'is foolish'.[30] Khoury believed that Nazis created the 'Jewry legend' to distract the German people with constructed theories of racial superiority.[31] He argued that, 'with the death of Nazism, the vein that feeds this movement would be cut'.[32] Referring to Jews as a minority that had witnessed all kinds of persecution in the world, Khoury tore through Nazism's various excuses– Judaism, Bolshevism, capitalism, and the stipulations of the Versailles treaty – to justify their actions. He refuted Nazism's claims against Judaism by rhetorically asking, how can Judaism be both capitalist and communist? For the Nazis, 'Capitalist Britain is Jewish, and capitalist America is Jewish. And communist Russia is Jewish, and all that is not Nazi is Jewish, and everything that does not serve Nazism is Jewish.' Khoury added that anything that opposed Nazism would be considered its enemy, therefore 'you, for example, are Jewish. I am Jewish. My words are Jewish.'[33] In that line, he argued, Judaism can be used for any excuse for Nazism, including blaming Nazism on a Jewish conspiracy in case Hitler ever gets caught and tried.[34] Only the defeat of fascist forces in Europe would halt the urgency for European Jews to create a national home in Palestine. Therefore, the Palestinian fight for independence was a fight against fascism as much as it was against Zionism and colonialism.

In its inaugural meeting in 1939, the League decided to send a letter of support to the anti-fascist conference taking place in Paris on 13–14 May, asking solidarity with the Syrian-Lebanese League.[35] Although it would not hold another public conference until December 1942, the League grew throughout the early years of the Second World War, with several branches opening in various cities around Syria and Lebanon. The lag between the first congress in 1939 and 1941 when the League's journal *al-Tariq* appeared might be explained by the takeover of Lebanon by pro-German Vichy French forces from June 1940 until July 1941 in which anti-fascist activities were curbed. The non-aggression pact signed between Germany and the Soviet Union in August of 1939, just before the war erupted, caused further confusion and disappointment within leftist ranks. Between the 'liberation' of Syria and Lebanon from Vichy in 1941 and the defeat of the Axis powers in North Africa in 1942, anti-fascist activities increased in Lebanon. By 1942 the League had established branches in Tripoli, Zahle, Homs, Aleppo, Damascus, and Jerusalem. These branches organised lectures, parties, and opened offices and meeting halls to increase interaction between the leadership of the League and the people.[36]

In April of 1942, League representatives organised a tour from Beirut to Syria, with stops in Tripoli, Homs, and Aleppo. They met other League members in these areas, as well as some local political leaders and French officials.[37] Later that summer, a committee of the Beirut central branch made a trip to Damascus to meet with the city's women's branch,[38] the Democratic Student League, and the Communist Party office in the city.[39] Between 100 to often 500 people attended some of the public meetings across Lebanon where it seems gatherings attracted more people than just the members of the League.[40]

The second conference of the League, which was held on 18–20 December 1942, proved the extent of the work its members had done in spreading the anti-fascist message. There were 38 representatives from 9 different participating branches in Lebanon and Syria: Beirut, Damascus, Homs, Tripoli, the Shuf region, Aleppo, the Alawite region, Biqa', and Marji'yun. Speakers emphasised the dangers of fascism and Nazism on cultural, intellectual, social, and political life.[41] The conference attendees again argued for the connectivity of national struggles around the world and their relation to the fight against fascism.[42] More importantly, the League again pushed for the fulfilment of wartime French promises of independence for Lebanon and Syria.

Despite prioritising the need to fight fascism and therefore allow for a 'marriage of convenience' with their colonisers, League members used anti-fascism to challenge France and Britain and hold them accountable for their promises. They underlined the need to rectify the French-Syrian and French-Lebanese treaties and a solution to the problem in Palestine. The decisions also tackled French policies in Lebanon and Syria towards fascist propaganda, demanding the French government's respect of democratic freedoms of the people and upholding of democratic principles. In their declaration of support to France, leftists who continuously invoked the democratic principles of the French revolution, used that support as a bargaining chip to demand the implementation of these principles within the mandates that France ruled over.

The events of November 1943 in Lebanon, primarily the imprisonment of the main figures of government and the president of the republic by the French authorities in an attempt to curtail demands for national independence, were also framed by several leftist intellectuals as a result of the connection between the national struggle and the anti-fascist struggle. *Al-Tariq* published a direct declaration in the name of the League addressed to the French High Commissioner, denouncing French actions – suspension of the constitution and dissolution of parliament, and the imprisonment of political figures – as demonstrating a fascist-like spirit.[43] Fascism and Nazism had provided a model for totalitarian and authoritarian rule, and those who opposed this model increased the calls for democratic rule. Leftists understood that only democracy would guarantee a future world with peace and independence to all its people.[44] For feminists organising within the leftist anti-fascist movement during the Second World War, this democracy was lacking without political rights for women.

Fascism, the enemy of women

Leftist feminists identified fascism as a reactionary force that stood against progress. Linking women's advancement to human progress, they argued that fascism was ultimately the enemy of women.[45] Maqbula al-Shalaq was one of the main speakers during the first League conference held in May 1939 in Beirut, and the only female speaker as far as we know.[46] We do not have an exact date and details, however, we do know that a women's section of the League was established at some point during the Second World War with branches in Lebanon, Syria and Iraq.[47] These various branches of the Women's League Against Nazism and Fascism held regular meetings and gatherings, and were a direct affiliate of the main League which continued to host women in its meetings, public lectures, and its publications.[48]

The women involved in the League, both its main section and the women's section, used that venue and the outlet of the journal *al-Tariq* to raise their voices against fascism while making a strong argument for the advancement of women in the public sphere. Much like their male counterparts, they saw the world divided between a fascist and a democratic struggle, and called for taking a direct stand against forces of fascism. They viewed the League, its activities, and its efforts to unite men and women in the struggle against fascism, as part of the process of the liberation of women.[49]

Maqbula al-Shalaq's speech at the first conference of the League in 1939 echoed the general sentiments of that meeting regarding the dangers of fascism and the necessary struggle for freedom. Speaking in the name of women in Syria and Lebanon, she wondered 'what kind of woman who has a heart does not resent fascism?'[50] This resentment to fascism should come because of two main reasons, she argued, since fascism stood against democracy, and since fascism was the enemy of women. Al-Shalaq declared, 'We are democratic Arab women, and we say proudly that we resent fascism … and nothing will stop us from resisting it fiercely … Isn't it (fascism) the enemy of Arab women?'[51] She went on to describe fascism's treatment of women more generally, underlining the unequal treatment of women in Germany and their confinement to the kitchen and the 'prison of house walls', and the fascist impediments for women's education.[52] Furthermore, fascism 'looks at women as a tool to be sold and bought cheaply, and forgets that nature has granted her the same it granted man from senses and intellect'.[53] Most significantly, fascism took back women to the age of servitude and imprisonment that they have fought so long to get out of; it therefore reversed progress for women. Al-Shalaq elaborated on this point by explaining how Nazism was discouraging women from going to schools and forbidding them from working outside their homes.[54]

Drawing on a historical overview of women's suffrage movements and successes to attain the vote from late nineteenth century Bohemia to the Soviet example of gender equality, Emily Fares Ibrahim noted in an article that the countries that have given women the right to vote were fighting along the democratic front against Nazism and fascism.[55] Fares Ibrahim, a Lebanese intellectual and a force within the Arab women's movement, argued that not only did fascism deny women their rights, but Hitler and Mussolini were responsible for reversing some of the political rights achieved by women in their countries, primarily the right to vote and run for office.[56]

Feminists argued that fighting fascism together as men and women provided a space in which both genders were equal. The idea of a struggle common to both men and women, despite acknowledging separate and traditional gender roles, allowed these women to insert themselves into the plural possessive pronoun in which 'we' was used and 'our' to designate a common possession of the homeland and of its freedom. Since the speakers were women themselves, the 'we' that they used, although not broken down into male and female, emphasised this inclusion. Al-Shalaq stated in her League speech in 1939:

> Let fascism know that in our country there are men who are awake and not happy with its actions! … Let fascism know that we have women whose hearts repulse at the mention of its name (fascism) …! […] And let the supporters and servants of fascism know, that *we* (my emphasis) resist it and will not allow it to fulfill its dreams in *our* homeland, whose freedom and independence *we* will redeem with our hands, our blood, and our souls.[57]

Within the anti-fascist movement, women, 'whether mothers, comrades, or sisters, should enlist to fight this disease with all the means they have'.[58] Moreover, fighting fascism placed women within the public realm. When women became men's partners in fighting this enemy, they achieved a greater status in public affairs. Women could then 'walk side by side the enlightened men of our country'; they could be the 'vanguard of the people fighting this oppressive system'.[59]

Fighting fascism was therefore a fight for the homeland and for the nation, and it placed women within that nationalist struggle. Maqbula al-Shalaq declared in a speech at a gathering of the Women's League in Damascus that 'we fight with honour against Nazism and fascism because we fight for our independence'. She urged women 'to fight Nazism and its traitor agents for the preservation of our homeland, culture, honour, and nationalist aspiration'.[60]

At a gathering of the Iraqi Women's League in Baghdad on 6 May 1943, Afifi Ra'uf, the president of the League, gave a speech 'al-Naziya 'Aduwwat al-Mar'a' (Fascism the Enemy of Women), arguing that Nazism would only bring backwardness to the East. For women, Nazism would colonise their country as well as enslave them and turn them into production machines. Therefore, women cannot be neutral, especially since women have proven over time to be at the forefront of the convoy moving towards progress and liberation. Ra'uf declared:

> To my sister, fascism is your personal enemy, robbing you of the right to fight for liberation, and stopping historical progress [...] in this war, our destiny is linked with the destiny of oppressed people, believe that victory is ours.[61]

Saluting women of the world fighting fascism, including women of Britain, US, China, and Soviet Union, Ra'uf urged Iraqi women to stand at the forefront of the global struggle, and that 'by joining the League Against Fascism, you have joined the ranks of these fighters'.[62]

Fighting fascism became a cause of women's progress and fight for equality with men.[63] Al-Shalaq argued continuously that,

> We should fight this monster (fascism) with all of the strength we have, to elevate the status of women in our country, and provide prosperity to our people, so that our countries can march to the zenith/pinnacle of civilisation and culture.[64]

Emily Fares Ibrahim went even further to argue that some of her countrymen had been attracted to fascism's appeal to their masculinities. This appeal came from its appearance of disciplined organisation, its promises of a national renaissance for the disempowered nation (*umma*) as well as its propagation of a strong leader (*za'īm*), that would be given the sole authority to lead.[65] Fares Ibrahim questioned the democracy of Lebanon in the absence of basic rights for women: 'who told them (men who refuse to give women their rights) they are fit for a complete democratic rule when there are (women) in their country who have been denied their basic political rights?'[66] She went on to identify two forms of democracy, a complete and humane democracy, and a deficient/incomplete democracy.[67] She further intensified her attacks, and in a typical manner reserved for the era of the Second World War, went after her male contemporaries stating her surprise that 'the men excited about the principles of democracy' were not aware that they were 'more nazi than the Nazis themselves by denying us (women) the right to run for office.[68]

Feminists paralleled, on the one hand, the correlation between fighting fascism and gaining rights for women, and on the other hand, the correlation between the women's cause and the advancement of the nation. Since the antithesis of fascism was democracy, these feminists framed their opposition to fascism within the language of democratic rule and argued for the incompleteness of democratic rights without political rights for women.

Taking a stand while looking at the past: democracy and the Arab renaissance

Leftists who debated democracy and called for it in the Arab context built a lineage between their arguments and Arabo-Islamic heritage. This trend was not confined to leftist intellectuals nor to that time period but was rather a common trope that emerged with the Arabic *nahda* (Renaissance) in the nineteenth century and characterised the late Ottoman period. Leftists in the interwar period saw themselves as a continuation of that tradition of Arabic renaissance and therefore engaged with those debates. In a lecture he gave in Damascus at a cultural meeting held by the League Against Nazism and Fascism in 1942, Khoury embarked on an overview of the conditions in which Arabs were living before the advent of Islam and concluded that they were a people in need of a renaissance (*nahda*) from a life that was backward economically, socially, intellectually, and ethically, and that they embraced Islam as a way towards a renaissance from this backward life.[69] Khoury, himself a Christian, reasoned that Islam worked as a unifier between the various warring tribes, as a breaker of idols and intellectual backwardness, as a supporter for women, for the poor against the wealthy merchants, and as a defender against ignorance, oppression, and humiliation.[70] He brought in examples from early Arab history of how Islam managed to achieve these.

What the Arabs had developed in common with other cultures – and here, he cited the French revolution's '*contrat social*' and Jean-Jacques Rousseau – was the responsibility of power as a covenant given to the ruler by his subjects, a trusteeship in the hands of the ruler handed to him by his people. 'If they (the rulers) mistreat it (the trusteeship)', Khoury argued, 'they were considered unfit for the trusteeship and justly ridden of it'.[71] Khoury gave examples from the rule of Mu'awiya and the poetry of al-Farazdaq, and how Mu'awiya's moves towards absolute rule found resistance among the Arabs. He added that for those who allege that the Arabs love individual dictatorship rule, for those who want the Arabs to abandon their position regarding the ongoing world struggle, 'it is enough to know that we are Arabs, meaning nothing will deter us from the main goal we, and the people of the world, are calling for, the goal of freedom and true democracy to the world'.[72] Drawing from the example of Abu Bakr al-Siddiq, the companion of the Prophet Muhammad and the first Muslim Caliph, who entrusted his army not to commit treason, murders against women and children, and killing of animals and cutting of trees, 'How could you want us to find an inch of common ground to stand on alongside the Nazi tyrants … slayers of the freedoms of weak people […] burners of books',[73] he asked, comparing the Nazis to the Mongol siege of Baghdad in the thirteenth century and its destruction of the libraries of Baghdad. He concluded by making the link between Arab heritage and anti-fascism, 'Are we not then, brothers, … in fighting Nazism and Fascism, trustees upon the spirit of the great Arab national heritage …? … Indeed!'[74] Khoury then ended on a high note, arguing that whatever victories Hitler may be scoring were but his final breaths for his end was near, and adding that 'Then, (when Hitler is defeated) Arabism will occupy its organic place in a free, democratic, and prosperous world. And the old Arab *nahda* current will fuse with its new current.'[75]

When Ra'if Khoury argued for a long Arab national heritage of just and democratic rule by referencing reactions to Mu'awiya's ruling tactics, the mercy of Abu Bakr al-Siddiq, and al-Ma'mun's love of knowledge, what mattered was not the validity of the arguments he made. One can hardly make anachronistic democratic claims for those Arab leaders, regardless of their character and rule. What mattered however, was the conviction, the tenacity, and the purpose with which Khoury made his argument. He created a lineage for a just, liberal, and democratic 'spirit' in Arab history to convince his readers and listeners of the importance of democracy as a system of rule, and its significance in the face of rising fascism. Therefore, embracing democracy became part of fighting fascism, and vice versa. The lineage was also his argument towards placing Arab history and ultimately Arab realities and future as part and parcel of the world and its destiny.

Khoury's ideas were echoed by other leftists who argued for a longer Arab history of opposition to forces of oppression. Contributors to *al-Tariq* referenced anecdotes from Arab history to argue for fighting fascism. 'Our national heritage is the heritage of freedom, equality, and fraternity', argued Qadri al-Qal'aji in a speech he gave at a League gathering in Tripoli, in a clear nod to the principles of the French revolution.[76] Since Nazism and fascism represented the opposite of these ideals, then they were antithetical to Arab heritage and a threat to it. Therefore, fighting fascism meant fighting for Arab heritage, it was a national duty. Moreover, contributors identified Nazism as directly threatening Arab cultural heritage, and therefore preserving and reviving it was part of the League's mission so that free Arab thought could play its rightful role in preserving humanity.[77] The members of the League saw themselves as the 'inheritors of Arab national heritage and its continuation', and the League made it its mission to create interest in studying Arab history.[78]

This *nahdawi* approach of searching for the roots of ideas and movements within Arabo-Islamic heritage echoed across the political spectrum as well. The Beiruti newspaper *Lisan al-Hal*, the Aleppine *al-Hadith*, and the Saida based *al-'Irfan* also published editorials and articles discussing democracy and linking its roots to an Arabo-Islamic heritage. *Lisan al-Hal* and *al-'Irfan* argued that the Arab-Muslim world had stood with democracy throughout the war because the Prophet, and Islam as a religion, had always upheld democratic principles and supported the French maxim of freedom, equality, and fraternity – establishing links between Islam and democracy.[79] Salah al-Asir on French Radio Orient and through *al-Hadith* made a link between the 'East' and democracy, arguing that based on this link, it was the East's duty to counter fascism and Nazism.[80] Jubran al-Tuwayni argued in the Beiruti journal *al-Adib* for the inherent existence of democratic principles in Arab civilisation.[81] *Al-Adib*, which published contributions that spanned the political spectrum,[82] pushed a recurring theme of humanism and human rights throughout the range of these contributions. Writers also linked racial theories to discussions on imperialism.

The Arabo-Islamic heritage was one side of the discussion of a democracy, the other concentrated on the continuous debate on progress and the need to achieve it. The treatment and engagement with the theme of progress, primarily on the pages of the journal *al-Tariq*, predominantly adhered to a positivistic understanding of the world, arguing for the significance of science and for the linearity of history. *Al-Tariq* very early on declared the importance of uncovering truths, and that it would provide its readers with evidence and true knowledge, to reveal reality.[83] This reality was that two forces were fighting in the world, democratic forces and regressive forces, respectively representing progress and backwardness:

> Fascism or Nazism, this regressive dark movement, wants to stand against historical progress [...] that is why we are the staunch enemies of Nazism and fascism; historical progress placed in front of humanity a higher goal of moving forward [towards a democracy].[84]

Since the victory of fascism and Nazism meant the victory of these regressive forces and the beginning of a period of oppression for all peoples of the world, opposing it was a duty for all those who saw progress as the way for humanity to move forward.[85] The war itself represented an impediment to the evolution of humanity and its progress, and only when it was over could the world continue to move towards a just system of equality.[86]

Furthermore, intellectuals who discussed the issue of progress emphasised the advancement of the 'West' and the lag of the 'East'. This signalled an engagement with debates on modernity that permeated Arab intellectual life from the late Ottoman period. 'Umar Fakhuri, a Lebanese leftist intellectual, questioned the categories of 'east' and 'west', arguing that in the *longue durée* of human history, cultural exchanges have shown that civilisational progress shifts from one centre to the other, between east and west and within these categories. Moreover, Fakhuri argued, after the First World War, the West had questioned its civilisation and progress. However, much of the consensus was that the East had stayed behind – the term used was almost always 'slept' – while the West advanced.[87]

The backwardness of the 'East', and specifically the Arab east, however, had begun to end with the awakening of the nineteenth century. *Al-Tariq* not only mentioned and discussed the Arab renaissance of the nineteenth century, but its contributors constantly positioned themselves as a continuation of that intellectual and cultural movement. They highlighted the ideas of the late nineteenth and early twentieth century *nahda* by republishing and quoting the works of main *nahdawi* figures and by referencing them as the predecessors.[88]

For leftist intellectuals, the backwardness of the 'East' had been challenged by one particular 'eastern' power that had proven its worth among the advanced nations of the world, the Soviet Union. This particular cartographic framing of the Soviet Union as part of the 'East', and often 'Asia', was not only deliberate but also multidirectional. The Soviet Union projected itself as an 'eastern' power, upholding the rights of the 'oppressed peoples of the East', as much as leftists in the colonised 'East' saw it as such.[89]

The Soviet Union: the cornerstone of civilisation and a model for progress

For Arab leftists, the Soviet Union represented a 'miraculous' case, a success story of a country that managed to rapidly modernise and even exceed the levels of progress and sophistication of western nations. When Nazi Germany attacked the Soviet Union in 1941, leftists rallied around the Red Army and followed intently events on the Eastern Front. The war intensified the attractiveness of the Soviet Union in the eyes of leftists who were not hesitant to declare their support and admiration towards it, even when these declarations were emanating from outside the parameters of communist parties. Standing first against colonialism, and then steadily against fascism and Nazism, the Soviet Union became a model of progress achieved through socialism, and this in turn worked to increase its appeal for intellectuals, activists, and the general public. An important indicator of this appeal was the increase in membership of the Communist Party of Lebanon and Syria in the 1930s, from several hundred in 1933 to around three thousand plus members in 1939.[90]

At the second conference of the League in 1942, Antun Tabit announced that the war has reached a turning point against fascism and Nazism, and that was made possible through one factor alone, the strength and victories of the Red Army.[91] In an almost overwhelming majority of articles that filled the pages of *al-Tariq* and League speeches, contributors agreed that the Soviet Union constituted the one example in the world of a group of people who had been suffering from that backwardness but have managed to progress and even surpass the 'west' in a very short matter of time.[92]

The highest point of fascination with the Soviet Union was its military might, manifested clearly in its successes in the face of the German war machine. A majority of the covers of the journal were dedicated to showcasing the might of the Soviet Red Army against Nazi soldiers, often with a Red Army soldier representing the Soviet Union crushing a Swastika, or in another instance, stabbing a dragon that had the face of Hitler.[93] A special double issue of *al-Tariq* was dedicated to the anniversary of the Red Army in 1943.[94] Articles highlighted the army's exceptionalism in fighting Axis forces, describing almost miraculous and legend-like stories of the Soviets' prowess and might.[95] The victories of the Red Army were the reason the Arab lands were spared Nazi invasion, argued Fakhuri in his speech during a celebration of the Red Army, and therefore the 'friendship' with the Soviet Union was largely based on admiration of the achievements of the Red Army during the war.[96] Fakhuri argued that the Soviet Union was 'the cornerstone for building a new world … for building a new humanity'.[97]

'Umar Fakhuri established *Jam'iyyat Asdiqa' al-Ittihad al-Sufyati* (Friends of the Soviet Union) in 1942 to bring together intellectuals who saw the Soviet Union as the defender of freedom, justice and democracy around the world.[98] The organisation was made up of a handful of intellectuals and activists who constituted the same leftist circles of the League, *al-Tariq,* and previously *al-Tali'a.*[99] It sought to educate people about the Soviet Union and its significance to the world, stating in its manifesto that was published in *al-Tariq* in 1942 that, 'there is no one today than can doubt that the stability of world peace, the flourishing of civilisation and culture, and the independence of small nations depends on the victory of the Soviet Union and its democratic allies'.[100] The Friends of the Soviet Union called for all those who believed that the Soviet Union was the upholder of democracy and civilisation in the world, to join their ranks and support their cause. According to Fakhuri, the Soviet Union 'is today paying the highest price to defend the freedom of the world and its civilisational heritage' from the Nazi hoards, adding that 'we did not intrude and impose our friendship on this great friend. 'Rather this friend had reached out since its inception towards the smaller nations and built its policies in line with the right of nations to self-determination'.[101]

Two gatherings were organised by the Friends of the Soviet Union in Beirut and Damascus to commemorate the anniversary of the October Revolution in November 1943.[102] Those gathered praised the Soviet Union as the place where the destiny of humanity was being decided. They saw the Soviet Union as standing free and strong in the face of forces that have managed to oppress even the most evolved and independent people of the world (in reference to western Europe). It had also managed to do so without resorting to colonialism and oppression, and by supporting other people's freedoms and rights.[103] The Soviet Union had therefore become 'the firmest pillar of civilisation',[104] advancing centuries of historical progress in a matter of years.[105]

Conclusion

For the intellectuals and activists who drew closer to the Soviet Union during the Second World War, the end of colonialism came with the end of the war, because colonialism and capitalism were the leading forces of that war. They believed that once fascism was defeated, the war would end, and that would also bring the end of imperialism across the world. They saw the Soviet Union as the sole power that stood against both colonialism and capitalism; it was the hero of that war and the world that was to emerge after it.

Speaking about the purpose of anti-fascist activism during the war, 'Umar Fakhuri explained, 'We should not only live … we should think of how we are supposed to live'.[106] The war, according to him, came down to a fight over how they should live as individuals, but also as nations. He continued that therefore, 'there is no escape for us from choosing a position with regard to this fight'.[107] Fakhuri and his fellow anti-fascists understood the dangers of fascism, and they vehemently opposed it; however, their stance did not stop at simply opposition. They demanded that democratic principles apply to them as well, by specifically challenging colonialism and therefore linking anti-fascism to anticolonialism. They placed Arab and Islamic heritage within a political lineage that opposed oppression and sought progress and democracy. They also argued for suffrage and women's rights as the only possible culmination and fulfilment of a true democracy. While mobilising against fascism, leftists utilised the cultural currency of their time to challenge their colonial and unjust realities. Therefore, the history of anti-fascism in Syria and Lebanon is about more than just taking sides with or against fascism, more than simply rejecting neutrality; it is about what the 'side' they took stood for and looked like, not only during the war, but in the future to follow.

Notes

1 Ra'if Khoury, 'Taqrir al-Lajna al-Tahdiriyya fi Mu'tamar Mukafahat al-Fashistiyya', *al-Tali'a* 5, No. 5, May 1939, p. 359.
2 Ibid.
3 Maqbula al-Shalaq, 'al-Fashistiyya 'aduwwat al-Mar'a', *al-Tali'a* 5, No. 5, May 1939, p. 365.
4 Of those parliament representatives who sent in letters in support of the League's conference, Shukri al-Quwatli and Fayiz al-Khuri. See articles on the League in the journal *al-Tali'a* (the Avant-Garde) published by leftist intellectuals in Damascus from 1935 to 1939, particularly *al-Tali'a* 5, No. 5, May 1939, and the article 'Mukafahat al-Fashistiyya' (Fighting Fascism), *al-Tali'a* 5, No. 5, May 1939, p. 247.
5 For instance, during the 1920s, Arab nationalist Shakib Arslan was active through the Syrian-Palestinian Congress and the League of Nations. In 1927, he represented the Arab delegation at the League Against Imperialism congress, an organisation closely linked in the years to follow to the Communist International. During the war years, he came under the German umbrella and mobilised against French and British colonialism from Berlin. For more on Arslan see, William L. Cleveland, *Islam against the West: Shakib Arslan and the Campaign for Islamic Nationalism* (Austin, TX: University of Texas Press, 1985). For interwar and wartime activism in European capitals, see for Paris Michael Goebel, *Anti-Imperial Metropolis: Interwar Paris and the Seeds of Third World Nationalism* (Cambridge: Cambridge University Press, 2015); for Berlin see Fredrik Petersson, 'Hub of the Anti-Imperialist Movement: The League against Imperialism and Berlin, 1927–1933', *Interventions*, Vol. 16, No. 1, 2012, pp. 49–71; and David Motadel, *Islam and Nazi Germany's War* (Cambridge, MA: Harvard University Press, 2017).
6 Christoph Schumann, 'The Experience of Organized Nationalism: Radical Discourse and Political Socialization in Syria and Lebanon, 1930–1958', in Thomas Philipp & Christoph Schumann (eds), *From the Syrian Land to the State of Syria* (Würzburg: Ergon in Kommission, 2004), pp. 343–358; Orit Bashkin, *The Other Iraq: Pluralism and Culture in Hashemite Iraq* (Stanford, CA: Stanford University Press, 2009); Israel Gershoni (ed.), *Arab Responses to Fascism and Nazism: Attraction and Repulsion* (Austin, TX: University Of Texas Press, 2015); Peter Wien, *Iraqi Arab Nationalism: Authoritarian, Totalitarian and pro-Fascist Inclinations, 1932–1941* (New York: Routledge, 2006); Götz Nordbruch, *Nazism in Syria and Lebanon: The Ambivalence of the German Option, 1933–1945* (New York: Routledge, 2009).
7 In various instances, the appeal of fascism had been linked to the rise of authoritarian regimes in Iraq, Syria, and Egypt, see Lukasz Hirszowicz, *The Third Reich and the Arab East* (London: Routledge & Kegan Paul, 1966); Robert Lewis Melka, 'The Axis and the Arab Middle East, 1930–1945', PhD dissertation, 1966. For Iraq see Reeva S. Simon, *Iraq between the Two World Wars: The Creation and Implementation of a Nationalist Ideology* (New York: Columbia University Press, 1986). On Syria and Palestine see Cleveland, *Islam against the West*; Klaus Gensicke & Alexander Fraser Gunn, *The Mufti of Jerusalem and the Nazis: The Berlin Years* (Portland, OR: Vallentine Mitchell, 2011); Philip Mattar, *The Mufti of Jerusalem: Al-Hajj Amin Al-Husayni and the Palestinian National Movement* (New York: Columbia University Press, 1988).
8 Motadel, *Islam and Nazi Germany's War.*

9 David Motadel, 'The Global Authoritarian Moment and the Revolt against Empire', *The American Historical Review*, Vol. 124, No. 3, 2019, pp. 843–877.

10 The main individuals behind the League were Antun Tabit, Ra'if Khoury, 'Umar Fakhuri, Yusuf Ibrahim Yazbik, and Qadri al-Qal'aji. While Tabit and Qal'aji were members of the Communist Party, the rest of the organisers behind the League were either former members, such as Yazbik, or fellow travellers.

11 Ilham Khuri-Makdisi, *The Eastern Mediterranean and the Making of Global Radicalism, 1860–1914* (Berkeley, CA: University of California Press, 2010).

12 The historiography of the Communist Party of Lebanon, which became the Communist Party of Lebanon and Syria before splitting into two parties in 1943, was established in Lebanon in October 1924 under the name Hizb al-Sha'b al-Lubnani (Lebanese People's Party, LPP). For personal and historical accounts on the foundation of the party see Muhammad Dakrub, *Judhur al-Sindiyana al-Hamra': Hikyat Nushu'; al-Hizb al-Shuyu'i al-Lubnani, 1924–1931* (Beirut: Dar al-Farabi, 1974); Yusuf Ibrahim Yazbik, *Hikayat Awwal Nawwar fi al-'Alam wa fi Lubnan: Dhikrayat wa-Tariikh wa-Nusus* (Beirut: Dar al-Farabi, 1974); Artin Madoyan, *Hayat 'Ala al-Mitras: Dhikrayat wa-Mushahadat* (Beirut: Dar al-Farabi, 2011); Fu'ad al-Shamali, *Asas Al-Harakat Al-Shuyu'iyya Fi Al-Bilad Al-Suriyya Wa-l-Lubnaniyya* (Beirut: Matba'at al-Fawa'id, 1935).

13 In 1928, at the Sixth Congress of the Communist International, Fu'ad al-Shamali was in Moscow representing the Communist Party of Syria. The Comintern had agreed to officially recognise the party that had originated in Lebanon, but stipulated a change in its name for the sake of greater inclusivity. The Comintern continued to view the Palestine Communist Party 'responsible' towards the prospects of communism in Lebanon and Syria and rather placed the PCP in control of Syrian communists. The Oriental Secretariat of the Comintern sent Eli Teper to Aleppo in 1927 to organise communist centres around various Syrian cities and towns and to start sending Syrian communists to study in Moscow. See Hanna Batatu, *The Old Social Classes and the Revolutionary Movements of Iraq: A Study of Iraq's Old Landed and Commercial Classes and of Its Communists, Ba'thists, and Free Officers* (Princeton, NJ: Princeton University Press, 1978), pp. 384–386. For the history of the Communist Party of Palestine see Musa Budeiri, *The Palestine Communist Party 1919–1948: Arab and Jew in the Struggle for Internationalism* (Chicago, IL: Haymarket Books, 2010).

14 Al-Shamali led the CP from 1928 until 1932 when Khalid Bakdash, a Syrian recruit into the CP, executed a coup that ousted and purged al-Shamali from the Party and its circles. The new leadership under Bakdash would gear the party into a new phase that was more in line with the Comintern's policies and recommendations.

15 For a history of this milieu, see Sana Tannoury Karam, 'The Making of a Leftist Milieu: Anti-Colonialism, Anti-Fascism, and the Political Engagement of Intellectuals in Mandate Lebanon, 1920–1948', PhD thesis, Northeastern University, 2017.

16 Of those parties influenced by fascist organisation in Lebanon and Syria, the Syrian Nationalist Social Party founded by Antun Sa'ada in 1932 that advocated for unity between Syria, Lebanon, Palestine, Transjordan, Cyprus, and northern parts of Iraq – what was known as the fertile crescent, and the Kata'ib, or Lebanese Phalange, founded by Pierre al-Jumayyil in 1936, influenced by the 1936 Olympic Games in Munich and the discipline of the Hitler youth. See Nordbruch, *Nazism in Syria and Lebanon*.

17 Sana Tannoury-Karam, 'This War is Our War: Antifascism among Lebanese Leftist Intellectuals', *Journal of World History*, Vol. 30, No. 3, 2019, pp. 415–436.

18 Motadel, 'The Global Authoritarian Moment and the Revolt against Empire'.

19 Tannoury-Karam, 'This War is Our War'.

20 Ra'if Khoury, 'Lubnan fi Nafsihi wa-fi-l-'Alam', *al-Tariq* 2, No. 20 (29 December 1943), pp. 8–9.

21 Ra'if Khoury, "Nahnu wa-al-Fashistiyya", *al-Tali'a*, December, 1936, p. 844.

22 For more on Ra'if Khoury's arguments against fascism and their relation to nationalism, see Tannoury-Karam, 'This War is Our War'.

23 Khalid Bakdash, 'al-Fashistiyya wa-l-Shu'ub al-'Arabiyya', *al-Tali'a* 5, No. 5, May 1939, pp. 369–370.
24 Khalid Bakdash, *Al-Arab wa-l-Harb al-Ahliyya fi Isbaniya* (Damascus, 1937), p. 18.
25 Antun Tabit, 'Kalimat al-Ustaz Antun Tabit Ra'is 'Usbat Mukafahat al-Fashistiyya', *al-Tali'a* 5, No. 5, May 1939, p. 395.
26 Ra'if Khoury, 'Jihad Filastin', in Ilyas Shakir (ed.), *Thawrat al-Fata al-Arabi: A'mal Mukhtara min Turath Ra'if Khoury* (Beirut: Dar al-Farabi, 1984), pp. 127–150.
27 Khoury, 'Jihad Filastin', pp. 130–131. According to Khoury, the revolt had started as a spontaneous movement from the people, but with the guidance of intellectuals had developed into a conscious organised movement with specific demands. When these demands weren't acknowledged by the government, the movement became more violent to counter the violence of the colonisers. Khoury did not condemn the violence but rather saw it as necessary in the face of colonialism. Furthermore, he refuted the accusations the British were spreading about the support of fascist Italy to the revolting Arabs, arguing that this could not be possible since Italy and Britain were one and the same with respect to colonial ambitions towards the Arabs.
28 Ibid., p. 141.
29 Khoury, '*Nahnu wa-l-Fashistiyya*', p. 845.
30 Ibid.
31 Ra'if Khoury, 'Al-Naziyya wa-l-Qawmiyya', *al-Tariq* 2, No. 21 (15 December 1942), pp. 10–11.
32 Ibid.
33 Ibid.
34 Ibid.
35 'Muqarrarat Mu'tamar Mukafahat al-Fashistiyya', *al-Tali'a* 5, No. 5, May 1939, pp. 390–391.
36 Antun Tabet, 'Taqrir al-Sukritar al-'Am Antun Tabit', *al-Tariq* 1, Special Issue, December 1942, p. 24
37 See *al-Tariq* 1, No. 8 (30 April 1942).
38 The women's branch meeting was attended by around 250–300 women and speeches were given by Maqbula al-Shalaq (secretary of the women's branch of the League), 'Umar Fakhuri, and Ra'if Khuri, see *al-Tariq* 1, No. 13, July 1942.
39 'Fi Dimashq al-'Arabiyya', *al-Tariq* 1, No. 13, July 1942, pp. 21–24.
40 'Usbat Mukafahat al-Naziyya wa-l-Fashistiyya fi Zahle' and 'Bayan 'Usbat Mukafahat al-Naziyya wa-l-Fashistiyya bi-Dimashq', *al-Tariq* 1, No. 15 (31 August 1942), pp. 16–17.
41 'Umar Fakhuri, 'al-Watan, Watan al-Jamahir', *al-Tariq* 1, Special Issue, December 1942, pp. 2–4.
42 Wasfi al-Banna, 'A'da' li-l-Fashistiyya li-Annana 'Arab', *al-Tariq* 1, Special Issue, December 1942, p. 7; Qadri al-Qal'aji, 'Sira' al-Qawmiyyat fi al-Harb al-Hadira', *al-Tariq* 1, Special Issue, December 1942, pp. 18–21.
43 'Fi Sabil al-Istiqlal', *al-Tariq* 2, No.19 (7 December 1943), p. 32.
44 'Umar Fakhuri, 'Tahiyya min 'Umar Fakhuri ila al-Shabab al-Muthaqqaf', *al-Tariq* 1, no.8 (30 April 1942), p. 10.
45 Maqbula al-Shalaq, 'al-Fashiyya 'Aduwwat al-Mar'a', *al-Tali'a* 5, No. 5, May 1939.
46 Maqbula al-Shalaq attended the Syrian University in Damascus, unveiled, and was the first woman to graduate with a law degree from that institution and in Damascus. She published novels, poetry, and articles in various newspapers. See Nizar Abaza, *Mu'jam Shahirat al-Nisa' fi Suriya'* (Damascus: Dar al-Fikir, 2002), pp. 124–125; Thompson, *Colonial Citizens*, p. 241.
47 The Iraqi branch of the Women's League was established in May of 1943.
48 It seems to have been the case that the women's branch was established to cater for the need to have female-only assemblies and associations, which was not uncommon since a male-dominant organisation might have discouraged some women from participation.
49 Maqbula al-Shalaq, 'Wajib al-Mar'a al-'Arabiya fi al-Harb al-Hadira', *al-Tariq* 1, No. 14 (15 August 1942), p. 19.

50 al-Shalaq, 'al-Fashistiyya 'aduwwat al-Mar'a', p. 365.
51 Ibid.
52 Ibid., p. 366.
53 Ibid.
54 Ibid.
55 Imili Faris Ibrahim, 'Sawt al-Mar'a, Huquq Jadida', *al-Tariq* 2, No. 20 (29 December 1943), pp. 15–17.
56 While German women gained suffrage in 1918 under the Weimar Republic, the Nazi Party discouraged women from entering the Party as well as getting involved in politics more generally. The Party further propagated the domesticity of women, and the image of child-bearing women who did not seek work outside their house. For more on women within Nazi Germany see Jill Stephenson, *Women in Nazi Germany* (Harlow & New York: Longman, 2001); Katherine Thomas, *Women in Nazi Germany* (New York: AMS Press, 1981); Claudia Koonz, *Mothers in the Fatherland: Women, the Family, and Nazi Politics* (New York: St. Martin's Press, 1987); Renate Bridenthal, Atina Grossmann, & Marion A Kaplan, *When Biology Became Destiny: Women in Weimar and Nazi Germany* (New York: Monthly Review Press, 1984); and Anna Maria Sigmund, *Women of the Third Reich* (Richmond Hill, Ont.: NDE Pub., 2000).
57 al-Shalaq, 'al-Fashistiyya 'aduwwat al-mar'a', p. 367.
58 Imili Faris Ibrahim, 'Muhimmat al-Mar'a fi al-Karitha al-'Alamiyya al-Hadira', *al-Tariq* 1, No. 4 (20 February 1942), p. 5.
59 Maqbula al-Shalaq, 'Wajib al-Mar'a al-'Arabiya fi al-Harb al-Hadira', *al-Tariq* 1, No. 14 (15 August 1942), p. 19.
60 Ibid., p. 18.
61 Afifi Ra'uf, 'al-Naziyya 'aduwwat al-Mar'a', *al-Tariq* 2, No.9 (1 June 1943), p. 22.
62 Ibid.
63 al-Shalaq, 'al-Fashistiyya 'Aduwwat al-Mar'a', p. 366.
64 Ibid.
65 Imili Faris Ibrahim, 'Nahwa 'alam Jadid', *al-Tariq* 3, No. 15/16 (31 August 1944), p. 11–12.
66 Ibid., p. 15.
67 Ibid., pp. 11–12.
68 Imili Faris Ibrahim, 'Sawt al-Mar'a, Huquq Jadida', *al-Tariq* 2, no. 20 (December 29, 1943), p. 16.
69 Ra'if Khoury, 'al-Turath al-Qawmi al-Arabi: Nahnu Humatuhu wa-Muk-mi-luh' (Arab National Heritage: We are its protectors and its continuance) in *Ma'alim al-Wa'i al-Qawmi wa-Maqalat Ukhra* (Beirut: al-Markaz al-'Arabi li-l-Abhath wa-Dirasat al-Siyasa, 2015), p. 159.
70 Ibid., pp. 160–165.
71 Ibid., p. 166.
72 Ibid., p. 167.
73 Ibid.
74 Ibid., 169.
75 Ibid., p. 175.
76 Qadri al-Qal'aji, 'al-Muthaqqafun wa-l-Siyasa', *al-Tariq* 2, No.12 (18 July 1943), p. 15.
77 'Risalat al-'Usba', *al-Tariq* 1, No. 1 (20 December 1941), p. 22; Abd al-Qadir Isma'il, 'Harb al-Nur wa-l-Zulma', *al-Tariq* 1, No. 3 (1 February 1942), pp. 3–4.
78 Qadri al-Qal'aji, 'al-Muthaqqafun wa-l-Siyasa', *al-Tariq* 2, No. 12 (18 July 1943), p. 13 in reference to Khoury's 'al-Turath al-Qawmi al-Arabi: Nahnu Humatuhu wa-Mukmiluh'.
79 Götz Nordbruch, 'A Challenge to the Local Order: Reactions to Nazism in the Syrian and Lebanese Press', in Israel Gershoni (ed.), *Arab Responses to Fascism and Nazism: Attraction and Repulsion* (Austin, TX: University Of Texas Press, 2015), p. 48.
80 Ibid.
81 Ibid., p. 51.

82 Contributors included prominent Arab nationalists such as Qustantin Zurayq and Edmond Rabbat, as well as leftists such Ilyas Abu Shabaka, 'Umar Fakhuri, Qadri al-Qal'aji, and Ra'if Khoury.
83 'Risalat al-'Usba', pp. 1, 22; Wasfi al-Banna, 'Raj'iyya Qadima wa-Raj'iyya Jadida', *al-Tariq* 1, No. 1 (20 December 1941), pp. 6–7.
84 Bahith 'Arabi, 'Ma Hiya al-Dimuqratiyya', *al-Tariq* 1, No. 4 (20 February 1942), p. 19.
85 Ibid.
86 'Risalat al-'Usba', p. 22.
87 'Umar Fakhuri, 'Kalimat al-Shabab', *al-Tariq* 1, No. 13, July 1942, pp. 2 and 24.
88 Of those main figures featured were Muhammad Abduh, Abd el-Rahman al-Kawakibi, Adib Ishaq, and Shubli al-Shumayyil. For more on the concept of *al-sābiqūn* (the predecessors), see Leyla Dakhli, *Une Génération d'Intellectuels Arabes: Syrie et Liban, 1908–1940* (Paris: IISMM, 2009).
89 Carolien Stolte's work on Asianism particular argues for the placement of the Soviet Union in 'Asia' and as part of the 'East' by South Asian leftists. See Carolien Stolte, 'Uniting the Oppressed Peoples of the East: Revolutionary Internationalism in an Asian Inflection', in Raza Ali, Franziska Roy, and Benjamin Zachariah (eds), *The Internationalist Moment: South Asia, Worlds, and World Views, 1917–1939* (New Delhi: SAGE Publications, 2015).
90 Walter Laqueur, *Communism and Nationalism in the Middle East* (New York: Praeger, 1957), p. 145.
91 Tabit, 'Taqrir al-Sukritar al-'Am Antun Tabit', pp. 22–23.
92 Some of the articles on the Soviet Union in volume 1 alone of *al-Tariq*: 'al-Hayat al-'Amma fi al-Ittihad al-Sufyati', No. 2; 'al-dimuqratiya al-sufyatiya', No. 11; 'Yusuf Stalin', No.12; 'Masadir Quwat al-Ittihad al-Suvyati', No. 13; 'Khitab Stalin', No. 20; 'Fi Stalingrad', No.20; 'Mukafahat al-Bagha' fi al-Ittihad al-Sufyati', No. 21; 'al-Atfal fi al-Ittihad al-Sufyati', No. 16.
93 See covers of *al-Tariq* 1, No. 3 and No. 4.
94 *al-Tariq* 2, No. 3/4 (20 March 1943). The issue included articles on the Soviet Union generally – education, economy, intellectual life … etc., including 'Umar Fakhuri's seminal article 'al-Ittihad al-Sufyati Hajar al-Zawiya' – as well as on the Red Army.
95 Khaled Bakdash gave his speech 'al-'Arab wa-l-Jaysh al-Ahmar' at a gathering celebrating the anniversary of the Red Army, *al-Tariq* 2, No. 3/4 (20 March 1943), pp. 2 and 46.
96 On the Friends of the Soviet Union see 'Nida' Min Jam'iyyat Asdiqa' al-Ittihad al-Sufyati', *al-Tariq* 1, No. 2, November 1942, p. 24. 'Fakhuri, 'al-Ittihad al-Sufyati Hajar al-Zawiya', p. 20.
97 Ibid., p. 23.
98 'Nida' Min Jam'iyyat Asdiqa' al-Ittihad al-Sufyati', *al-Tariq* 1, No. 2, November 1942, p. 24.
99 Some of those who signed the manifesto on the pages of *al-Tariq*, signifying their belonging to this organisation were: 'Umar Fakhuri, Kamil 'Ayyad, Yusuf Ibrahim Yazbik, Imili Faris Ibrahim, Raja Hourani, Wasfi al-Banna, and Niqula Shawi.
100 Ibid.
101 'Umar Fakhuri, *Adib fi-l-Suq* (Beirut: Dar al-Makhsuf, 1944), p. 76.
102 *al-Tariq* 2, No. 19 (7 December 1943).
103 Qadri al-Qal'aji, 'Rasul al-Salam wa-Nasir al-Shu'ub al-Da'ifa', *al-Tariq* 2, No. 18/19 (7 December 1943), pp. 2–3, 31; and 'Umar Fakhuri, 'al-Dunya al-Fadila', *al-Tariq* 2, No. 18/19 (7 December 1943), pp. 7–8.
104 al-Qal'aji, 'Rasul al-Salam wa-Nasir al-Shu'ub al-Da'ifa', p. 31.
105 'Umar Fakhuri, 'al-Dunya al-Fadila', p. 8. See also *al-Tariq* 3, No. 8, April 1944, reports on the exhibit in Damascus, and later Beirut, 'The Soviet Union During the War'.
106 'Umar Fakhuri, 'Qalil min al-Siyasa', *al-Tariq* 1, No.4 (20 February 1942), pp. 12–13.
107 Ibid.

PART II

Transnational lives, radical internationalism

8

ANTI-COLONIALISM, SUBALTERN ANTI-FASCISM AND THE CONTESTED SPACES OF MARITIME ORGANISING

David Featherstone

Introduction

In a recent paper on the Antwerp Group, a group of anti-fascist German merchant seafarers who together with key figures from the International Transport Workers' Federation waged 'a campaign against the Nazi government', Jonathan Hyslop draws attention to some of the distinctive ways in which maritime spaces inflected internationalist antifascist politics. Hyslop argues that the 'unique character of ports as cities of ships as social spaces' together with the particular 'social worlds of international trade unionism and left-wing politics – portside pubs, boarding houses, the crew quarters aboard ship […] provided a particularly generative environment for the development and defence of resistance politics'.[1] Through engaging with these sites and connections Hyslop suggests that a focus on maritime networks can make a distinctive contribution to work on global anti-fascisms which has sought to transcend the limits of 'methodological nationalism'.[2] He demonstrates that a focus on movements like the Antwerp Group can signal both diverse geographies and left political trajectories shaped in relation to anti-fascism.

This chapter develops this concern with the distinctive articulations of maritime spaces and organising and uses it to probe the relation between anti-fascist internationalisms and subaltern politics. It does this through engaging with the political trajectories of black seafarers from the Caribbean and West Africa who were in contact with anti-colonial agitators such as Padmore and were integral to organisations such as the London-based Negro Welfare Association (NWA). The chapter engages in particular with activities connected to the ports of Cardiff, London and North Shields which were significant in relation to various transnational political networks around anti-fascism and anti-colonialism. It argues that some of the forms of organising shaped in relation to these ports offers potential for thinking about the global connections and trajectories that shaped anti-fascisms and some of the 'subaltern lives' that were articulated through such political activity.[3] To reconstruct these activities, solidarities and relations the chapter draws on a range of sources. These include the writings and interventions of seafarers themselves, the papers of unions and political organisations and the more voluminous materials of intelligence reports and files. It uses these materials both to explore how such 'subaltern' figures articulated anti-fascist and anti-colonial politics through their organising work and their critical negotiation of some of the political spaces of communist internationalism. Through so doing the chapter makes a broader contribution to thinking about the contested dynamics between anti-colonialism, anti-fascism and left internationalisms.

Anti-fascism, anti-colonialism and maritime spaces

Hyslop's account of the various antifascist activities of the Antwerp group, which was 'a breakaway from one of the German-based but globally networked Comintern organisations of the early 1930s, the International of Seafarers and Harbour Workers (ISH)', suggests some of the ways in which seafarers could use their position in maritime networks to effect forms of political agency. Thus he notes that during the Spanish Civil War Antwerp group members were 'able to deliver high-quality intelligence on arms shipments' with one sailor 'who worked on the SS *Sostris* out of Hamburg' passing information to the International Transport Workers' Federation 'about the Swedish-flagged SS *Allegro*, which was taking German troops and war materials to Spain'.[4] This speaks to interventions in transnational relations of power which have been highlighted in Peter Cole's recent comparative study of dockworkers in Durban and the San Francisco Bay Area. He traces how through their activism they 'translated their beliefs in the need for and possibilities of solidarity into tangible actions: boycotting ships to protest apartheid and other forms of authoritarianism'.[5] Through doing so Cole locates understandings of such radical trade unionism in the dockers' 'transnational' labour process.

This work positions maritime actors such as seafarers and dockers as having both shaped transnational connections and being situated in relation to them. Thus both Cole and Hyslop demonstrate how their knowledge of the cargoes they handled and the connections they made between places were integral to their political interventions and agency. The terms on which maritime spaces and left politics were articulated, however, was rarely smooth. Thus Hyslop has usefully cautioned against positioning maritime actors as necessarily behaving in ways which straightforwardly acted out roles expected by left or anti-colonial figures.[6] This speaks to a broader ambivalence about maritime spaces and workers on the part of established left figures and organisations despite a recognition of the important strategic function maritime routes could play in shaping left internationalisms. A sense of the distance between some left activists and parties and maritime worlds is underlined by Len Wincott's account of the Invergordon Mutiny in 1931.

Wincott was involved in the mutiny which occurred when sailors in the British navy struck off Scotland and went on to become an activist with the Communist

Party of Great Britain (CPGB). Wincott notes in his account of the events, however, that the CPGB's response had been to send a woodworker and a miner to Portsmouth 'after the ships involved in the mutiny had arrived in home ports' obviously 'for the purpose of inciting the Fleet to further rebellious activity'. He argued that the choice of these unsuitable figures indicated 'the Communists' complete ignorance of the lower deck'.[7] Such attitudes were not confined to the CPGB. In 1924 Antonio Gramsci argued as follows:

> Italy lives from the sea and not to deal with the problem of the seas is one of the most essential problems, one to which the Party has to devote its greatest attention, would mean not thinking in concrete terms about the revolution. When I think that for a long time our policy vis-à-vis the sailors was in the hands of a youngster like Caroti's son I get the shudders.[8]

The pressure such disconnections between the left and maritime organising and cultures emerges exerted on transnational anti-fascist solidarity emerges in correspondence between Edo Fimmen of the International Transport Workers' Federation and Fenner Brockway and James Maxton, key figures in the UK Independent Labour Party (ILP), during the Spanish Civil War. Edo Fimmen's correspondence with Brockway and Maxton related to the ILPs attempts to break Franco's blockade of maritime trade to key ports such as Bilbao. Brockway and Maxton were seeking to purchase a ship to take food to Spain and sought Fimmen's advice on how to proceed. Fimmen, however, advised Brockway to avoid this cause of action, as he feared that they would be fleeced because of their ignorance of and distance from maritime concerns. Instead he suggested they liaise with a contact who he was prepared to find 'who knows the port of St Jean de Luz and neighbourhood, knows the people in the port, and knows the fishing trade' and to try and 'get in touch with fishermen who are prepared to take over the cargoes of the vessels concerned and run them to Bilbao'.[9]

What is of particular significance here is the way that a concern with these particular spatialities of connection and articulation can suggest how particular maritime spaces functioned as a means for globalising anti-fascisms. This in turn can help to generate a more dynamic and processual sense of the ways in which anti-fascist solidarities were generated and articulated. Such an engagement with global anti-fascist activity can also rework existing accounts by foregrounding often neglected articulations of anti-fascisms and anti-colonialisms. A central figure in recent work at the intersection of anti-fascism and anti-colonialism has been the Trinidadian Marxist and anti-colonial agitator George Padmore who developed significant connections with maritime workers and networks during his period working with the Comintern organisation the International Trade Union Committee of Negro Workers (ITUCNW).[10] Padmore's analysis of fascism and anti-fascism emphasised the need to think about transnational articulations of internationalism which stretched between 'metropolitan' and 'colonial' spaces.

It also emphasises how such forms of analysis were shaped by exchanges and solidarities between intellectuals and activists from the Caribbean and Africa and left movements in imperial cities such as London and Paris. If, as Richard Iton argues, nation-centred framings of radicalism and internationalism are inadequate for asserting the political trajectories and intersections constructed by black radical figures and/or Communists such as George Padmore, then this raises the question of what alternative maps of their activity might be constructed.[11] This is significant as the terms on which fascism was brought into contestation shaped different political trajectories and solidarities. It is also important as influential work on anti-fascism continues to position such antagonisms within a decidedly European-centred framing.[12] To engage with the dynamic terms on which fascism and anti-fascism were theorised and articulated the rest of this section traces some of the different ways in which Padmore theorised fascism and anti-fascism locating these theoretical engagements in the context of Padmore's changing relationship with the Comintern. This is important for the anti-fascist trajectories of black maritime actors discussed later in the chapter given that many, for at least a time, were allies and collaborators with Padmore.

Fascism was defined by the fifth congress of the Communist International in July 1924 as 'one of the classic forms of counter-revolution in the epoch when capitalist society is decaying, the epoch of proletarian revolution, particularly where the proletariat has taken up the struggle for power but, where, for lack of revolutionary experience, and in the absence of a leading revolutionary class party, it has been unable to organise the proletarian revolution and to intensify the insurrection of the masses to the point of establishing the proletarian citizenship'.[13] The Fifth Congress concluded that 'fascism and social democracy were "two sides of a single instrument of capitalist dictatorship"'. This in part laid the terrain for the emergence of the concept of 'social fascism' which was integral to the 'class-against-class' line of the Comintern's Third Period. As David Beetham notes, the 'notorious concept of "social-fascism", which became influential in the Comintern from 1929 onwards positioned "Social Democracy" as the "moderate" wing of fascism, because it provided the bourgeoisie with a means for securing consent to reactionary policies which did not involve the use of violence'.[14]

George Padmore's first major text, *Life and Struggles of Negro Toilers*, published in 1931 while he was still working for the Comintern, made a significant intervention in terms of these debates by applying an analysis rooted in understandings of social fascism to anti-imperialist politics. Padmore articulated a position where the 'oppression of Negroes' was seen as 'on the one hand oppressed as a class, and on the other as a nation'. This anti-imperialist communist internationalism was explicitly defined against other articulations of anti-colonial/anti-imperial politics in line with the Comintern's 'class against class' line. Thus Padmore critiques the 'national reformist misleader Marcus Garvey', 'black reformist trade union leaders' such as 'Kadalie and Champion in South Africa, Randolph and Croswaith in the United States' and, crucially, social democratic articulations of internationalism associated with the Amsterdam International/the Second International. In the introduction to the book he notes that 'it is also necessary for the workers in the capitalist countries to understand that it is only through the exploiting of the colonial workers, from whose sweat and blood super-profits are exhorted that the imperialists are able to bribe the reformist and social fascist trade union bureaucrats and thereby enable them to betray the struggles of the workers'.[15]

This analysis was defined by actively drawing antagonisms between Communist parties and Communist-linked union organisations such as the International Trade Union Committee of Negro Workers and labour movement organisations and social democratic parties which were dismissed as reformist. The ways in which Padmore combined an 'analysis' of social fascism and fascism 'proper' is developed in his discussion of the racial politics of the United States later in *Life and Struggles of Negro Toilers*. Thus he notes that 'In order to break up' the emerging 'alliance between the whites and blacks' in organisations like the Communist Party of the USA and the Trade Union Unity League and 'weaken the counter-offensive of the workers against the capitalists, the bourgeoisie, with the aid of their social-fascist lackeys of the Socialist party and the American Federation of Labour, as well as the open fascist organisations like the *Ku Klux Klan*, the *Black Shirts*, the *American Legion*, etc., have launched a new wave of white terror (lynching) against the Negro masses'.[16]

Padmore's use of the distinction between 'social' and 'open' fascism positions Padmore within the conventions of Communist International theoretical orthodoxy. The terms of his engagement with the articulations between fascism/anti-fascism and anti-imperialism was nonetheless a significant intervention. These arguments also pre-figure the attention to fascism in colonial contexts which would be integral to his analysis in texts such as *Africa and World Peace*.[17] Thus in a section of *The Life and Struggles of Negro Toilers* on 'Spanish and Italian Africa' he argued that 'In the Italian colonies fascism rules with all the bloody ruthlessness that labour is subjected to in Italy. By means of bayonets and machineguns the population in Somaliland is forced to work for the dictators'. Such an analysis directly links a critical analysis of fascism with a direct sense of the violence of processes of colonialisation. This position resonates with articles in the *Negro Worker* at this time which under Padmore's editorship shaped an analysis of fascism/anti-fascism which placed them directly in relation to processes of colonialism and imperialism. Writing in response to the banning of the paper in Trinidad in 1932, 'A.R.', for example, noted:

> Governor Hollis, the Mussolini of Trinidad, in his effort to discourage and suppress the Trade Unions in the British West Indies, has by an order in Council under the Seditious Publication Law, an ordinance enacted during the last imperialist war prohibited the importation and circulation of the NEGRO WORKER, the official organ of the ITUCNW.[18]

Such interventions, then, shaped a political culture where fascism and colonialism were understood as connected and where the geographies of fascism were seen as produced in relation to repression in colonial contexts. This focus on the geographies of fascism, colonialism and anti-fascism was innovative. While Comintern discourse on anti-fascism at times engaged with anti-colonialism, leading figures in the Communist International rarely articulated the kind of integrated analysis developed by Padmore. Thus Palmiro Togliatti made clear the importance of Abyssinia in his speech on the twentieth anniversary of Gramsci's death. He argued that the 'war of aggression against Abyssinia had after all ended in success; tyrannical regimes similar to that of Italy dominated a good part of Europe and enjoyed the benevolent support of the Western democracies'.[19] Despite drawing on Lenin's argument that countries like Italy were constructing an 'imperialism in rags' he did not fully incorporate an anti-colonial perspective into his analysis of fascism.[20]

Thus the 'Lectures on Fascism' which Togliatti delivered to Italian comrades at the Lenin school in Moscow in the 1930s include critical discussions of the Italian Marxist Arturo Labriola's legitimation of Italian colonialism. Colonialism remains a peripheral analytic in these lectures and Togliatti failed to develop its implications for thinking about anti-fascist strategy or organising.[21] Engaging with Padmore's analysis of fascism and anti-fascism, by contrast, emphasises the need to think about transnational articulations of internationalism which stretched between colonial/coloniser spaces and which were shaped by exchanges between intellectuals and activists from the Caribbean and Africa and left movements in imperial cities such as London and Paris. Padmore's contacts and engagements with politicised seafarers were key to shaping these transnational linkages and connections and they were shaped by particular maritime spaces and circuits. The following sections engages with the political trajectories of these seafarers to develop a focus on the productive and contested intersections shaped through articulations between communism and black internationalism which were integral to forms of anti-colonial and anti-fascist organising in the late 1920s/1930s and which shaped particular political constructions of blackness.

Maritime organising, anti-colonialism and contested articulations of left politics

Subaltern articulations of transnational anti-fascism were generated by seafarers from the Caribbean and West Africa who worked with George Padmore and were integral to his anti-colonial organising while he was still connected with communist internationalism. The terms through which Padmore envisioned their relation to anti-imperial communist organising are made clear in a report of the International of Seamen and Harbour Workers' (ISH) conference in Altona near Hamburg in 1932. He emphasised 'that it is the task of the ISH and its affiliated sections to give the Negro workers active help in breaking through the barriers set up by imperialist, terror and reformist treachery to strengthen their already existing organizations and to create new ones in the colonies'.[22] Padmore used politicised seafarers from the Caribbean and West Africa as couriers for ITUCNW publications, engaged with their struggles and sought to support organisations they were involved in.[23] He also collaborated with the West African labour organiser Tiemoko Garan Kouyaté, from the French Sudan, who worked with Antillean and West African seafarers and dockers in French ports, to challenge, the way that the Parti Communiste Francais (PCF) and the CPGB closed down of spaces for anti-colonial work.[24]

Seafarers from the Caribbean and West Africa who were in contact with Padmore were integral to organisations in London such as the Negro Welfare Association (NWA). The NWA was apparently founded on the initiative of two Afro-Caribbean communists Arnold Ward and Chris Jones who both had seafaring experience, though throughout its existence had strong links to the League Against Imperialism.[25] The NWA acted as a node of translocal anti-imperial and anti-fascist politics. This role was partly shaped by the diverse trajectories of seafarers who were involved in the organisation. Thus when the *Negro Worker* was banned by Cunliffe Lister in Trinidad in 1932 the NWA noted that 'the Negro workers in England held a meeting under the auspices of the Negro Welfare Association in London' and issued a statement to the press exposing 'the lying hypocrisy about British democracy in the colonies'. The NWA was central to the assertion of a militant black presence in the capital in the 1930s and was a communist-led organisation linked to the networks of the League Against Imperialism (LAI) and the International Trade Union Committee of Negro Workers (ITUCNW).

The statement by the NWA positions the repression in Trinidad in a broader imperial context noting that 'Whether or not Negroes are denied the right to organize in Trinidad, it is a fact that in almost every other colony of the British Empire, Negroes when they attempt to organize, are beaten up, arrested, and shot'.[26] As the annual report of the British section of the League Against Imperialism in 1934 reveals, the organisation brought together diverse left political trajectories. It noted that the Chairman is Reginald Bridgeman, International Secretary of the League Against Imperialism, the Treasurer was the London-based communist Hugo Rathbone and the Secretary Arnold Ward, a Barbadian who was a seafarer and had been interned in Ruhleben in 1915. The report also noted the first aim of the NWA was to 'work for the complete liberation and independence of all Negroes who are suffering from capitalist exploitation and imperialist domination and to cooperate with all peoples who are struggling against all forms of colonial oppression'.[27]

The NWA was part of broader black internationalist circuits of organising and connectivity which were shaped by the black communist left. Thus in correspondence with Ward the influential African-American communist William L. Patterson noted that 'Every effort should be made to utilize these Negroes who are now employed as seamen as an acting link with the colonies. Through them we should try to get our literature and other correspondence into such colonial countries as they have contact with.'[28] A letter by Padmore in late 1931 noted that, the ITUCNW was 'now in direct contact with comrade A. Ward and his organization'.[29] Thus Jim Headley, a Trinidadian radical, seafarer and contact of Padmore, played a significant role in bridging between the NWA and the *Negro Welfare,*

Cultural and Social Association in Trinidad. Metropolitan Police files indicate that in 1932 he was a committee member of the NWA, along with the Sierra Leonean seafarer Rowland Sawyer, the Barbadian Chris Braithwaite, who I refer to in the rest of this essay by his pseudonym Chris Jones, and Nancy Cunard, the renegade heiress to the Cunard shipping line who had diverse contacts among black internationalists.[30] As Hakim Adi argues the white leadership of the NWA caused significant tensions throughout its existence.[31]

Headley and Ward were also central to the organising work of the Seamen's Minority Movement (SMM) with 'colonial seafarers' in the early 1930s. The SMM was part of the communist-affiliated National Minority Movement which sought to organise a left alternative to the Trade Union Congress, and was affiliated to the Red International of Labour Unions. Led by George Hardy who had been involved with the Industrial Workers of the World in North America and Fred Thompson, the SMM made significant attempts to co-ordinate opposition to the National Union of Seamen (NUS) which under the leadership of Havelock Wilson had failed to observe the 1926 General Strike and supported a 'non-political' mining union in Nottinghamshire which sought to undermine the Miners' Federation's six-month dispute. It also sought to challenge the NUS's status as one of the bulwarks of what Jon Hyslop has termed as 'white labourism'.[32]

The NUS's predecessor organisation the National Seamen and Firemen's Union (NSFU) was also challenged by syndicalist seafarers such as the Liverpool political activist and writer George Garrett. Garrett was part of the 'Seamen's Vigilance Committee' and was one of a number of 'Vigies' who were expelled from the NSFU in September 1921 for belonging to the organisation.[33] Syndicalist organising could still be shaped strongly by discourses of white labourism; a key demand of the Amalgamated Marine Workers Union (AMWU) was the 'Abolition of Chinese and Asiatic labour west of the Suez Canal'.[34] Garrett, however, explicitly refused the racialised constructions of the 'Britisher' that were central to NUS organising and rhetoric. Addressing a demonstration of unemployed workers in Liverpool in 1921 he commented that 'I don't tell people I'm a Britisher', arguing that 'All workers are slaves to the capitalists, no matter what the race, colour or creed is, and there is more slavery under the Union Jack than under any other flag.'[35] While there were activists of colour such as Straker in Cardiff and Chris Jones in London who were involved in the NSFU/NUS in the 1920s their involvement in the union was fraught and they were subject to racist treatment from leading officials which they both contested.[36]

Maritime connections and networks nonetheless offered potential for relations between anti-colonial and left politics despite such ambivalences and tensions. Thus Joe Jacobs, a Jewish tailor, in recalling his time as a communist militant in Stepney in the East End of London, in the 1930s gives a vivid sense of the way communist anti-fascist politics was shaped by internationalist and anti-imperial imaginaries. He was a local member of the International Labor Defense (ILD) which was directed by William Patterson. He recalls how the SMM and the ILD worked together in support of 23 striking seafarers from the SS *Ionic* who 'were given 21 days for "refusing" duty and disobeying order'.[37] Jacobs also recounts his involvement in different campaigns where concerns with anti-fascism and anti-colonialism intersected in significant ways. These included the campaigns in support of the Scottsboro' boys, in support of the Meerut prisoners, opposition to the invasion of Ethiopia and colonialism in Palestine. This was combined with ongoing struggles against the British Union of Fascists on the streets of the East End which culminated in the Battle of Cable Street in 1936. He notes, however, his consternation at the liquidation of the ILD in the early 1930s which he suggests actively undermined the strength of communist internationalist political cultures in places like London's East End.[38]

Jacob's focus on the SMM is significant in terms of exploring the relations between left maritime organising and place-based political cultures where anti-fascism and anti-colonialism became linked. The SMM was part of pioneering attempts to organise black and Asian seafarers in British ports and in 1931 set up a 'Committee of 18 negroes was erected to form a national Movement of coloured workers'.[39] Inaugurated at 'a meeting at the International Seamen's Club, 233 High Street, Poplar, held under the auspices of the Seamen's Minority Movement' on 3 December 1931, police reports suggest that the meeting was addressed by Arnold Ward, Chris Jones, and Jim Headley who was appointed to head the committee.[40] The intersections shaped by organisations such as the SMM and NWA were integral to producing maps of internationalist political activity which cross-cut metropolitan and colonial spaces.

While key activists such as Jones and Ward would eventually leave the NWA, disillusioned with the Communist Party, there were continuing connections between the organisation and multi-ethnic seafarer's organising. Thus a Special Branch report contained in the secret services' file on Peter Blackman, the Barbadian communist and poet who was the chair of the NWA in the late 1930s notes that he 'was one of the speakers at a meeting' on 'Trade Unionism in the West Indies' which was held at the Public Hall, Canning Town, under the auspices of the Negro Welfare and Colonial Seamen's Association on 5.12.37'.[41] The latter organisation had been set up to fight the 1935 British Shipping Assistance Act and included Jones as president and the Indian seafarers' leader and communist Surat Alli as secretary.[42] While the NWA was a London-based organisation it nonetheless appears to have been significant for black left politics in other UK ports. Thus writing to Blackman after the NWA's demise in 1940 the Guyanese Cardiff-based seafarer's organiser Harry O'Connell, lamented that the end of organisation 'means that all news, and any other information concerning our people comes to an end'.[43]

O'Connell's letter suggests the importance of these political networks in shaping and circulating information on Black Left politics. In this regard maritime workers forged important spaces of connection which were shaped by, and in relation to, subaltern actors who worked together with leadership figures such as Padmore. The importance of some of these transnational connections and flows of radical information/ideas can be demonstrated through discussing a Liverpool based seafarer who was from Sierra Leone, Ernest Foster Jones. Ernest Foster Jones was a

Sierra Leonean who was 'one of the leaders of the Freetown-based United Seamen's Club, a social and welfare organisation originally formed in 1923, which represented the seamen in talks with their employers'.[44] Padmore recommended Foster Jones as 'the Secretary to the new International Seamen's Club they are founding in Sierra Leone'. Foster Jones's activity in the early 1930s exemplifies how seafarers contributed to the broader organising work directed by Padmore on behalf of the ISH/ITUCNW. According to UK police reports on the activity of the SMM and ISH Foster Jones was acting as a courier for the ISH/ITUCNW between Hamburg and West Africa. Thus an account from November 1931 noted that 'in the middle of October' of that year he was on board the SS *Holmelea* at Freetown Harbour, Sierra Leone and 'was acting as a courier, and conveying propaganda material, messages etc between Nigeria and Freetown, as well as a diversity of centres in French West Africa, and the International Committee at 8, Rothesoodstrasse, Hamburg'.[45] Further it noted that the SS *Holmelea* was 'due in Hamburg about the 5th November, and should from there go to London, when it is indicated that Jones may bring parcels for Fred Thompson and the Seamen's Minority Movement'.

This positions ISH activists as part of broader circulation of left and anti-colonial ideas and integral to their exchange and transmission. Such relations were not, uncontested however. Correspondence relating to the visit to UK ports of Richard Krebs from the ISH headquarters in Hamburg indicate that the organisation generated internationalist connections through racialised encounters. Accounts of his visit demonstrate the intense racism which structured the ways in which Krebs interacted with activists from racialised minorities. Thus accounts of Krebs interactions with Harry O'Connell in Cardiff note that he used racist language[46] and that he sought to sideline O'Connell by pushing him only to do 'colonial work'.[47] Krebs accounts of his interactions with O'Connell suggest, however, that O'Connell held his own against him.

Krebs also clashed with the Barbadian seafarer Chris Jones, noting that he had expelled him from the SMM and advocated his expulsion from the CPGB, though it wasn't until in 1932 that Jones did leave the Party.[48] He then became a powerful and vociferous critic of the limits of communist positions on imperialism.[49] Jones was to work with Padmore, James and Amy Ashwood Garvey in the International African Friends of Abyssinia/Ethiopia and contributed a column 'Seamen's Notes' to International African Opinion, the publication associated with their International African Service Bureau. He argued that 'colonial seafarers' could use the mobility afforded to them by their labour to shape transnational organising networks.[50] Jones's trajectory emphasises, however, that seafarers could refuse the strategic roles for them envisioned by left political projects, despite the strategic centrality of seafarers to trade networks was one of the reasons why the ISH wanted to engage with them.[51] The next section explores how such contested relations between black political activists, maritime organising and communist internationalism impacted on the opposition to the invasion of Ethiopia by Mussolini in October 1935.

Maritime internationalisms, anti-fascism and 'workers' sanctions'

In early to mid-1935 maritime workers, particularly those of the Black diaspora, used their strategic role in transnational flows to exert pressure on the preparations being made by the Italian fascist government for the invasion of Ethiopia. Thus the 7 September edition of *Umsebenzi*, the paper of the South African Communist Party, noted that 'the local committee of the Communist Party' in Durban had 'issued an appeal last June to the dock workers' and 'had called upon them to refuse to handle cargo destined for Italian East Africa. It called upon them to keep a sharp lookout for Italian ships loading meat at Durban'. Further it noted that the 'first of these ships arrived last week and docked at the Congella Wharf. A gang of 60 Native stevedores refused to handle the frozen meat. Unfortunately all the dockers did not exhibit the same degree of political consciousness and another gang was taken on by the employers'.[52] Peter Cole notes that the Durban Committee of the South African Communist Party declared 'If we, workers of South Africa, allow this food to be sent to East Africa we shall be helping Mussolini to conquer and enslave the people of Abyssinia'.[53] *Umsebenzi* reported further:

> In Capetown last Sunday the dockworkers (the majority of whom are Coloured) have refused to load the Italian vessel *Sabbia* with a cargo of South African chilled meat which is destined for the Italian army, because they will not be a party to any action which will promote the war now threatened.

This was part of broader left political opposition to the invasion in South Africa. Thus the South African police recorded a meeting on 6 October of 1935 with T. Thibedi as the chairman which was held in Sophiatown in Johannesburg and which 'had been called for the purpose of bringing to the notice of the people the war between Italy and Abyssinia'.[54] Such organising was articulated in ways which exceeded some of the moderate appeals to the League of Nations which structured some forms of labour internationalism. It challenged the limited dominant forms of labour internationalism such as those envisioned by the British TUC. These stayed within the limits of League of Nations position and shied away from the more militant 'workers' sanctions' position. As PS Gupta notes the official UK Labour Party and TUC position was different from that advocated by anti-imperialists such as Fenner Brockway who 'favoured international working class action to 'black' essential supplies to Italy'.[55] Opposition to some of the colonial imaginaries which inflected such official positions in the British labour movement was articulated by differently placed anti-colonial commentators.

Thus an article in the Indian nationalist paper *Amitra Bazar Patrika*, on 8 September 1935, which also carried new of the refusal of dockers in South Africa to load cargo on to an Italian vessel the *Perla*, noted the passing of a resolution by the British Trade Union Congress 'declaring faith in the collective peace system within the League of Nations, calling upon the British Government, in co-operation with the League, to use all necessary pressures provided by the Covenant to prevent

Italy's "unjust and rapacious attack" upon the territory of a fellow member of the League'. It argued, however, that the 'resolution' was 'likely to prove no more than a pious wish and a hope, for the British policy, as far as one can understand it is being guided not so much by the spirit of the covenant of the League as by the fear that British Imperial interests might be jeopardized by Italy's rapacious attack on Abyssinia'. The article concluded that the 'British TUC should rather strike at the root of the evil than seek to cure the maladies that are bound to be produced by the end'.

These solidarities then, challenged the colonial imaginaries of labour organising which inflected organisations like the TUC and the Labour Party. While there were figures in the party such as the Labour MP, Arthur Creech Jones, who had a strong interest in colonial matters, they nonetheless expected labour organisers in the 'colonies' to adopt the structures and moderate approach associated with the British labour movement. The mobilisations in opposition to Mussolini's invasion of Ethiopia, such as those in Trinidad had significant effects and were shaped by assertive and independent political trajectories which refused to be subordinated to colonial labour geographies.[56] Thus Elma Francois and other activists involved in the Negro Welfare Cultural and Social Association (NWCSA) to which Jim Headley belonged, became interested in the war in Ethiopia after receiving and reading copies of the *New Times* and *Ethiopian News* edited by Sylvia Pankhurst.[57] According to the NWCSA activist Dudley Mahon the 'Abyssinian War awakened the consciousness of the Trinidad working class' and became articulated with political articulations of blackness.[58] The NWCSA organised a mass meeting on 10 October 1935 in Port of Spain where 'speakers denounced France for its lukewarm attitude and also renounced England for refusing to sell arms to Ethiopia. They called on all Negroes to boycott French and Italian goods and stevedores were asked to refuse to unload Italian ships'.[59] Dockers took action in Port of Spain later that year on 15 November 1935, refusing to unload the Italian ship *Virgilo*.[60] This took place in a context where, as Margaret Stevens notes, the British Union of Fascists had a presence on Trinidad, and she quotes US intelligence reports indicating that a former American citizen Edward York had sought to 'make plans for the formation of Fascist nuclei in Bermuda, British Honduras, the British West Indies and British Guiana'.[61]

The NWCSA continued to make links between anti-colonialism and anti-fascism. At the Mayday demonstration in Port of Spain in 1938 Rhoda Reddock observes that slogans included: 'Long live the International', 'Long live Jim Barrette!' (then in prison on sedition charges), 'No Trinidad Oil for Franco!' and 'This is not Rhodesia!' She also notes that in August 1939 eleven Spanish refugees fleeing from France who passed through Port of Spain in the sloop Alexandrina were welcomed by NWCSA members who made a 'statement against fascism'. The refugees presented to the NWCSA a 'picture of Black American anti-imperialist Paul Robeson singing to Spanish workers in the trenches'. This emphasises how organisations like the NWCSA mobilised opposition to Franco as part of a broader opposition to imperialism in different contexts.[62] While these anti-fascist connections had some linkages to the circuits of communist internationalism, Holger Weiss dissects the claim of the ITUCNW head Otto Huiswoud to have orchestrated boycotts by maritime workers. Weiss argues that his claim was 'overblown'. He notes that in Trinidad 'the Longshore Workers Branch had started its activities before it was contacted by the ISH secretariat' and 'were asked to join a world-wide boycott of Italian ships in September 1935'.[63] As Bayerlein notes elsewhere in this volume the ISH boycott was itself opposed by the Comintern and was quickly stood down (see Chapter 11, this volume).

Examining some of the different and contrasting trajectories of activists who had been involved in the SMM/ISH enables a focus on the different terms on which these forms of black internationalism, maritime organising and anti-fascism intersected. While there was a strong presence of different left wing organisations in contesting the invasion of Ethiopia there were also significant struggles on the left over the terms on which the invasion was contested. In London there was a significant communist presence in relation to opposition to Mussolini's invasion of Ethiopia. Thus Tom Mann spoke at a Communist Party meeting held on 17 October 1935 for Dockers and Seamen at St George's Hall, Shadwell in London's dockside communities.[64] The meeting organised around the slogans 'Stop the fascist murder of men, women and children in Abyssinia' and 'Not a ship must sail from London docks which carries supplies to the Italian invaders'. As the report of the meeting Tom Mann addressed in Shadwell indicates maritime workers were a key target of this organising and they were encouraged to stop Italian ships carrying supplies, particularly munitions.

The ILP leader Fenner Brockway recounts, however, that in London in particular ILP member 'went on to the streets with leaflets and speech-making, confident that they had a working-class policy with which to meet the campaign of the Labour and Communist parties, both of which were demanding Governmental action which in our view would lead to war'.[65] CLR James made important contributions to debates within the ILP making what Brockway described as a 'typically torrential speech', but the fact that James had appealed as 'a black worker for help for the black population of Abyssinia' was used to dismiss his case as nationalist rather than socialist.[66] Makalani observes, however, that if 'some on the British Left needed convincing, black workers were actively pursuing workers' sanctions'.[67]

These tensions had a material effect on the construction of alliances in relation to anti-fascism. The influential London Trades Council, for example, withdrew its support from a conference that had been jointly arranged with the Socialist League due to the League's 'attitude to official Labour policy on the Italian-Abyssinian dispute'.[68] That this was directly related to contrasting positions in terms of sanctions – is made clear by discussion at LTC delegate meeting in September 1935.[69] Thus seconding an unsuccessful move to 'reference back' the recommendation to withdraw from supporting the conference, Mr Jacobs Junior of the NAFTA no. 15 branch argued that he 'was in favour of sanctions being imposed upon Italy because he looked upon such action as correct against fascist Italy':

> He could not believe that anyone was prepared to allow this fascist state to act as an aggressor against Abyssinia. His reason for supporting sanctions was in line with a true revolutionary socialist's position. That is that it was right in every case to take part in any action calculated to resist the menace of Fascism.[70]

Despite the ambivalence of some sections of the left to workers' sanctions and maritime workers, circuits of Black Internationalism shaped the emergence of opposition to Italy's invasion of Ethiopia in important ways. Thus one of the ships targeted as part of attempts to effect a maritime blockade was the SS *Holmelea*, the United Africa Company steamer, which Foster Jones had been engaged on in the earlier 1930s. In August 1935 Sierra Leonean crew members of the ship made their captain sign a resolution which denounced Mussolini's preparations for an invasion.[71] In late July 1935 representatives of the crew had spoken at a meeting in London organised by the International African Friends of Abyssinia. They noted their concern about the 'war threat of fascists and Imperialists against coloured people in Africa', and pledged to stop the ship from sailing in the event of the vessel being loaded with munitions.[72] Information about this event was circulated in the *Sierra Leone News* and the *Negro Worker*.

Intelligence material relating to the Barbadian communist Peter Blackman positions this action in relation to ongoing political connections and solidarities forged between North Shields and Freetown. In the late 1930s Blackman was based in London, was involved in the NWA and was being used as a '"contact" with colonial seamen' by Reginald Bridgeman and the Colonial Information Bureau and reports indicate that he had spoken to a meeting of 'coloured seamen' at 20 Clive Street, North Shields in November, 1937.[73] Blackman's surveillance file contains a description of an intercepted letter of 24 January 1938 from A. G. Watkis, the General Secretary of North Shields Branch of the Coloured Nationals Mutual Association, to Peter Blackman, which notes that Watkis had asked Blackman 'to send him some literature for distribution by comrades who were going to Freetown and other ports in South [*sic*] Africa'.[74] Though reports based on an informant suggested that 'most of the members of the North Shields Branch of the Coloured Nationals Mutual Association were not in favour of Communism'.[75]

In Cardiff Harry O'Connell was arrested for allegedly threatening to lead a march from the shipping office yard in Butetown to Cardiff's Italian consulate.[76] The *Rino Carrada*, an Italian vessel, was targeted by harbour workers and coal trimmers in Cardiff who stopped it being loaded with coal.[77] Harry O'Connell also recounted being involved in anti-fascist mobilisations in relation to the Spanish Civil War. The anthropologist St Clair Drake who did research in Cardiff for his PhD in the late 1940s recounts that while he was walking back from the 1948 May Day parade in Cardiff to the multi-ethnic, dockside area of the city known as Butetown that O'Connell told him 'This isn't like it was in the days of the Spanish war. In those days we formed our own parade in the Bay – with all the Spaniards marching together and a lot of our people – and we marched up to meet the main parade. But now nobody from the Bay marches in May Day parades.'[78]

This conversation emphasises the diverse and temporary articulations that made up anti-fascist left political cultures in particular port cities. There were key connections between figures involved in mobilising maritime opposition to Franco and anti-colonial communist activists such as O'Connell. Thus Jimmie Henson, a long-standing maritime union activist in South Wales was vice-president of the Colonial Defence Association, an organisation headed by O'Connell.[79] Henson continued to be involved in internationalist work in relation to Spain after the defeat of the Republic in 1939. The minutes of a Cardiff Trades Council meeting held on 5 October 1944 noted that a letter had been received from 'Mr Henson drawing attention to the Spanish Republican's position in Spain'.[80] O'Connell's remarks to St Clair Drake emphasise, however, the temporary character of some of the political alliances forged in relation to anti-fascist mobilisation in the 1930s, but it also signals their enduring significance for some of the activists involved.

Such tensions are made more explicit in intercepted correspondence between O'Connell and Peter Blackman in January, 1940. Writing in relation to the decision to close the Colonial Information Bureau, effectively liquidating the anti-colonial work of the CPGB, O'Connell observed to Blackman that this was 'a very serious mistake, in fact an unforgiveable one'. He continued:

> It seems to me if we can do for ourselves, and are making any successes, then all these friends are prepared to wave flags along with us, their conduct certainly drives the Col [people of colour] miles away from them, it is painful to think of the continual mistakes the people make with the work.[81]

It is interesting to note here the distancing way in which O'Connell refers to 'friends', suggesting only a partial identification and incorporation within the Communist Party. This is particularly significant given that unlike many of his ISH/SMM contemporaries O'Connell would remain a loyal communist into the post-war period.[82]

In this regard many activists from the SMM/ISH found that to pursue a consistent anti-colonial position necessitated breaking with communism.[83] The response to the invasion of Ethiopia proved to be a particularly significant rupture here. This was the case both in terms of black communists breaking with the party but also in terms of the Party's presence in relation to broader organising in relation to the conflict. Thus while Ward could assert confidently to William Patterson that on leaving the Comintern Padmore 'would fade away' and that 'the Garvey days are over' by the mid-1930s his assessment had changed.[84] Thus Holger Weiss notes that Ward responded to chiding from Huiswoud's about the inactivity of NWA, by stressing the negative impacts of 'the CPGB's disinterest and George Padmore's resumed activities' on the NWA.[85] He noted that Padmore's articles 'on Abyssinia in the Crisis is well read here among Negroes and you can well judge for yourself' has done 'the NWA a lot of harm. The inactivity of the *AWM*, the LAI and the CP on the Abyssinian question brings GP and Marcus Garvey right in the limelight. Sak and I are bound to be pessimistic.'[86] This was compounded by the actions of the USSR, most notably of the failure of the Soviet Union to condemn Italian aggression in April of 1935.[87] As Christian Høgsbjerg notes: 'When the news broke that the Soviet Union had sold oil to Mussolini, most of the few black activists still involved with the CPGB and organisations like the LAI broke with them overnight.'[88]

As Bernhard Bayerlein notes elsewhere in this volume this represented 'the premature termination of the Soviet Union's anti-colonial and anti-imperialist tradition'. In this context Padmore's activities outside communist circles became increasingly significant and also involved connections with many black radicals who had been formerly involved with different communist organisations such as the ISH. Padmore and Kouyaté continued to work together after they were both expelled from/left the Comintern 'plotting out protest' against Mussolini's threatened invasion of Ethiopia, from Paris in February in 1935.[89] Kouyaté was particularly important in shaping solidarities between black and Arab international networks and in forging relations with black maritime circuits and networks.[90] These activities generated a set of imaginative articulations between anti-fascism, anti-racism and anti-colonialism. Such articulations were a fragile achievement that resonated with diverse attempts to generate solidarities and alliances between anti-fascism, anti-racism and anti-colonialism which existed in increasingly unfavourable and dangerous circumstances in the 1930s. These political interventions were increasingly constructed beyond the institutions of communist internationalism and through an anti-Stalinist lens as is indicated by Hyslop's discussion of the Antwerp group. The relations between anti-fascism, anti-colonialism and communism became increasingly fraught through the 1930s. As Matthew White has noted for anti-fascists such as Virgil Morris in Spain to be associated with IWW linked unions- such as the Marine Transport Workers was to invite suspicion, imprisonment and beatings.[91]

These tensions also shaped political organising at the intersection of anti-colonialism and anti-fascism in London. Thus as CLR James notes Chris Jones became key to maritime organising in relation to Ethiopia working with Padmore, James and Amy Ashwood Garvey in the International African Friends of Abyssinia. Thus he notes how Jones was central to the movement for support of 'workers' sanctions' in 'opposition to proposals for League of Nations sanctions against Italy', and that 'We had one or two people who worked on the waterfront. They gave the pamphlets to seamen and people in boats. In that way it went around.'[92] He noted that Chris Jones was one of these seamen, locating Jones's role as part of a broader challenge to the position of the CPGB on imperialism. Jones was also present at key rallies speaking, for example, at a 'mass rally of the IAFA in Trafalgar Square' in August 1935, 'alongside Amy Ashwood Garvey, CLR James, George Padmore […] and the Kenyan nationalist Jomo Kenyatta'.[93] Jones later wrote in an article 'Why the Colonial Workers oppose conscription' in June 1939 that 'we shall never forget the shameful betrayal of Abyssinia by the so-called League of Nations dominated by the great democracies Britain and France'.[94]

Conclusions

This chapter has sought to contribute to emerging discussions of the relations between anti-fascism and anti-colonialism through a focus on the political trajectories of black seafarers from the Caribbean and West Africa who were active in British ports in the inter-war period. Through developing Hyslop's focus on the way a focus on maritime networks can stretch and engage with anti-fascisms in different ways I have sought to reconstruct some of the ways such actors intervened in anti-fascist activity. By focusing on the specific political trajectories, contributions and experiences of key organisers I have also sought to go beyond some of the rather broad invocations of the strategic importance of maritime workers. The chapter has sought to position their interventions as generative of intersections between anti-fascist and anti-colonial internationalisms. By examining some of the disjunctures between left figures and maritime spaces and some of the racist practices that black seafarers faced in left internationalist networks it has also developed a focus on some of the contested processes through which maritime anti-fascisms were articulated.

These interventions have allowed the chapter to sketch out some of the ways in which internationalist anti-fascist politics was constituted 'from below' particularly in relation to pivotal organising such as the opposition to Mussolini's invasion of Ethiopia in 1935. Further through tracing some of the political trajectories of figures such as Harry O'Connell, Chris Jones and Jim Headley who had different movements through networks such as the ISH and SMM the paper has demonstrated the importance of understanding the different terms on which anti-fascist, anti-colonial and maritime spaces and organising were envisioned and negotiated. By locating these actors in some of the dynamic and processual ways in which anti-fascist solidarities were generated and articulated this has contributed to ways of thinking about the specific geographies through which 'global anti-fascisms' were produced. It also emphasises that there were subaltern articulations of such political discourses and practices which speak to causes, individuals and practices which have often been rather occluded within dominant left narratives of anti-fascisms.

Notes

1 Jonathan Hyslop, 'German Seafarers, Anti-fascism and the Anti-Stalinist Left: The "Antwerp Group" and Edo Fimmen's International Transport Workers' Federation, 1933–40', *Global Networks*, Vol. 19, No. 4, 2019, pp. 499–520, quote on p. 501.
2 Kasper Braskén, *The International Workers' Relief, Communism and Transnational Solidarity: Willi Münzenberg in Weimar Germany* (London: Palgrave Macmillan, 2015); Hugo García, 'Transnational History: A New Paradigm for Anti-fascist Studies?', *Contemporary European History*, Vol. 25, No. 4, 2016, pp. 563–572.
3 Clare Anderson, *Subaltern Lives: Biographies of Colonialism in the Indian Ocean, 1790–1920* (Cambridge: Cambridge University Press, 2012), see also Andrew Davies, 'Identity and the Assemblages of Protest: The Spatial Politics of the Royal Indian Navy Mutiny, 1946', *Geoforum*, Vol. 48, 2013, pp. 24–32.
4 Hyslop, 'German Seafarers, Anti-fascism and the Anti-Stalinist Left', p. 513.
5 Peter Cole, *Dockworker Power: Race and Activism in Durban and the San Francisco Bay Area* (Urbana, IL: University of Illinois Press, 2018), p. 210.

6 Jonathan Hyslop, 'Guns, Drugs and Revolutionary Propaganda: Indian Sailors and Smuggling in the 1920s', *South African Historical Journal*, Vol. 61, No. 4, 2009, pp. 838–846.
7 Len Wincott, *Invergordon Mutineer* (London: Weidenfeld and Nicolson, 1974), pp. 136–137.
8 Antonio Gramsci, *A Great and Terrible World: Pre-Prison Letters, 1908–1926*, edited and translated by Derek Boothman (London: Lawrence and Wishart, 2014), p. 231.
9 Fimmen to Brockway, 19 April 1937, International Workers Federation Papers, 157/3/c/6/17, Modern Record Centre, Warwick University. See also Hyslop, 'German Seafarers, Anti-fascism and the Anti-Stalinist Left', p. 514.
10 See Leslie James, *George Padmore and Decolonization from Below: Pan-Africanism, the Cold War and the End of Empire* (London: Palgrave Macmillan, 2015), pp. 40–45; Matthew Quest, 'George Padmore's and CLR James's International African Opinion', in Fitzroy André Baptiste & Rupert Lewis, *George Padmore: Pan-African Revolutionary Kingston* (Miami, FL: Ian Randle Publishers, 2009), pp. 105–132; and Priyamvada Gopal, *Insurgent Empire: Anti-Colonial Resistance and British Dissent* (London: Verso, 2019), pp. 355–394.
11 Richard Iton, *In Search of the Black Fantastic: Politics and Popular Culture in the Post-Civil Rights Era* (Oxford: Oxford University Press, 2010), p. 61.
12 Enzo Traverso, *Fire and Blood: The European Civil War, 1914–1945* (London: Verso, 2016) e.g. p. 246.
13 Jane Degras, *The Communist International 1919–43*, Volume II (London: Oxford University Press, 19560), pp. 137–139.
14 David Beetham, 'Introduction', in David Beetham (ed.), *Marxists in the Face of Fascism: Writings by Marxists on Fascism from the Interwar Period* (Manchester: Manchester University Press, 1983), p. 19.
15 Georg Padmore, *The Life and Struggles of Negro Toilers* (London: International Trade Union Committee of Negro Workers, 1931), pp. 5, 6.
16 Ibid., p. 109, emphasis in original.
17 Georg Padmore, *Africa and World Peace* (London: Secker and Warburg, 1937).
18 A.R., Trinidad, '"Negro Worker" Banned by Imperialists', *Negro Worker*, 15 June 1932, pp. 14–17.
19 Palmiro Togliatti, *On Gramsci and Other Writings* (London: Lawrence and Wishart, 1979), p. 143.
20 Padmore, *Life and Struggles*, p. 45; Beetham, *Marxists in the Face of Fascism*, p. 57.
21 Palmiro Togliatti, *Lectures on Fascism* (New York: International Publishers, 1976); see also David Featherstone, 'Black Internationalism, International Communism and Anti-fascist Political Trajectories: African American Volunteers in the Spanish Civil War', *Twentieth Century Communism*, No. 7, 2014, pp. 9–40.
22 George Padmore 'World Congress of Seamen', *Negro Worker*, Vol. 2, No. 6, 1932, pp. 23–25, quote on p. 25.
23 Ibid., pp. 23–25; James, *George Padmore and Decolonization from Below*.
24 Brent Hayes Edwards, *The Practice of Diaspora: Literature, Translation, and the Rise of Black Internationalism* (Cambridge, MA: Harvard University Press, 2003). Kouyaté, from the French Sudan, led the Paris based anti-colonial group 'Ligue de défense de la race Nègre', editing its paper *Le cri des Nègres*.
25 See Matthew Worley, *Class Against Class: The Communist Party in Britain Between the Wars* (London: I. B. Tauris, 2002), pp. 226–228.
26 A.R., Trinidad, '"Negro Worker" Banned by Imperialists', pp. 14–17.
27 Hull History Centre, League Against Imperialism Papers, British Section, Bridgeman, U DBN/25/1.
28 Cited by Susan D. Pennybacker, *From Scottsboro to Munich: Race and Political Culture in 1930s Britain* (Princeton, NJ: Princeton University Press, 2009), p. 48.
29 The UK National Archives, (hereafter TNA), CO 323/1164/114.
30 TNA MEPO 38/9, 11A.
31 Hakim Adi, *Pan-Africanism and Communism: The Communist International, Africa and the Diaspora, 1919–1939* (Trenton, NJ: Africa World Press, 2013), p. 259.

32 On the support of the NUS for 'non-political unions', see Arthur Ivor Marsh; & Victoria Ryan, *The Seamen: A History of the National Union of Seamen, 1887–1987* (Oxford: Malthouse Press, 1989), pp. 126–127; Jonathan Hyslop, 'The Imperial Working Class Makes Itself "White": White Labourism in Britain, Australia, and South Africa Before the First World War', *Journal of Historical Sociology*, Vol. 12, No. 4, 1999, pp. 398–421. See also Holger Weiss, '"Unite in International Solidarity!" The Call of the International of Seamen and Harbour Workers to "Colonial" and "Negro" Seamen in the Early 1930s', in Stefano Bellucci & Holger Weiss (eds), *The Internationalisation of the Labour Question* (London: Palgrave Macmillan, 2020), pp. 145–162.

33 University of Warwick, Modern Records Centre, Mss 175/1/1/4, minutes of NSFU executive council meeting, 26 September 1921.

34 Modern Record Centre, University of Warwick, MSS 175/6/AMW/4/1–22: Amalgamated Marine Workers Union (1921) 'Programme and Prospectus', *The Marine Worker*, Vol. 1, No. 4, May 1922, p. 16.

35 Mike Morris, Tony Wailey & Andrew Davies, 'Introduction to *Ten Years On the Parish*', in Mike Morris, Tony Wailey & Andrew Davies (eds), *Ten Years on the Parish: The Autobiography and Letter of George Garrett* (Liverpool: Liverpool University Press, 2017), p. 31.

36 See Laura Tabili, *'We Ask For British Justice': Workers and Racial Difference in Late Imperial Britain* (Ithaca, NY: Cornell University Press, 1994).

37 Joe Jacobs, *Out of the Ghetto: My Youth in the East End: Communism and Fascism 1913–1939*, 2nd edition (London: Phoenix Press, 1991), p. 116.

38 Ibid., pp. 162–163.

39 TNA CO 323/1164/114.

40 TNA CO 323/1164/114.

41 TNA KV2 1838/ 105. See also the entry on Blackman in David Dabydeen, John Gilmore & Cecily Jones (eds), *The Oxford Companion to Black British History* (Oxford: Oxford University Press, 2007), p. 58.

42 See David Featherstone, 'Maritime Labour, Transnational Political Trajectories and Decolonisation From Below: The Opposition to the 1935 British Shipping Assistance Act', *Global Networks*, Vol. 19, No. 4, 2019, pp. 539–562.

43 TNA KV2 1838/ 105 letter from Harry O'Connell to Peter Blackman, 30 January 1940. See also Adi, *Pan-Africanism and Communism*, p. 290.

44 Adi, *Pan-Africanism and Communism*, p. 138.

45 TNA CO 323/1164/114.

46 See David Featherstone, 'Maritime Labour and Subaltern Geographies of Internationalism: Black Internationalist Seafarers' Organizing in the Interwar Period', *Political Geography*, Vol. 49, 2015, pp. 7–16.

47 TNA KV2/1102/53a.

48 Christian Høgsbjerg, *Mariner, Renegade and Castaway: Chris Braithwaite, Seamen's Organizer and Militant Pan-Africanist* (London: Socialist History Society and Redwords, 2013), p. 39.

49 Ibid.

50 Jones was later to argue in his column Seamen's Notes for the *International African Opinion* that it was 'up to us … as coloured seamen, to enlighten our fellow colonial workers during our travels that we underdogs have nothing to gain by fighting in the interests of the imperialist robbers', see David Featherstone, Solidarity: Hidden Histories and Geographies of Internationalism (London: Zed Books, 2012), p. 89.

51 Holger Weiss, *Framing a Radical African Atlantic: African American Agency, West African Intellectuals and the International Trade Union Committee of Negro Workers* (Leiden: Brill, 2014).

52 'Native and Coloured Dockers' Anti War Strike- Refuse to Load Italian Ships at Durban and Capetown', *Umsebenzi,* 7 September 1935 in *South African Communists Speak* (London: Inkululeko Publications, 1981), p. 124–125.

53 Cole, *Dockworker Power*, p. 191.

54 South African Police Office of the Deputy Commissioner, Witwatersrand Division, Marshall Square, Johannesburg, 10 October 1935, National Archives of South Africa, NTS 339/400.

55 Partha Sarathi Gupta, *Imperialism and the British Labour Movement, 1914–1916* (Cambridge: Cambridge University Press), p. 238.
56 Rhoda Reddock, *Elma Francois: The NWCSA and the Workers Struggle for Chance in the Caribbean in the 1930s* (London: New Beacon Books, 1988); Kevin A. Yelvington, 'The War in Ethiopia and Trinidad, 1934–1936', in Bridget Brereton & Kevin A. Yelvington (eds), *The Colonial Caribbean in Transition: Essays on Postemancipation Social and Cultural History* (Barbados: The Press University of the West Indies, 1999), pp. 189–225.
57 Reddock, *Elma Francois*, pp. 18–19.
58 Cited by Reddock, ibid., pp. 18–19; Yelvington, 'The War in Ethiopia and Trinidad', pp. 189–225; see also Jerome Teelucksingh, *Labour and the Decolonization Struggle in Trinidad and Tobago* (London: Palgrave Macmillan, 2014).
59 Reddock, *Elma Francois*, pp. 18–19.
60 Weiss, *Framing a Radical African Atlantic*, p. 651; *Negro Worker*, Vol. 11, No. 5, 1935, p. 28.
61 Margaret Stevens, *Red International and Black Caribbean: Communists in New York City, Mexico and the West Indies, 1919–1939* (London: Pluto, 2017), p. 173.
62 Yelvington, 'The War in Ethiopia and Trinidad', p. 206, Reddock, *Elma Francois*, pp. 44, 48.
63 Weiss, *Framing A Radical African Atlantic*.
64 *Daily Worker*, 17 October 1935.
65 Fenner Brockway, *Inside the Left: Thirty Years of Platforms, Press, Prison and Parliament* (London: Georg Allen & Unwin, Ltd., 1947), p. 326.
66 Ibid., p. 326.
67 Minkah Makalani, *In the Cause of Freedom: Radical Black Internationalism From Harlem to London, 1917–1939* (Durham, NC: University of North Carolina Press, 2011), p. 203.
68 'Unions Disown Sir Stafford Cripps- Loyal to Party Policy', *Daily Herald*, 13 September 1935.
69 London Metropolitan Archives, London Trades Council Papers, ACC 3287/01/21, Minutes of Delegate Meeting held in Club Union Buildings, Clerkenwell Road, London on Thursday, 12 September 1935.
70 London Metropolitan Archives, London Trades Council Papers, ACC 3287/01/21.
71 S. K. B. Asante, *Pan-African Protest: West Africa and the Italo-Ethiopian Crisis, 1934–1941* (London: Longman, 1977), p. 130.
72 *Negro Worker*, Vol. 5, No. 11, 1935, pp. 12–13.
73 TNA KV2/1838–2.38. In this context it is worth noting that the Seamen's Minority Movement had a significant presence in South Shields where it constructed alliances between white and Arab seafarers in campaigns against the racialized politics of the NUS, see David Byrne, 'Class, Race and Nation: The Politics of the "Arab Issue" in South Shields, 1919–39', *Immigrants and Minorities* Vol. 13, No. 2–3, 1994, pp. 89–103, here p. 96–97; and Richard Lawless, *From Ta'izz to Tyneside: An Arab Community in the North-East of England during the Early Twentieth Century* (Exeter: Exeter University Press, 1995), p. 135.
74 TNA KV2/1838–1.38 summary of intercepted letter from A. G. Watkis, General Sec, The Coloured Nationals Mutual Association, North Shields Branch to Peter Blackman, 53, Grays Inn Road, London, WC1 dated 24 January 1938.
75 TNA KV2/1838–1.38.
76 Mid Glamorgan Record Office P/S CBO 3/210 Friday, 18 October 1935.
77 H. Morice, 'The Marine Workers' Fight Against Italian War', *Negro Worker* Vol. 6, No. 2, 1936, pp. 24–26.
78 St Clair Drake 'Cardiff Diary and Notes', Schomburg Center for Research in Black Culture, St Clair Drake Papers 62/3; Tabili, *'We Ask For British Justice'*.
79 Drake 'Cardiff Diary and Notes'.
80 Cardiff University Special Collections, minutes of an executive committee meeting of Cardiff Trades Council held on 5 October 1944.
81 TNA KV2 1838/ 105 letter from Harry O'Connell to Peter Blackman, 30 January 1940.

82 David Featherstone, 'Harry O'Connell, Maritime Labour and the Racialised Politics of Place', *Race and Class*, Vol. 57, No. 3, 2016, pp. 71–87; Marika Sherwood, 'Racism and Resistance: Cardiff in the 1930s and 1940s', *Llafur*, Vol. 5, No. 4, 1991, pp. 51–70.
83 See James, *George Padmore and Decolonisation From Below.*
84 Ward cited in Pennybacker, *From Scottsboro to Munich*, p. 85.
85 Weiss, *Framing A Radical African Atlantic*, p. 656.
86 Ward cited by Weiss, *Framing A Radical African Atlantic*, pp. 656–657.
87 Mark Naison, *Communists in Harlem during the Depression* (Chicago, IL: University of Illinois Press, 2005), p. 157.
88 Høgsbjerg, *Mariner, Renegade and Castaway*, p. 49.
89 Joseph Fronczak, 'Local People's Global Politics: A Transnational History of the Hands Off Ethiopia Movement of 1935', *Diplomatic History*, Vol. 39, No. 2, 2015, pp. 245–274, 277.
90 Tiemeko Garan Kouyaté 'Black and White Seamen Organize for Struggle', *Negro Worker*, Vol. 1, No. 12, 1931, pp. 19–20, Pennybacker, *Scottsboro to Munich*, p. 341, Jonathan Derrick, *Africa's 'Agitators': Militant Anti-Colonialism in Africa and the West, 1918–1939* (New York: Columbia University Press, 2008), pp. 221–226.
91 M. White, '"The Cause of the Workers Who are Fighting in Spain Is Yours": The Marine Transport workers and the Spanish Civil War' in Peter Cole, David Struthers & Kenyon Zimmer (eds), *Wobblies of the World: A Global History of the IWW* (London: Pluto Press, 2017), p. 223.
92 C. L. R. James, 'C. L. R. James and British Trotskyism: An Interview', Interview with Al Richardson, Clarence Chrysostom & Anna Grimshaw, 1986, online at www.marxists.org/archive/james-clr/works/1986/11/revhis-interview.htm (accessed 15 January 2020).
93 Høgsbjerg, *Mariner, Renegade and Castaway*, p. 47.
94 *New Leader*, 9 June 1939, reproduced in Høgsbjerg, *Mariner, Renegade and Castaway*, p. 107.

9

TRANSNATIONAL ANARCHISM AGAINST FASCISMS

Subaltern geopolitics and spaces of exile in Camillo Berneri's work

Federico Ferretti

This chapter addresses the life and works of transnational anarchist and anti-fascist Camillo Berneri (1897–1937). It draws upon Berneri's writings, rarely available in English, and on the abundant documentation available in his archives, especially the Archivio Berneri-Chessa in Reggio Emilia. Berneri is an author who is relatively well known in Italian scholarship, and these archives have been explored by many Italian historians: in this chapter, I extend this literature by discussing for the first time Berneri's works and trajectories through spatial lenses, together with their possible contributions to international scholarship in the fields of critical, radical and subaltern geopolitics. An anti-fascist exile between Switzerland, France, Belgium, Netherlands, Germany and Luxembourg in 1926–1936 and then a revolutionary and anti-fascist fighter in Spain in 1936–1937, Berneri produced scholarly outputs which can still nourish current debates.[1]

Exploratory studies have addressed the idea of 'anarchist geopolitics',[2] in association with the notion of subaltern geopolitics, which encompasses a wide range of experiences generally associated with post-colonialism and with the rise of counter-powers and counter-hegemonies.[3] An important notion to be considered addressing spaces, places and contexts of anarchist activism is exile, a condition which has been discussed in postcolonial contexts[4] and which now constitutes a pillar of recent approaches to anarchism as an intrinsically transnational movement. According to this new scholarship, anarchism must be understood in its relational and transnational nature by analysing contexts, places, mobilities and processes of transculturation that characterised the nomadic existence of its activists. Italian-speaking anarchism is considered as an exemplar case in these studies.[5] Activists' transnationalism was often a forced condition, due to exile for political reasons, or for economic migration, but it could also be related to internationalism and mobility for propaganda reasons. This means that contextual and spatial-sensitive approaches are indispensable to understand anarchism.

While authors like Davide Turcato have convincingly demonstrated the globality of the networks characterising Italian anarchism across the Atlantic in the Age of Empire,[6] recent studies similarly address the transnational nature of Spanish anarchism, which likewise 'benefitted from inspiration and cross-fertilization with Argentina and Cuba'[7] and other overseas regions. Moreover, transnational approaches characterise new scholarship on broader European anti-fascisms demonstrating that the 'cultural battle' of transnational anti-fascism started in the 1920s, well before what was argued in former contributions.[8] The Italian case exemplified by the figure of Berneri confirms this scholarship, showing how anti-fascists started their active resistance in 1920, even before Mussolini seized power. In addition, it underpins the notion of 'cross-fertilisation' between different national traditions given that, while Italian anarchists brought their patrimony of ideas and practices to global anti-fascisms, their strategies were impacted by the places and experiences that characterised their exile.

Drawing upon the literature referred to above, I explore Berneri's life spaces and works to make sense of his geopolitical contribution to global anti-fascisms. My argument is twofold. First, I challenge Italian liberal scholarship arguing that Berneri was an 'unorthodox' or an 'heretic' in the anarchist field. I do that by showing Berneri's exemplar insertion in the spaces and contexts of a generation of Italian anarchists. Most of them were compelled to escape from Italy after Mussolini took the power in 1922 to seek refuge in other European countries (and to a lesser extent in North and South America). Then, in 1936–1939, they fought in Spain, and those who survived Spanish fascism and the Second World War came back to Italy in 1943–1945 to participate in the armed Resistance against Nazi-Fascism. Therefore, transnational anti-fascism is a key element in understanding this generation of Italian anarchists.

Berneri was one of the most representative figures in this trajectory and a leading member of its main organisations, such as the Italian Anarchist Union (UAI) and the Italian Syndical(ist) Union (USI). Second, I argue that Berneri's writings on the geopolitical problems that the Spanish revolution had to face from 1936, such as defence from Franco's troops and from Mussolini's imperialism in the Balearic Islands, can nourish present-day debates by exposing examples of internationalist and stateless geopolitics. The prickliness of Berneri's analyses, published in the journal of the Italian anarchists fighting in Spain, *Guerra di Classe*, can explain why he was murdered by Stalinist agents during the Bloody May (*Mayo Sangriento*) 1937 in Barcelona, just a few days after delivering a radio speech where Berneri gave a moving tribute to another Italian anti-fascist, Antonio Gramsci, who had just died in a fascist prison in Italy. In this sense, Berneri's awareness of the globalisation of revolutionary challenges that global totalitarianisms entailed allows us to consider Berneri's works as a resource for contemporary spatial reflections on global networks of anti-fascist solidarity.[9]

In the first part of this chapter, I question the idea of Berneri's 'unorthodoxy' in Italian scholarship by focusing on his position in spaces and contexts of his activists' generation, one which was especially marked by anti-fascist activities.

In the second part, I discuss places, politics and scholarly implications of his exile experience in several European countries between 1926 and 1936. In the third part, I analyse anarchist and anti-fascist geopolitics performed by Berneri in Spain in 1936 and 1937, providing a contextual and space-sensitive reading of his contribution to Italian and global anti-fascisms.

Anarchism, anti-fascism and orthodoxy

Among Italian anarchists, anti-fascism was the principal activity of what Ugo Fedeli (1898–1964) defined as 'thirty years of anarchist activity'[10] from the First World War to 1945, whose legacy has been ceaselessly claimed by activists of following generations until the present day.[11] Analysing Berneri's role in this generation, and in its places and trajectories, is essential to understanding his idea of anti-fascism. This included Berneri's participation in armed resistance in Spain, but even before in the little-known experience of the *Arditi del Popolo* squads, groups organised by anarchists and other anti-fascists who performed early barricades resistance to the street violence of early fascist squads from 1921.[12] For the anarchists, this implied discussing matters on ethics, especially on the legitimacy of violence, whose use was rejected as a principle but admitted as a defensive practice in the tradition established by authors such as Errico Malatesta (1853–1932). According to another transnational anarchist anti-fascist, Luce Fabbri (1908–2000), Berneri's work was instrumental in refreshing this tradition and bringing it to the following activists' generations.[13] More recently, authors such as Gianni Carrozza and Claudio Strambi noticed how 'practically all Berneri's production from 1921 deals with antifascism'.[14]

In Italy, the literature on Berneri's life and works is abundant and particularly contentious. As discussed by Carrozza,[15] Berneri's thinking was forced to fit disparate agendas. Indeed, the Italian anarchist spent most of his career in exile and politically persecuted, being finally murdered at the age of only 40. Therefore, he did not have the opportunity to establish a systematic theoretical opus, and his works and thoughts are scattered in numerous pamphlets, journal articles and fragments, including correspondence and work notes whose use is disputed. According to Carrozza, Berneri was first 'sanctified' as an anarchist 'martyr' who only ever had excellent ideas. Indeed, the first editors of his works and curators of his archives, Cesare Zaccaria (1897–1961), Aurelio Chessa (1913–1996) and Berneri's wife Giovanna Caleffi (1897–1962) did not hesitate to hide from the public some of Berneri's writings which challenged their own views.[16] To understand Berneri's later interpretations, what I consider important is that activists like Chessa were far from representing the entire 'anarchist movement', being akin to the so-called 'Galleanist' tendency, inspired by the figure of Luigi Galleani (1861–1931) and internationally represented by *L'Adunata dei Refrattari*, an Italian journal published in the United States and circulated worldwide. Ironically, this corresponded to the anti-organisational tendencies (not necessarily individualistic but often akin to anarcho-individualism) of the movement. Albeit influential, anti-organisational anarchists were ostensibly a minority in relation to the organisational anarcho-communist tendencies represented by the *Unione Anarchica Italiana* (founded in 1920), later *Federazione Anarchica Italiana* (1945),[17] and the anarcho-syndicalist ones represented by the *Unione Sindacale Italiana* (1912).

Indeed, the 'anti-organisers' were the main adversaries of Berneri, and several historians have implicitly considered them as the 'orthodox anarchists', in order to highlight Berneri's allegedly 'heretical' positions within the movement and to argue that he was 'an atypical liberal rather than an anarchist'.[18] This was the case with some works by Nico Berti, and especially by Pietro Adamo and Carlo De Maria.[19] According to Carrozza, these works are methodologically flawed by the fact that, especially in the cases of Adamo and De Maria, the authors develop their arguments by putting an over-emphasis on some unpublished and often incomplete writings, without a clear discussion on what an unpublished note or fragment tells us about 'what Berneri [decided to publish] when he was alive'.[20] Matching Carrozza's views, I would contend that reading Berneri as a liberal rather than an anarchist thinker is completely misleading and does not consider contents, contexts and places of communist, anti-fascist and organisational anarchism at Berneri's time.

In the following paragraphs, I discuss some of the key ideas that Berneri contributed to anarchist debates, considered in the contexts, spaces and daily practices of the transnational Italian-speaking movement of his day. As a geographer, I would argue that anarchism should be understood in its places, networks and flows of ideas and activists,[21] and to avoid anachronisms such as pretending that Berneri would have been a 'heretic'. In this vein, it is worth noting that Berneri's travels and travails from Italy to France, Germany, Switzerland, Netherlands, Belgium and Luxembourg, and finally to the Spanish Revolution, corresponded to the spatial patterns which characterised the mobility of the very 'mainstream' (if any) of communist and organisational anarchists trying to find a difficult way among the concurrent persecutions of Nazism, Stalinism and liberal democracy. These life trajectories are now displayed by invaluable works like the *Dizionario Biografico degli Anarchici Italiani*[22] where the biographical pathways of approximately 2,000 early activists can be compared. Therefore, while anarchism has always been a plural and heterogeneous movement and it would be odd to identify one 'anarchist orthodoxy', I would contend that, if any mainstream tendency has existed in twentieth-century Italian anarchism, it was the organisational anarcho-communism inspired by Malatesta, of which Berneri was one of the most important, and even 'orthodox' exponents.

A leitmotiv of those who deem Berneri a 'heretic' are his frequent polemics with the *Adunata*'s director Raffaele Schiavina (1894–1987), whose pen name Max Sartin (seemingly a tribute to Max Stirner) is indicative of how little this activist can be considered representative of any 'orthodoxy', given the unpopularity of authors such as Stirner and Nietzsche in the Italian anarcho-communist tradition.[23] Yet, Schiavina/Sartin should be praised for his open-mindedness, as he regularly published Berneri's writings which clearly countered his own views and always kept a cordial relationship with him as shown by the correspondence they exchanged.[24]

Amazingly, Berneri was such a 'liberal' that, in one of these polemics with Sartin, he was charged with being too 'philo-Soviet' because he claimed that the original idea of the Soviets was that of 'a fruitful gymnasium of self-administration which can prepare the people to systems of major autonomy',[25] one which matched anarchist principles and should not be confused with Bolshevik bureaucracy and Stalinist rule. In his response to Berneri, Sartin continued to foster confusion between the original idea of Soviets and Bolshevik authoritarianism.[26] Considering the writings of the most prominent Italian and international anarchists in the early years of the Russian revolution[27], and the enthusiasm of USI activists for worker's councils,[28] the true 'orthodox' in relation to the anarchist tradition was not Sartin but Berneri.

Another point on which Berneri was defined as a 'heretic' is abstentionism. Again, the idea of 'heresy' is a remarkable mix of misunderstanding and lack of contextualisation. Berneri fumed sarcastically at what he called 'abstentionist cretinism'[29] which drew harsh critiques by Sartin and other anarchists. However, the target of Berneri's polemics was not the principle of abstentionism from political elections,[30] but its transformation in an immutable dogma to be applied at any cost and in any circumstance. Berneri criticised silly extensions of the abstentionist principle to occasions where voting did not entail sending a delegate to the Parliament and had the value of direct democracy, like raising one's hand in an assembly, or participating in a local referendum for opening 'a neighbourhood's public library'.[31] Crucially, Berneri repeatedly advocated the moral authority of authors such as Bakunin and Malatesta, arguing that 'Malatesta's [past] heresies are now principles'.[32] He also received the support of respected international activists such as Luigi Bertoni (1872–1947), editor of the influential journal *Il Risveglio/Le Réveil* in Geneva, and Gigi Damiani (1873–1953), former co-editor of *Umanità Nova* with Malatesta,[33] who were not exactly peripheral figures in Italian-speaking anarchism. It is worth noting that these discussions occurred in the context of a wider anti-fascist debate. The choice made in February 1936 by the Spanish CNT, for instance, which gave up a strong abstentionist campaign on the occasion of the Spanish elections, and thereby facilitated the victory of the Popular Front. This decision was motivated by material stakes because the political Left had committed to free all political prisoners including thousands of anarchists. Although this CNT's choice was often criticised in anarchist literature, the centrality of 1936 Spain in anarchist history allows us to appreciate how some electoral 'possibilism', though highly contentious, was also part of the anarchist tradition.

Adamo and De Maria also considered Berneri's views on the state, and especially his federalism and communalism, as radically alternative to the anti-statism of the anarchist tradition. Ironically, in his discussion on federalism, Berneri was so much of a 'heretic' that he took as his main reference point one of the most 'classical' anarchists, Peter Kropotkin, and his critique of bureaucracy and centralism.[34] The other big inspiration for Berneri was the Risorgimento federalist Carlo Cattaneo (1801–1869), something which is likewise deemed an element of 'anarchist unorthodoxy' by the authors mentioned above. Yet, any scholar familiar with relations between early anarchism and the federalist tradition of the Risorgimento should hardly be surprised by the interest of an Italian anarchist in Cattaneo, or in other federalists such as Carlo Pisacane (1818–1857) and Giuseppe Ferrari (1812–1876).[35] This interest was shared by Malatesta, who quoted Cattaneo among the most respected names of the Risorgimento alongside Garibaldi and Mazzini,[36] and especially by another leading figure of Italian anarchism, Luigi Fabbri (1877–1935), in whose circuit the names of Cattaneo and Ferrari 'have always been familiar'.[37] This leads us to again question what 'orthodoxy' might mean: Adamo admits that, in his late years, even Malatesta 'gained a reputation of "revisionist"',[38] which should suggest that labels such as 'revisionist', 'unorthodox', 'heretic' and similar should be used cautiously in anarchist contexts.

Another point on which Adamo deems Berneri 'heretical' is his declared humanism, allegedly opposed to 'the leftist revolutionary vulgate … and its strong classist vocation'.[39] Again, this looks misleading, first because in his text on anarchist humanism, Berneri clearly advocates the anarchist tradition, from Kropotkin's 'dreams of human emancipation'[40] to 'Malatestian humanism',[41] mentioning a range of 'noble' figures including Louise Michel and Pietro Gori. Second, Berneri's (and in general anarchist) humanism was never opposed to class struggle, because Berneri was one of the strongest supporters of anarcho-syndicalism, that is one of the most genuinely proletarian social movements in the twentieth century.[42] His discussions with Luigi Fabbri, who always was Berneri's friend and collaborator,[43] evoked by Adamo, concerned their different assessment of the relations between syndicalism and 'specific' anarchist organisation, a leitmotiv of anarchist debates from the 1907 Amsterdam congress onwards.[44] However, it is worth noting that between anarcho-syndicalists and anarcho-communists there was generally operational convergence, especially in the anti-fascist resistance, despite some ideological differences: like many activists of his generation, Berneri was concurrently part of the UAI (anarchist organisation) and the USI (anarcho-syndicalist organisation).[45] In the early years of fascist repression in Italy, he served as the link between Malatesta and international activists like Max Nettlau, and as one of the Italian correspondents for the anarcho-syndicalist Congress of Berlin in 1922.[46] In his letters to Fabbri, Berneri identified individualism as the first target of his polemics. 'If I criticise individualism, it is because, while the individualistic trend has little numeric importance, it managed to influence almost all the movement'.[47] When Berneri mentioned 'pure anarchism',[48] this was clearly in the context of a discussion on anarcho-communism and anarcho-syndicalism and not to support liberalism instead of anarchism.

Thus, if any 'anarchist orthodoxy' has ever existed in the first half of the twentieth century in Italian-speaking milieus, we should count Berneri among its possible representatives. He continued to be a self-declared anarchist throughout his short life and shared, with most of his comrades, a trajectory including activism in the UAI and in the USI after the Red Biennial (1919–1920), anti-fascist exile in several countries, and finally the experience of the Spanish Revolution with the CNT-FAI (Confederación Nacional del Trabajo – Federación Anarquista Ibérica), bringing decisive ideas to the entire field of anarchist anti-fascism as I explain in the following sections.

Transnational anarchism and anti-fascist exile

Berneri's full insertion into the typical anarchist trajectory of his day is confirmed by a spatial history of his exile experiences, which exemplify the transnational nature of Italian-speaking anarchism.[49] Born in Lodi, near Milan, in 1897, Berneri started his political activities when he was an adolescent in Reggio Emilia, where he followed his mother Adalgisa Fochi, a schoolteacher and later a campaigner for the truth about her son's assassination.[50] In Reggio, Berneri was first an activist in the youth organisation of the Socialist Party, and then joined the local anarchist group, a worker's collective where Camillo was the sole student, mentored by bookbinder Torquato Gobbi (1888–1963). 'Gobbi was my teacher, in the foggy nights under the Via Emilia's arcades, resounding with my attempts to resist his placid dialectic'.[51] However, Berneri retained the 'socialist humanism'[52] that he learned at the school of Reggio socialist leader Camillo Prampolini (1859–1930). Despite being a key figure of moderate socialism, Prampolini had collaborated with the anarchists in his youth and was generally respected by them due to shared values of tolerance.[53] After being mobilised for the First World War, Berneri lived in Florence, where he studied modern history supervised by socialist and future anti-fascist exile Gaetano Salvemini (1873–1957), and became acquainted with some socialist and liberal scholars who would become part of the broader Italian anti-fascist movement, such as Ernesto Rossi (1897–1967), Piero Gobetti (1901–1926) and the brothers Carlo (1899–1937) and Nello (1900–1937) Rosselli.[54] Later, Berneri taught in several secondary institutes in Tuscany and Marche, until fascist aggression and political isolation compelled him to quit Italy in 1926, shortly followed by his family, comprising Giovanna Caleffi, Maria Luisa Berneri (1918–1949) and Giliana Berneri (1919–1998), all future anarchist activists and writers.[55]

In France, the odyssey which led Camillo to be defined as 'the most expelled anarchist in Europe' started in the late 1920s. His exile was a harsh experience not only for the material difficulties that exile always entails, but also for the war at distance that the fascist regime fought against its exiled opponents. Mussolini's government exerted pressure on other European governments to expel anti-fascists and sent abroad a number of spies and *agents provocateurs* who rendered the exiles' milieus especially precarious.[56] Committed to organising a sort of counterespionage service to unmask these agents, Berneri played key political and organisational roles in the exile circuits of Italian anarchists. Many militants either formally or informally recognised him as the 'successor' to the most respected leaders who were forcibly isolated. In these years, the elderly Malatesta remained in Rome under the strict surveillance of the fascist police until his death in 1932,[57] while Fabbri quit Europe in 1929 to finding refuge in Uruguay, where he died of an illness in 1935.[58] For these reasons, Berneri was a main target for the provocateurs. His implication in the so-called 'Menapace affair' – a spy who managed to compromise several activists by circulating firearms and explosives to attack fascist exponents, served as pretext for the international police harassment which Berneri suffered, all documented in his archives and recollections.

One document details Berneri's peregrinations in the period 1928–1931. Brought from France to the Belgian frontier in December 1928 and immediately re-expelled from there, Berneri obtained a provisional permit, but was arrested in December 1928 in Brussels and sentenced to 5 years in prison for a 'false passport and for carrying prohibited firearms'.[59] In May 1930, he was 'expelled from Belgium; arrested in Rosendhal, Netherlands, and compelled to come back to the Belgian territory',[60] where he was sentenced to one more month in prison for breach of his expulsion decree. He was then accompanied to the frontier with Luxembourg in June 1930. There, he was arrested and expelled at the French frontier, where he was arrested again, and brought to the German border in August 1930. In October, he was expelled from Germany and went to France again, where his case interested the League for Human Rights and the International Committee for Political Prisoners. Jailed from October 1930 to May 1931, protest meetings were organised in Berneri's favour. He then obtained a presidential pardon and was accompanied to the Spanish frontier but was finally allowed to remain in France. After other expulsions, all suspended by French tribunals, Berneri's situation in 1933 was the following: 'Without passport; refused by the Luxembourg Embassy, by the Berlin Consulate, by the Paris consulate … Formally expelled from France and Belgium; informally expelled from Luxembourg; forbidden to stay in Switzerland and Netherlands; expelled from Germany.'[61]

Berneri's recollections *Pensieri e battaglie*, published posthumously in 1938, can be considered a masterpiece in exile literature. Among others, Edward Said highlighted the de-humanising nature of twentieth-century mass exile in relation to former 'romantic' traditions. Drawing upon these postcolonial contributions, I would argue that anarchist stories can question the divide between elites and masses: anarchists were part of mass displacements in the era of totalitarianisms, but they remained a conscious minority of manual and intellectual workers. It is worth noting that anarchists did not have a bureaucratic apparatus able to secure income for 'party executives', therefore anarchist intellectuals had to generally live off their manual work while exiled, including Berneri who worked as a bricklayer when he lived in France. They did not escape from what Said called 'the crippling sorrow of estrangement',[62] exemplified by Berneri's comment that he 'remained alone, as one is alone in Paris',[63] which anticipated Said's remarks that: 'Paris may be a capital famous for cosmopolitan exiles, but it is also a city where unknown men and women have spent years of miserable loneliness: Vietnamese, Algerians, Cambodians, Lebanese, Senegalese, Peruvians'.[64] It was also the case with the anarchists, whose proclaimed internationalism, however, allowed them, in Saidian terms, to 'lend dignity to a condition legislated to deny dignity'.[65] Thanks to a certain internationalist pride, anarchist exiles embraced the cosmopolitanism that characterised exiled people, generally aware of more than 'one culture, one setting, one home'.[66] While they remained sensitive to the call of home, as shown by the attempts to return to Italy, the mobility of the most expelled anarchists in Europe chimes with recent contributions to notions of postcolonial exile as something unsettling irenic ideas of home.[67] They likewise provide an alternative to nationalism, being that during their exile they became active in addressing the revolutionary challenges arising in their places of residence. This is especially true in relation to the Spanish events of 1936–1939.

The exile experience also reinforced internationalist and anti-statist anarchist ideas about the absurdity of political frontiers and their de-humanising nature. Berneri stressed how several of his expulsions were illegal because the neighbouring nations which tried concurrently to get rid of him lacked a formal agreement on this issue. Therefore, he did more than once undertake 'clandestine passages'[68] from one country to another, pushed by the police of the former and trying to avoid the police of the latter to reach the closest town. This led to Kafkaesque situations such as Berneri's 1930 expulsion from Luxembourg, when he reported that: 'I called their attention on the fact that I was already banished from France, Belgium, Switzerland and Netherlands.'[69] Thus, Luxembourg policemen tried to organise a discrete transfer to France, but Berneri broke this plan by screaming and opposing resistance to be arrested by the French police in the middle of a crowd: 'This way I obtained all what I could obtain: calling public attention on my case.'[70] Significantly, this did not occur in 'totalitarian' states, but in the Western European countries which pretended to represent democracy and universal rights. In matters of human rights and tolerance, an amazing anecdote concerns Berneri's discussion with a French policeman who was violently threatening him during a detention, when the Italian exile noticed the image of Voltaire on his pipe and commented on the philosopher's thought. Astonished that a stranger, whom he considered a criminal and an exponent of the worst scum, was familiar with Voltaire, the man became suddenly dialogic and kind. For Berneri: 'In this way, in 1928, Voltaire contributed to humanising a policeman. I think that this was not his smallest contribute to the fight for tolerance.'[71] Conversely, observing the despising attitude towards a community of gypsies shown by the residents of a Berlin neighbourhood where he stayed for a while in 1930, Berneri wrote some pessimistic remarks on conformism and xenophobia, that he defined as 'the aversion of the majority for everybody and everything which does not match the Rule'.[72] These exile experiences had doubtlessly the effect of further internationalising the Italian movement creating a new generation of cosmopolitan and multilingual activists, but they were likewise characterised by sadness and sorrow. For the intellectuals, this was often 'the impossibility of attending conferences, registering with a library, studying or writing seriously'.[73]

This stresses the importance of considering authors' material lives, contexts and positionality to assess their work. In the case of Berneri and his fellows, their exile experiences were key to informing their contributions to global anti-fascisms. While the anarchists criticised the 'official' group of Italian anti-fascist political parties in France, the Antifascist Concentration (also boycotted by the communists), Berneri was one of the most active anarchists in seeking collaboration with other groups available for anti-fascist unity of action. This was especially the case with the so-called 'liberal-socialist' movement *Giustizia e Libertà* (GL) led by the brothers Carlo and Nello Rosselli, and in general with the area that Berneri identified as 'the anarchists, the GL people and the republican/socialist action'.[74] This was an attempt to take initiative beyond the most moderate sectors of the Concentration and the isolationist line of the Italian Communist Party led by Palmiro Togliatti, following Joseph Stalin's instructions from Moscow. This situation involved multiple challenges for the anarchists, who were committed to anti-fascist unity but had to struggle, in Berneri's words, 'against both right/wing fascism and left/wing fascism',[75] which meant being opposed at the same time to liberal democracy and to fascist and Stalinist totalitarianisms. About the communists, in addition to their critiques of the Russian regime and the processes against Trotskyists and left/wing dissidents, Italian anarchists were disappointed with the so called 'Appeal to the Fascists', a document that communist leaders sent to Italy in 1936, trying to recruit activists from the fascist ranks by claiming the original 'social inspiration' of fascism.[76] Against such tactics, deemed opportunistic, the anarchists preferred to support anti-fascist actions such as attacks against Mussolini and his men, and to prepare for a possible insurrection in Italy.[77]

Berneri was aware that fascism was not only a phase in the expansion of great capital, but an ideology permeating culture and mentality in dangerous ways. His activities as an intellectual touched several themes and disciplines, including psychoanalysis. For instance, Berneri's analysis of Mussolini's personality and his performances as a 'great actor' tried to explain why, in the early 1920s, one of the strongest workers' movements in Europe was defeated by people of so low political and intellectual level as the fascist leaders.[78] Some of Berneri's main scholarly contributions stood in continuity with the tradition of anarchist geographers Reclus and Kropotkin and their efforts to use science against racism and colonialism.[79] In 1935, Berneri published a pamphlet, *El delirio racista*, firstly issued in Buenos Aires, countering the pseudo-scientific bases of Nazi-fascist antisemitism and racial myths, and defining the 'racist delirium' as a 'true collective psychosis'.[80] Yet, Berneri predicted the racist turn that Italian fascists would take in the following years (the 1938 'Racial Laws'), suggesting that racism 'might become necessary'.[81] Berneri's notion of 'race' as a literary invention to justify policies like colonialism in the nineteenth century and Nazi-Fascism in the twentieth century was doubtlessly ground-breaking and can even speak to contemporary critical race studies.

Berneri's transnational activities clearly spanned beyond Europe, especially through his collaborations with transnational anarchists of Italian origin in the Americas. These networks included the North-American group of *L'Adunata* and anti-fascist refugees in South-America such as Fedeli, Gobbi and the Fabbris, exiled in Montevideo, Uruguay, who extensively corresponded with Berneri on matters of anti-fascism and on the political situations in the respective countries.[82] It was probably the Fabbris who served as intermediaries in publishing *El delirio racista* in Argentina, while the journal they founded in Montevideo, *Studi Sociali*, published some of Berneri's anti-fascist articles[83] and one of the first obituaries denouncing his assassination, authored by Luce Fabbri,[84] who was likewise one of the first to write to Berneri's wife and daughters to offer support and solidarity.[85] From Montevideo, Luigi Fabbri remained in touch with Berneri until his last days, while Berneri's first 'anarchism's teacher' Gobbi often wrote from Uruguay to inform Camillo of his continuing commitment to anti-fascism.[86]

Meanwhile, in 1935, the Rossellis proposed 'an anti-fascist revolutionary alliance'[87] to the anarchists, who were also given heart by hopes that the Fascist regime would fall following a possible defeat in the colonial war in Ethiopia. In October of that year, Italian anarchists from all France, Belgium and Switzerland celebrated their first general conference for more than 10 years, in Sartrouville, organised by Berneri and other Paris-based activists. Despite the constraints that a clandestine meeting entailed, the most important point discussed was how to organise a return to Italy in case of the regime's crisis. First, the mass armed return of all the exiles was deemed necessary to make the regime collapse. Then, the crucial issue of anti-fascist unity was addressed by supporting alliances with movements like GL and excluding permanent unions with political parties. As summarised by Luigi di Lembo, this meant: 'Acting in synergy with the other antifascist forces, but maintaining our political and armed independence, ready to defend ourselves at the first sight of prevarication'.[88] Among the conference reports, presented under pseudonyms for security reasons, the 'A' document, signed by the organising group and probably written by Berneri,[89] established a distinction between the 'formula of the free Soviets'[90] desired by the anarchists, and the Bolshevik-like solutions. This was clarified in the document's aims: 'Destroying the structure of the fascist state and impeding that … under the cover of a provisional pseudo-revolutionary government, a government for democratic-social-liberal conservation or a Bolshevik dictatorship is possibly put in place.'[91] In defining GL and left/wing sectors of the republican and socialist parties as the preferred anti-fascist partners, the anarchists acknowledged that 'we should seek help in fields akin to ours, to get rid of an enemy that we cannot defeat alone'.[92] Importantly, this conference was the last of this genre until the Carrara Congress of 1945 because the circumstances did not allow any other similar meeting. Therefore, the principles established in Sartrouville were applied by the Italian anarchists to the anti-fascist struggle in Spain from 1936 to 1939 and to Italian Resistance from 1943 to 1945. This further demonstrates that the figure of Berneri was not marginal, but absolutely central to the Italian anarchist movement.

Crucially, the 1935 invasion of Ethiopia by Fascist Italy reinvigorated traditional anarchist anti-colonial critiques, which were key for Berneri's analysis. From the 1910s, Berneri had identified anti-militarism and anti-colonialism as qualifying points for anarchism, reproaching moderate socialists like his friend Prampolini for having been 'responsible for the insufficient resistance to fascist squads and, formerly, to colonialism [1911 Libya War] and interventism [World War First]'.[93] In the early 1920s, Berneri likewise observed with special interest anti-colonial movements within the British Empire: 'In the Orient, we see an awakening which will overthrow John Bull's domination, and we see Ireland in ebullition.'[94] In the following decade, he denounced how 'in Libya, the fascist government started the systematic extermination of the Arabs',[95] and called for the retreat of Italy from her colonies. This included leaving 'hospitals, railways and schools built by the administration to the indigenous, as reparation'.[96] Berneri protested against the Italian aggression of Ethiopia, fuming at 'that butcher of Ethiopians and Italians named Mussolini'.[97] He argued that this war was a continuation of early Italian imperialism in Eritrea fostered by Prime Minister Francesco Crispi and King Umberto I. Berneri highlighted the ineffectiveness of the League of Nations in hindering Mussolini's imperial ambitions and the complicity of the main colonial powers, Britain and France, denouncing an 'Anglo-French-Italian aggression to Abyssinia'.[98] Berneri concluded that 'our struggle should be directed against capitalism and against the state and not just against Italian fascism, which is only a form of worldwide fascism'.[99] This analysis informed the subaltern and anti-colonial geopolitics which Berneri would deploy in Spain in the last year of his life.

Geopolitics of the social revolution

As revealed in the introduction to this chapter, critical, anarchist and subaltern geopolitics increasingly question state and state affairs as the main framework of geopolitical studies. As a case in point, let us consider Berneri's articles published in the journal of the Italian anarchists fighting fascism during the Spanish Civil War (1936–1939), *Guerra di Classe*, and his study on Italian imperialism in the Mediterranean Sea, *Mussolini alla conquista delle Baleari*. Berneri's analysis of fascism and his critiques of Mussolini's imperialism in Africa and in the Mediterranean underpinned his exhortation to the Spanish republican government to support the struggle of Moroccan people for independence. According to anarchist critics like Berneri's son-in-law Vernon Richards,[100] failure to listen to Berneri and other anarchist intellectuals advocating Moroccan independence like Gonzalo de Reparaz (1860–1939)[101] was one of the biggest blunders of the republican front. The racist propaganda often deployed by republican leaders against the Moroccan mercenaries appointed by Franco has been discussed on the scholarship on the engagement of Afro-American volunteers in the republican front[102] and on this latter's deficiencies in constructing 'an anticolonial understanding of fascism'.[103]

In Spain, Berneri took a leading position among Italian anarchist volunteers and co-directed with Carlo Rosselli the Italian section of the CNT-FAI Ascaso Column, composed of anarchists and GL activists, fighting around Huesca in the Northern Aragon Front. Returning to Barcelona because his comrades deemed him more useful as a writer than as a soldier,[104] Berneri started his journalistic activity, coupled with researching on documents of the Italian consulate in Barcelona, whose headquarters were occupied by the Italian anti-fascists after the departure of the consul.[105] According to Berneri, these documents proved the plans of Mussolini for Italian expansion in the Western Mediterranean to counter the British maritime power and to possibly cut communications between France and her North African colonies.

Berneri's strategic aim was to highlight the contradictions between Italian and French-British imperialisms before it was too late for Spain to avoid the victory of Franco, and a new world war. In his work, Berneri compared the Italian intervention in Spain with Mussolini's colonial endeavours. 'As [Italy] speculated on alleged barbarity to conquer Ethiopia, so she is speculating on "red barbarity" to conquer Spain.'[106] While this was the ideological cover for supporting the 'Voluntary Troops', a label invented to circumvent the French–British 'non-intervention' committee, Mussolini's availability to keep troops and materials in Mallorca, from which he would have proceeded to bomb Barcelona, constituted a de facto occupation of the archipelago, meaning that 'Spain appeared to Italian fascism as a country to be colonised'.[107] Then, Berneri perceived how opportunistic Mussolini's support for Franco was, with the Italian dictator aware of the Balearic Islands' 'importance in the game of Mediterranean forces'.[108] Berneri meticulously studied the documents, denouncing an Italian colonial interest lasting from the 1920s, when Italian public opinion was entertained by press campaigns showing the touristic interest of the archipelago:

> As in colonial conquest, the explorer comes first, followed by the missionary, then by the soldier, then by the tradesman. … Now there is the journalist. He is the one who discovers oil … who solemnly speaks of 'the rights of civilisation' and so on.[109]

Also the documents presenting the Balearic Islands as a good place for Italian businesses and investments were read by Berneri as motivated 'by the essential strategic value of the Balearic Islands for Italian imperialism'.[110] At the level of his geopolitical analysis of Italian fascism and imperialism, Berneri concluded that 'fascist power in the Mediterranean is becoming a matter of fact; Mussolini can instigate Egypt against England and Tunisia, Algeria and Morocco against France, while he strengthens his colonial domination in Tripolitania and Ethiopia'.[111] As Claudio Venza observed, Berneri was one of the most lucid analysts of the increasing globalisation of fascisms, well beyond the Spanish fronts.

At the level of geopolitical analyses for the concrete needs of the anti-fascist struggle, Berneri started a series of papers in *Guerra di Classe* in October 1936, where he tried to exert a public role as a combatant intellectual, proclaiming that, even in the rear-guard of the antifascist front: 'I grab my pen as I would grab a gun or a rifle.'[112] Analysing the international situation around the Spanish conflict, Berneri criticised the international committee for non-intervention, that Spanish revolutionaries considered to be a measure which favoured the Fascists, hindering the arrival of weapons for the Republican front but allowing the massive intervention of expedition corps from Fascist Italy and Nazi Germany. In this context, Berneri considered the choice of the Republican government to refuse independence to Morocco a serious mistake. For the anarchists, an anti-colonial revolt would have been one of the winning moves for the anti-fascist war: 'We must intensify the propaganda for Moroccan autonomy in the entire area of Pan-Islamic influence. We must impose to Madrid unequivocal statements for Spain abandoning her colonies in Morocco with the help of Moroccan activists.'[113]

In November 1936, one of Berneri's key texts concerned the decision of the CNT to enter the Republican government and was significantly titled: 'A dangerous turning point: warning!'. This raised multiple issues that the Spanish anarchists and their international fellows had to contend with. First, the dilemma 'war or revolution', which meant conciliating the needs of social revolution, namely, the ongoing collectivisation of Spanish fields and Barcelona industries,[114] with the need to defeat Franco's troops. This task implied an alliance with the liberals, the republicans, the Catalan nationalists, the socialists and the communists, political forces which were not always favourable to collectivisation and in most cases strongly opposed to social revolution. Berneri strongly supported those anarchists arguing that the choice between anti-fascist war and social revolution was a false alternative, because war and revolution would have been unescapably won or lost all together. On the military side (again matching Reparaz's positions) Berneri argued that 'we should shift from a war of position to a war of movement, attacking with a general and solid plan'.[115] Concurrently, he claimed that the war had to be won by further mobilising Spanish proletarians and extending the revolution beyond merely getting weaponry, and warned against possible militarist degeneration. 'The anarchists who now serve as generals should remember their experiences as revolutionaries'.[116] Berneri countered the position of the moderate governmental sectors, supported by the Communist Party in particular, that called for the formal 'militarisation of the militias'[117] as a solution to the alleged lack of discipline of anarchist brigades. Yet, these militias had defeated the fascist military insurrection in most of Spain in July 1936, also with thanks to the participation of many women whom the militarisation would exclude from the front. For Berneri, war discipline (including 'self-discipline') was obviously needed, but this was not to be confused with political control of the militias. For Berneri, 'the government of Madrid is an enemy of social revolution', and for this reason it was unwilling to send weapons to Barcelona.[118]

In these months, one of the prickliest aspects of Berneri's journalistic activity was his constant and sharp denunciation of the growing hegemony that the Communist Party was gaining in the Republican Front. Communists were a small minority in Spain until 1936, but they were becoming powerful thanks to Soviet support and to their choice of defending small property, becoming 'the Foreign legion of Spanish democracy and liberalism',[119] which allowed them to recruit many members of the petty bourgeoisie scared by the collectivisation. Berneri also criticised those CNT leaders who tried to please such a thorny ally, arguing for instance that, 'in exalting the USSR government, *Solidaridad Obrera* reached the peak of political naiveté'.[120] But the main problem with the Communist Party was not (only) its commitment 'to defend [bourgeois] democracy and private property'[121] against the ongoing collectivisation: it was its willingness to exert an authoritarian control over republican Spain. 'Barcelona is now surrounded between Burgos, Rome, Berlin, Madrid and Moscow. A siege … But we can do miracles. Taken between Prussia and Versailles, the Paris Commune lighted a fire which still enlightens the world … The Godeds[122] of Moscow shall be aware of this.'[123] These articles attracted the attention of Russian consul Antonov-Ovshenko who met an 'influential member of the government'[124] to apply pressure to silence Berneri.

In Berneri's analysis, the fear for revolution was likewise blinding Western democracies on the dangers of Nazi-Fascism, an exemplar case being the leader of French *Front populaire* Léon Blum, who preferred to take the risk of having his country encircled by fascist forces rather than having a revolution close to home. Highlighting the inadequacy of liberal democracy for countering fascisms, the Italian anarchist predicted a forthcoming world war if the Spanish massacres, such as the ferocious Nazi bombing of Madrid, failed to raise public awareness:

> Today on the sky of Madrid, tomorrow on that of Barcelona, and the day after tomorrow in Paris. The European war resumed. It is the airplanes of Mussolini's Italy and Hitler's Germany which massacre and disgrace Madrid. Does not this abomination shake your conscience? Therefore, it is the bombs that will awaken it.[125]

The most famous of these documents was the 'Open letter to comrade Federica Montseny', a CNT leader and member of the Largo Caballero government, published in April 1937, few weeks before Berneri's assassination. In this letter, Berneri complained about the action of Stalinist forces in the rear-guard and the increasing paranoia against the so-called 'uncontrolled'. Instead of fighting the enemy, richly armed police corps were left far from the front seizing guns and rifles from revolutionary groups.[126] Berneri reproached Montseny for her shy behaviour within the Spanish government: 'You sit in a government which offered advantages to England and France in Morocco, while we should have officially proclaimed Moroccan independence'.[127] As a result of these choices, and of the deteriorating military situation, Berneri observed that the revolutionary war was increasingly becoming a national war of resistance for mere survival. For Berneri, the people responsible for that were the Stalinists, also favoured by:

> The silence of [Spanish] anarchist press on the dictatorial crimes of Stalin and on the abominable process against the Trotskyist and Leninist opposition … [including] the plan announced by the *Pravda* on 17 December 1936: 'In Catalonia, the cleansing from Trotskyist and Anarcho-Syndicalist elements has started and will be carried out with the same energy as it was accomplished in the USSR.'[128]

In these weeks, Berneri was also one of those who publicly stood up against the Stalinist persecution of the POUM (*Partido Obrero de Unificación Marxista*), denouncing its 'unprecedented violence and pretextual nature'[129] and praised the constructive role that the anarchists played in trying to moderate the dispute between the PSUC (*Partido Socialista Unificado de Cataluña,* the Catalan branch of the Spanish Communist Party) and the POUM in Catalonia. For Berneri, it was this dispute, and not the possible action of few *incontrolados*, which constituted 'a breach of war discipline'.[130] He noticed that, despite their ideological distance from the anarchists, the Marxists of the POUM 'sided with the FAI and the CNT in the heroic resistance against the military/fascist putsch, and organised columns which brought 8,000 men to the fronts'.[131] Against Stalinist repression, Berneri urged Montseny to use her prestige to call for an intensified revolutionary action, arguing that: 'The dilemma "war of revolution" does no longer make sense. The sole dilemma is: victory over Franco through the revolutionary war or defeat.'[132]

Berneri paid for his outspokenness with his life during the tragic Barcelona 'Bloody May' of 1937, when several hundreds of anti-fascists of various belongings died in violent street clashes between the anarchists and the Catalan nationalists supported by the PSUC. On the same day of Berneri's assassination, 5 May 1937, *Guerra di Classe* published his last article denouncing the alliance between the PSUC, the Catalan nationalists and the 'petty-bourgeoisie which entered the Popular Front'.[133] Berneri finally mentioned the names of their leaders Santiago Carrillo, Juan Comorera, together with '*Acció Catalana*, the right/wing components of the PSUC, [socialist minister Angel] Galarza, etc. Here you are the forces of counter-revolution.'[134] Nobody knows the name of the material executors of Berneri: according to direct witnesses, he was arrested at home by anonymous agents after that he remained confined in his building, which was behind the governmental lines in the crazy urban geography that characterised Barcelona in these days. However, the political responsibility for his murder was publicly claimed by the journal *Grido del Popolo*, organ of the Italian Communist Party led by Togliatti, a journal that wrote a few days later that 'Berneri has been executed by the democratic revolution, which was in its legitimate right of self-defence.'[135]

While the political responsibility of the Stalinists (and of their occasional Catalanist allies), is largely recognised by historiography, some less convincing hypotheses have been recently made by other Italian authors. They attributed Berneri's murder to agents of Angel Galarza, following an amazing 'thriller story' concerning some suit-cases replete with gold, allegedly stolen by Galarza in Madrid which then fell into the hands of the Italian anarchists.[136] However, these works are methodologically flawed. Their authors strongly rely on the internal reports of fascist spies without questioning the reliability of these documents, and by the fact that they do not provide any decisive evidence in support of their final statements.[137] Most importantly, these 'new' hypotheses don't modify the political field from which Berneri's assassination was commissioned, that is the governmental one, and namely the persons and parties that he had denounced as 'counter-revolutionaries'.

Conclusion

With reference to the anarchist historiography mentioned above, it is possible to conclude that the transnational and anti-fascist contexts of Berneri's work reveal his central position in a political and organisational pathway shared by most of Italian anarchists, demonstrating how Berneri, whom some liberal historians pretended to be an 'heretic' of anarchism, was paradoxically more 'orthodox' than many others (if any 'anarchist orthodoxy' has ever existed). His contribution to anarchist theories and praxes complements similar figures of activists and intellectuals such as Fabbri and Malatesta, which remain to this day important references for the organised anarchist movement.[138]

The anti-fascist exile that Berneri shared with his fellows shows the specificity of anarchist transnationalism. On the one hand, exile was consistent with anarchist internationalist postulates and conferred pride and moral authority. On the other, anarchist exiles did not escape from the sense of extraneity highlighted by Said: without being nationalist, they continued to reclaim forms of rootedness and willingness to return 'home' to accomplish their revolutionary work. This confirms recent scholarship arguing that anarchism is not incompatible with open and inclusive ideas of nation,[139] especially in the context of anti-colonial struggles.

Anti-colonialism was one of the key notions for Berneri's anarchist and subaltern geopolitics. He sought a dialectic between internationalism and national liberation (the latter being a rhetorical device which was widely deployed in republican Spain) and performed geopolitical and geostrategic analyses questioning statist frameworks. For Berneri and his anarchist fellows, struggling for political freedom and social equality meant fighting against fascism and for social revolution at the same time, occupying an increasingly narrow and uncomfortable political space where operational alliances were not prejudicially excluded.

Finally, it is worth stressing the relevance of the theoretical and practical example of Berneri, an exiled, imprisoned and persecuted intellectual, who had to do manual work to earn a living, and to grab alternatively a rifle and a pen to do his revolutionary job. In a world which is once more increasingly shaped by walls and barriers, intolerance and xenophobia, Berneri's conclusion for *Mussolini alla conquista delle Baleari* can still inspire current critical scholarship: 'I am not impartial, because I have been an exile for 11 years and I am in the middle of the battle – Impartiality is an illusion, honesty is a duty.'[140]

Notes

1 Klaus Dodds, Merje Kuus and Jo Sharp (eds), *The Ashgate Research Companion to Critical Geopolitics* (Farnham: Ashgate, 2013).

2 Federico Ferrett & Jacobo García-Álvarez 'Anarchist Geopolitics of the Spanish Civil War (1936–1939): Gonzalo de Reparaz and the "Iberian Tragedy"', *Geopolitics* 2019, online at www.tandfonline.com/doi/full/10.1080/14650045.2017.1398143

3 Ruth Craggs, 'Subaltern Geopolitics and the Post-Colonial Commonwealth, 1965–1990', *Political Geography* 65, 2018, pp. 46–56.; James Sidaway, Virginie Mamadouh and Marcus Power, 'Reappraising Geopolitical Traditions', in Klaus Dodds, Merje Kuus and Jo Sharp (eds), *The Ashgate Research Companion to Critical Geopolitics* (Farnham: Ashgate: 2013), pp. 165–187; Jo Sharp, 'Subaltern Geopolitics: Introduction', *Geoforum* Vol. 42, No. 3, 2011, pp. 271–273.

4 Edward Said, *Reflections on Exile and Other Essays* (London: Granta Books, 2000); Andy Davies, 'Exile in the Homeland? Anti-colonialism, Subaltern Geographies and

the Politics of Friendship in Early Twentieth Century Pondicherry', *Environment and Planning D: Society and Space* Vol. 35, No. 3, 2017, pp. 457–474.

5 Constance Bantman & Bert Altena, *Reassessing the Transnational Turn: Scales of Analysis in Anarchist and Syndicalist Studies* (New York: Routledge, 2015); Pietro Di Paola, *The Knights Errant of Anarchy, London and the Italian Anarchist Diaspora (1880–1917)* (Liverpool: Liverpool University Press, 2013); Davide Turcato, *Making Sense of Anarchism: Errico Malatesta's Experiments with Revolution, 1889–1900* (Oakland, CA: AK Press, 2015).

6 Davide Turcato, 'Italian Anarchism as a Transnational Movement, 1885–1915', *International Review of Social History* Vol. 52, No. 3, 2007, pp. 407–444.

7 Martha Ackelsberg, 'It takes more than a village! Transnational Travels of Spanish Anarchism in Argentina and Cuba', *International Journal of Iberian Studies* Vol. 29, No. 3, 2016, pp. 205–223, here p. 209.

8 Kasper Braskén, 'Making Antifascism Transnational: The Origins of Communist and Socialist Articulations of Resistance in Europe, 1923–1924', *Contemporary European History* Vol. 25, No. 4, 2016, pp. 573–596.

9 David Featherstone, *Solidarity: Hidden Histories and Geographies of Internationalism* (London: Zed, 2012).

10 Ugo Fedeli, *Un trentennio di attività anarchica* (Cesena: L'Antistato, 1953).

11 See the journal of the Italian Anarchist Federation, *Umanità Nova*, www.umanitanova.org.

12 Marco Rossi, *Arditi non gendarmi* (Pisa: BFS, 1997).

13 Luigi Fabbri, 'Camillo Berneri', *Studi Sociali*, Vol. VIII, No. 6, 1937, pp. 4–6.

14 Gianni Carrozza, 'Berneri e il fascismo: Problemi e chiavi di lettura', *Rivista Storica dell'anarchismo* 16, 2001, pp. 23–44, here p. 40. Claudio Strambi, *Inquieta attitudine: Camillo Berneri e la vicenda politica dell'anarchismo italiano* (Pisa: Kronstadt, 2015).

15 Gianni Carrozza, 'Prefazione', in Camillo Berneri, *Scritti Scelti* (Milan: Zero in Condotta, 2007), pp. 7–12. All quotes from texts originally in Italian, Spanish and French have been translated by the author.

16 Pietro Adamo, 'Tra epistemologia e politica: La "crisi" dell'anarchismo nella riflessione di Camillo Berneri', in Camillo Berneri, *Anarchia e società aperta: Scritti editi e inediti a cura di Pietro Adamo*, Milan (Milan: MB, 2001), pp. 7–90; Gino Cerrito, 'Introduzione', in Camillo Berneri, *Scritti Scelti*, (Milan: Zero in Condotta, 2007), pp. 13–41.

17 Federico Ferretti, 'Organisation and Formal Activism: Insights from the Anarchist Tradition', *International Journal of Sociology and Social Policy* Vol. 36, No. 11–12, 2016, pp. 726–740.

18 Carrozza, 'Prefazione', p. 9.

19 Adamo, 'Tra epistemologia e politica'; Giampietro Berti, *Il pensiero anarchico dal Settecento al Novecento* (Mandura: Lacaita, 1998); Carlo De Maria, *Camillo Berneri tra anarchismo e liberalismo* (Milan: Angeli, 2004).

20 Carrozza, 'Prefazione', p. 12.

21 Federico Ferretti, Gerónimo Barrera de la Torre, Anthony Ince & Francisco Toro (eds), *Historical Geographies of Anarchism: Early Critical Geographers and Present-day Scientific Challenges* (Abingdon: Routledge, 2017).

22 Maurizio Antonioli, Giampietro Berti, Santi Fedele, & Pasquale Iuso (eds), *Dizionario biografico degli anarchici italiani*, 2 vols (Pisa: BFS, 2003–2004).

23 Ferretti, 'Organisation and Formal Activism'.

24 Camillo Berneri, *Epistolario inedito*, 2 vols. (Pistoia: Archivio Famiglia Berneri, 1980–1984).

25 Camillo Berneri, *Scritti scelti* (Milan: Zero in Condotta, 2007), p. 136 [orig. Sovietismo, anarchismo].

26 Ibid., pp. 138–142.

27 Errico Malatesta, *Pagine di lotta quotidiana*, 2 vols. (Carrara: Movimento Anarchico Italiano, 1975); Emma Goldman, *Living my Life* (New York: Garden City Publishing, 1934).

28 Maurizio Antonioli, *Armando Borghi e l'Unione Sindacale Italiana* (Manduria: Lacaita, 1990).

29 Berneri, *Scritti scelti*, p. 163 [orig. Le elezioni in Spagna].

30 Francisco Madrid Santos, 'Evolución e interpretaciones del pensamiento berneriano', in G. Berti and G. Sacchetti (eds), *Un libertario in Europa, Camillo Berneri tra totaitarismi e democrazia* (Reggio Emilia: Biblioteca Panizzi, 2010), pp. 123–148.
31 Camillo Berneri, *Anarchia e società aperta: Scritti editi inediti a cura di Pietro Adamo* (Milan: MB, 2001), p. 228.
32 Berneri, *Anarchia e società aperta*, p. 227.
33 Adamo, 'Tra epistemologia e politica', p. 65.
34 Camillo Berneri, *Peter Kropotkin, his federalist ideas* (London: Freedom press, 1943) [original edition *Un federalista: Pietro Kropotkin* (Rome: Edizioni di Fede!, 1925)].
35 Giorgio Mangini, 'Libero pensiero, repubblicanesimo, anarchismo: L'incontro Fabbri-Ghisleri', in Maurizio Antonioli and Roberto Giulianelli (eds), *Da Fabriano a Montevideo, vita e idee di un intellettuale anarchico e antifascista* (Pisa: BFS, 2006), pp. 39–76; Arthur Lehning, 'Michel Bakounine et le *Risorgimento Tradito*', *Bollettino del Museo del Risorgimento di Bologna* No. 17/19, 1972–1974, pp. 266–292; Pier Carlo Masini, *Eresie dell'Ottocento* (Milan: Editoriale Nuova, 1978); Nello Rosselli, *Carlo Pisacane nel Risorgimento italiano* (Turin: Bocca, 1932).
36 Errico Malatesta, *Un lavoro lungo e paziente, il socialismo anarchico dell'Agitazione 1897–1989* (Milan: Zero in Condotta/La Fiaccola, 2011), p. 188.
37 Luigi Fabbri, *Luigi Fabbri, storia di un uomo libero* (Pisa: BFS, 1996), p. 144.
38 Adamo, 'Tra epistemologia e politica', p. 27.
39 Berneri, *Anarchia e società aperta*, p. 172.
40 Ibid., 172 [orig. Umanesimo e anarchismo].
41 Ibid., 174 [orig. Umanesimo e anarchismo].
42 Bertrand Russell, *Roads to Freedom: Socialism, Anarchism and Syndicalism* (London: Allen & Unwin, 1973).
43 Gaetano Manfredonia, *La lutte humaine, Luigi Fabbri, le movement anarchiste italien et la lutte contre le fascisme* (Paris: Editions du Monde libertaire, 1994).
44 Antonioli, *Armando Borghi e l'Unione Sindacale Italiana*; Fabbri, *Luigi Fabbri*.
45 Francisco Madrid Santos, *Camillo Berneri* (Pistoia: Archivio Famiglia Berneri, 1985); Gianni Carrozza, 'Camillo Berneri', in Maurizio Antonioli, Giampietro Berti, Santi Fedele & Pasquale Iuso (eds), *Dizionario biografico degli anarchici italiani*, vol. I (Pisa: BFS, 2003), pp. 142–149.
46 Amsterdam, International Institute of Social History (IISH), Nettlau Papers, 222, 1922–1926, Correspondence between Camillo Berneri and Max Nettlau.
47 Berneri, *Anarchia e società aperta*, p. 137.
48 Ibid., p. 141.
49 Di Paola, *The Knights Errant of Anarchy*; Turcato, 'Italian Anarchism as a Transnational Movement'.
50 Adalgisa Fochi, *In difesa di Camillo Berneri* (Forlí: Cooperativa Industrie Grafiche, 1951).
51 Camillo Berneri, *L'operaiolatria* (Pistoia: Archivio Famiglia Berneri, 1987) [original edition: Brest, Gruppo d'edizioni libertarie, 1934].
52 Madrid Santos, *Camillo Berneri*, p. 45.
53 Fabrizio Montanari, *L'utopia in cammino, anarchici a Reggio Emilia 1892–1945* (Reggio Emilia: Maestrale, 1993).
54 Marco Scavino, 'Berneri, Gobetti e la rivoluzione italiana', *Rivista Storica dell'Anarchismo*, No. 7, 1997, pp. 73–84.; Rodolfo Vittori, 'Elogio dell'eresia, Ernesto Rossi e gli anarchici', *Rivista Storica dell'Anarchismo*, No. 19, 2003, pp. 5–48.
55 Giorgio Sacchetti, *Eretiche: il Novecento di Maria Luisa Berneri e Giovanna Caleffi* (Milan: Biblion, 2017); Fiamma Chessa & Giorgio Sacchetti, 'Giliana Berneri', in Maurizio Antonioli, Giampietro Berti, Santi Fedele & Pasquale Iuso, *Dizionario biografico degli anarchici italiani*, vol. I. (Pisa: BFS, 2003), pp. 149–151.
56 Aldo Garosci, *Storia dei fuorusciti* (Bari: Laterza, 1953).
57 Giampietro Berti, *Errico Malatesta e il movimento anarchico italiano e internazionale* (Milan: Angeli, 2003).
58 Fabbri, *Luigi Fabbri*.
59 Berneri, *Epistolario inedito*, Vol. 2, p. 259.

60 Ibid.
61 Berneri, *Epistolario inedito*, p. 260.
62 Said, *Reflections on Exile and Other Essays*, p. 225.
63 Camillo Berneri, *Pensieri e Battaglie* (Paris: Comitato Camillo Berneri, 1938), p. 140.
64 Said, *Reflections on Exile and Other Essays*, p. 227.
65 Ibid., p. 227.
66 Ibid., p. 239.
67 Davies, 'Exile in the Homeland?'.
68 Berneri, *Pensieri*, p. 67.
69 Ibid., p. 73.
70 Ibid., p. 74.
71 Ibid., p. 67.
72 Ibid., p. 195.
73 Ibid., p. 69.
74 Ibid., p. 218
75 Ibid., p. 222.
76 Palmiro Togliatti, *Appello ai fascisti* (Catania: La Talpa, 1978).
77 *L'antifascismo rivoluzionario tra passato e presente* (Pisa: BFS, 1993).
78 Camillo Berneri, *Mussolini grande attore* (Pistoia: Archivio Famiglia Berneri, 1983).
79 Federico Ferretti, *Anarchy and Geography: Reclus and Kropotkin in the UK* (Abingdon: Routledge, 2018).
80 Camillo Berneri, *Mussolini normalizzatore e il delirio razzista* (Pistoia: Archivio Famiglia Berneri, 1986), p. 31.
81 Ibid., p. 39.
82 Fabbri, 'Camillo Berneri'.
83 Carrozza, 'Berneri e il fascismo'.
84 Fabbri, 'Camillo Berneri'.
85 Carlo De Maria (ed.), *Giovanna Caleffi Berneri: Un seme sotto la neve, carteggi e scritti* (Reggio Emilia: Biblioteca Panizzi, 2010), pp. 3–4.
86 Berneri, *Epistolario inedito*, I, p. 94.
87 Luigi Di Lembo, *Guerra di classe e lotta umana, l'anarchismo in Italai dal biennio rosso alla Guerra di Spagna* (Pisa: BFS, 2001), p. 190.
88 Ibid., p. 192.
89 Carrozza, 'Berneri e il fascismo'.
90 *Convegno d'intesa degli anarchici italiani emigrati in Europa (Francia-Belgio-Svizzera): ottobre 1935* (Pistoia: Archivio Famiglia Berneri, 1980), p. 12.
91 Ibid., p. 18.
92 Ibid., p. 18.
93 Berneri, *Pensieri*, p. 39.
94 Ibid., p. 39.
95 Camilllo Berneri, 'Via dalle colonie', *L'Adunata dei Refrattari*, 30 July 1932, pp. 6–7.
96 Ibid., p. 6–7.
97 Berneri, *Pensieri*, p. 39.
98 Ibid, p. 3.
99 Ibid., p. 3.
100 Vernon Richards, *Lessons of the Spanish Revolution (1936–1939)* (London: Freedom Press, 1953).
101 Ferretti & García-Álvarez, 'Anarchist geopolitics of the Spanish Civil War'.
102 David Featherstone, 'Black Internationalism, Subaltern Cosmopolitanism, and the Spatial Politics of Antifascism', *Annals of the Association of American Geographers*, Vol. 103, 2013, pp. 1406–1420.
103 David Featherstone, 'Black Internationalism, Antifascism and the Makings of Solidarity', *Soundings: A Journal of Politics and Culture*, No. 55, 2013, pp. 94–107, here p. 92.
104 Umberto Marzocchi, 'Ricordando Camillo Berneri', in *Camillo Berneri nel cinquantesimo della morte,* (Pistoia: Archivio Famiglia Berneri, 1986), pp. 47–80.

105 Claudio Venza, 'Prefazione', in Camillo Berneri, *Mussolini alla conquista delle Baleari* (Casalvelino Scalo: Galzerano, 2002), pp. 5–22.
106 Camillo Berneri, *Mussolini alla conquista delle Baleari* (Casalvelino Scalo: Galzerano, 2002) [original edition: Barcelona: Oficina de Propaganda CNT-FAI, 1937], p. 73.
107 Ibid., p. 74.
108 Ibid., p. 75.
109 Ibid., p. 79.
110 Ibid., p. 125.
111 Ibid., p. 157.
112 Camillo Berneri, *Guerra di classe in Spagna 1936–37* (Genoa: RL, 1979), p. 12 [orig. Una svolta pericolosa].
113 Ibid., p. 7 [orig. Che fare].
114 Myrna Breitbart, *The Theory and Practice of Anarchist Decentralism in Spain, 1936–1939*, PhD thesis, Clark University, 1978.
115 Berneri, *Guerra di classe in Spagna*, p. 12 [orig. Una svolta pericolosa].
116 Ibid., p. 12 [orig. Una svolta pericolosa].
117 Ibid., p. 13 [orig. Una svolta pericolosa].
118 Ibid., p. 13 [orig. Una svolta pericolosa].
119 Ibid., p. 13 [orig. Una svolta pericolosa].
120 Ibid., p. 14 [orig. Una svolta pericolosa].
121 Ibid., p. 20 [orig. La Guerra e la rivoluzione].
122 Manuel Goded was the general who led the fascist insurrection in Barcelona and was then executed by the Catalan people.
123 Berneri, *Guerra di classe in Spagna*, p. 20 [orig. La Guerra e la rivoluzione].
124 Madrid Santos, *Camillo Berneri*, p. 386.
125 Berneri, *Guerra di classe in Spagna*, p. 17 [orig. Madrid la sublime].
126 Ibid., p. 33 [orig. Lettera aperta].
127 Ibid., p. 33 [orig. Lettera aperta].
128 Ibid., p. 37 [orig. Lettera aperta].
129 Berneri, *Scritti scelti*, p. 234 [orig. Noi e il POUM].
130 Ibid., p. 237 [orig. Noi e il POUM].
131 Ibid., p. 239 [orig. Noi e il POUM].
132 Berneri, *Guerra di classe in Spagna*, p. 37 [orig. Lettera aperta].
133 Ibid., p. 43 [orig. La controrivoluzione in marcia].
134 Ibid., p. 44 [orig. La controrivoluzione in marcia].
135 Madrid Santos, *Camillo Berneri*, p. 387.
136 Roberto Gremmo, *Bombe, soldi e anarchia: l'affare Berneri e la tragedia dei libertari italiani in Spagna* (Biella: Storia Ribelle, 2008); Saverio Pechar, *Il caso Berneri* (Rome: ANPPIA, 2017).
137 An internal report surviving at the IISH accounts for a clandestine investigation that some anarchists did in Barcelona to discover Berneri's murderers, an endeavour which had to stop 'due to repression', but which led to the identification of an unnamed individual close to the PSUC circuits. IISH, CNT Archive 005F.9, 'Informe sobre el asesinato de los compañeros Camilo Berneri y Francesco Barbieri'. Barbieri (1895–1937) was another Italian transnational anti-fascist, who had become an anarchist in South America before acting as an activist in France, Switzerland and Spain. See A. Orlando & A. Pagliaro, *Chico il professsore: Vita e morte di Francesco Barbieri, l'anarchico dei due mondi* (Ragusa: La Fiaccola, 2013). About Berneri's and Barbieri's assassination, Pechar's theories are also implicitly contradicted by recent archival findings by Agustín Guillamón, *Insurrección: Las sangrientas jornadas del 3 al 7 de mayo de 1937* (Barcelona: Descontrol, 2018).
138 Ferretti, 'Organisation and Formal Activism'.
139 Davide Turcato, 'Nations without Borders: Anarchists and National Identity', in Constance Bantman & Bert Altena (eds), *Reassessing the Transnational Turn: Scales of Analysis in Anarchist and Syndicalist Studies* (New York: Routledge, 2015), pp. 25–42.
140 Berneri, *Mussolini alla conquista delle Baleari*, p. 157.

10

'AID THE VICTIMS OF GERMAN FASCISM!'

Transatlantic networks and the rise of anti-Nazism in the USA, 1933–1935

Kasper Braskén

Anti-fascism became one of the main causes of the American left-liberal milieu during the mid-1930s.[1] However, when looking back at the early 1930s, it seems unclear as to how this general awareness initially came about, and what kind of transatlantic exchanges of information and experiences formed the basis of a rising anti-fascist consensus in the US. Research has tended to focus on the latter half of the 1930s, which is mainly concerned with the Communist International's (Comintern) so-called popular front period. Major themes have included anti-fascist responses to the Italian invasion of Ethiopia in 1935, the strongly felt solidarity with the Spanish Republic during the Spanish Civil War (1936–1939), or the slow turn from an 'anti-interventionist' to an 'interventionist/internationalist' position during the Second World War.[2]

The aim of this chapter is to investigate two communist-led, international organisations that enabled the creation of new transatlantic, anti-fascist solidarity networks only months after Hitler's rise to power in January 1933. They were called the World Committee against War and Fascism and the World Relief Committee for the Victims of German Fascism. Both organisations were established in Paris in 1933 and they quickly formed separate US sections known as the American League against War and Fascism (American League, or ALAWF) and the National Committee to Aid the Victims of German Fascism (National Committee) respectively. During the 1930s the American League would become the largest anti-fascist organisation in the US. However, besides Nigel Copsey's and Christopher Vials's most recent studies on the subject, the American League has remained largely under-researched. Meanwhile, the National Committee has been almost completely overlooked in previous research, although I will argue here that it played a profound role in the shaping of transatlantic and US anti-fascism.[3] Rather than offering a general history of these two anti-fascist organisations, I will focus on the connections between American anti-fascists and German, British and French anti-fascists established though these organisations from 1933 to 1935. This will provide new insights to the ways anti-fascist ideas and practices were circulated, but it also reveals how frictions between these transnational efforts and the Communist Party of the USA (CPUSA) became a veritable obstacle for the formation of a broader anti-fascist consensus in the US. The chapter is based on archival research in the Comintern archives in Moscow and supplemented by new findings from the German Federal Archives, the German Foreign Ministry Archives, the Akademie der Künste in Berlin, the Tamiment Library in New York, and the Swarthmore College Peace Collection in Pennsylvania.[4]

Although the fight against international fascism was the main concern of these organisations, it is important to remember that they were created in the concluding phase of the Comintern's sectarian class-against-class line. This line had been established in 1928/1929 and declared unequivocally that social democracy was the main enemy of the communist movement. The Comintern's slow turn to the anti-fascist popular front period commenced in late 1934 but did not become its official line until August 1935. In practice, the period under investigation contained a number of internal contradictions and tensions as, on the one hand, the CPUSA continued pushing uncompromising, sectarian politics and enhanced their attacks against social democracy. On the other, the newly established communist-led global networks of anti-war and anti-fascist committees advocated the creation of broader united front initiatives and solidarity campaigns. While the former indulged only in united fronts 'from below' with workers of various left-liberal orientation, the latter welcomed co-operation with socialist politicians and intellectuals years before the Comintern's official turn to Popular front politics.[5] The chapter can be seen as a contribution to a growing field of research on transatlantic anti-fascism, but it clearly differs from the recent work of Michael Seidman whose study is focused on the years between 1936 and 1945 and as a result completely overlooks the role of such international anti-fascist organisations in the formation of transatlantic anti-fascism on the civil society level.[6]

Although anti-fascism had already become a major concern during the 1920s among Italian radical migrants in the US (see e.g. Chapter 1, this volume),[7] transatlantic anti-fascist connections significantly intensified as a consequence of the rise of Nazi Germany. They were also significantly diversified as German, British, French and American anti-fascist activists took an increasingly important role on the global stage. Moreover, the establishment of the Third Reich resulted in an unprecedented cultural and political exile from Germany and led to a dramatic restructuring of the transnational anti-fascist movement in Europe and the Americas. Hitler had used the democratic system to undermine democracy itself, but it was with the burning of the Reichstag (the German parliamentary building) on 27 February 1933 that a pretext to unleash an unprecedented wave of terror and repression against the communist and socialist movements in Germany was provided. It is vital to keep in mind that the Nazi seizure of power did not result in a moment of united broad resistance in Germany, but delivered instead a cataclysmic defeat to Europe's most powerful Marxist parties and trade unions. If the possibilities for resistance inside Nazi Germany seemed hopeless, the global popular struggle against Nazi Germany, connected to the fight against every form of fascism, offered much more promise.

Here, the role of German communists, socialists, scientists, and cultural figures, many of whom were Jewish, was pivotal in re-establishing and reconfiguring of the transnational anti-fascist movement, and for the global spread of anti-fascism. Like many Italians before them, the German exiles did not start their exile politically or ideologically unprepared. Several of the key activists had concerned themselves with the threat of fascism for years, if not for a whole decade.[8] In the process in March 1933 Paris was transformed into the anti-fascist capital of Europe and the world.[9] One of the key anti-fascist hubs was formed around the so called 'Münzenberg network', which since 1921 had been supported by a large number of intellectuals, socialists and liberals. From Paris it organised some of the most prominent global anti-fascist solidarity campaigns of the 1930s. The German communist Willi Münzenberg was then the leader of the International Workers' Relief organisation (IWR), which was one of the Comintern's most successful international organisations that sought broader unity beyond party divisions. Münzenberg was seen by many as Joseph Goebbel's primary rival in the propaganda war between the Nazis and the political left. Since 1921, from its headquarters in Berlin, the IWR had organised popular international solidarity campaigns for the Soviet Union, and it had mobilised relief to working class victims of major calamities, class conflicts and strikes all around the world. Through its efforts, it had become connected to a global community of left-liberal activists and provided a transnational network and organisational structure to civil society actors who otherwise might not have connected across borders and continents, including the USA, where its headquarters were located in New York City.[10] Thanks especially to the IWR, but also to the International Red Aid (in the US known as the International Labor Defense), many critical connections to intellectuals, artists and sympathisers predated 1933, which in a significant way made the transnational and transatlantic anti-fascist mobilisation much faster and effective.

After 1933, the anti-fascist gateway to America went through New York City. A metropolis made of immigrants, many of whom were now directly affected by and connected to the political events in Europe. As Tyler Anbinder notes in his epic history of immigrant New York, the rise of Mussolini, and Hitler above all, divided New York immigrants. Anbinder argues that Italian and German Americans tended to 'take national pride in the prosperity and respect' that their new fascist leaders had given to their countries.[11] However, the German-Americans or the Italian-Americans were by no means the only groups affected by the fascist menace as Jewish, Austrian, African-American, and later, with the onset of the Spanish Civil War, Spanish communities were directly affected too.

Many on the political left in the US, irrespective of nationality/ethnicity, were nevertheless deeply engaged in opposing every form of fascism. Anti-fascism was also directly related to threats posed by home-grown Nazis and far right groupings. As Cathy Bergin's chapter shows in this volume, it became easy to compare Nazi racism with US racial laws, Jim Crow and the KKK.[12] In Paris and London, such interpretations of 'American fascism' were also repeatedly circulated in the left-wing press. These transatlantic circulations show how German fascism was not only used as a frame for understanding fascism in the USA, but how the unique examples of American fascism helped the anti-fascist movement analyse international fascism and its relation to racism and white supremacy.[13] Besides American far-right movements, openly Nazi organisations were also established in the US. Among the most notorious groups were the Friends of the New Germany (*Bund der Freunde des Neuen Deutschlands*). Originally founded in mid-1933, this was reorganised under Fritz Kuhn's leadership into the German American Bund (*Amerikanische Volksbund*, generally referred to as 'the Bund') in March 1936. US anti-fascism was thus never only about European prospects, but closely connected to an understanding of fascism as an international phenomenon, integrally bound to capitalist society, and crucially present in American society and politics on the national and local level.[14] In the following, I will analyse some of these key issues and campaigns that principally concerned protests against Nazi terror and the mobilisation of aid and solidarity to anti-fascist political prisoners in Germany.

Solidarity for the victims of German fascism

The first transnational anti-fascist organisation created as a response to Hitler's rise to power was the World Relief Committee for the Victims of German Fascism (World Relief Committee). This was a direct initiative of the 'Münzenberg Network' and was launched in Paris in early April 1933. It had two main missions. Firstly, it sought to mobilise help and helpers for the fight against fascism. Secondly, it aimed to 'construct a dam' against the flood of lies coming out of Hitler's Germany. The aim was to keep world opinion informed and expose the truth about the brown terror in Nazi Germany. Through wide circulation of anti-fascist newspapers, journals, pamphlets and books its intention was to collect and publish facts about political murders, terror, violence and anti-Semitic actions that were denied or downplayed by the German government and its pro-Nazi newspapers. The aim was to document what was actually going on in Nazi Germany and to form alternative news outlets that could influence world opinion.[15]

Nazi officials, just as Franco's side during the Spanish Civil War, deemed all such efforts as 'atrocity propaganda', which today might perhaps best translate as a form of 'fake news'. Clearly it was not a neutral endeavour, but constituted a critical anti-fascist perspective that sought to see through Nazi propaganda and expose the brutal inner workings of the regime and the Nazi movement.[16] Despite its restrictions, it was the only international organisation created for the purpose to make the Nazis accountable for their actions. It is important to keep in mind that most countries strived to maintain good foreign relations to Germany even after 1933, or at least remain neutral, which in practice meant abstaining from 'meddling' in Germany's domestic affairs, irrespective of how horrific they were. US–German relations were, for example, diplomatically cordial at least during the first two years, while thereafter the US government increasingly isolated itself from European affairs. Hitler himself, of course, spoke during these years of 'freedom and international peace' while secretly preparing for war and conquest. This led many people to erroneously give his regime the benefit of the doubt, or to accept a wait-and-see mentality.

While the world's official governmental representatives were ambiguous or silent in their public statements on the new Germany, an increasing importance was bestowed to civil society and social movements in the democratic countries. When all German independent, critical news agencies were shut down by the regime, foreign correspondents resident in Berlin and alternative news outlets became even more important as critical and independent sources of information. Among the most critical American voices were such personalities as Edgar A. Mowrer and Dorothy Thompson who both played significant roles in reporting Nazi atrocities. They were also both expelled from Germany due to these activities.[17] The ability to access information from inside the Nazi dictatorship was increasingly difficult and relied largely on clandestine contacts, underground work, and non-governmental networks and independent news outlets willing to sacrifice good relations and publish critical reports for the world to read.

Within days, the World Relief Committee had established separate French, German, and British sections. The French section was supported by intellectuals such as Henri Barbusse, Guston Bergéry, Jean Richard Bloch and Romain Rolland.[18] The British Committee was led by Isabel Brown (Secretary of the IWR's British Section) and Dorothy Woodman (Member of the Labour Party).[19] These three sections would become the central hubs for the world wide struggle to influence public opinion against Hitler. Moreover, long before the popular front, these anti-fascist unity organisations managed to form an embryo of the forthcoming popular front as communists, social democrats and liberals participated in the campaigns and took official posts in the anti-fascist organisations. So, when the first international meeting of the World Relief Committee was held in Paris on 16 April 1933 it was chaired by the British Labour MP, Lord Marley. The honorary presidents were German Nobel Prize winner Albert Einstein and the French professor of physics Paul Langevin.[20] In the US, the so-called *National Committee* was formed through the IWR's American Section. Alfred Wagenknecht functioned as the National Secretary of both US organisations, although they at least officially functioned as separate entities. He was moreover on the National Executive Committee of the American League. Born in Germany in 1881, Wagenknecht emigrated with his parents to the USA as a young boy. Before the First World War he came to have leading positions in the Socialist Party of America and he had been one of the founding figures of the US communist movement in 1919. Wagenknecht was the central contact to both the World Relief Committee in Paris and the CPUSA leadership in New York. He remained a pivotal transnational figure in America until he resigned from both organisations in December 1934 to become the CPUSA's district organiser in St Louis instead. His departure left the

National Committee without its strongest advocate within the CPUSA leadership and thereafter the National Committee and the US section of the IWR also lost much of its significance.[21]

The historically more well-known American League was formed at the 'US Congress against War' held in New York City, 30 September–1 October 1933. Importantly for the chronology of US anti-fascism, the congress in New York was planned and realised first and foremost as a congress against the 'imperialist war danger'. Originally it had been inspired by the Amsterdam anti-war congress of 1932, which had nothing to do with anti-fascism. Following the merger of the Amsterdam anti-war movement with the European anti-fascist congress movement in August 1933, the US Congress against War eventually gave birth to the American League against War and Fascism. As it declared in its manifesto, 'the rapid rise of Fascism is closely related to the increasing war danger', and therefore it subsumed both the anti-war and anti-fascist causes.[22] However, in the process a problematic, or at least confusing, parallelism emerged within the communist camp. There seems to have been a lack of understanding especially among the CPUSA's functionaries and leadership why the National Committee was needed as a separate organisation after the formation of the American League. In an effort to clarify the matter, the CPUSA tried to advise its local leadership that while the American League was the organisation 'for struggle against war and fascism', the National Committee was concerned with 'solidarity support in aid of victims of German fascism and in the campaign for the liberation of [Ernst] Thälmann and all anti-fascist prisoners in Germany'.[23] Organisationally they were completely different animals. For example by March 1934 the National Committee had created committees in 25 American cities, but only half were 'functioning fairly well'.[24] The American League's founding congress had again been attended by 2616 delegates from 35 states, which shows its immediate organisational supremacy in the USA.[25] It moreover launched its own illustrated journal in late November 1933 titled *The Fight against War and Fascism* (generally known as *The Fight*) which provided it with a visually striking platform to distribute its program. It also formed a transatlantic platform as *The Fight* published articles by leading figures from Europe, such as John Strachey, Rajani Palme Dutt, Jennie Lee, Fenner Brockway, Henri Barbusse and Gabrielle Duchene.

A final misfortune for the National Committee was that several local CPUSA leaders had decided to 'liquidate' existing National Committees in order to 'benefit' the establishment of the American League. This was the case in Cleveland, Minneapolis, Los Angeles and Milwaukee where it was felt that there was not enough space for both organisations to operate.[26] Nonetheless, between May and November 1933 the National Committee remained the primary anti-fascist organisation in the US and based its anti-fascist mobilisation on strong transatlantic connections to Paris and London.

The National Committee in New York first stepped into the public eye through a 'Call to Action' in June 1933 where it specifically depicted the hardship and terror experienced by the German people:

> Workers and their leaders are being jailed, tortured and killed. Their families suffer extreme hardship. [...] Pogroms against the Jewish people of Germany and against other national minorities continue in full force, notwithstanding all official denial. [...] All the civil rights granted by the Weimar Constitution have been completely obliterated under the iron heel of Hitler.

The Call narrated the sorrow of the thousands of widows and orphans and families separated from their breadwinners due to the fascist terror. It told of homeless refugees and exiles scattered all over Europe. It declared: 'These victims of German Fascism, people of varying political, cultural and religious views, of various races and nationalities *are in desperate need of help*' (original emphasis). It explained that as long as the Nazis were in power, persecution and atrocities would continue. 'This is the fascist program', it declared. It 'earnestly and urgently' appealed to the American people, 'regardless of race, creed, nationality or political affiliation' to 'form a solid wall of support' for these victims. It was perceived as an opportunity for Americans to join a 'world-wide movement' for the collection of funds and relief in support of the persecuted and exiled.[27] In essence it constituted the broadest possible call to aid and strived for the mobilisation of transnational anti-fascist solidarity and practical relief to anti-fascist refugees and exiles.

Next, an Anti-Fascist Demonstration Day was proclaimed for 24 June 1933. The movement was clearly conscious of the ethnic structure of political activism in New York City and it declared how American, German, Jewish, Hungarian, Italian, Balkan, and workers of other ethnicities were going to march together under the banners of their respective organisations to Union Square. These included besides the National Committee, such organisations as the German Anti-Fascist Action Committee, the Italian United Front for Anti-Fascist Action, the Jewish Workers and Peoples Committee against Fascism and Pogroms, the Hungarian Anti-Fascist League, and the Balkan Anti-Fascist Alliance.[28] They urged all to seize the opportunity to 'strike a blow at Hitler Terror'. The lessons of the past months were clear: the Nazis had inaugurated a 'regime of bloody terror'. In a devastating tone, it was declared how 'all gains made by the German working class through many decades of struggle against the bankers and industrialists' had now been 'wiped out by the Fascist regime'. The trade unions had been sized by the Nazis and 'converted into instruments of exploitation'. Strikes had been outlawed, the workers press had been banned and all workers organisations had been raided and closed down. Hitler had promised salvation, but four months in power had seen him set in motion parades, orgies, bonfires, persecution, and 'Jew-baiting'. Moreover, the fake anti-capitalism advocated earlier by Hitler had finally been exposed: He had openly become 'the tool of the industrialists and bankers', the anti-fascists declared.[29] Although many such calls for solidarity and relief underlined the need to aid the victims of terror in Germany, there still was a stubborn belief in the German working class's ability to rise in resistance. The Nazis had overpowered the German workers, but they had not broken their fighting spirit. It was believed that the German workers were 'gaining momentum', organising, striking and, allegedly the factories and streets of Germany were 'flooded' with newspapers and leaflets issued by underground militant organisations.[30] In this way they were not aiding helpless victims, but workers who were heroically fighting for their existence.

Reminiscent to something like an anti-fascist pledge the National Committee distributed a roll call where people could declare their opposition to 'Hitler fascism and all it stands for'. An American anti-fascist in 1933 thereby declared:

> I hereby sign my name as an opponent of Hitler Fascism and all its barbarism, persecution and torture. I oppose the activities of Hitler agents in this country. I am unalterably opposed to pogroms against Jewish people and against the spread of anti-Semitism. I declare myself in favor of asylum in the United States for political refugees from Germany. I declare myself in favor of boycott of German commodities. I declare myself for the immediate release of the Reichstag fire defendants and of all Hitler prisoners, whether Unionists, Socialists, Pacifists, Christians, Jews, Free Thinkers, Communists, physicians, scientists, educators, attorneys, authors. I declare myself in favor of aiding the victims of Hitler fascism, their orphans and children.[31]

This pledge from summer 1933 included major elements that can be seen as universal to 20th century anti-fascism, including the expressions of international solidarity and the will to give practical aid to all those who are persecuted or victims of fascist terror (irrespective of religion, social background or political conviction), a strong stand against anti-Semitism, and a desire to actively boycott fascist countries. It called for the opening up of US borders to anti-fascist exiles and refugees and framed anti-fascism in strong internationalist terms as well.

Socialists, communists and the prospects of an anti-fascist united front

Although the National Committee never grew into a mass membership organisation, it did forge significant transatlantic connections, especially through organisation of speaking tours by British, French and German anti-fascists in the US. In the other direction, it brought US lawyers and intellectuals to anti-fascist conferences and rallies in Europe. The World Relief Committee's first tour organised in the US was for the Chairman of the World Relief Committee, Lord Marley, Labour MP and Deputy Speaker of the House of Lords. He had been one of the main speakers at a major anti-fascist rally organised at Kingsway Hall in London on 22 January 1934 together with John Strachey and Dorothy Woodman. Shortly afterwards, between 6 and 28 February 1934, Marley gave speeches in 13 US cities, including Detroit, Chicago, Los Angeles, San Francisco, Pittsburgh, Philadelphia, Boston and New York.[32] In New York a special welcome committee had been elected where prominent authors, activists and intellectuals such as John Dewey, Sherwood Andersson, Roger Baldwin, W. E. B. Du Bois, Elmer Rice and Ella Winter provided their support.[33] On arrival Lord Marley also had an official meeting with New York's mayor Fiorello La Guardia. After touring around the

US, Lord Marley was welcomed back in New York City at the Mecca Temple on 24 February for a last 'anti-Hitler' protest rally. The relevance of this transatlantic connection was emphasised by the National Committee as it was advertised as an opportunity to get 'first-hand information on the latest developments in Germany'.[34]

Wagenknecht explained in a confidential letter to Earl Browder, general secretary of the CPUSA, that the aim of the tour had been to 'unify and broaden the united front of organisations for activity against Hitler fascism and its agents in this country, and for the relief of Hitler victims. Secondly, the aim was to involve in our movement as many of the professional elements, the educators, intellectuals, etc., as possible.' Luncheons and banquets with Lord Marley had been organised for liberals and, according to Wagenknecht, they had been generally successful. The public meetings had apparently not all enjoyed mass attendance, although the event in San Francisco stood out as especially successful. However, it seems that its success was not dependent of the CPUSA's support. Wagenknecht noted to Browder that 'in nearly all cities where Lord Marley spoke, the Party gave very little or no cooperation'. As a whole the Lord Marley tour had been able to collect funds and opened up new areas of co-operation between communists, socialist and liberals through their common commitment to fight Hitler.[35]

Ironically, Lord Marley's tour coincided with significant conflict between the CPUSA and the Socialist Party of America. The CPUSA was still acting according to the Comintern's sectarian class-against-class line, but as noted by Fraser O. Ottanelli, it was also a significant transition period with many inherent conflicts, contradictions and ambiguities. Events unfolding in Europe crucially affected the dynamics and character of anti-fascism in the USA. This became painfully clear when the Austrian Social Democrats engaged in a short-lived and unsuccessful armed resistance against the right wing dictatorship headed by Engelbert Dolfuss on 12 February 1934. The Socialist Party of America organised a protest meeting at Madison Square Garden in New York on 16 February 1934, which was attended by 18,000 people. However, instead of joining the anti-fascist demonstration of the Socialist Party, 1,000–2,000 communists under the leadership of Robert Minor and the editor of the CPUSA's newspaper *Daily Worker*, Clarence Hathaway, disrupted the meeting.

Afterwards, in a CPUSA publication, it was explained that the socialist doormen and ushers at the entrance had targeted all communist workers and confiscated all banners and communist literature: Accordingly, the communists claimed that 'the workers coming to the meeting to demonstrate against fascism saw a fascist staring at them at the door. One need not describe their mood once they seated themselves in the hall.'[36] Things escalated rapidly and soon, according to the *New York Times*, 'chairs were flung from the balconies, and screams and shrieks of women, mingled with boos, yells and catcalls, drowned the voices of speakers at the platform'.[37] The gathering more or less ended with the Afro-Caribbean socialist Frank Crosswaith shouting in response to the communist instigated chaos at the Garden that the communists would 'remain pigs because it is the nature of Communists to be pigs'.[38] Afterwards, even the communists described the outcome as 'regrettable' for the anti-fascist united front but, on the other hand, it had allegedly divulged to all workers that the socialist leaders were indeed 'enemies of the united front', while the common socialist workers had realised the importance of a joint struggle across party lines.[39]

The sectarian attack on their fellow anti-fascists was broadly condemned by the CPUSA's sympathisers, and had direct repercussions on the anti-fascist campaign work. As a result 25 anti-fascists, including John Dos Passos, Edmund Wilson, John Chamberlain and Anita Brenner signed an open letter that condemned the action: 'This meeting ended in shameful disorder. Instead of working-class unity, factional warfare ruled.' Quoting the *Daily Worker*'s earlier remark that 'anyone who splits the ranks of the workers at this time helps the fascists', the signatories stated how they, 'with horror', observed how the communists were 'playing the part against which it itself warned'.[40] The CPUSA's actions also resulted in the resignation of J. B. Mathews, the president of the American League against War and Fascism. He was joined by six other Socialist Party members, who had been part of the League's national executive committee.[41] In its reply the League did not show any understanding as it had not been directly involved in the incident. 'For this reason the League is compelled to consider the reasons given for these resignations pure and simple desertions.' It continued by lambasting that 'a resignation from the League can be justified only on the grounds either that the League no longer adheres to its purpose of fighting against war and fascism, or that the resignee no longer adheres to the purposes of the League'. It naturally argued that it was the latter case, bitterly adding that these people had taken the first chance to abandon the fight and that they lacked 'faith in the masses of workers'.[42]

While the American League was chiefly affected by these events, the National Committee seems to have been spared from larger membership loss and could continue its solidarity work for the victims of fascism. Tellingly, Lord Marley could continue his US tour for the anti-fascist united front, and he carried on supporting the work of the World Relief Committee.

The Reichstag fire and German political prisoners

February 1934 represented, for different reasons, a watershed moment for the National Committee. Since its foundation it had been fully committed to reporting and defending the communists charged for incinerating the German parliamentary building, the Reichstag, on the night of 27/28 February 1933. It had been used by the Nazi government to stage a major crack-down of German communism. The first person arrested at the scene of the fire was the erratic and confused Marius van der Lubbe who originated from the Netherlands. The government's hunt for alleged communist culprits led to the arrest of the Bulgarian communists Georgi Dimitrov, Blagoy Popov and Vassil Tanev on 9 March 1933 in central Berlin. Soon afterwards, the leader of the KPD's parliamentary group Ernst Torgler was also arrested and charged as a co-conspirator.[43] The trial was set for the German

High Court in Leipzig, but as news about the forthcoming trial spread around the world, it was increasingly called out as an unjust political trial. In the US, International Labor Defense (ILD) had together with the American Civil Liberties Union (ACLU) been fighting prominently against class justice and for the rights of political prisoners for over a decade. Starting with the Sacco and Vanzetti case in the 1920s and the defence of the Scottsboro Boys in the early 1930s, the American left-liberal milieu had a direct understanding of what the Reichstag Trial was all about: a plot against innocent political activists put on trial to strengthen the political position, aims and needs of those in power.[44] As a counter-measure the World Relief Committee organised an International Legal Commission of Inquiry of the Reichstag Fire consisting of lawyers from Europe and the US, including Arthur Garfield Hays, one of the co-founders of the ACLU in 1920 and well-known as one of the defence lawyers for Sacco and Vanzetti. The trial in Leipzig began on 21 September 1933 and continued to captivate the world's attention until its conclusion on 23 December. It ended with the acquittal of the three Bulgarians and Torgler due to 'lack of evidence', while van der Lubbe was sentenced to death and was quickly executed. The others remained imprisoned, leaving the world's public uncertain as to what their final fate would be.[45]

The chief innovation of the Münzenberg Network in Paris had been the launch of a powerful counter-narrative that claimed that the Nazis themselves had burned the Reichstag. The World Relief Committee was responsible for the world famous publication *The Brown Book of the Reichstag Fire and Hitler Terror* (published in English translations in London and New York). Before the beginning of the trial the World Relief Committee organised a counter trial in London in mid-September 1933 where Arthur Garfield Hays functioned as the American representative. When Hays returned to New York, he published a widely circulated protest declaration to the German Federal Court of Justice on 27 November where he opposed the way the process in Leipzig was being handled. The declaration was circulated to all the American contacts of the National Committee. By 15 December the protest resolution had been signed by 250 American intellectuals. The collection of supporters continued and a list of 378 Americans demanding the liberation of Dimitrov, Torgler, Popov and Tanev was published by the World Relief Committee in Paris. These names were further accompanied by 252 French university professors who also joined the international protest movement. Such publications played a crucial role in showing that the American and European public was deeply concerned about the developments in Nazi Germany, and enhanced the establishment of a transatlantic anti-fascist community long before the Italo-Ethiopian war or the Spanish Civil War.[46] As the American League's monthly illustrated journal *The Fight* declared:

> This is a situation intolerable to workers and anti-Fascists of the world, whose great champions Dimitrov and his comrades have become. Protests must pour into German consulates as never before! These protests, wherever possible, should be borne with mass demonstrations![47]

In the end the Bulgarians were all granted citizenship in the USSR and on 27 February 1934 they were quietly put on a plane to Moscow. A cult of personality was constructed around Dimitrov, but after his release the main focus of the global anti-fascist public shifted towards the liberation of the German communist leader Ernst Thälmann who also had been arrested in March 1933.[48] While Thälmann today represents a forgotten cause, the campaign for his release formed a central element of the transatlantic anti-fascist campaign work after the Reichstag Fire campaign. Thälmann was above all constructed into a symbol of the anti-fascist struggle, where his liberation was connected to all other imprisoned anti-fascists, including communists, left-socialist, social democrats, and liberals, and functioned as a symbol of the terror and injustice in the Third Reich. Dimitrov himself was central in producing this shift. He telegrammed the National Committee in June 1934 declaring that 'this fight for Thälmann [...] is [at the] same time [a] fight to save thousands of German political prisoners. [...] this fight will determine our future struggle against Fascism'.[49]

When it came to re-thinking the logics of Comintern sectarianism, the leadership of the German CP was less than helpful. In a letter to the CC of the CPUSA sent on 20 March 1934 it thanked the American communists for their avid anti-fascist mass demonstrations and for protesting against the German 'swastika ambassador' Dr Hans Luther in Washington. The KPD leadership claimed that the American anti-fascist struggle had been well received in Europe and thus 'awakened an enthusiastic echo among the fighting German Comrades of our Party who are unafraid of death'. The American help to liberate Dimitrov, Popov and Tanev was defined as a 'very important element' in the international protest wave. Now, similar efforts for Thälmann were called for, but instead of expecting a broad campaign for his release, the KPD stated that 'we know that in all countries the Social-Fascists are sabotaging the mass struggle for the release of Thälmann. Because they hate Thälmann who has always conducted an untiring principled struggle against social-democracy. [...] The Social-Fascists of all countries will gladly consent to the murder of Thälmann [...].'[50] In a similar tone Earl Browder described at the CPUSA's party convention in the beginning of April 1934 that the Socialist Party leadership should still be understood as social fascist, and defined them as the main enemy of the communists.[51] In early 1934, instead of unity, the US anti-fascist movement seems to have been in a state of disarray and bitter rivalry.

Anti-fascist tours in the USA

Under these challenging circumstances the World Relief Committee decided to organise a new campaign tour in the USA in summer 1934. This time, a prominent trio was sent across the Atlantic, consisting of Willi Münzenberg, the German left-socialist and prominent lawyer Kurt Rosenfeld, and the Welsh born Member of Parliament Aneurin Bevan, who was of the British Labour Party's left-wing.[52] Rosenfeld, born in 1877 in Germany to a Jewish family, had acted as Prussian

Minister of Justice in the Weimar Republic. Rosenfeld had extensive experience of political trials as a defence lawyer of socialists and communists in Germany. He had also been a signatory to one of the first international anti-fascist protest letters to Mussolini that publicly demanded an end to the fascist terror in Italy in 1926.[53] Bevan, born in 1897 in a South Wales mining community, had for decades been engaged in trade union work and was also deeply involved in the 1926 British general strike and miners' lockout. In 1929 he was elected into Parliament as a Labour MP. According to his biographer, Bevan was a 'convinced Marxist but never a Communist'. Like many left-socialists Bevan was outraged by the Labour Party Executive's stance taken in the *Democracy versus Dictatorship* resolution that called for the equal condemnation of Nazism and Soviet communism as totalitarian enemies of democracy in March 1933. It was no surprise to him that a united front between the parties was ruled out, but the Labour Party Executive's stance towards all 'auxiliary or subsidiary' organisations was incomprehensible. Bevan had stood together with communists and members of the Independent Labour Party (ILP) at demonstrations and rallies, but now the Labour Executive stated that the united front was incompatible with Labour Party membership. In other words, if Bevan took part without the permission of the Labour Party's National Executive in anti-fascist rallies with communists, he could be ousted from the party. Nonetheless, he still joined the World Relief Committee's tour in the USA in summer 1934. Apparently, Bevan's wife Jenny Lee who was a MP for the ILP, and herself a member of the British Relief Committee had persuaded Bevan to finally accept the invitation to travel to the US. It had first been envisaged as a short visit to New York, but had quickly been expanded into a tour spanning across the whole of North America.[54]

Both Rosenfeld and Bevan first appeared at a public hearing of the 'American Legal Commission of Inquiry of the Brown Terror' in New York on 2 and 3 July 1934. The aim of the inquiry was to collect facts about the situation in Germany. During its first session, 38 witnesses were called to give testimony who, according to Rosenfeld, gave a devastating image of the bloody terror in Nazi Germany. Rosenfeld himself acted as witness and told about the collapsing justice system and the installation of the arbitrary 'people's courts' in Germany. Bevan also appeared at the inquiry with reference to his long background in trade union work. According to Rosenfeld, Bevan criticised the German trade unions strongly for not resisting the rise of fascism in any way. The idea behind the Legal Inquiry had been to repeat the success of the London Counter Trial and to fend of, in a formal way, Nazi allegations that the left-liberal critics had a tendency to exaggerate and overplay reports on the terror in Nazi Germany.[55]

For the CPUSA, the star of the World Relief Committee's tour was Münzenberg. A mass meeting was organised on 6 July 1934 at the Madison Square Garden that assembled 16,000 people. There the secretary of the CPUSA, Earl Browder, introduced Münzenberg as a 'member of our heroic German brother party' to the crowd. Münzenberg entered the stage and, according to a report submitted to the Comintern, one second of complete silence followed, until an 'indescribable jubilation' broke loose and thousands gave a standing ovation to Münzenberg. The crowd started singing the *Internationale,* which further emphasised the inherent internationalism of the moment. Münzenberg spoke in German as it was the only language he mastered. Although the report to the Comintern noted that it was a foreign language for most of the assembled, it seems to have been sufficient that he represented a flesh and blood representative of German communism and the European anti-fascist movement. (Despite such statements, it must be assumed that the audience included representatives of the over 230,000 Germans or 120,000 Austrians resident in New York at the time).[56] Münzenberg informed the assembled New Yorkers about the brutal 'Night of the Long Knives', also known as the Röhm Purge, of 30 June 1934, and the escalating aggressive and hostile stance of Nazi Germany. In his speech, Münzenberg argued that because German fascism was in an ever weaker position and lacked mass support, the more it had to rely on brutality and 'blood and iron'. With the rising levels of terror it was of outmost importance to save Thälmann from the hands of the brutal regime, Münzenberg explained. Such statements provided a new a sense of urgency to Thälmann's cause and to the entire anti-fascist mobilisation campaign in the USA.[57]

The rally at Madison Square Garden was concluded with the presentation of an appeal by the National Committee. It required all organisations affiliated to the World Relief Committee to send a minimum of 500 protest telegrams to Hitler. Apparently, the mass meeting in New York resulted in a new wave of campaign activity at the grass roots level in the US, including picketing of the German embassy and consulates around the country. One of the goals, as presented in the CPUSA's newspaper *Daily Worker* on 12 July 1934, was to gather in ten days an 'Ehrenrolle', a sort of honorary list of all organisations in the United States that supported Thälmann's liberation. This list was then to be handed over to Münzenberg on his departure back to Europe, so that the German CP could show to all of its members the achievements of the Americans.[58]

Together with Rosenfeld and Bevan, Münzenberg then commenced their speaking tour. The trio travelled from one mass demonstration to the next, visiting Detroit, Cleveland, Milwaukee, and Chicago, thereafter Münzenberg returned to New York for some concluding rallies. Bevan and Rosenfeld continued their tour all the way to the West Coast, visiting among others St Louis, Denver, Los Angeles, San Francisco, Portland, and Minneapolis.[59] In a typescript preserved among the Kurt Rosenfeld papers in Berlin, he offers an elaborate analysis of his tour experiences. He had then been on the road for two months. It reveals that he also had visited Montreal, Toronto, and Winnipeg in Canada. Rosenfeld was altogether very impressed by the publicity achieved during the tour. They had been interviewed by local newspapers, and 'objective' reports about the public meetings had been published. Only the Fascists (as described by Rosenfeld), and especially the newspapers closely associated to the German fascists in the US, had been hostile. Rosenfeld was convinced that the meetings had improved the general political atmosphere in the US and Canada, supported the anti-fascist movement, and had advanced the united front. Rosenfeld's detailed account provides a unique insight into the general mood at the various rallies and meetings. According to Rosenfeld, the composition of the audience reflected directly the political orientation of the local organising committees. In many places the International Labor Defense had organised the meetings, at other places individual communists or socialists. Apparently, the organisers oscillated from pure bourgeois to completely communist committees and meetings. In some cases they were even supported by anti-communist persons and committees. In one location the translator of Rosenfeld's speech had, shortly before the meeting, noted that he had made some 'improvements' to Rosenfeld's manuscript. It turned out that the translator had completely erased the section on Thälmann. The mentioning of Thälmann's name seems to have been an especially sensitive issue and, according to Rosenfeld, it was the best way to measure the political character of the audience. Despite these variations, it seems that the more typical audiences consisted of a mix of various social groups and political orientations.[60]

In Milwaukee, where a large German-American population resided, Münzenberg had been particularly warmly welcomed, and two mass meetings were organised where over 10,000 German and American workers gathered. In New York, Münzenberg was one of the main speakers at a writers' conference held on 26 July 1934, where 100 authors listened in to Münzenberg's plea to the intellectuals to form a united front together with the working class. Münzenberg's aim was to mobilise all intellectuals who still remained 'neutral' to form the strongest possible propaganda for Thälmann's liberation. Münzenberg also addressed a crowd of 500 New York doctors for the formation of an 'intellectuals' committee' in the New York Relief Committee. Moreover, he requested that a delegation of doctors would be dispatched to investigate the medical condition of imprisoned anti-fascists and especially Thälmann. A protest resolution was accepted by the assembled doctors, and an official demand for a delegation of doctors was to be handed over to the German consulate general. It was also proposed that a delegation of lawyers were to be sent to meet Thälmann and to acquaint themselves with the details of his forthcoming trial.

In the meantime, the American League was also preparing the dispatch of a 12–15-person-strong women's delegation for the Women's World Congress against War and Fascism organised 28–30 July 1934 in Paris. The plan was that the women's delegation would continue with a tour of German prisons to inspect the conditions of female anti-fascists.[61] These examples show that a central component of the transatlantic anti-fascist mobilisation was realised through an active exchange of information about the real conditions in Nazi Germany and, where possible, people were sent to inspect the state of affairs in the Third Reich. On their return to the US, they were expected to tour and give public talks about their experiences. One could indeed argue that these efforts formed a mirror image of the Soviet Friendship delegations that Münzenberg through the IWR and Olga Kameneva at the VOKS (All-Union Society for Cultural Relations with Foreign Countries) had organised since the 1920s to showcase the construction of socialism in the Soviet Union.[62] Now, on the global anti-fascist movement's initiative the same method was used in reverse to divulge the terror and hardship in the Third Reich.

On Münzenberg's last day in New York, 27 July 1934, together with the Anti-Nazi Federation of New York, the National Committee organised a mass meeting at the Bronx Coliseum. It was conceptualised as a 'Thälmann Day' and functioned as a 'mass anti-fascist rally' and a farewell banquet in honour of Münzenberg. On the cultural side, the program included a performance of 'Set Ernst Thälmann Free' (translated from the German by Anne Bromberger and Frances May) by the Workers' Music League, and a performance of the play 'Free Ernst Thälmann' by the Workers Laboratory Theatre. Greetings were presented, for example, by Euquile McKeithen and Mother Bloor, who both were delegates to the Women's International Congress Against War and Fascism, soon to convene in Paris. Earl Browder of the CPUSA and Münzenberg concluded the event with speeches.[63]

All these events emphasised how the American campaign was an integral part of a worldwide campaign, and how the American experiences, perspectives, and valuable new insights to the campaign could be used to commence the 'Generalangriff' [general attack] on all fronts against German fascism. The Thälmann campaign was therefore seen as a campaign both *producing* and *being produced* by a 'world-wide solidarity' and 'anti-fascist internationalism'. In accordance with the anti-fascist movement's global aspirations, it was stated that Münzenberg's finest accomplishment was that the Thälmann campaign in the USA had been connected to all Thälmann campaigns of the whole world. Those who before Münzenberg's tour had not been a part of this 'great movement', were finally absorbed into it, it was enthusiastically declared in a report by the World Relief Committee.[64]

During the tour Aneurin Bevan had been confronted with the fact that the National Committee had been much more influenced by the communists than the British Relief Committee. Unfortunately, no detailed account of Bevan's impressions have been found. What we do know is that when Bevan returned to Britain he attended the Labour Party Conference at Southport in October 1934. There he expressed his fury at the Labour Party's decision to blacklist the World Relief Committee as a communist front organisation, which clearly indicates Bevan's positive stance towards its anti-fascist mission. In a counter to the party leadership, he questioned their authority to restrict what organisations and committees members were permitted to associate with. Bevan concluded his speech in Southport: 'If you are going to expel a man from this Party merely because he meets [Louis] Gibarti, or [Willi] Münzenberg, or talks to Harry Pollitt [...] then this Party will get itself laughed out of court.' Unsurprisingly, the conference voted to prohibit just the kinds of anti-fascist activities that Bevan had been engaged in.[65] The Labour Party's stance against anti-fascist collaboration also limited the potential that the British Labour Party's anti-fascism could play on the global stage. In due course, such important figures as Bevan, Dorothy Woodman and Lord Marley were all forced to resign from their official positions in the aforementioned anti-fascist organisations.

The tours to the USA did not cease, however, and the World Relief Committee dispatched the German proletarian composer Hanns Eisler, who was a close associate to Bertolt Brecht, on a concert tour in the US. His travels between March and May 1935 took him from the East to the West Coast, and according to a report sent to the Comintern, he performed at 25 major and 150 smaller meetings. Many of the meetings had been attended by Germans or German-Americans, but apparently several of them had attracted an assorted crowd of anti-fascists. When Eisler arrived to New York a special 'Eisler welcome committee' had been formed of 32 famous American anti-fascist intellectuals and artists, including the composers Georg Gershwin, Aaron Copland and Louis Gruenberg, and the authors Michael Gold, Edward Dahlberg and Josephine Herbst. Gold was a Jewish American writer and communist, and at the time editor-in-chief of the New York based illustrated journal *New Masses*. Dahlberg had visited Germany in 1933 where he penned critical articles about the Third Reich for the London *Times*. In 1934 he had published the novel *Those Who Perish*, which has been described as the first American anti-Nazi novel. Josephine Herbst would later, in 1936, author an anti-fascist survey of Nazi Germany titled *Behind the Swastika* (published by the Anti-Nazi Federation in New York). Moreover, 14 proletarian cultural and fighting organisations had signed up to the Eisler welcome committee. To the Comintern it was reported that the most memorable rally was organised at the Mecca Temple on 2 March 1935 where 4,000 anti-fascists had gathered.[66] Overall the World Relief Committee assessed that the tour had constituted a 'great cultural political success'.[67] Eisler's example reveals that the anti-fascist alliance between liberals and the left was, despite continuous party sectarianism, finding ways to encourage anti-fascist unity through alternative practices and cultural encounters.

Conclusions

Despite the many calls for his liberation, Thälmann's incarceration continued for over a decade. In the end, he was moved to the Buchenwald concentration camp where in 1944 he was executed by the Nazis. Ironically, he would outlive several of the anti-fascists campaigning for his release, including Barbusse (1935), Münzenberg (1940) and Rosenfeld (1943). However, many of the anti-fascist practices developed especially by the World Relief Committee and the National Committee during these first crucial years after the Nazi seizure of power continued after the dissolution of the National Committee in 1935. Here the American League was especially important in staging energetic solidarity and protest campaigns as well as maintaining transatlantic anti-fascist networks that transferred knowledge about terror and atrocities committed in Nazi Germany, Austria, Italy, Ethiopia and Spain. Thälmann's imprisonment and fate was shared by innumerable anti-fascists in fascist prisons and concentration camps whose life stories and victimhood was powerfully brought to the attention of the global public thanks to the World Relief Committee and other anti-fascist organisations, activists and reporters.

This chapter has shown that the transatlantic anti-fascist solidarity networks managed already in summer 1933 to inspire local activism across the US which was crucial for raising awareness of the fascist danger and why it had to be opposed. Still, the time period investigated here was filled with contradictions and ambiguities. It shows the presence of serious efforts to unite people against fascism, but it also reveals how the anti-fascist agenda was severely muddled by the communists. Equally important was the omnipresence of a significant fear among non-communists that anti-fascism was merely used as a manoeuvre by the communists, that the communist-led calls for unity were disingenuous or not based on an actual will to fight fascism.

Yet documents discussed earlier, such as the 'Roll Call' published in summer 1933 by the National Committee, seem to tell a different kind of story that is clearly linked to the radical roots of the US civil rights movement. They show that there were indeed solemn attempts to form broad coalitions in the fight against fascism when devastating news about pogroms, terror and political violence started pouring out of Nazi Germany: In the face of this brutal fascist dictatorship, the protection of civil rights and the safeguarding of all victims of fascism irrespective of their 'race, creed, nationality or political affiliation' became the foremost mission of the global anti-fascist movement. In a significant way it directed the anti-fascist movement's full focus to the international threat posed by Nazism which re-defined anti-fascism as anti-Nazism in the US. Still Nazism was consistently defined as 'German fascism', not losing touch with the fact that it constituted a part of an international fascist movement, variously present in different societies across the Atlantic, but sharing the same distinct oppressive, anti-democratic nature. The transatlantic anti-fascist bond after 1933 was based on this common realisation and the shared will to offer relief to the victims to fascism in Germany and to aid all those who were willing to resist its spread globally.

Notes

1 Michael Denning, *The Cultural Front: The Laboring of the American Culture in the Twentieth Century* (London: Verso, 1996); Alan M. Wald, *Trinity of Passion: The Literary Left and the Antifascist Crusade* (Chapel Hill, NC: The University of North Carolina Press, 2007); Christopher Vials, *Haunted by Hitler. Liberals, the Left, and the Fight against Fascism in the United States* (Amherst, MA: University of Massachusetts Press, 2014), pp. 26, 32, 36.

2 See e.g. William R. Scott, *The Sons of Sheba's Race: African-Americans and the Italo-Ethiopian War, 1935–1941* (Bloomington, IN: Indiana University Press, 1993); Justus D. Doenecke & John E. Wilz, *From Isolation to War, 1931–1941* (Chichester: Wiley Blackwell, 2015); Adam Hochschild, *Spain in Our Hearts: Americans in the Spanish Civil War, 1936–1939* (Boston, MA: Houghton Mifflin Harcourt, 2017).

3 Nigel Copsey, 'Communists and the Inter-War Anti-Fascist Struggle in the United States and Britain', *Labour History Review,* Vol. 76, No. 3, 2011, pp. 191–192; Vials, *Haunted by Hitler.*

4 The chapter is based on a larger book manuscript focusing on transatlantic anti-fascism. A first draft of the chapter was presented at the ENIUGH Congress in Budapest 2017 and the Åbo Akademi History research seminar. I am grateful for all constructive comments.

5 See e.g. Fraser M. Ottanelli, *The Communist Party of the United States: From the Depression to World War II* (New Brunswick, NJ: Rutgers University Press, 1991); James Ryan, 'A Final Stab at Insurrection: The American Communist Party, 1928–1934', in Matthew Worley (ed.), *In Search of Revolution: International Communist Parties in the Third Period* (London: I. B. Tauris, 2004), pp. 203–219.

6 Micheal Seidman, *Transatlantic Antifascisms: From the Spanish Civil War to the End of World War II* (Cambridge: Cambridge University Press, 2018).
7 See e.g. John P. Diggins, 'The Italo-American Anti-Fascist Opposition', *Journal of American History,* Vol. 54, No. 3, 1967, pp. 579–598; Marcella Bencivenni, *Italian Immigrant Radical Culture: The Idealism of the Sovversivi in the United States, 1890–1940* (New York: New York University Press, 2011).
8 Kasper Braskén, 'Making Antifascism Transnational: The Origins of Communist and Socialist Articulations of Resistance in Europe, 1923–1924', *Contemporary European History,* Vol. 25, No. 4, 2016, pp. 573–596.
9 See further Anson Rabinbach, 'Paris, Capital of Anti-Fascism', in Warren Breckman et al. (eds), *The Modernist Imagination: Intellectual History and Critial Theory: Essays in Honor of Martin Jay* (New York: Berghahn Books, 2009), pp. 183–209.
10 On the global history of the IWR (in English speaking research also referred to as the WIR), see Kasper Braskén, 'In Pursuit of Global International Solidarity? The Transnational Networks of the International Workers' Relief, 1921–1935', in Holger Weiss (ed.), *International Communism and Transnational Solidarity: Radical Networks, Mass Movements and Global Politics, 1919–1939* (Leiden: Brill, 2017), pp. 130–167.
11 Tyler Anbinder, *City of Dreams: The 400-Year Epic History of Immigrant New York* (Boston, MA: Houghton Mifflin Harcourt, 2016), p. 493.
12 See for example Glenda Elizabeth Gilmore, *Defying Dixie: The Radical Roots of Civil Rights, 1919–1950* (New York: W. W. Norton & Company, 2008); Susan D. Pennybacker, *From Scottsboro to Munich: Race and Political Culture in 1930s Britain* (Princeton, NJ: Princeton University Press, 2009).
13 See Kasper Braskén, 'Whether Black or White, United in the Fight: Connecting the Resistance against Colonialism, Racism, and Fascism in the European Metropoles, 1926–1936', *Twentieth Century Communism,* No 18, 2020, pp. 126–149.
14 See e.g. Daniel Geary, 'Carey McWilliams and Antifascism, 1934–1943', *Journal of American History,* Vol. 90, No. 3, 2003, pp. 912–934. On the development of US fascism and Nazi organisations in the US, see e.g. Bradley W. Hart, *Hitler's American Friends: The Third Reich's Supporters in the United States* (New York: Thomas Dunne Books/St Martin's Press, 2018).
15 Deutsches Hilfs-Komitee gegen faschistischer Terror; March 1933 [Amsterdam], Russian State Archive of Socio-Political History (RGASPI) 495/30/939, 1; Gemeinsamer Kampf – Gemeinsamer Hilfe, *Mitteilungsblätter des Hilfskomitees für die Opfer des deutschen Faschismus*, Nr. 1, 15 April 1933 (Basel).
16 See discussion on atrocity propaganda in Hugo García, *The Truth about Spain! Mobilizing British Public Opinion, 1936–1939* (Brighton: Sussex Academic Press, 2010).
17 Michaela Hoenicke Moore, *Know Your Enemy: The American Debate on Nazism, 1933–1945* (Cambridge: Cambridge University Press, 2010), pp. 41–101; Klaus P. Fischer, *Hitler and America* (Philadelphia, PA: University of Pennsylvania Press, 2011), pp. 46–49.
18 Report by Fritz Globig; Moscow, 8 April 1933, RGASPI 495/30/937, 1–2.
19 IAH report, Paris, 1 April 1933, RGASPI 495/30/937, 3.
20 Committee report '500.000 Francs Hilfe – Neue Aufgaben', RGASPI 495/30/937, 20.
21 A short biography of Wagenknecht from 1936 is preserved in RGASPI 515/1/4033, 19–20.
22 'Manifesto and Program of the US Congress against War', published by the American League against War and Fascism, New York, 1933.
23 Alfred Wagenknecht to Barth, 15 August 1934, RGASPI 515/1/3696, 33.
24 Wagenknecht to Earl Browder; 20 April 1934, RGASPI 515/1/3696, 9–10.
25 Call to the Second US Congress against War and Fascism, RGASPI 515/1/3700, 17.
26 Wagenknecht to Brown, 19 November 1934, RGASPI 515/1/3700, 72.
27 Call to Action: To the Aid of the German People. National Committee to Aid Victims of German Fascism, 1933, RGASPI 538/2/98, 117.
28 All Out – Union Sq., New York, 24 June 1933, RGASPI 538/2/98, 120.
29 Strike a blow at Hitler Terror, June 1933, RGASPI 538/2/98, 120 (backside).

30 All Out – Union Sq., New York, 24 June 1933, RGASPI 538/2/98, 120.
31 Vote against Hitler Fascism; National Committee, 1933; RGASPI 538/2/92, 62.
32 *Menschen in Not. Bulletin zum Winterhilfswerk*, No. 1 [1934].
33 'Riesenkundgebung in den Vereinigten Staaten gegen Hitler erheben die Forderung auf Freilassung von Dimitroff und Thälmann', *Menschen in Not: Informationsdienst über den Terror in Hitlerdeutschland für die Presse, Organisationen und alle Hilfskomitees für die Opfer des Hitler-Faschismus*, No. 3, 1934.
34 Wagenknecht to Louis Gibarti, New York, 20 February 1934, RGASPI 495/30/1059, 27–29; 'Anti-Hitler Protest Rally: Lord Marley', RGASPI 538/2/98, 121.
35 Wagenknecht to Earl Browder; 15.3.1934, RGASPI 515/1/3696, 3–4.
36 Sam Peazner, 'Austria and Madison Square Garden', *The New Order*, No. 2, March 1934, pp. 4, 9. The number of people in the audience is according to the ACLU investigation published shortly afterwards. See *ACLU Report of Commission of Inquiry to the Board of Directors on Madison Square Garden Mass Meeting, February 16, 1934 (March 1934)*, reprinted in Bernard K. Johnpoll (ed.), *A Documentary History of the Communist Party of the United States*, Vol. III (Westport: Greenwood Press, 1994), pp. 5–20.
37 Quote from *Times* is reprinted in Ottanelli, *The Communist Party of the United States*, p. 56.
38 Jack Ross, *The Socialist Party of America: A Complete History* (Nebraska: Potomac Books, 2015), pp. 338–339.
39 Peazner, 'Austria and Madison Square Garden'.
40 An open letter to the Communist Party, February 1934, RGASPI 515/1/3700, 1.
41 Ottanelli, *The Communist Party of the United States*, p. 56.
42 Comment on resignations from the ALAWF due to events on 16 February 1934 in Madison Square Garden, New York, RGASPI 515/1/3700, 46–47.
43 Marietta Stankova, *Georgi Dimitrov: A Biography* (London: I. B. Tauris, 2010), pp. 103–114.
44 See e.g. James A. Miller, Susan D. Pennybacker & Eve Rosenhaft, 'Mother Ada Wright and the International Campaign to Free the Scottsboro Boys, 1931–1934', *American Historical Review*, Vol. 106, No. 2, 2001, pp. 387–430; Mary Anne Trasciatti, 'Elizabeth Gurley Flynn, the Sacco–Vanzetti Case, and the Rise and Fall of the Liberal–Radical Alliance, 1920–1940', *American Communist History*, Vol. 15, No. 2, 2016, pp. 191–216.
45 See further in Benjamin Carter Hett, *Burning the Reichstag: An Investigation into the Third Reich's Enduring Mystery* (Oxford: Oxford University Press, 2016).
46 'Massenprotest der Intellektuellen in USA gegen Leipziger Prozess', *Alarm: Bulletin des Welthilfskomitees für die Opfer des Hitlerfaschismus* (London-Paris), No. 10, 26 December 1933; 'Weitere 128 amerikanische Intellektuelle protestieren!', *Alarm*, No. 13, 30 December 1933; 'Ein antifaschistisches Dokument', *Unsere Zeit*, No. 1, 20 January 1934.
47 David Zablodowsky, 'Dimitrov – Workers' Hero', *The Fight* (February 1934).
48 The outlines of the campaign are described in Anson Rabinbach, 'Freedom for Thälmann! The Comintern and the Orchestration of the Campaign to Free Ernst Thälmann, 1933–1939', in Hugo García, et al. (eds), *Rethinking Antifascism: History, Memory and Politics, 1922 to the Present* (New York: Berghahn Books, 2016), pp. 23–42. See also Kevin Morgan, *International Communism and the Cult of the Individual: Leaders, Tribunes and Martyrs under Lenin and Stalin* (London: Palgrave Macmillan, 2017), pp. 185–203.
49 Telegram from Dimitrov to 'New York National Committee Defence Political Prisoners', 6 June 1934, SAPMO–BArch, SgY 15/V 243/30, 28.
50 Letter from the CC of the KPD to the CC of the CPUSA; 20 March 1934, SAPMO–BArch, RY 1/I 2/3/224, 40–41.
51 Ottanelli, *The Communist Party of the United States*, p. 57.
52 On the Thälmann campaign in the USA, see: Bericht des Welthilfskomitees für die Opfer des Hitlerfaschismus, RGASPI 495/30/1058, 26–48.
53 'Gli intellettuali di Europa contro il regime di terrore del fascismo in Italia' [1926], RGASPI 513/1/541a, 3.
54 Michael Foot, *Aneurin Bevan: A Biography. Volume One: 1897–1945* (London: Macgibbon & Kee, 1962), pp. 147, 168–172. The Labour Party's stance was clearly put forward

in the pamphlet: *The Communist Solar System: The Communist International* (London: The Labour Party, Labour Publications Dept., 1933).
55 Akademie der Künste, Kurt Rosenfeld Archiv, Folder 3, 1–6.
56 Population numbers from Anbinder, *City of Dreams*, pp. 572–573.
57 Bericht des Welthilfskomitees, RGASPI 495/30/1058, 43.
58 Ibid., 43–44.
59 Ibid., 44–45.
60 Akademie der Künste, Kurt Rosenfeld Archiv, Folder 6, 1–9.
61 American League against War and Fascism, 14 April 1934, RGASPI 515/1/3700, 5; Bericht des Welthilfskomitees, RGASPI 495/30/1058, 44–46.
62 See Micheal David-Fox, *Showcasing the Great Experiment: Cultural Diplomacy and Western Visitors to the Soviet Union, 1921–1941* (Oxford: Oxford University Press, 2012).
63 Thälmann Day, Bronx Coliseum, 27 July 1934, RGASPI 538/2/98, 114.
64 Bericht des Welthilfskomitees, RGASPI 495/30/1058, 43, 46.
65 Foot, *Aneurin Bevan*, pp. 172–176.
66 Bericht über den Organisationsstand und die Aktionen des Welthilfskomités für die Opfer des Hitlerfaschismus im Verlauf des letzten halben Jahres, 27 May 1935, RGASPI 495/30/1058, 15–25, here 21.
67 'Millionen singer seine Lider – Millionen verstehen ihn'; Paris, 25 March 1935, RGASPI 495/30/1059, 6.

Acknowledgement

The research for this chapter was completed within the framework of Kasper Braskén's Academy of Finland research project 'Towards a Global History of Anti-Fascism: Transnational Civil Society Activism, International Organisations and Identity Politics Beyond Borders, 1922–1945'.

11

ADDIS ABABA, RIO DE JANEIRO AND MOSCOW 1935

The double failure of Comintern anti-fascism and anti-colonialism

Bernhard H. Bayerlein

This chapter originates from a sequence of simultaneous yet contradictory events that took place in Africa and Latin America. When Benito Mussolini's imperial war against Ethiopia began in October 1935, the Soviet Union 'unofficially' backed it. As a result, the transnational anti-fascist movement was only ever half-heartedly mobilised in defence of Abyssinia. However, just one month later, the Comintern supported a military uprising against the government of Getúlio Vargas in Brazil backed by a so-called 'anti-imperialist popular front'. This uprising failed in a pitiful way. Both the 'Hands off Abyssinia' campaign and the uprising of the *Aliança Libertadora Nacional* (ALN) in Brazil seemingly reveal a contradictory entanglement. Significantly, this entanglement demonstrates the profound ambiguities of international communist anti-fascism and anti-colonialism.

This chapter uses the Ethiopian and Brazilian cases to reveal the nature of global communist anti-fascism in the 1930s, approaching this history mainly from a 'top down' perspective. This history can only be reconstructed meaningfully if one takes into account the multifaceted interplay of different forces and actors. My methodological approach is based on the understanding that this interplay was governed by a triangular relationship. Firstly, it consisted of the national or regional communist parties (with their different local and regional networks and substructures) and the widespread minority movements that had their diverse communication channels to Moscow. Secondly, we have the Communist International (Comintern) that functioned as an intermediary organisation. Thirdly, there was the Soviet Union as a state structure with its ruling communist party and its ever-changing foreign and domestic politics, supported by its powerful secret intelligence services. Since the opening of the Soviet archives almost 30 years ago, it has become possible to apply this model of 'entangled' history.

Global communist anti-fascism had an ambivalent character. Contrary to the official propaganda that focused on creating a global anti-fascist mythology, this chapter shows that for the leadership of international communism in the Stalin period, anti-fascism was either secondary or subordinate, and mostly used in a technical-instrumental way. What is more, Ethiopia stands not only for the (more or less open) renunciation of anti-fascism, but also for the abandonment of the anti-colonial and anti-imperialist tradition of the Soviet Union invoked in Lenin's time and largely implemented after the October Revolution.

On the other hand, especially since the German defeat of 1933, the transnational anti-fascist movement and social movements in, for example, France, Spain, and Chile responded with anti-fascist politics that only partially generated a response from the Comintern. There was a basic contradiction between the willingness to act on the grassroots level by the anti-fascist movement, and the heavily bureaucratised leadership of the Comintern and most of the communist parties. The anti-fascist movement continued to advocate for strikes and blockades to defend national liberation but encountered bureaucratic obstacles erected by the Comintern or the Red International of Labour Unions (RILU/Profintern). During the whole Third Period of the Comintern from 1928/29 to 1934/35, Left Socialism, Trotskyism, international trade unions like the International Federation of Transport Workers (ITF), and anarcho-syndicalism represented the avant-garde of anti-fascism, all of them fiercely contested by communists. Moreover, the Comintern's international anti-fascist campaigns were subordinated to international anti-war issues. As a consequence, inter-organisational fractures, hybridisation and bifurcation became evident. Despite the overwhelming transnational anti-fascist impulse of 1933, the USSR and the Comintern tried until the end of 1934 to undermine this unitarian anti-fascist reflex and rejected any unity and common activity with the 'social-fascists' or the 'anarcho-fascists' against fascism (with some exceptions mostly carried out by Willi Münzenberg and his circle in Paris).[1]

At the beginning of the period of the 'anti-fascist Popular Front' – the starting point was the Comintern intervention in France and in Spain – global anti-fascism was at first a flexible response to the growing anti-fascist movement on the left, the international trade unions, and the liberal intelligentsia. In this first period, anti-fascism's hidden character as a technical instrument of the Stalinist regime was not so easily recognisable. In particular, Willi Münzenberg through non-party organisations and committees, such as the World Committee Against War and Fascism, the *Brown Book* of the Reichstag fire or the international campaign against the Reichtsag fire trial, painted over it in a virtuoso manner. Even so, Münzenberg's anti-fascist convictions were beyond doubt. In letters to Stalin he sharply criticised the passivity of the Comintern apparatus and the manipulation of anti-fascism by the KPD (German Communist Party). Like many other party members, Münzenberg probably did not yet know that he had turned to the wrong addressee and that Stalin was, at the same time, secretly pursuing rapprochement with Nazi Germany at the expense of the Comintern. Consequently, most of Münzenberg's global anti-fascist ventures and movements were disbanded in 1936/1937 due to directives from Stalin and Georgi Dimitrov who then acted as General Secretary of the Comintern.

It has to be remembered that global anti-fascism in the interwar period under Stalin was never an official political orientation of the Soviet Union. As revealed by Russian historians after the opening of the archives, a bifurcation of global anti-fascisms emerged between Soviet and Comintern politics.[2] A twin-track system was created. This lasted until 1939 when the pact between Stalin and Nazi Germany removed the last remnants of Comintern anti-fascism.

With regards to anti-colonialism and anti-imperialism, the new *Cambridge History of Communism* argues that Stalin and the Soviet Union continued to pursue revolutionary goals for the global South in the interwar period. This is highly misleading.[3] The recently deceased neo-Stalinist historian, philosopher and Gramsci specialist Domenico Losurdo also argues that there was an uninterrupted continuity between the anti-colonial and anti-imperialist revolutionary mission of the Soviet Union during the Stalin period.[4] Fortunately, more recent transnationally oriented studies, for example on South Asia or the Atlantic region,[5] have revisited these research questions and provide further empirical substance to the earlier work of pioneers of communism research, such as Isaac Deutscher, Moshe Lewine, Pierre Broué and Hermann Weber. Newer contributions and portrayals of central anti-colonial actors from Africa and India such as Georg Padmore, M. N. Roy, Virendranath Chattopadhyaya, or C.L.R. James further illuminate processes and caesuras of the 'internationalist moment' of the 1920s and 1930s. In reality, Stalinism became increasingly detached from the anti-imperialism of the original Bolshevism. The retreat from world revolutionary concepts was comprehensive and overlapping.

Logics of a turn

In the Brazilian and Ethiopian case, key strategic and global concerns of the transnational communist movement - anti-fascism, anti-imperialism and national self-determination - were at stake. Intrinsically linked to the fundamental question of internationalism ('Is ONE world possible?') was the concept of the national self-determination of peoples as a civilising mission. It runs like a 'red thread' throughout the history of the workers' internationals. Its significance was derived from the idea that the class question always occurred in combination with the national question or national liberation, and that this applied especially to the Global South. As a class, the workers and peasants were both objects of exploitation and members of a nation oppressed by wars, economic exploitation and/or political repression.

Conceptually, this chapter assumes a striking caesura – a moment of discontinuity – between Lenin's nationality policy in the multi-ethnic state and subsequent Sovietisation. Internal colonial structures of the Russian Empire were partially broken after the October Revolution, but, promoted by the militarisation and bureaucratisation of war communism, it was not possible to achieve the original goals of Lenin's nationality policy. This original policy gave way to the restitution of the empire under Stalinism. 'The concept of a united multinational Soviet people (remained) pure fiction'.[6]

After the epoch of European 'primary nationalism', the 'liberation nationalism' of the twentieth century was supposed to bring the fulfilment of modernity to the national and ethnic minorities in the European empires. However, from the second half of the 1920s, a retrograde development occurred and in this context the Comintern's strategic shift took place. The so-called 'Third Period' – the 'defence of the Soviet Union by all means', and 'social-fascism', – constituted the official line from 1928–1929 to the end of 1934. This period saw the climax of the Stalinisation process, which impacted on a global scale, particularly so for the Latin American communist parties.

The universal demand for national self-determination had belonged to the guiding principles of the Russian revolutionary social democrats who constituted themselves as Bolsheviks in 1903. Shortly after the October Revolution, a fundamental break took place in the implementation of the nationality question. This occurred as early as 1921, when the Red Army occupied independent Georgia. Soviet Russia itself appeared then as an imperial power, and the social-democratic government of the Democratic Republic of Georgia, formed as a result of the Russian February Revolution, was removed. This was implemented by the nationality commissar Stalin, and his helpers, whom Lenin fought unsuccessfully against. A second, and more fundamental break took place in 1925/1926 with the 'tragedy of the Chinese Revolution', when the VKP(b) and the Comintern, under the decisive influence of Stalin and Bukharin, forced the Chinese workers and communists into a coalition with the national bourgeoisie in the Kuomintang. As a result, the Chinese communists were massacred in their thousands.[7] What followed was the collapse of the open attitude towards the smaller peoples and nations. An 'affirmative action empire', as originally conceptualised by Lenin, was now replaced with a model encompassing the superiority of the Soviet workers over the workers of the other national republics and nations, and by the superiority of the Soviet communist party over the other communist parties.[8]

Despite the subsequent 'Asian turn' of the Comintern (to China, Indonesia and India), and increased attention to the global South as a whole, the 'restraint on possible revolutions in the colonies and developing countries' was obvious.[9] Historiography has paid little attention to the fact that a major transformation had already taken place in 1925 at a time when transnational anti-colonial movements were approaching a climax. As anti-imperialist moments, the Rifkabyls' uprising under Abd el-Krim in Morocco, the 30 May movement in China and the great Syrian uprising, were insufficiently embraced by the Comintern. One explanation is provided by the 'new colonial position' introduced at about the same time, which turned out to be an elastic formula, if not a national-populist doctrine, that shifted the focus in the global South from the workers to the peasants and prioritised peasant revolutions.[10]

The 'tragedy of the Chinese revolution', as reported by Harold R. Isaacs in the years 1926–1927, demonstrated the failures of the Comintern, which also included the Indonesian uprisings in Java and Bali in 1926.[11] Another indication was the withdrawal from the revolutionary incursions of Sandino in the Caribbean and – in structural terms – the lack of representation of the (semi-)colonial countries in the governing organs of the Comintern. The radical language and the militant habitus of the communist parties concealed the fact that, even under the 'Third Period', revolutionary approaches in a polycentric sense diminished – not only in the centre but also in the global South. This also pointed to the new alliances required with factions of the national bourgeoisie in the (semi) colonial countries.

During the first half of the 1930s, international anti-fascist activities were subordinate to international anti-war campaigns like those of the *International of Seamen and Harbour Workers* (ISH) and the *International Trade Union Committee of Negro Workers* (ITUCNW) that protested against Japanese imperialism in Manchuria and Italian imperialism in Ethiopia. These 'Hands off China' and 'Hands off Abyssinia' campaigns were mainly organised by the Red International of Labour Unions and affiliated organisations. Nevertheless, as Holger Weiss rightly states, the calls for international solidarity were constantly accompanied by a hostility towards competing socialist, social democratic or syndicalist organisations.[12] In a more obvious way than the Manchurian crisis (starting with the Mukden incident in 1931 and concluding with the Japanese occupation of Manchuria), the Ethiopian crisis 'marked a break in political mobilisation' of the communist movement 'especially in the African Atlantic'.[13]

The main event for the communist movement and world history was undoubtedly the German catastrophe of 1933. It was a tragedy for the Communist Party of Germany and it shook up the whole Comintern system. When the world's strongest working-class movement was hopelessly defeated by Hitler – without a major fight – it represented a political and cultural trauma. It reflected the crisis of both the Stalin regime and Communist anti-fascism which had been oriented towards the fight against 'social fascism' (that is social democracy, and not fascism or Nazism).

The events in Brazil and Ethiopia fell into the incipient period of the so called 'Popular Fronts'. By this time, anti-fascism was the new doctrine (albeit a kind of anti-fascism always linked to the more general theme of anti-war propaganda). This started in 1935 and lasted until 1938/39. During this period, Stalin told his inner circle that he believed that Hitler would eventually come back to the table and seek an alliance with the Soviet Union. In the meantime, he initiated a tactical shift towards the Western democracies. Therefore, all kinds of socialist transformations or revolutions abroad, especially in the core countries, were no longer deemed effective. It was not by historical coincidence that the moment of the 'Frente Popular' arrived alongside state terror in the USSR and the re-nationalisation and even de-internationalisation of party communism.

The Abyssinian tragedy

In order to advance to the question of how these seemingly conflicting campaigns (Brazil and Ethiopia) are related to one another, I will consider the African case first. The Abyssinian war began with the Italian declaration of war on 2 October

1935, followed by the neo-imperial colonial attack the next day. It led to the annexation of Ethiopia, the last independent African state (with Liberia), on 9 May 1936. This devastating outcome was not only enabled by the hegemonic pressure of the fascist regimes but also by the predominant appeasement policy of the Western powers and the League of Nations, and also by the supposedly neutral attitude of the Soviet Union that resulted in a gentle treatment of Mussolini. His coup represented the 'highest game a statesman has ventured since World War I', according to the German ambassador in Rome, Ulrich von Hassel.[14] Significantly, it also resulted in the premature termination of the Soviet Union's anti-colonial and anti-imperialist tradition.

The Soviet Union had now largely resigned itself to fascism, the 'plebeian form of counterrevolution'.[15] Officially, the USSR's position in the conflict was neutrality, which was underpinned by the ritually repeated 'desire for peace'. This was further demonstrated by the founding of the Rassemblement Universel pour la Paix (RUP) on 25 September 1935 with the support of Willi Münzenberg. Officially this initiative was launched by the Soviet Federation of Trade Unions as a reaction to the Ethiopian war.[16] However, inter-organisational contradictions soon became evident between the transnational anti-fascist grassroots movements and the bureaucratic obstacles set from above, from the leadership of the Comintern to the leadership of the RILU. So while the ISH advocated an active boycott of Italian ships, the Comintern and the USSR opposed it. The Hands off Abyssinia campaign in the spring of 1935 did not even get off the ground before it was terminated.[17]

In fact, the internal documents of the highest political Soviet body speak a clear language. These files reveal the Russian Politburo's secret motives. One day after the Italian attack, this body passed secret instructions to the representative of the USSR in the League of Nations, Vladimir Potemkin, which amounted to protection of the aggressor. Litvinov, the People's Commissar for Foreign Affairs (but not a member of the Politburo), was even threatened by Stalin because he advocated some kind of protest and even boycott of Italy. Only if the assembly of the League of Nations enforced a resolution against Italy's aggression would the Soviet Union's representative support such a course of action. In the wording of the Politburo, a sharp condemnation of Italy should be avoided.[18]

Significantly, on 11 December 1935, the Politburo rejected a request by Ethiopia regarding the provision of weapons and instructors, allegedly because the USSR did not have enough of them itself.[19] Like the League of Nations as a whole, the Soviet Council of People's Commissars actually supported some import and export sanctions and financial restrictions against Italy. At the same time, a directive to Litvinov on 15 October 1935 stated that 'with regard to the sanctions against Italy' no 'greater zeal should be developed than other states'.[20] On 14 December 1935, the so-called Laval-Hoare Plan for the division of Ethiopia (which contained advances to Italy) was rejected by the League of Nations with reference to the protection of territorial integrity. The Soviet Politburo, however, stated that in case Ethiopia itself agreed, the plan was acceptable.[21]

At the beginning of 1936, the Politburo records indicate that the Soviets believed that the destruction of the Ethiopian state had become an irrefutable fact. Stalin damned Litvinov for arguing that he should not defend 'the mandates [...] of the factually non-existent Abyssinian state'.[22] Again, if the League of Nations decided to impose sanctions against Italy, the USSR should be ready to join these measures.[23] Nevertheless, the Soviet Union left a back door open and in March 1936, it did give the green light to receive a messenger from Emperor Haile Selassie.[24]

This was the context for the Comintern and the Communist Parties' 'Hands off Abyssinia' campaign. The effectiveness of the campaign must therefore be questioned. As a matter of fact, the Soviet Union covered about 40 per cent of the Italian demand for petroleum during this period.[25] On the question of a boycott, the Soviet Union was not to take any initiative on oil sanctions against Italy. Mussolini later stated that the Italian troops would have lasted only eight days if a boycott decision had been made by the League of Nations, which would have led to an Italian withdrawal from Ethiopia. Two months later, on 10 July 1936 when Abyssinia had been annexed into Italian East Africa, the Soviet Politburo decided that the Council of People's Commissars should issue a press statement. It declared that all sanctions on Italy and Italian imports should be lifted.[26]

The thesis that Soviet policy towards Italy was governed by the need to stop Hitler's Germany from expanding is not convincing either. For Stalin also pursued an appeasement policy towards Hitler. In Stalin's view, Germany should be a central component in an overarching East–West alliance of European States. This necessitated rapprochement with Hitler and may explain that, for the first time, the dualism of Communist-Stalinist politics now became vividly clear: anti-fascism functioned as a doctrine for the Comintern but not for the Soviet Union.[27] The problem for the international communist movement was that this went against the transnational anti-fascist trend of the social movements. Some of the Comintern's mass and non-party organisations such as the League against Imperialism or the International of Seamen and Harbour Workers (ISH) entered the active boycott of Italian ships, but soon stepped down.[28] This process was accompanied by the deliberate financial and organisational retrenchment of the League Against Imperialism which had been founded in 1926 by Willi Münzenberg. The League had been the most important international anti-colonial and anti-imperialist organisation of the interwar period, a transnational hub and reference point for those fighting for the right to national self-determination.[29]

At the same time, the Labour and Socialist International (LSI) as a representative voice of the workers' movement complained not only on the neo-colonial diplomatic game on Abyssinia but also on the 'perforation of the world boycott against the Hitler regime'. The 'weak policy of the governments' were, as the LSI stated, 'determined in fact by short-sighted special interests against the fascist attack on Abyssinia'. Instead, it urged for an 'extensive coordination of the policies of Great Britain, France and the Soviet Union to prevent all attacks and violations of the treaties'.[30]

The Ethiopian events not only deepened the existing split in the international workers' movement, but aided the emergence of a new type of global bifurcation and caesura within the power relationship of Soviet and Comintern politics. The scissors opened even further, when poison gas attacks and massacres perpetrated by the Italian troops caused a wave of international protests to which the League of Nations also joined. Stalin in the Soviet Politburo categorically opposed all types of aid, including that provided by the Red Cross to the distressed population or a trade boycott against Italy. This had been discussed in the League of Nations and initially supported internally by the Foreign Commissariat under Litvinov.[31]

Soviet policy did not go unopposed. The US National Association for the Advancement of Colored People (NAACP) sent Litvinov a telegram criticising him for his apparent failure to defend the Ethiopian peoples.[32] Reactions on the communist party level were quite mixed. While a housewives' consumer group in the US began to organise a boycott against Italy,[33] black women's organisations engaged in defending Italian women against fascism – but did not engage in solidarity activities with Ethiopia. Calls for a boycott of Italy by the International Transport Workers' Federation remained unheeded. Although the Comintern had made preparations for an international campaign for Ethiopia since the beginning of 1935, the Comintern's General Secretary Dimitrov only made an offer to the LSI in late September 1935, much too late to be serious. It was consequently rejected as a tactical and instrumental manoeuvre.[34]

Under the conditions of the new Popular Front line that stipulated an alliance with the 'democratic' liberal parties in the world it is not surprising that the CP's anti-colonial efforts built during the 1920s,[35] especially in the metropolis of the colonial empires, like Great Britain and France, had to significantly tone down their anti-colonial articulations. This radical break with anti-colonialism is the topic of a new historical debate. Some authors like Nils Federn and Marika Sheerwood shed light on the inactivity of the Communist Parties, especially the CP of Great Britain in this field, resulting in a significant exodus of the African and Caribbean members from the party.[36] A manifold discussion from below was under way on the transnational level: George Padmore, the former secretary of the Comintern inspired International Trade Union Committee of Negro Workers (ITUCNW), who had been expelled from the Comintern, but who continued his outstanding transnational panafrican engagement, criticised this rupture and declared that it was a consequence of the USSR's political turn.

The case of Ethiopia appears as the definitive assertion of the primacy of Soviet foreign policy, which did not intend to risk its good relations with Mussolini, but which also wanted to maintain its ties with the Western colonial empires. In conclusion, Abyssinia stands for the abandonment of the anti-colonial and anti-imperialist tradition of the Soviet Union. Indeed, in August 1936, the Italian Communist Party had declared itself ready, together with the 'Brothers in the Black Shirts' (Fratelli in camicia nera), to realise the fascist programme of 1919 and to march 'hand in hand with all fascists', 'whatever rank they occupy in the hierarchy of the party and the state'.[37]

The Brazilian tragedy

As if the differences could not be greater, the case of Brazil coming soon after the fall of Ethiopia represents probably the only case in Comintern history where a military rebellion was prepared to overthrow a constitutional government in power. The German October of 1923 was planned not as a military uprising, but as a workers' revolution with support of the German Communist Party, which had been transformed into a pseudo-military organisation. Despite the differences, both events ended in disastrous failures. In the Brazilian case, twelve years later, responsibility was assigned to military circles around Luís Carlos Prestes (who had been recruited by the party at the instigation of Moscow). In Brazil, the Communist Party was excluded from the operative preparation of the rebellion because this was considered a danger for the clandestine preparations realised with the Comintern.

Between 23 and 28 November 1935, a mostly military rebellion was carried out on behalf of the Aliança Nacional Libertadora (ANL) (a kind of Brazilian Popular Front) against the government of Vargas beginning in the north-eastern state of Natal. Despite widespread social unrest and an institutional crisis with mass strikes, the four-day rebellion was only supported in the north of the country by a greater part of the population (nevertheless failing in Recife). It failed particularly in Rio de Janeiro, where during the night of 27 to 28 November the insurgents of the Third Infantry Regiment could only hold the barracks at the 'Praia Vermelha' for a few hours.[38] Due to the weak military and even weaker popular participation, the rebellion was severely suppressed, and followed by a relentless repression by the political police. Anti-fascism suffered another major failure. This defeat was a precondition for Getúlio Vargas's putsch on 10 November 1937, which closed down the congress and cancelled elections, and founded the era of the "Estado Novo" until 1945. It is worthwhile noting that there existed a connection between Rome and Rio de Janeiro: the Brazilian dictatorship of the Estado Novo was inspired by Italian fascism of the corporatist type, like his Portuguese predecessor under Salazar.

The rebellion miscalculated principally on two fronts. Firstly, Prestes's assessment of the willingness and the preparedness of the officers to take part in the uprising and, secondly, the Comintern's confidence in the possibilities of a spontaneous insurrection in a 'semi-colonial' country. Arthur Ewert, who functioned as the head of the international communist delegation in Brazil had too much confidence in the military leader of the rebellion, the charismatic 'Cavaleiro da Esperança' Prestes (called 'the Knight of Hope' by famous Brazilian writer Jorge Amado).

The current trend to present the uprising unilaterally as the result of a 'mass movement in defence of national and democratic interests, extraordinarily broad for the time, and stimulated by the National Liberation Alliance', is not convincing due to new evidence from the Comintern Archives in Moscow.[39] It can no longer be denied that the coup attempt in Brazil was another link in the long chain of the Comintern's fatal defeats and that of its specific form of anti-fascism, both in the core countries as in the Global South. At the time the magnitude of the defeat was hidden by the subsequent campaigns for the liberation of Prestes, his companion

Olga Benario, Arthur Ewert and his wife Elisabeth and others arrested, who had mostly been at the service of the Comintern or the Soviet military counter intelligence. A certain parallel with the Ethiopian case is the solidarity campaign with the victims of the uprising, organised by the Comintern under the slogan 'Liberty for Prestes and Olga Benario'. As it is well known, Willi Münzenberg, with great talent, managed not only to launch anti-fascist campaigns but also to transform devastating defeats into moral victories. Nevertheless, in this special case, this campaign seems to have failed. The 'financial difficulties' and the 'slowness of the organising committee' were mentioned as the main reasons, and it was soon overshadowed by the Spanish Civil War.[40] There was also another problem: Madame Willard from Belgium, chairman of the committee set up for this purpose, had earlier sent a delegation to Berlin, who after returning, had praised the prison conditions in Germany.[41]

How do we explain such disparities between the strangling of solidarity in the case of Abyssinia and the offensive to the utmost in the case of Brazil? How did agenda-setting work in the case of Brazil? Without any doubt, the striking feature of agenda-setting in Brazil was that strategically and logistically the rebellion had been prepared by Prestes and the Comintern instructors with some support by the Russian military intelligence apparatus (of course, in complete secrecy). A large delegation of instructors had been sent to the country (mostly to Sao Paulo and Rio de Janeiro) for this purpose, including the German KPD 'Conciliator' Ewert, the Argentinian Rodolfo Ghioldi, the American Victor Allan Barron, the Italian Amleto Locatelli, the German sailor 'Jonny' de Graaf and others.

If one tries to classify the events strategically, the insurrection seems at first to be in contradiction with the new 'democratic' line of anti-fascism in the Popular Front period. It is true that the undertaking was already prepared during the Comintern's 'Third period'. Nevertheless, French historian Pierre Broué argues correctly that it was not a 'leftover', a sort of latecomer from the Third Period, which the Comintern had failed to cancel at the right moment. A military insurrection for the national liberation of the people (insurreicão nacional libertadora), was perfectly compatible with a special 'form of the People's Front in a semi-colonial country' as a so-called 'anti-imperialist unity front' as defined by the Seventh Comintern Congress some months before. Furthermore, the mobilisation of North Eastern social banditism (the cangaçeiros) must not obscure the fact that the Brazilian military oppositional tradition of the lower ranking officers (tenentistas) was part of a broader social movement against the authoritarian rule of Getúlio Vargas and against the Great Landowners, especially the coffee plantation oligarchy.[42] This form of 'tenentismo' had been declared compatible with the Popular Front at the Third conference of Latin American communist parties in October 1934 in Moscow although it had already failed during the 1920s.[43] Secondly, it fitted within the Popular Front line because a revolutionary outcome in the socialist sense was not at stake.[44] In accordance with the Popular Front concept for the core countries, the bourgeois regime as such should not be affected. It had been decided the same year by the Third Conference of the Latin American

Communists, that the upheaval as a 'national-liberatory' revolution should be led – in the wording of Arthur Ewert as head of the Comintern delegation in Brazil – by a national liberation alliance representing 'the largest Popular Front (workers, peasants, petty bourgeoisie and that part of the bourgeoisie which is against imperialism)' and should be followed by the installation of 'a revolutionary national popular government with Prestes to lead, and in which the above mentioned strata will be represented' – and supported 'above all, by the national-revolutionary parts of the army'.[45]

Concerning the erroneous analysis, some of the causes of the failure seem evident. It was more than inept to put forward at an early stage the slogan 'All power to the Aliança Libertadora Nacional'. In doing so, the strategy was revealed which led to a lockdown during the preparation of the campaign. The top down perspective addressed issues of local agency only as subordinated to the successful military part of the uprising. This was supported by Ewert and the Comintern delegation even without a major interference of the workers' and peasants' struggles.[46] However, the overwhelming number of soldiers and officers remained firmly on the side of the government. With a few exceptions in north-eastern Brazil, the popular masses kept away from the struggle.

There can be no longer any doubt concerning Moscow's decision to start the armed uprising. This has been recently confirmed by Russian historian Fridrich Firsov, who is the leading expert on the cyphered Comintern telegrams. The new evidence contradicts a good deal of the historiography on the subject, which claims that the Comintern did not order the uprising. This is still the official view of the Communist Party of Brazil.[47] Already on 21 July 1935, the Comintern Secretariat cabled the CC of the Brazilian CP that the establishment of armed communist groups in the north-east was on the agenda.[48] In terms of their central content, the documents reveal that the ECCI Secretariat, while setting the line for the insurrection, left the timing to the comrades in Brazil.

The Russian version of the telegram, signed by Palmiro Togliatti, Dmitry Manuilsky, Wang Ming, Klement Gottwald, Wilhelm Florin, Otto Kuusinen, André Marty und Wilhelm Pieck also reveal that the translations circulating in the published studies so far have been inaccurate on one crucial point. The central passage in the telegram was not, as William Waack and Anita Leocádia Prestes, among others allege, 'the decision for the revolt must be made by you yourself'.[49] Instead, the decision to strike had already been made, and only the specific point in time was left to the Comintern delegation in Brazil: 'The question of the general advance [the uprising] is to be decided by yourself as soon as you consider it necessary [Vopros o vseobshchem vystuplenii reshaite sami, kogda sochtete nuzhnym]'.[50] The fact that the telegram arrived when the fighting had already begun and most of them had already collapsed does not change the evidence.[51] This interpretation is supported by another telegram from Dimitrov to Ercoli (i.e. Palmiro Togliatti), Moskvin, and Wang Ming from 22 November, predating the aforementioned telegram and attesting to the decision-making process in the ECCI. There, Dimitrov wrote: 'We suggest to leave the decision on the moment and the forms of the advance to the Brazilian comrades.' While the decision-making was left to the 'Brazilian comrades', it is merely the decision on time and form, not on whether to proceed with the uprising or not. That said, misunderstandings or false apprehensions in historical writing may also be traced back to the language in which the telegram was communicated to Rio de Janeiro.

The tragic outcome was that, like in many other cases, the Comintern and the Soviet Union did not even succeed in freeing their own comrades from the hands of the police. The events in Brazil opened another chapter of the traumatic defeats of international communism following Germany in 1933. Just like the pregnant Olga Benario, Ewert's wife Elisabeth Saborowsky was handed over by the Vargas regime to Hitler's Germany. Both women were killed by Nazi persecution while Ewert himself, a most intelligent and able German communist who had been ousted from the German CP's leadership after a personal intervention by Stalin in 1928, was tortured to madness. Prestes was released in 1945, becoming a heroic Stalinist-communist leader. Since then, he rejected all claims that liberation of his wife Olga and the others would have been possible. He died in 1990. In response to all criticism about the uprising, he remained faithful to his motto: 'There has been no instruction from the International, none of this is true, all must be denied.'[52]

On ruptures, revolutions and neo-imperial rearrangements: conclusion

The events in Brazil, particularly in Rio de Janeiro in the autumn of 1935, reveal the extent to which the twofold failure of the Comintern in Ethiopia and Brazil can be regarded as a turning point and transformation of official communist anti-fascism and anti-colonialism. If one summarises the cases of Rio de Janeiro, Addis Ababa and Moscow as strategic and intertwined entanglements of communist world politics, my initial hypothesis can be confirmed: the Comintern's military defeat in Brazil and the events in Ethiopia formed an entangled history that represented a double failure of anti-fascism and anti-colonialism. That said, the Soviet and Comintern intervention in the Spanish Civil War, an intervention incomparably more comprehensive and massive than the tentative solidarity campaigns for Ethiopia and Brazil, once again stimulated anti-fascism. Even so, the Soviet Union and the Comintern still did not pursue the victory of the republican camp with a consistent anti-fascist policy. The stark reality is that in the inter-war period, anti-fascism never became a doctrine of the Soviet Union. Inside the Soviet Union, the Pandora's box was opened with the failure of the Ethiopian and Brazilian campaigns: the systemic paranoia of Stalinism and terror led to the political massacre of communists and the brutal, genocidal deportations of national minorities and entire peoples. It is no coincidence that some of the active organisers of the Brazilian uprising were neither killed in Brazil nor by the Nazis, but in the Soviet Union.

These events were also linked to the interwar period's ongoing imperial rearrangements. From the 1930s onwards, the disentanglement of the Soviet Union from the world revolutionary context necessarily involved a period of strategic eclecticism in its international politics. In this respect, just as the myth of anti-fascism, the thesis of the Soviet Union's policy of collective security as a new-found mission in world politics, does not hold up to a critical review from a global historical perspective. The global collective security map was, as we now know, drawn by Stalin principally as an East-West pact including Germany. Walter Krivitsky's thesis is worth mentioning here, according to whom a neo-imperial rearrangement of the Stalinist USSR with German fascism was already being considered by Stalin during the Spanish Civil War.[53]

With the Spanish defeat, the pendulum in Europe definitely turned in the direction of fascism and the Soviet Union's alliance with Nazism. At this point, the fate of the Comintern was already sealed. With the Hitler–Stalin pact of 1939 the bifurcation was once again reinforced and escalated the dissolution of the Comintern four years later. The striking disentanglement between the Comintern and the Soviet Communist Party on anti-fascism and anti-colonialism, which has been described here, was never entirely reversed. This was certainly the main reason for the dissolution of the Comintern.[54] In an unequal but combined process, revolutionary communism necessarily fell victim to totalitarian bureaucratic absolutism long before the Stalinist and post-Stalinist system finally imploded.

Notes

1 Bernhard H. Bayerlein, 'El Significado internacional de Octubre de 1934 en Asturias. La Comuna Asturiana y el Komintern', in Gabriel Jackson et al., *Octubre 1934: Cinquenta años para la reflexión* (Madrid: Siglo XXI Editores Espana, 2002), pp. 19–40.

2 See Natal'ja Lebedeva & Michail Narinskij (eds), *Komintern i Vtoraja Mirovaja Vojna, C [tsch]ast' I: Do 22 Ijunja 1941 g., II: Posle 22 Ijunja 1941 g.* (Moscow: Pamjatniki Istoric [tsch]eskoj Mysli., 1994 & 1998).

3 Silvio Pons & Stephen A. Smith (eds), *The Cambridge History of Communism: Vol. 1: World Revolution and Socialism in One Country 1917–1941* (Cambridge: Cambridge University Press, 2017). Similarly also Sabine Dullin & Brigitte Studer, 'Communisme + transnational. L'équation retrouvée de l'internationalisme (premier XXe siècle)', *monde (s)*, Rennes, No. 10, 2016, pp. 9–32, 29.

4 Domenico Losurdo, *Stalin: Geschichte und Kritik einer schwarzen Legende* (Cologne: Papyrossa, 2012). For the critique, see Christoph Jünke, 'Zurück zu Stalin!? Domenico Losurdos Feldzug gegen die Entstalinisierung', *Emanzipation*, Vol. 4, No. 2, 2014, pp. 58–73.

5 See Nirode K. Barooah, *Chatto: The Life and Times of an Indian Anti-Imperialist in Europe* (Oxford: Oxford University Press, 2004); Ali Raza, Franziska Roy & Benjamin Zachariah (eds), *The Internationalist Moment: South Asia, Worlds, and World Views, 1917–39* (New Delhi: Sage, 2015); Holger Weiss, *Framinga a Radical African Atlantic: African American Agency, West African Intellectuals and the International Trade Union Committee of Negro Workers* (Leiden: Brill, 2014); Christian Høgsbjerg: *C. L. R. James in Imperial Britain* (Durham, NC: Duke University Press, 2014).

6 Dittmar Schorkowitz, *Staat und Nationalitäten in Russland: Der Integrationsprozeß der Burjaten und Kalmücken, 1822–1925* (Stuttgart: Steiner, 2001), p. 471.

7 Harold R. Isaacs, *The Tragedy of the Chinese Revolution*, 2nd revised edition (Stanford, CA: Stanford University Press, 1966) (1st. ed. in London 1938).

8 Terry Martin, *The Affirmative Action Empire: Nations and Nationalism in the Soviet Union 1923–1939* (Ithaca, NY: Cornell University Press, 2001).

9 Ragna Boden, 'Jakarta, 1965: Zur Rolle kommunistischer Parteien in der Dritten Welt', in Andreas Hilger (ed.), *Die Sowjetunion und die Dritte Welt: UdSSR, Staatssozialismus und Antikolonialismus im Kalten Krieg 1945–1991* (Munich: Oldenbourg, 2009), pp. 121–141, quote from p. 128.
10 Baruch Hirson, 'Bukharin, Bunting and the Native Republic Slogan', *Searchlight South Africa* Vol. 1, No. 3, 1989, pp. 51–66 (online at www.marxists.org/archive/hirson/1989/native-republic.htm), p. 7. Concerning the CP of France, see David H. Slavin, 'The French Left and the Rif War: Racism and the Limits of Internationalism', *Journal of Contemporary History* Vol. 26, No. 1, 1991, pp. 5–32.
11 Isaacs, *The Tragedy of the Chinese Revolution.*
12 Holger Weiss, 'Against Japanese and Italian Imperialism: The Anti-War Campaigns of Communist International Trade Union Organizations, 1931–1936', *Moving the Social: Journal of Social History and the History of Social Movements*, No. 60, 2018, pp. 121–146.
13 Ibid.
14 Hans Woller, *Mussolini: Der erste Faschist* (Munich: C. H. Beck, 2016).
15 Analogous to Marx, Jacobinism in the French Revolution is described as 'die plebejische Abrechnung mit den feudalen Feinden der Bourgeoisie', see Bernhard H. Bayerlein, 'L. Trockij und seine Auseinandersetzung mit dem Faschismus: Grundlagen und methodischer Zugang', Francesca Gori (ed.), *Pensiero e Azione politica di Lev Trockij*, II (Florence: Leo S. Olschki, 1982), pp. 667–692; here 667–671.
16 See a part of the archives of this undertaking in the International Institute of Social History, Amsterdam (IISG), ARCH01165, online at http://hdl.handle.net/10622/ARCH01165.
17 Weiss, 'Against Japanese and Italian Imperialism', pp. 23f.
18 Russian State Archive of Social and Political History (RGASPI), Moscow, 17/162/18, 172–173. Document published in G. Adibekov, A. Di Bijadžo, F. Gori et al. (eds), *Politbjuro CK RKP(b) – VKP(b) i Evropa. Rešenija 'Osoboj Papki' 1923–1939* (Moscow: ROSSPEN, 2001), pp. 328–330.
19 See Bernhard H. Bayerlein, 'Deutscher Kommunismus und transnationaler Stalinismus: Komintern, KPD und Sowjetunion 1929–1943: Neue Dokumente zur Konzeptualisierung einer verbundenen Geschichte', in Hermann Weber, Jakov Drabkin, Bernhard H. Bayerlein & Aleksandr Galkin (eds), *Deutschland, Russland, Komintern:* Vol. I: Überblicke, Analysen, Diskussionen: Neue Perspektiven auf die Geschichte der KPD und die Deutsch-Russischen Beziehungen (1918–1943) (Berlin: De Gruyter, 2014), pp. 325f.
20 Adibekov et al., *Politbjuro*, pp. 328–330, (RGASPI 17/162/20, 8). Published in ibid., p. 338, Fn. 1. (RGASPI, 17/162/18, 178). Published in ibid., p. 331.
21 Adibekov et al., *Politbjuro*, p. 333.
22 See Hermann Weber, Jakov Drabkin & Bernhard H. Bayerlein (eds), *Deutschland, Russland, Komintern,* Vol. II: Dokumente (1918–1943), Vol. 2 (Berlin: De Gruyter, 2014), p. 1139 a.o.
23 RGASPI 17/162/19, 32, published in Adibekov et al., *Politbjuro*, p. 334. See also Aleksandr V. Šubin, *Mir na kraju bezdny: Ot global'noj katastrofy k mirovoj vojnje, 1929–1941 gody* (Moscow: Veče, 2004), p. 188.
24 Ibid., p. 177.
25 Ibid., p. 188.
26 Weber et al., *Deutschland, Russland, Komintern,* Vol. II, p. 1139.
27 For this assumption, see Weiss 'Against Japanese and Italian Imperialism'. See also Bayerlein, 'Deutscher Kommunismus und transnationaler Stalinismus', pp. 325 e.a.
28 Weiss, *Framing a Radical African Atlantic.*
29 See Fredrik Petersson, *Willi Münzenberg, the League against Imperialism and the Comintern (1925–1933)* (Queenston: Edward Mellen Press, 2013).
30 Franz Osterroth & Dieter Schuster, *Chronik der deutschen Sozialdemokratie: Vom Beginn der Weimarer Republik bis zum Ende des Zweiten Weltkrieges*, electronic edition (Bonn: FES Library, 2001), online at http://library.fes.de/fulltext/bibliothek/chronik/spdc_band2.html (accessed 4 December 2019).

31 RGASPI 17/162/19, 13.
32 Denise Lynn, 'Fascism and the Family: American Communist Women's Anti-fascism During the Ethiopian Invasion and Spanish Civil War', *American Communist History*, Vol. 15, No. 2, 2016, p. 178.
33 Lynn, 'Fascism and the Family', p. 182.
34 *Die Einheit wird siegen!: Dimitroffs Ruf zur internationalen Aktionseinheit und die Antwort der Sozialistischen Arbeiterinternationale* (Strasburg: Prometheus Verlag, 1935).
35 Neil Redfern, 'British Communists, the British Empire and the Second World War', *International Labour and Working Class History* No. 65, Spring 2004, pp. 117–135, cited from Evan Smith, 'National Liberation for Whom? The Postcolonial Question, the Communist Party of Great Britain, and the Party's African and Caribbean Membership', *International Review of Social History* Vol. 61, No. 2, 2016, p. 288.
36 Concerning the lack of activity of the communist parties in this field, especially the CP of Great Britain, see Neil Redfern, 'British Communists, the British Empire and the Second World War', pp. 117–135; Marika Sherwood, 'The Comintern, the CPGB, Colonies and Black Britons, 1920–1938', *Science & Society,* Vol. 60, No. 2, 1996), pp. 137–163. Against this thesis see: John Callaghan, 'Colonies, Racism, the CPGB and the Comintern in the Inter-War Years,' *Science and Society,* Vol. 61, No. 4, 1997, pp. 513–525. For a more recent contribution, see Smith, 'National Liberation for Whom?', which supports Callaghan's thesis.
37 Adibekov et al., *Politbjuro*, p. 315.
38 See Marly de Almeida Gomes Viana, *Revolucionários de 1935* (São Paulo: Cia. das Letras, 1992).
39 Humberto Jansen & Marly A.G. Vianna (eds), *A Insurreição da ANL em 1935. O Relatório Bellens Porto* (Rio de Janeiro: Editora Revan, 2015) (stated in the blurb).
40 William Waack, *Camaradas* (São Paulo: Companhia das Letras, 1993), pp. 145, 288.
41 Ibid., pp. 289, 45.
42 Pierre Broué, *Histoire de l'Internationale Communiste 1919–1943* (Paris: Fayard, 1997), p. 668.
43 Anita Leocadia Prestes, 'A Conferência dos Partidos Comunistas da América do Sul e do Caribe e os levantes de novembro de 1935 no Brasil', *Crítica Marxista*, No. 22, 2006, pp. 132–153, online at www.ifch.unicamp.br/criticamarxista/arquivos_biblioteca/artigo211artigo7.pdf (accessed 4 December 2019).
44 Waack, *Camaradas*, pp. 56, 100.
45 Jansen & Vianna, *A insurreição da ANL*, p. 38.
46 William Waack, *Die vergessene Revolution. Olga Benario und die deutsche Revolte in Rio* (Berlin: Aufbau Taschenbuch Verlag, 1994), p. 148.
47 For the 'deniers', see Anita Leocádia Prestes, *Luiz Carlos Prestes e a Aliança Nacional Libertadora: Os caminhos da luta antifascista no Brasil 1934–35* (São Paulo: Brasiliense, 2008), p. 140; Ronald Friedmann, *Arthur Ewert: Revolutionär auf drei Kontinenten* (Berlin: Dietz, 2015). Friedmann's book is based on his PhD thesis from the University of Potsdam, 2015. For the Comintern documents, see Waack, *Camaradas*, p. 102 e.a.
48 Fridrich Firsov, *Sekret'nye kody istorii Kominterna 1919–1943* (Moscow: AIRO-XXI, 2007), p. 38.
49 Waack, *Die vergessene Revolution*, p. 152; Waack, *Camaradas*, p. 203. Here the Portuguese translation of the telegram, which was originally sent in English and French, is also partly misleading: 'Questão da ação (o levante) geral decidam vocês mesmos quando acharem necessário.' It is ambiguous, but in the most common translation it means 'decide for yourselves when you feel the need [on the timing]'.
50 Firsov, *Sekret'nye kody istorii Kominterna,* pp. 41–42. The classified document 'Vkhod. 1935 iz Kislovodska, received on 22 November 1935' is preserved in RGASPI 495/184/20.
51 Waack, *Camaradas*, p. 153 (Waack, *Die vergessene Revolution*, p. 152); Prestes, *Luiz Carlos Prestes*, p. 140 (quoted in Friedmann, *Arthur Ewert*, p. 354).
52 Ibid.

53 Walter G. Krivitsky, *In Stalin's Secret Service: An Exposé of Russia's Secret Policies by the Former Chief of the Soviet Intelligence in Western Europe* (New York: Harper Brothers, 1939).

54 See Bayerlein, 'Deutscher Kommunismus und transnationaler Stalinismus', p. 325 a.o.; and Bernhard H. Bayerlein, 'Transnationalisierung und weltrevolutionäres Scheitern: Die Komintern und Revolutionsvorbereitungen deutscher Kommunisten in der Zwischenkriegszeit', in Jörg Ganzenmüller (ed.), *Verheißung oder Bedrohung: Die Oktoberrevolution als globales Ereignis* (Cologne: Böhlau, 2019), pp. 47–74.

12

'WORLD CAPITAL OF ANTI-FASCISM'?

The making – and breaking – of a global left in Spain, 1936–1939

Hugo García

Studying anti-fascism in the Spanish Civil War might seem redundant, so closely associated are the two terms in collective memory. In fact, the relevant literature is compartmentalised along national and party lines, and the existing overviews reach different conclusions. Collotti, Droz and Hobsbawm gave sympathetic views of the conflict as the great cause which arose the political consciousness of a generation, anticipating Resistance movements in the Second World War.[1] Furet reframed the war as 'a showcase for Soviet propaganda', a legend designed by the Comintern to mask the Communist satellisation of the Republic.[2] More recently, Seidman has reinterpreted it as a failed rehearsal, a case of 'revolutionary antifascism' that would be outperformed by Churchill's, Roosevelt's and de Gaulle's 'more inclusive', and effective, 'counter-revolutionary' anti-fascist coalitions.[3]

Seidman's stimulating comparative study timely reminds us that foreign support for the Republic came above all from the left, but poses at least two problems. First, it downplays the disputes among Spanish and foreign anti-fascists during the war – in particular, over social revolution and national liberation – and their impact on the content and following of the cause. Second, it disregards the circulation of activists and ideas on which the movement was based, a crucial aspect of its coalescence in the years 1933–1937 and unravelling in 1938–1939. This chapter explores the dynamic and transnational dimension of anti-fascism by looking at the discourse and actions of the foreigners who supported the Republic during the war, and examining the ways in which the movement and the conflict shaped each other. It tries to synthesise and push forward the literature on both topics by discussing whether a transnational public sphere built on the idea of anti-fascism emerged and functioned in this period, as well as its wider impact in and outside Spain.

Ultimately, the chapter uses the war to engage with recent research on internationalism.[4] It shows how local movements can broaden their audience by reaching out to parallel efforts in the name of shared values, and the fascinating hybridisations these exchanges produce. It also seeks to complicate the notion of a 'twentieth-century global left', as advanced by Fronczak in the context of the Hands Off Ethiopia campaign of 1935–1936.[5] The Aid Spain movement built on previous protests to forge a broad front against *fascism*, and succeeded like few others in history in creating spaces for cooperation among competing forces. For the same reason it was an arena of dispute over everything, including its name and goals, and became increasingly fragile as the Republic suffered under the double burden of fascist intervention and democratic non-intervention. As other varieties of international solidarity, anti-fascism was a laborious construction, an effort to build bridges across national and cultural barriers which involved a considerable degree of wishful thinking.[6] This chapter reassesses its achievements and limits, and the light they shed on its world and age.

The making of a global left in/over Spain, 1936–1939

The illusion of a global left loomed large in Republican discourses about the war. Francisco Largo Caballero's coalition government responded to the recognition of the Burgos Junta by Germany and Italy, on 21 November 1936, by proclaiming that it was supported by 'the international Popular Front', besides Mexico, the Soviet Union and 'the majority of the world's democratic peoples'.[7] The Anarchist Iberian Federation (FAI) called for an 'international anti-fascist conference' in February 1937, whereas the Spanish Popular Front appealed for an 'Anti-fascist international alliance' in November.[8] The Republic's foreign supporters thought along similar lines; British author John Langdon-Davies interpreted the military rebellion as the work of a 'Fascist International' and wondered whether 'an anti-Fascist International' could stop it.[9] His French colleague Romain Rolland agreed that the war had 'consecrated the internationalism of all parties' (including fascisms), but anticipated the victory of 'the immense bloc of peoples from all nations'.[10]

Besides their obvious mobilising purpose, these statements raise a problem that has inspired much recent research on anti-fascism: how coherent was the movement, and to what extent was the Republic's voice 'heard in every part of the world', as Communist leader Dolores Ibárruri claimed as early as September?[11] Attempting to answer this question requires a prior engagement with the concept of anti-fascism itself. Recent literature has tended to broaden its scope in order to highlight the neglected but significant contributions of liberal, conservative and religious groups.[12] Here I will adopt a more conventional, but perhaps more functional definition of anti-fascism as a stance requiring both an explicit self-definition and an active involvement in an organised struggle against actual or perceived fascism. This amounts to rehabilitating the old-fashioned view of the movement as primarily 'a left-wing phenomenon', though, as we will see, its boundaries were shifting.[13] Despite the active role played by some liberals (and a few conservatives) in the Spanish campaign, the major liberal and republican parties remained predominantly non-interventionist, except in the UK, Italy and Spain itself.[14]

A large number of contemporary texts represented the world as a vast front between two hostile camps, fascism and anti-fascism, engaged in a global civil war of which Spain was the metaphor and centre. The Soviet writer Mikhail Koltsov expressed it with cinematographic vividness at the Second International Congress for the Defence of Culture, held in Republican Spain and Paris in July 1937: this unprecedented front, he argued, 'start[ed] at the Madrid trenches and cover[ed] all Europe and the world', leaving no spot for 'silence, calm and neutrality'.[15] This view had been taking shape since the electoral victories of the left in Spain and France in February and May 1936 materialised the ideal of an 'international Popular Front' doomed to clash with the mounting fascist tide.[16] Speaking in Madrid on 22 May, French novelist André Malraux warned his audience that 'the differences that oppose us to Fascists will one day have to be resolved with machine guns'.[17] The July military rebellion fulfilled his prophecy, though the boundaries of this front remained uncertain as the international situation kept changing. Langdon-Davies's 'Anti-fascist International' was composed of 'Russia, nine-tenths of France, one-half of England, and some smaller and more civilized countries, such as the Scandinavian'.[18] The editors of the Argentine journal *Contra-Fascismo* claimed in early 1937 that the 'international fascist bloc' was growing in number and aggressiveness, but the 'democratic and pacifist bloc' led by the Soviet Union, and supported by China, Spain, France, Mexico and the United States was also growing in number and force.[19]

Anti-fascists looked at Republican Spain as the 'heart' of this front and the key to a future of peace and freedom. This metaphor, later popularised by W. H. Auden and Pablo Neruda, was used by the Argentine socialist Augusto Bunge as early as 2 August 1936.[20] It spread above all during the Nationalist siege of Madrid in October-November, when Republican propaganda proclaimed the city to be the 'world capital of anti-fascism' and 'heart of the world'.[21] Herbert Kline played with the word in *Heart of Spain*, a documentary on Dr Norman Bethune's work in the Republican blood-transfusion service and a broad narrative of Spain's role in the struggle against fascism which was watched by millions in North America and Europe.[22] A fair estimate of the conflict's strategic importance and a sign of its deeply emotional dimension, the metaphor symbolised international solidarity with the Republic until its fall.

The importance that anti-fascists gave to this crusade explains the strenuous efforts they made on its behalf through public statements, demonstrations, committee work, economic or material relief, visits of solidarity, industrial action and armed combat. Categorising such diverse activities as *anti-fascism* may seem reductionist, yet they were most often discussed and performed as part of a single struggle. A chronicle by Cuban communist writer Pablo de la Torriente on two meetings held in New York City on 24–25 July 1936, written shortly before he left for Spain in September, reflects how collections, propaganda and volunteering merged in early mobilisations for the cause.[23] Torriente described with enthusiasm these meetings –attended by 20,000 people according to the left-wing press, and 2,000 to 'reactionary' papers– that had spread from Spanish and Spanish-American exiles 'to all the colonies, races and languages'. Among other interesting details he highlighted the protesters' ethnic diversity (Italians, Germans, Jews, Russians, Japanese, Chinese, American, French), their hostility towards international 'fascism' and expressions of fraternity with other peoples through speeches, posters and the singing of The Internationale. The selling of newspapers and pamphlets in various languages, the presence of newsreel cameras and the concluding calls to match the large sums that would be raised all over Latin America suggest that the organisers were well aware of the mediatic and transnational dimension of their cause.

As Torriente, who went to Spain as a press correspondent and ended up as a political commissar in the International Brigades before he was killed by a stray bullet in December 1936, many supporters of the Republic switched roles throughout the war. Writer-combatants such as André Malraux, Italian Randolfo Pacciardi, German Ludwig Renn and American Louis Fischer; diplomat-propagandists such as Mexican Narciso Bassols and journalists-military advisers-secret agents such as Koltsov are just the best-known examples of versatility among anti-fascists. Overlapping between humanitarianism and politics was certainly not automatic, but it was frequent, perhaps because the naked facts of the war invited the indignant cry 'Franco the baby-killer' used by pro-Republicans in Britain.[24] Mixed motivations are evident in American Jewish communists such as Irene Goldin, who went to Spain as a nurse 'to fight against fascism'; or James Neugass, a short-sighted poet who volunteered to drive an ambulance in Spain as a surrogate for enlisting.[25] For Swiss socialist Clara Thälmann, one of the 200 competitors in Barcelona's People's Olympiad who joined the Republican militias in July 1936, swimming and fighting could be equally valid ways to fight fascism.[26]

Far from being self-evident, what being an anti-fascist involved was discussed throughout the war in practical as well as moral terms. Many activists criticised relief as an insufficient or inadequate means of help. In February 1937, Swiss journalist René Bertholet, a member of the Internationale Sozialistiche Kampfbund, demanded comrades abroad, and especially in England and France, 'a more active sympathy', reminding them 'that we are in danger of being defeated in spite of this mass of greetings and good wishes which are quite platonic'.[27] Others saw relief, arms smuggling, volunteers and propaganda as equivalent. Speaking at a Socialist and Labour conference on Spain held in London in March 1937, Belgian representative Isabelle Blume argued that 'relief was essential' and might also become 'a means of propagation of interest'.[28] In a report read to the International Conference for aid to the wounded, widows, orphans and refugees from Republican Spain held in Paris on 16–17 January 1938, physicist Paul Langevin emphasised the link between 'moral' and 'material' aid to Spain, which reflected the characteristics of 'the fascist offensive' itself.[29]

It is tempting to read such views as bourgeois or female versions of anti-fascism: in fact, pro-Spain campaigns were usually led by women to highlight their non-partisan character, regardless of the highly political profile of figures such as

Gabrielle Duchêne, Ellen Wilkinson or Blume herself.[30] However, it is doubtful whether these women or combatants such as Thälmann or Mika Feldman dared to embrace a specifically 'feminine and feminist interpretation' of anti-fascism which could challenge its masculinised ethos.[31] Feldman, an Argentine Jew who fought as captain of a POUM battalion on the Madrid front, felt forced to behave as a 'woman-soldier' after her husband was killed in battle in August 1936, choosing to 'serv[e] in this revolution with the maximum efficacy and fuck the small pull of the flesh'.[32]

Similarly, combatants often sneered at mere 'war tourists' showing off at the fronts.[33] Yet some writers alternated between these two roles with impressive fluency: Malraux, in particular, moved from organising an airplane squadron in August 1936 to making a successful fundraising lecture tour across North America in early 1937, attending the above-mentioned Writers' Congress in July, writing a novel on the conflict in 1938 and making a film out of it in 1939. Described by Manès Sperber as 'the Saint-Just of anti-fascism' for his friendship with German and Italian émigrés in Paris, Malraux did much to popularise the anti-fascist role model combining action and reflection, sympathy for victims and a resolute acceptance of violence for a just cause.[34] The recollections of Maurice Constant, a University of Toronto student who volunteered after listening to the French star lecture on Spain 'accompanied by a stunning French blond', attest to its appeal.[35]

The heated debates over Non-Intervention that took place in France and other democracies over the war show that the debate over violence that took up much of the energy of the left in the late 1930s transcended gender divides. While some members of the Vigilance Committee of Anti-fascist Intellectuals defended Non-Intervention with the argument that 'the true anti-fascist is … completely pacifist', others accused them of having a 'Platonic anti-fascism' which, in practice, turned them into 'anti-anti-fascist'.[36] The dispute was never settled, though the disastrous course of the conflict favoured a belligerent approach that was arguably its main contribution to anti-fascism. Even Gandhi had trouble preaching pacifism for Spain: as he put it in a letter in September 1937, 'I do not know how the message of non-violence can be delivered to China as I do not how it can be delivered to Spain.'[37]

Anti-fascist discourses on the Spanish war reflect the utopia of a *popular* or *united front* capable of stopping the fascist dystopia, and a mobilising myth aimed at making this possible. Once created, the myth proved self-sustaining. The ignorance of most visitors about Spain did not prevent them from becoming deeply involved in the imagined community of anti-fascism. As Jef Last put it at the Writers' Conference, his stay transformed the very nature of his anti-fascism: 'it is no longer intellectual: it has gone over into my blood'.[38] Witnesses of the battle of Madrid, including well-informed British and American correspondents, felt deeply moved by the courage of Spanish Loyalists: Ernest Hemingway would recall these months as 'the happiest period of our lives'.[39] Lois Orr, a 19-year-old American socialist who worked for the POUM's foreign propaganda service, remembered the burial of FAI leader Buenaventura Durruti in Barcelona on 23 November 1936 as a turning point which committed her 'emotionally and intellectually ... to the anti-fascist revolution as a noble and wonderful human experiment'.[40] A result of the war experience and/or the Republic's techniques of hospitality, this emotional identification affected even impartial observers such as the students from the Université Libre de Bruxelles who, after visiting Catalonia on a humanitarian mission in the summer 1937, created a Comité Estudiantin d'Aide à l'Espagne Républicaine.[41]

The politics of anti-fascism

The urge to act for Spain did not necessarily imply a willingness to do it with anyone, as the movement tended to impose. The unitary logic of anti-fascism contributed more to its success than its vague utopian dimension, as it offered a solution to the practical problems posed by the conflict and the perceived failures of the left in previous clashes with *fascism*. But it challenged the modus operandi of the organisations which headed the global left in the 1930s, and carried the weight of the campaign: socialists, communists (orthodox and dissident) and anarchists. Their traditions, agendas, phobias, inner struggles and different conceptions of anti-fascism thwarted the Republic's repeated calls for an 'international people's front', echoed by the Comintern and left-wing socialists such as H. N. Brailsford.

The war split all the families of the left, but proved particularly divisive for the Labour and Socialist International and the International Federation of Trade Unions. When UGT general secretary Pascual Tomás asked the IFTU to hold a joint meeting 'with all class-conscious international Trade Union and political organisations ... inspired by the hate of Fascisme [*sic*]', on 20 November 1936, he had to accept a conference of IFTU and LSI members on the pretext that any other would be incompatible with Socialist statutes.[42] The proceedings of the conference reflect a thinly veiled tension among national and ideological factions: while Spanish delegates Tomás and Manuel Cordero (PSOE) emphasised that Spain needed 'firm actions' and continued to advocate 'an all-inclusive conference', their British hosts Walter Citrine and Ernest Bevin (Trade Unions Congress) insisted on rejecting the all-in conference (as Bevin bluntly put it, 'please let us manage our own affairs') and claiming that public opinion was not ready to go to war over Spain, before putting their guests before the dilemma of 'work[ing] with us' or with Russia.[43] The French, Italian, Belgian, Dutch, Scandinavian and American delegations agreed on the failure of non-intervention but disagreed on everything else, with a majority defending the Spanish proposals and a minority supporting the British approach. The latter eventually prevailed in the recommendations of the conference, which emphasised the need to redouble Socialist efforts 'to rouse that world public opinion on which, in the last resort, the outcome of the conflict depends'.[44] The circular logic of this strategy condemned subsequent efforts to create a united front for Spain at the political, humanitarian or trade union level, deepening the fracture within the LSI-IFTU and coalition governments in France, Belgium and Sweden.

Unity was easier to achieve at the national or local levels, where institutional and cultural constraints were weaker and grassroots initiatives stronger. A number of extended popular fronts including anarchists were created in North Queensland in Australia, surviving in some cases beyond May 1937.[45] Even in France, Spain promoted a short-lived consensus after the Soviet Union announced its decision to leave the Non-Intervention Agreement on 24 October 1936. On 6 December, all the members of the Rassemblement Populaire and the Union Anarchiste called for the lifting of the embargo at the Vélodrome d'Hiver in Paris, under the slogan 'Down with war, but long live the Spanish revolution!'[46] This superficial agreement concealed substantial differences, with CGT leader Victor Basch expressing his support to Léon Blum's government and SFIO dissenters Jean Zyromsky and Marceau Pivert openly criticising Non-Intervention, but temporarily put the French left on the same wavelength as the Spanish one. Young anti-fascists were also receptive to ecumenical approaches: after hearing the report of their Spanish colleagues at the first World Youth Congress in Geneva in September 1936, one hundred delegates from socialist, communist and anarchist organisations agreed on starting joint actions for Spain in all continents, including a European Conference in Paris in December.[47] The 'formidable international and juvenile single front' advocated by CNT-FAI delegate Félix Martí Ibáñez did not materialise, but it was at least contemplated.

Factional competition often had the salutary effect of inducing emulation in recruiting, collecting and propaganda efforts.[48] The international organisations to which the Spanish parties belonged played a key role in explaining their cause abroad. Even the Spanish government initially put its foreign publicity in the hands of Willi Münzenberg, the architect of the Comintern's transnational anti-fascist and anti-imperialist campaigns since 1923.[49] Münzenberg's media network did much to build the illusion of a solid Spanish front by circulating images of combat taken by artists such as John Heartfield and Robert Capa.[50] As in previous campaigns for Francisco Ferrer in 1909, Sacco and Vanzetti in 1927 or Ethiopia in 1935–1936, the left's media network fostered transnational mobilisation, giving anti-fascists an evidence of their collective existence that ignored differences in contexts and details.[51] Thanks to the 'political grammar' of anti-fascism – the verbal equivalent of Heartfield's brilliant photomontages - the Spanish metaphor was easy to translate into other languages and resonate with various projects of emancipation.[52]

Framing the war as a universal issue helped to produce solidarity with Spain, but it was not enough. A number of studies reflect the movement's dependence on the local left and exile communities, which were often interlinked as in the case of the Jewish diaspora.[53] For refugees from Eastern and Central Europe or Jews from Mandatory Palestine, supporting the Republic made sense on political and national grounds, especially given their precarious economic and political situation.[54] But 'push factors' combined with a systematic attempt by the left, and especially the Comintern, to connect with local traditions. The KPP reminded Poles that 'Hitler is preparing for Poland the same lot as for Spain'.[55] Likewise, Josip Broz and other leaders of the KPJ explained the war against the 'Spanish četniks' to 'the Croatian peasant masses' 'in the context of their own experiences and on the basis of Croatian examples'.[56] In an apparently paradoxical case of nationalist internationalism, which connected it to a long tradition of 'revolutionary romanticism', the Republican cause was identified with national minorities, and fascism with their oppression.[57]

The similarities in culture and political context turned Latin America into a fertile ground for Loyalist propaganda. Throughout the subcontinent, many workers and democrats regarded anti-fascism as a useful tool against the spread of military dictatorships.[58] In Mexico, with the Soviet Union the country that most supported Spain during the war, President Lázaro Cárdenas admitted as early as August 1936 that his Government had sold weapons to the Republic and declared his solidarity with its struggle against 'international fascism'.[59] Vicente Lombardo Toledano, a prominent Labour leader and editor close to the Communist Party, saw helping the Republic as a way to consolidate the Revolution's work and combat 'creole fascism'.[60] Ernesto Giudici, a Communist author and secretary general of the Comité Antifascista Argentino, described in April and September 1936 a 'universal fascist phenomenon' which, in Argentina, adopted the form of a 'semi-colonial fascism' and served to protect Anglo-American imperialist interests.[61] Uruguayan poet Blanca Luz Brum put the same idea in verse: 'Who can remain at home / if Spain's children are / America's children? / And Europe's fascism is / the same which threatens us.'[62]

Western and especially Communist activists regarded liberation struggles around the world as part of a historical and geographical continuum. 'Spain – wrote the Jewish-American volunteer Edwin Rolfe – is yesterday's Russia, tomorrow's China / yes, and the thirteen seaboard states.'[63] The two great causes of the late 1930s drew inspiration from each other, or at least attempted to join forces.[64] An American journalist noted 'the intense interest' with which the Chinese Reds followed the Spanish war, and the frequency with which Spain's 'People's Front' was compared with the 'United Front' in China, and Germany and Italy described as the 'Fascist allies' of Japan.[65] Kuomintang General Yang Hucheng, the head of a Chinese delegation to Spain in October 1937, also linked both struggles, dubbing Shanghai China's 'heroic Madrid, capital of anti-fascism in the Orient'.[66] Some one hundred Chinese volunteers from China, the United States, Cuba and France joined the Brigades, the largest national group from a diverse Asian collective including Philippines, Indians, Vietnamese, Japanese and Indonesians.[67] Reciprocally, Spanish intellectuals declared in April 1938 that 'the struggle which takes place in China is identical to the one waged by the Spanish people'.[68]

Indian socialists also identified with the Spanish resistance. In January 1939, after visiting Spain in June 1938 and before travelling to China, Congress leader Jawaharlal Nehru proclaimed that 'The frontiers of our struggle lie not only in our own country but in Spain and China also.'[69] His party extended to the Republic its belief in 'the commonality of anti-imperialist struggles', though Nehru's speeches for British audiences emphasised that one could only be anti-fascist if one was anti-imperialist. His support – partly ideological, partly a strategic attempt to raise India's international status and display her readiness for independence – worked through left-wing channels rather than Indian civil society, and produced little material aid.[70]

Elsewhere, attempts to insert the Popular Front strategy into anti-colonial efforts were hampered by the movement's 'imperial' assumptions.[71] While European activists such as Nancy Cunard found it natural to embrace 'anti-colonial anti-fascism', Marxist Pan-Africanists such as George Padmore and C. L. R. James pointed out the contradiction between the Spanish Government's calls for Muslim help and its reluctance to give up its Moroccan Protectorate.[72] What Padmore called the Republic's reluctance 'to make an anti-imperialist gesture to the Moors' alienated apparently well predisposed nationalists, such as Abdeljalek Torres in Morocco or the leaders of Étoile Nord-Africaine in Algeria.[73] The Republicans' stance stemmed partly from their wish to keep French support and partly from ingrained prejudices: the attempts by Ibnu Jala (pseudonym of the Palestinian communist Najati Sidqi) to rally anti-fascist Muslims in the fall 1936 failed due to widespread Spanish suspicion of the 'Moors'.[74] Their awkward calls for Islamic solidarity, which appealed at the same time to anti-fascism, revolution and Jihad, thus fell relatively flat, though the enlisting of 500 to 800 Arabs in the Brigades suggests that they were not altogether sterile.[75]

The voice of Spain resonated even less strongly South of the Sahara.[76] Ahmed Din Josef's decision to join the Garibaldi Battalion made great publicity about 'Abyssinian warriors', but did not represent the detached attitude of the Ethiopian exile, which corresponded to the Republic's watchword during the Battle of Guadalajara, '*Madrid is not Addis Abeba*'.[77] A 1938 poem by Senegalese Léopold Sédar Senghor expressed African nationalists' understandable indifference towards the Spanish tragedy: 'While ten ships in unyielding line like thin-lipped mouths bombarded Almeria … / We talked of Africa.'[78] In telling contrast with the Ethiopian campaign, the only significant initiatives seem to have come from emigrant groups such as the Johannesburg Committee of the Friends of the Spanish Republic, composed by Lithuanian Jews, which sent a few volunteers to the Brigades and sponsored a 'SA Foodship for Spain' near the end of the war.[79] It was a wounded African-American volunteer in the Lincoln battalion, one of some 100 such combatants in this non-segregated military unit, who conceded, 'This ain't Ethiopia, but it'll do.'[80]

In short, the 'international Popular Front' was impressively broad, but did not achieve the unity nor the global reach that its supporters attributed to it. The movement had to adapt to hyper-fragmented political environments and a deeply unequal state system, which limited activists' agency and influence. Aid figures reflect a strong correlation between mobilisation for Spain and the local strength of the left: according to an IFTU report of June 1937, Sweden was the first collector in per capita terms, followed by Switzerland, Argentina, France and the UK.[81] Perhaps for the same reason, the largest figures came from the Soviet Union, where mobilising for Spain became a state policy after *Pravda* announced that Moscow workers had agreed to donate 0.5 per cent of their salaries to Spain on 3 August

1936.[82] This unleashed the most massive and sustained campaign for the Republic during the war, including obsessive media coverage, meetings attended by up to 100,000 people in the main cities and constant public displays of Stakhanovite solidarity. As André Gide's witness account suggests, the people only mobilised after *Pravda* gave the signal, though they did it passionately.[83] The war was seen both as a re-enactment of the Russian revolution and a chance to escape the massive purge against *Trotskyist* saboteurs that started exactly at the same time.[84] Requests to go fight in Spain in the fall 1936 reflect a cunning use of the official jargon to seek an escape from the terror, which eventually reached the architects of the anti-fascist campaign themselves.[85]

The (partial) breaking of the front, 1937–1939

The USSR of the Great Purge was no country for the global left, but something like it seemed to emerge in Spain in the fall and winter 1936, as the anarchist CNT-FAI and the Basque Catholic nationalists (the darling of conservative anti-fascists abroad) joined the Catalan and Central governments in a desperate attempt to save the beleaguered Republic. Besides the model of cross-party resistance that this enlarged Popular Front offered, a number of organisations created for military, political, humanitarian and propaganda reasons maintained the illusion of unity. The most influential one was by far the International Brigades, which accommodated some 40,000 volunteers from 53 countries from November 1936 to October 1938. Stalin's reasons to create them continue to be debated, but public relations concerns were probably among them: as Louis Fischer put it, 'To protect a victim of Fascist attack was … the proof of anti-Fascism.'[86] In this respect, the Brigades were a brilliant success, even if they were organised along national, rather than international lines (with exceptions such as the multiethnic Chapaev battalion) and admitted Spanish troops since March 1937.[87] Their propaganda emphasised their role as the 'glorious avant-garde of world anti-fascism' or, in Upton Sinclair's more inspiring phrase, 'Young rebels from a hundred nations and tribes proclaiming: *No Pasaran*!'[88] All political groups treated them as heroes throughout the conflict; their example incited many to emulate them or contribute more generously to the cause.[89]

The Spanish front went beyond the Brigades and units based on similar cross-party principles such as the International Column of the CNT-FAI at Pina de Ebro, described by Clara and Paul Thälmann as 'a motley crew of anti-fascists of all countries'.[90] It was also broader than the 'circus of intellectuals' which toured Republican Spain in July 1937, in an elaborate attempt to materialise what Willi Bredel called 'a cultural Popular Front'.[91] The conflict turned Spain into a cosmopolitan hub which competed with Paris as the centre of left-wing initiatives of a national or transnational character. Since the proclamation of the Second Republic in 1931, an 'anti-fascist bohemia' of refugees had chosen Barcelona and Madrid as places to live and continue their political struggles.[92] This process intensified during the war, as German anarchists created an International Committee of Anti-fascist Exiles in Barcelona in August 1936.[93] Since at least mid-1937, an International

Anti-fascist Club at the Casa degli Italiani in Barcelona hosted tributes to volunteers, public readings and theatre shows, published propaganda and sponsored conferences among different groups.[94] Associations of Portuguese and Cuban anti-fascists were set up in Madrid and Barcelona before or during the war, with Spanish support and funding.[95]

Besides giving economic and political assistance to these groups, the Republic inspired new political formulas based on a unitary logic. A complex and fluid situation and the lack of clear leadership gave local leaders and factions, for instance in the KPD, a large degree of autonomy to make decisions inspired by the military needs and the war spirit.[96] It also boosted the organisations which tried to eschew party structures and prioritise action over speculation, such as Carlo Roselli's Giustizia è Libertà, which described itself as 'the first totally antifascist European movement'.[97] Supra-party committees speaking for specific communities mushroomed from Barcelona to the International Brigades headquarters at Albacete and the Republic's second capital in Valencia.[98] Spain was the pretext, setting and inspiration of this process: Diego Martínez Barrio, the moderate president of the Republican *Cortes*, told a conference of German Communist, socialist and 'middle class anti-fascists' held in Paris on 10–11 April 1937 that 'in the blood shed by the fallen German, French and other volunteers, a firm, growing international people's front is being nourished ...'[99]

This unity was directly connected to the joint military struggle, and the Barcelona May Days of 1937 dealt it a serious blow. The rift between revolutionary and counter-revolutionary anti-fascists, caused as much by ideological differences as by the disastrous course of the war, received prompt and wide coverage in the international left-wing press. Following the Government and communist line, most papers interpreted the events as a victory of 'the anti-fascists' and a defeat of 'the putschists', which by allowing a 'more vigorous national unity' under a 'business-like' and 'responsible' new government led by Dr. Juan Negrín greatly increased the chances of victory.[100] Some echoed the Communist story of sabotage in Spain, imported from the Soviet Union, and called for the 'Trotskyist agents of fascism' to be 'rapidly eliminated from decent democratic society'.[101] Other papers, however, reproduced the alternative versions of the CNT-FAI, the philo-Trotskyist POUM and the many victims of the repression.[102]

The protest launched by anti-Stalinist Marxists such as Victor Serge through the Paris-based *Comité d'aide et de secours aux victimes de la contre-révolution espagnole* was as transnationally coordinated as the Aid Spain movement, and framed in a similar language.[103] In a report of his visit to Barcelona published in August, French syndicalist Robert Louzon compared the murder of POUM leader Andrés Nin by Soviet agents in June to that of Matteotti.[104] Katia Landau, the widow of an Austrian Trotskyist also murdered by the NKVD after the May Days, described Santa Ursula's prison in Barcelona as the 'Dachau' of Republican Spain.[105] German council Communist Paul Mattick, who had opposed CNT participation in government from the start, called on Spanish workers to fight against both 'Franco-Fascism and Moscow-Fascism'.[106] While advancing the anti-totalitarian narrative of the Cold War, this line of protest reflected the hegemony of and competition over anti-fascism within the international left. As criticism of the Republic mounted, even this supreme value was called into question. Scottish anarchist Ethel MacDonald, who escaped from Barcelona in September after having worked for the CNT's English-language broadcasts and saved many victims of the crackdown, described anti-fascism in August as 'the new slogan by which the working class is being betrayed'.[107] Similar doubts are reflected in Vernon Richards's *Spain and the World*, the 'Anti-Fascist fortnightly' which on 9 June renamed itself as 'Fortnightly dedicated to the anti-Fascist struggle and the Social Revolution in Spain' in order to mark the difference between both endeavours.[108]

The May Days, added to the purges in the Soviet Union, contributed to the gradual shrinking of the movement during the latter half of the war. Divisions over both issues weakened or destroyed Popular Front initiatives in Germany, Italy (especially after Carlo Roselli's murder by Fascist agents in June 1937) and France. Many revolutionary anti-fascists rallied around pacifist and anti-imperialist fronts, in ambiguous coexistence with fascistised groups such as Gaston Bergery's Parti Frontiste.[109] Disillusioned communists tried to create new platforms for transnational cross-party collaboration such as Willi Münzenberg's *Die Zukunft*.[110] The loss of revolutionary followers was partly the prize for Negrín's decision to woo liberals and conservatives, whom he saw as the key to the support of Western democracies. From mid-1937, a number of moderate observers expressed sympathy for his protection of owners and the Church and repression of extremists, on grounds of 'democracy' and because they considered this policy as the most effective to beat 'fascism'.[111] The anti-fascist front was split, but also reframed in ways that anticipate the 'counter-revolutionary' coalitions which fought and won the Second World War.[112]

While the war lasted, in any case, most participants abstained from criticising the Republic in order to avoid damaging the common cause. In April 1938 the CNT signed a much-publicised 'programme of unity of action' with the UGT and, after the fall of the Aragón Front and the ensuing government crisis, re-entered the government, turning the Popular Front into an 'Anti-fascist Popular Front'.[113] Trotskyist criticism of the Republic remained unpopular in anti-fascist circles, which avoided discussing Spanish domestic issues as much as possible.[114] Similar considerations dissuaded the leaders of the British Independent Labour Party from giving publicity to the alleged murder of its comrade Bob Smillie in a Spanish prison in May.[115] Willy Brandt, a young member of the tiny left socialist SAP, an associate of the POUM at the London Bureau, insisted on the need for unity in and outside Spain in a report to his comrades in July 1937, while reminding of the 'crucial' importance of the struggle of 'young anti-fascist Spain' for the International labour movement, freedom and socialism.[116]

Likewise, the very small number of anti-fascist writers who dared voice their dissatisfaction were censored or censored themselves –confirming the movement's either/or logic.[117] André Gide's article in defence of the Republic's anti-fascist prisoners was published by Bergery's *La Flèche* in December 1937 after being rejected by *Vendredi*, which refused to 'aggravate the divisions among Spanish communists and anarchists'.[118] Orwell's *Homage to Catalonia* was ignored when it was published in April 1938, after being rejected by the editors of the Left Book Club and *The New Statesman*.[119] Jean Cassou, the editor of *Europe* and founder of Les Amis de l'Espagne, justified his refusal to publish an article by US novelist Waldo Frank in August 1938 by sentencing: 'now the choice is made, and Spain appears to us only as a bloc, to be taken or rejected in whole, without making nuances'. Cassou proposed that Frank rewrite his article erasing inconvenient allusions to Republican politics, and Frank accepted.[120]

Neither did ideological differences hurt the volume of aid. Figures from Sweden and Switzerland indicate, on the contrary, a steady rise in collections, otherwise natural given the growing needs of Spanish civilians.[121] More interestingly, the CNT-FAI reacted to its defeat in the May Days by searching for allies beyond the anarcho-syndicalist movement under the banner of ... anti-fascism. Its decision to set up its own relief organisation in Barcelona, *Solidarité Internationale Antifasciste* (SIA), on 27 May 1937, was a deliberate attempt to compete with the Communist-controlled International Red Aid by presenting itself as a weapon of 'aid to all anti-fascists'.[122] Directed by the poet Lucía Sánchez Saornil since May 1938, SIA extended beyond the orbit of the International Workingman's Association by setting up some twenty national branches on five continents (including one in the UK, with Emma Goldman as secretary and sponsors such as Orwell and W. H. Auden). As its Communist competitor, the operation combined political manoeuvring and sincere conviction: as she organised the British section of SIA in December 1937, Goldman wrote to a colleague 'we cannot discard the term anti-Fascism. At least I cannot.'[123]

The growing certainty of defeat deepened the split at the front and the debate over responsibilities, especially after the fall of Barcelona in January 1939. Justified from the start by its alleged military effectiveness, anti-fascism was shaken by such a disaster. Trotsky lost no time in interpreting it as 'a terrible blow' that reflected 'the mechanics of the Spanish Popular Front as an organised system of deceit and treachery of the exploited masses'.[124] His former acolyte, the surrealist writer Pierre Naville, blamed it for frustrating the resistance of French workers to fascism since February 1934.[125] Mieczyslaw Bortenstein, a Polish-Jewish Trotskyist and International Brigade veteran, sentenced, soon before being sent to Auschwitz, 'By destroying the revolution, they lost the anti-fascist war'.[126] The Jamaican-born Pan-Africanist Claude McKay drew a different 'lesson': the Republic had ultimately been destroyed by its refusal to give up Morocco and thus take advantage of the natives' hostility to fascism.[127] The controversy continued for decades, producing bitter divisions and historiographical patterns based on largely symmetric memories of the conflict.

A failure of internationalism?

Just as they had predicted its victory thanks to the anti-fascist international, many friends of the Republic saw its demise as a failure of internationalism. On 28 January 1939, three months before hanging himself at his New York hotel room, his desk covered with photographs of Spanish children killed by bombs, German writer Ernst Toller wrote to his British colleague Stephen Spender about his recent six-month fund-raising tour across Europe and the US: 'one feels that all this ought to have been done ever so much earlier, that all of us have somehow failed'.[128] Toller's ambitious Spanish Relief Plan, a direct appeal to the heads of the wealthiest nations to provide the massive aid Spain needed, seemed to assume that the global left had not yet become a self-sufficient international actor. Herbert Read, the British anarchist art historian, also interpreted 'the Spanish tragedy' as a sign 'that the international solidarity of the working classes … [did] not yet exist', and called on his readers to 'create new bonds of international solidarity, free from the weaknesses inherent in parliamentary socialism'.[129] After receding during the Second World War this self-critical view revived during the Cold War: as Spender put it in 1951, 'the emotions and the arguments used by the anti-Fascists were taken over by the democratic governments in their war against Hitler … But the fact was that the anti-Fascist battle had been lost.'[130]

This was not an unreasonable conclusion in the light of the fractures of various kinds that had impeded joint action on behalf of the Republic throughout the war; but, as often with anti-fascists, it was not unanimous. For André Gide, Spain's 'atrocious agony' was a case of 'heroism scorned, good faith betrayed, victorious cheating'.[131] Edwin Rolfe preferred to blame democratic statesmen such as Blum and Chamberlain 'by emptying the available wells of Chinese blood, and African, and Spanish, by strangling the Viennese voices and the laughing streets of Prague'.[132]. Considering how popular appeasement had been in the democracies, even while a great majority of the public sided with the Loyalists, it is doubtful that a tighter unity would have made a great difference. The war shaped an anti-fascist public sphere that momentarily served, with all its contradictions, as a functional equivalent of a global left – but also showed that internationalism alone was not enough, unless backed by weapons as in the Axis variety. The 'international people's front' could not win the war; but it could, and did, sustain the Republic's resistance by giving her material and moral aid and validating its self-image as world capital of anti-fascism. In the process, it produced a mass of testimonies of genuine and manufactured emotion, which continue to draw our attention to this fleeting episode of imperfect left-wing unity.

Notes

1 Enzo Collotti, *L'Antifascismo in Italia e in Europa: 1922–1939* (Turin: Loescher, 1975); Jacques Droz, *Histoire de l'antifascisme en Europe: 1923–1939* (Paris: La Découverte, 2001); Eric Hobsbawm, *Age of Extremes: The Short Twentieth Century* (London: Abacus, 1994).
2 François Furet, *The Passing of an Illusion: The Idea of Communism in the Twentieth Century* (New Haven, CT: Yale University Press, 1995), p. 251.
3 Michael Seidman, *Transatlantic Antifascisms: From the Spanish Civil War to the End of World War II* (Cambridge: Cambridge University Press, 2017), p. 48.
4 Charlotte Alston, 'Transnational Solidarities and the Politics of the Left, 1890–1990 – Introduction', *European Review of History*, Vol. 21, No. 4, 2014, pp. 447–450.

5 Joseph Fronczak, 'Local People's Global Politics: A Transnational History of the Hands Off Ethiopia Movement of 1935', *Diplomatic History*, Vol. 39, No. 2, 2015, pp. 245–274.
6 David Featherstone, *Solidarity: Hidden Histories and Geographies of Internationalism* (London: Zed Books, 2012).
7 *ABC*, 22 November 1936, p. 1. All translations are mine unless otherwise indicated.
8 *Frente libertario*, 9 February 1937; *La Libertad*, 30 November 1937.
9 John Langdon-Davies, 'Introduction', in *A Short History of the Future* (London: Routledge, 1936), p. xix.
10 Romain Rolland, 'Le duel des internationalismes', *Regards*, No. 183, 14 July 1937, p. 3.
11 Dolores Ibárruri, 'Our Battle-Cry Has Been Heard by the Whole World!', *Komsomolskaya Pravda*, 15 September 1936, Marxists Internet Archive (henceforth MIA).
12 Nigel Copsey, 'Preface: Towards a New Anti-Fascist "Minimum"?', in Nigel Copsey and Andrej Olechnowicz (eds), *Varieties of Anti-Fascism: Britain in the Interwar Period* (London: Palgrave, 2010), pp. xiv–xxi.
13 Larry Ceplair, *Under the Shadow of War: Fascism, Anti-Fascism, and Marxists* (New York: Columbia University Press, 1987), pp. 2–3.
14 A full discussion of this issue would require a longer article. See especially Gilles Vergnon, *L'antifascisme en France de Mussolini à Le Pen* (Rennes: Presses Universitaires de Rennes, 2009), pp. 94–99; Marc D'Hoore, 'Les libéraux belges et la Guerre Civile espagnole', *Revue belge d'Histoire contemporaine*, Vol. 18, No. 1–2, 1987, pp. 451–456; and Martin Pugh, 'The Liberal Party and the Popular Front', *English Historical Review*, Vol. 121, No. 494 (Dec. 2006), pp. 1327–1350, here pp. 1333–1334.
15 Manuel Aznar Soler & Luis Mario Schneider (eds), *II Congreso Internacional de escritores para la defensa de la cultura*, Vol. III (Valencia: Generalitat Valenciana, 1987), p. 84.
16 *L'Humanité*, 18 April 1936, p. 1.
17 Richard Thornberry, *André Malraux et l'Espagne* (Geneva: Droz, 1977), pp. 24–25.
18 John Langdon-Davies, *Behind the Spanish Barricades* (New York: Robert McBride, 1937), p. 268.
19 *Contra-fascismo*, No. 3, January–February 1937, pp. 3–7.
20 Niall Binns, *Argentina y la guerra civil española* (Madrid: Calambur, 2012), pp. 168–171.
21 The former quote was published in *ABC* on 9 November 1936 and 5 February 1937, among other sources. The latter was printed in Lucía Sánchez Saornil, '¡Madrid, Madrid, mi Madrid!...' (1936), in Serge Salaün, *Romancero de la defensa de Madrid*, Vol. 2 (Barcelona: Ruedo Ibérico, 1982), p. 41.
22 Eric Smith, *American Relief Aid and the Spanish Civil War* (Columbia, MO: University of Missouri Press, 2013), pp. 53–56.
23 Pablo de la Torriente, *Cartas y crónicas desde España* (La Habana: Centro Cultural Pablo de la Torriente Brau, 1999), pp. 272–276.
24 Lewis H. Mates, 'Practical Anti-Fascism? The Spanish Aid Campaigns in North-East England, 1936–1939', in Nigel Copsey & David Renton (eds), *British Fascism, the Labour Movement and the State* (London: Palgrave, 2005), pp. 118–140.
25 Aelwen D. Wetherby, *Private Aid, Political Activism: American Medical Relief to Spain and China* (Columbia, MO: University of Missouri Press, 2017), pp. 31–32.
26 Raanan Rein, 'El desafío a los Juegos Olímpicos de Berlín 1936: Los atletas judíos de Palestina en la frustrada Olimpiada Popular de Barcelona', *Historia Contemporánea*, No. 56, 2017, pp. 147–50.
27 Pierre Robert [René Bertholet], *Spain Calling! Their Fight is our Fight* (London: International Publishing, 1937), pp. 23–24.
28 *Report of International Conference on Spain, held on March 10th and 11th 1937, at the Central Hall, Westminster, S.W.1*, Warwick Digital Collections, 292/946/21/37.
29 *Service d'Information* of the *Comité Internationale d'Information et de Coordination pour l'Aide à l'Espagne Républicaine*, n.d. [1938], Archives de la Ligue de Droits de l'Homme, Nanterre, BDIC F DELTA RES 798/61.

30 Laurence Brown, 'Pour Aider Nos Frères d'Espagne: Humanitarian Aid, French Women, and Popular Mobilization during the Front Populaire', *French Politics, Culture & Society*, Vol. 25, No. 1 (Spring 2007), pp. 30–48.
31 Julie Gottlieb, 'Varieties of Feminist Responses to Fascism in Interwar Britain', in Nigel Copsey and Andrej Olechnowicz (eds), *Varieties of Anti-Fascism: Britain in the Interwar Period* (London: Palgrave, 2010), p. 101.
32 Mika Etchebéhère, *Mi guerra de España* (Barcelona: Plaza y Janés, 1976), p. 150.
33 Richard Baxell, *Unlikely Warriors: The British in the Spanish Civil War and the Struggle Against Fascism* (London: Aurum Press, 2012), p. 303.
34 Jean-Michel Palmier, *Weimar in Exile: The Antifascist Emigration in Europe and America* (London: Verso, 2006), p. 192.
35 Michael Petrou, *Renegades: Canadians in the Spanish Civil War* (Vancouver: UBC Press, 2008), p. 46.
36 Claude Jamet, 'Front Populaire de la Vienne', 12 June 1937, in Vergnon, *L'antifascisme en France*, pp. 108–109; André Wurmser, 'Lettre ouverte à Pyrrhus non-interventionniste', *Regards*, No. 183, 14 July 1937, p. 21.
37 Gandhi to Gladys Owen, 5 September 1937, in *Collected Works of Mahatma Gandhi Online*, Vol. 72, p. 195.
38 Jef Last, *The Spanish Tragedy* (London: Routledge, 1939), pp. 200–201.
39 Paul Preston, *We Saw Spain Die: Foreign Correspondents in the Spanish Civil War* (London: Constable, 2008), pp. 43–48.
40 Lois Orr, *Letters from Barcelona: An American Woman in Revolution and Civil War*, edited by Gerd-Rainer Horn (London: Palgrave, 2009), p. 203.
41 Georgette Smolski, 'L'U.L.B. devant la guerre d'Espagne', *Revue belge d'histoire contemporaine*, Vol. 18, No. 1–2, 1987, pp. 419–446.
42 Pascual Tomás to George Stolz, 15 January 1937, Archives of the Trade Union Congress, Warwick Digital Collections, 292/946/10/41.
43 *Report of International Conference on Spain*, p. 59.
44 Ibid., p. 98.
45 Diane Menghetti, 'North Queensland Anti-Fascism and the Spanish Civil War'. *Labour History*, No. 42 (May 1982), p. 71.
46 Archives de la Préfecture de Police de Paris (APPP), BA 2160, File 59685.
47 Sandra Souto, *Paso a la juventud: Movilización democrática, estalinismo y revolución en la República Española* (Valencia: Universitat de València, 2013), pp. 378–382.
48 Bertil Lundvik, *Solidaritet och partitaktik: Den svenska arbetarrörelsen och spanska inbördeskriget 1936–1939* (Stockholm: Almqvist & Wicksell International, 1980), pp. 194–197.
49 Kasper Braskén, 'Making Antifascism Transnational: The Origins of Communist Articulations of Resistance in Europe, 1923–1924', *Contemporary European History*, Vol. 25, No, 4, 2016, pp. 573–596.
50 Cristina Cuevas-Wolf, 'A Defiant Spain: Münzenberg, Montage and Communist Media in France and Spain', in Jordana Mendelson (ed.), *Revistas, modernidad y guerra* (Madrid: Museo Nacional Centro de Arte Reina Sofía, 2008), pp. 53–71.
51 Daniel Laqua, 'Freethinkers, Anarchists and Francisco Ferrer: The Making of a Transnational Solidarity Campaign', *European Review of History*, Vol. 21, No 4, 2014, pp. 467–484; Lisa McGirr, 'The passion of Sacco and Vanzetti: A Global History', *Journal of American History*, Vol. 93, No. 4 (March 2007), pp. 1085–1115; Fronczak, 'Local People's Global Politics'.
52 Christopher Vials (ed.), *American Literature in Transition, 1940–1950* (Cambridge: Cambridge University Press, 2017), pp. 73–74.
53 Gerben Zaagsma, *Jewish volunteers, the International Brigades and the Spanish Civil War* (London: Bloomsbury Academic, 2017), pp. 4–7.
54 Nir Arielli, 'Induced to Volunteer? The Predicament of Jewish Communists in Palestine and the Spanish Civil War', *Journal of Contemporary History*, Vol. 46, No. 4 (October 2011), pp. 854–870.
55 Marek Jan Chodakiewicz, 'Affinity and Revulsion: Poland Reacts to the Spanish Right, 1936–1939 (And Beyond)', in Marek Jan Chodakiewicz & John Radzilowski

(eds), *Spanish Carlism and Polish Nationalism: The Borderlands of Europe in the 19th and 20th Centuries* (Charlottesville, VA: Leopolis Press, 2010), p. 69.

56 Vjeran Pavlakovic, 'Vladko Maček, the Croatian Peasant Party and the Spanish Civil War', *Contemporary European History*, Vol. 16, No. 2 (May 2007), p. 243.

57 Furet, *The Passing of an Illusion*, p. 259.

58 Andrés Bisso, 'El antifascismo latinoamericano: Usos locales y continentales de un discurso europeo', *Asian Journal of Latin American Studies*, Vol. 3, 2000, pp. 91–116.

59 Agustín Sánchez Andrés & Fabián Herrera León, *Contra todo y contra todos: La diplomacia mexicana y la cuestión española en la Sociedad de Naciones, 1936–1939* (Santa Cruz de Tenerife: Idea, 2011), p. 181.

60 Andrea Acle-Kreysing, 'Antifascismo: un espacio de encuentro entre el exilio y la política nacional: El caso de Vicente Lombardo Toledano en México (1936–1945)', *Revista de Indias*, Vol. LXXVI, No. 267, 2016, pp. 573–609.

61 Ernesto Giudici, 'Fascismo mundial y argentino', *Contra-fascismo*, No. 2, August-September 1936, pp. 3, 8–9; and Ernesto Giudici, 'Fascismo y fenómeno fascista universal', *Contra-fascismo*, No. 1, 25 April 1936, pp. 1, 7.

62 Blanca Luz Brum, 'Clamor por los niños ametrallados de Madrid', in *Cantos de la América del Sur* (Santiago de Chile: Ercilla, 1939), p. 19.

63 Edwin Rolfe, *Collected Poems* (Urbana, IL: University of Illinois Press, 1996), p. 130.

64 Tom Buchanan, '"Shanghai-Madrid Axis"? Comparing British Responses to the Conflicts in Spain and China, 1936–39', *Contemporary European History*, Vol. 21, No. 4, 2012, pp. 533–552.

65 Edgar Snow, *Red Star Over China* (London: Left Book Club, 1937), p. 407.

66 'Chinos en España', *Mundo Gráfico*, 27 October 1937, p. 4.

67 Nancy Tsou & Len Tsou, 'The Asian Volunteers in the Spanish Civil War: A Report', *Science & Society*, Vol. 68, No. 3, 2004, pp. 342–350.

68 *La Vanguardia*, 22 April 1938.

69 Jawaharlal Nehru, 'Homage to the Spanish Republic', 24 January 1939, in *China, Spain and the War* (London, 1940), p. 58.

70 Maria Framke, 'Political humanitarianism in the 1930s: Indian aid for Republican Spain', *European Review of History: Revue européenne d'histoire*, Vol. 23, No. 1–2, 2016, pp. 63–81; Michele L. Louro, *Comrades against Imperialism: Nehru, India, and Interwar Internationalism* (Cambridge: Cambridge University Press, 2018), pp. 236–241.

71 Tom Buchanan, '"The Dark Millions in the Colonies are Unavenged": Anti-Fascism and Anti-Imperialism in the 1930s', *Contemporary European History*, Vol. 25, No. 4, 2016, pp. 645–665.

72 Robert Shilliam, '"Ah, We Have Not Forgotten Ethiopia": Anti-Colonial Sentiments for Spain in a Fascist Era', in Gurminder K. Bhambra & John Narayan (eds), *European Cosmopolitanism: Colonial Histories and Postcolonial Societies* (London: Routledge, 2016), pp. 31–46; Featherstone, *Solidarity*, pp. 108–111.

73 Maria Rosa de Madariaga, *Los moros que trajo Franco: La intervención de tropas coloniales en la Guerra Civil española* (Barcelona: Martínez Roca, 2002), pp. 173–178; Benjamin Stora, 'La gauche socialiste, révolutionnaire, et la question du Maghreb au moment du Front Populaire (1935–1938)', *Revue française d'histoire d'outre-mer*, Vol. 70, No. 258–259, 1983, pp. 57–79.

74 Najati Sidqi, 'I Went to Defend Jerusalem in Cordoba, Memoirs of a Palestinian Communist in the Spanish International Brigades' [*al-Tali'a*, June 1938], *Jerusalem Quarterly*, No. 62, 2015, pp. 102–109.

75 Madariaga, *Los moros que trajo Franco*, pp. 321–346.

76 'The Fascist Rebellion in Spain', *Negro Worker*, Vol. VI, No. 8 (Oct. 1936); 'Support the Spanish People', *Negro Worker*, Vol. VII, No. 2 (Feb. 1937); 'Save the Spanish Republic, the Bulwark of Liberty and Peace!', *Negro Worker*, Vol. VII, No. 4 (April 1937).

77 Neelam Srivastava, *Italian Colonialism and Resistances to Empire, 1930–1970* (London: Palgrave, 2018), p. 174; Last, *The Spanish Tragedy*, p. 138.

78 Léopold Sédar Senghor, 'Méditerranée' [1938], in *Prose and Poetry* (London: Heinemann, 1976), p. 127.
79 Taffy Adler, 'Lithuania's Diaspora: The Johannesburg Jewish Workers' Club, 1928–1948', *Journal of Southern African Studies*, Vol. 6, No. 1, 1979, pp. 83–85.
80 Featherstone, *Solidarity*, pp. 112–126.
81 Nic Ulmi, et al., 'La solidarité populaire avec l'Espagne républicaine en Suisse', in Mauro Cerutti (ed.), *La Suisse et l'Espagne de la République a Franco* (Lausanne: Antipodes, 2006), p. 294.
82 Daniel Kowalsky, *Stalin and the Spanish Civil War* (New York: Columbia University Press, 2004), Chapter 4, online at www.gutenberg-e.org/kod01/frames/fkodimg.html.
83 André Gide, *Return from the USSR* (New York: Alfred Knopf, 1937), p. 44.
84 Karl Schlögel, *Moscow 1937* (London: Polity, 2014), pp. 95–108.
85 Gleb J. Albert, '"To Help the Republicans not just by Donations and Rallies, but with the Rifle": Militant Solidarity with the Spanish Republic in the Soviet Union, 1936–1937', *European Review of History*, Vol. 21, No. 4, 2014, pp. 501–518.
86 Louis Fischer, *Men and Politics* (New York: Duell, Sloan and Pearce, 1940), p. 413.
87 Lisa A. Kirschenbaum, *International Communism and the Spanish Civil War: Solidarity and Suspicion* (Cambridge: Cambridge University Press, 2015), pp. 83–116.
88 *Le volontaire de la liberté*, Paris, [1938], 2; Upton Sinclair, *No Pasarán! (They Shall Not Pass): A Story of the Battle of Madrid* (Pasadena, 1937), p. 95.
89 Antonio Elorza & Marta Bizcarrondo, 'Las Brigadas Internacionales: Imágenes desde la izquierda', *Ayer*, Vol. 56, No. 4, 2004, pp. 67–91.
90 Clara Thälmann & Paul Thälmann, *Combats pour la liberté: Moscou, Madrid, Paris* (Paris: La Digitale, 1983), p. 171.
91 Aznar Soler & Schneider, *II Congreso Internacional de escritores*, p. 77.
92 Julián Gorkin, 'Bohemia antifascista', *Luz*, 2 August 1933.
93 Carlos García & Harald Piotrowski, 'Emigración alemana en Barcelona a principios del siglo XX', in Dieter Nelles, et. al. (eds), *Antifascistas alemanes en Barcelona (1933–1939)* (Barcelona: Sintra, 2010), pp. 51–56.
94 See *Solidaridad Obrera*, 7 August 1937; *La Vanguardia*, 11 September 1937 and 11 January 1938; *La Voz*, 29 November 1937; *El Sol*, 7 December 1937; *The Volunteer for Liberty*, Vol. II, No. 6, 23 February 1938.
95 Cristina Clímaco, 'Portugal within the European Antifascist Movement, 1922–1939', in Hugo Garcia, Mercedes Yusta, Xavier Tabet and Cristina Clímaco (eds), *Rethinking Antifascism: History, Memory, and Politics, 1922 to the Present* (Oxford: Berghahn, 2010), p. 126; Comité Antifascista Cubano de Madrid to Comisión Ejecutiva of PSOE, 8 July 1936, Archivo Fundación Pablo Iglesias, Alcalá de Henares, AH-78–4.
96 Tim Rees, 'The Highpoint of Comintern Influence? The Communist Party and the Civil War in Spain', in Tim Rees & Andrew Thorpe (eds), *International Communism and the Communist International, 1919–43* (Manchester: Manchester University Press, 1998), pp. 149–161.
97 Stéphanie Prézioso, '*Aujourd'hui en Espagne, demain en Italie*: L'exil antifasciste italien et la prise d'armes révolutionnaire', *Vingtième siècle*, No 93, 2007, pp. 79–91; Stéphanie Prézioso, 'Antifascism and Anti-Totalitarianism: The Italian Debate', *Journal of Contemporary History*, Vol. 43, No. 4, 2008, p. 570.
98 Alejandro Andreassi, 'El KPD en la Guerra Civil española y la cuestión del Frente Popular: Algunas reflexiones', *Hispania*, Vol. LXXVI, No. 246, 2014, pp. 177–204.
99 Willi Münzenberg, 'The People's Front in Germany', *New Masses*, No. 7, 4 May 1937, p. 5.
100 James Hawthorne, 'Spain's Government Girds for War', *New Masses*, 22 June 1937, pp. 7–8.
101 James Hawthorne, 'Trotskyist agents in Spain', *New Masses*, 13 July 1937, pp. 15–18.
102 See, among many others, *Spain and the World*, 4 June 1937 and 2 July 1937; *L'Espagne Nouvelle*, 22 May 1937; *Guerra di Classe*, 25 May 1937; *One Big Union Monthly*, July and November 1937; *La Flèche*, 5 June and 7 August 1937; Orwell, 'Spilling the

Spanish Beans', *New English Weekly*, 29 July 1937 and 2 September 1937; Orr, *Letters from Barcelona*, pp. 185–200; Ture Nerman, *Spansk resa våren 1937*, MIA.

103 Victor Serge, *Memoirs of a Revolutionary* (Iowa City, IA: University of Iowa Press, 2002 [1951]), pp. 339–340; L.-P. Foucaud, 'Au secours des républicains espagnols', *La Flèche*, 4 September 1937.

104 Robert Louzon, 'Notes sur l'Espagne', *La Révolution Prolétarienne*, No. 253, 25 August 1937.

105 Katia Landau, 'Stalinism in Spain', Parts 1 & 2, *Revolutionary History*, Vol. 1, No. 2, 1988 [originally published as *Le stalinisme en Espagne*, Paris, 1938].

106 Paul Mattick, '*The Barricades Must Be Torn Down:* Moscow-Fascism in Spain', *International Communist Correspondence*, Chicago, Vol. 3, No. 7–8 (August 1937), MIA.

107 *Workers' Free Press,* October 1937, in Mark Shipway, *Anti-Parliamentary Communism: The Movement for Workers' Councils in Britain* (London: Palgrave, 1988), p. 159.

108 See also V[ernon] R[ichards], 'Anti-Fascism: Capitalist or Socialist?', *Spain and the World*, Vol. II, No. 47, 23 December 1938.

109 Stora, 'La gauche socialiste, révolutionnaire et la question du Maghreb', p. 70; Police reports on the French section of the anarchist 'Solidarité Internationale Antifasciste', APPP, BA 2159, File 59685.

110 Susan D. Pennybacker, *From Scottsboro to Munich: Race and Political Culture in 1930s Britain* (Princeton and Oxford: Princeton University Press, 2009), pp. 223–239.

111 Émile Hambresin, 'L'écrasement de l'anarchisme espagnol et la résurrection de l'Espagne', *Esprit*, No. 65 (février 1938), pp. 680–702. Similar views by Tory MP Michael Weaver, in 'An English Conservative on Spain', *The War in Spain*, No. 47, 10 December 1938, p. 186.

112 Cf. Seidman, *Transatlantic Antifascisms*, 84ff.

113 François Godicheau, 'L'existence et le nom du Front Populaire comme enjeu d'interprétation et d'appropriation', *Mélanges de la Casa de Velázquez*, Vol. 41, No. 1, 2011, online at http://journals.openedition.org/mcv/3815.

114 Robert Cohen, *When the Old Left was Young: Student Radicals and America's First Mass Student Movement 1929–1941* (New York: Oxford University Press, 1993), pp. 167–171; Luc Van Dongen, 'Solidarité ouvrière et antifascisme: Les amis de l'Espagne républicaine à La Chaux-de-Fonds (1936–1939)', *Cahiers d'histoire du mouvement ouvrier*, Vol. 13, 1997, p. 42.

115 Tom Buchanan, 'The Death of Bob Smillie, the Spanish Civil War, and the Eclipse of the Independent Labour Party', *The Historical Journal,* Vol. 40, No. 2, 1997, pp. 435–464.

116 Willy Brandt, *In Exile: Essays, Reflections and Letters 1933–1947* (London: Wolff, 1971), p. 164.

117 Anson Rabinbach, 'George Mosse and the Culture of Antifascism', *German Politics and Society*, Vol. 18, No. 4, 2000, pp. 37–38.

118 Jean Guéhenno, *Journal d'une 'revolution', 1937–1938* (Paris: Grasset, 1939), pp. 214–236.

119 Eric Hobsbawm, 'Intellectuals and the Spanish Civil War', in *Revolutionaries* (London: Abacus, 2007). Online version, Orwell Foundation. https://www.orwellfoundation.com/the-orwell-foundation/orwell/library/eric-hobsbawm-intellectuals-and-the-spanish-civil-war/.

120 Jean Cassou to Waldo Frank, 30 August 1938, Bibliothèque Nationale de France, Paris, Fonds Jean Cassou, JC 188 (6).

121 Lundvik, *Solidaritet och partitaktik*, p. 192; Van Dongen, 'Solidarité ouvrière et antifascisme', p. 38.

122 Valentin Cionini, 'Solidarité Internationale Antifasciste, ou l'humanitaire au service des idées anarchistes', *Diacronie*, No. 7, 2011, https://doi.org/10.4000/diacronie.3311.

123 Emma Goldman, *Vision on Fire: Emma Goldman and the Spanish Revolution*, edited by David Porter (Oakland, CA: AK Press, 2006), pp. 121–122.

124 Leon Trotsky, 'The Tragedy of Spain', *Socialist Appeal*, 10 February 1939, in Valentine Cunningham (ed.), *Spanish Front: Writers on the Civil War* (New York: Oxford University Press,1986), pp. 367–369.

125 Pierre Naville, '12 février 1934, la classe ouvrière écrase le fascisme, 12 février 1939, les dirigeants socialistes et communistes laissent Franco écraser les travailleurs d'Espagne', *La lutte ouvrière*, 12 February 1939.
126 Mieczyslaw Bortenstein (M. Casanova), *Spain Betrayed: How the Popular Front Opened the Gates to Franco* [*Quatrième Internationale*, No. 17, May 1939], MIA.
127 Claude McKay, 'Native Liberation Might Have Stopped Franco's Revolt', *New Leader*, 18 February 1939, in *The Passion of Claude McKay: Selected Poetry and Prose, 1912–1948* (New York: Schoken, 1973), pp. 285–289.
128 Ernst Toller to Stephen Spender, 28 January 1939, in Toller, *Briefe 1915–1939: Kritische Ausgabe* (Göttingen: Wallstein Verlag, 2018), pp. 1565–1566.
129 Herbert Read, 'Nearer to reality', *Revolt!*, Vol. III, No. 1, 11 February 1939.
130 Stephen Spender, *World Within World: The Autobiography of Stephen Spender* (Los Angeles, University of California Press, 1966), p. 262.
131 André Gide, 26 January 1939, in *Journal, tome 2: 1926–1950* (Paris: Gallimard, 1997), p. 639.
132 Rolfe, *Collected Poems*, p. 200.

Acknowledgements

I am grateful to Scott H. Krause for the idea, to the editors, and to Michael Seidman, Gilles Vergnon, Olga Glondys and José María Faraldo for their comments on earlier versions. This article is an outcome of the research project *Espacios emocionales: los lugares de la utopía en la Historia Contemporánea* ['Emotional spaces: spaces of utopia in Modern history'], funded by Spain's Ministry of Science and Innovation (Reference PGC2018-093778-B-I00), and directed by professor Juan Pro Ruiz.

13

AFRICAN AMERICAN INTERNATIONALISM AND ANTI-FASCISM

Cathy Bergin

Wes Bellamy, the Deputy Mayor of Charlottesville, eschewed the euphemism 'alt right' in the aftermath of the killing of Heather Heyer by the torch-wielding 'Unite the Right' rally in that city in the Summer of 2017. It is, he insisted 'important to call these people what they are: White supremacists.'[1] Some of the counter-demonstrators, equally under no linguistic illusions, explicitly named the beast that they were resisting, declaring the counter-campaign to be anti-fascist and anti-Nazi.[2] No neologism was required to describe what was afoot. Its lineage was clear from Jim Crow and the Klan, through the American-German Bund in the 1930s, and to McCarthyism in the mid-twentieth century with its anti-communist and racist witch hunts, and its exculpation of, and apologetics for, Nazi war criminals. Fascism has not been alien to the landscape of US race politics, and neither have resistances to it. One of the central resources for thinking about the relationship between anti-fascism and anti-racism is to be found in the US history of black radical writing about race and class, and the key determination of the race-class relation via the history of colonialism, slavery, and neo-colonialism. This chapter situates the Spanish Civil war in that wider formation of race/class politics instantiated by African American activists between the wars.

While the African American story of the Spanish Civil war remains relatively untrumpeted, there is a rich body of scholarship in this discrete area of black internationalist history.[3] This chapter focuses on the letters from brigadists and more specifically on the writings of African Americans in radical black and Communist publications. It is worth noting that the Spanish Civil War featured strongly in the African American Press as a whole, not least in the journalism of Langston Hughes, who is a focal writer for this chapter. As Robin Kelley has noted, African American newspapers generally were on the side of the Spanish loyalists.[4] Michael Thurston sees this allegiance in relation to the influence of left wing politics during the period, arguing that when the Spanish Republic was attacked 'black editors and writers acted on their historic sense of strategic connection with the Left'.[5] Black radicals writing about Spain can be thought of here as essential to creating a vital counter-public which insisted on the connections between fascism abroad and what was frequently referred to as 'domestic' fascism in the US in relation to Jim Crow.[6]

So, my focus is on black anti-fascism within the context of the black radical tradition more widely and on earlier twentieth century formations of black internationalism more specifically. The links made between racism and fascism by black activists are informed by the lived experience of 'race', and also by the ambitious and dynamic race politics of the black Left. As a literary and cultural historian I am interested in the powerful ways that transnational solidarity is articulated. While this chapter keeps a relatively local focus, that loci needs to be understood within the structuring paradigm of the transnational. If 'internationalism' is a political formation/outlook then 'transnationalism' points to the extra-national process/structuring of that formation. There is a productive problematic at play in focusing on transnational politics through an emphasis on local articulations of race/class politics. Black internationalism has been variously defined as forms of pan-Africanism, subaltern solidarities, cultural interconnectedness and shared diasporic histories rooted in slavery and colonialism.[7] All of these definitions are important when looking at African American anti-fascism in relation to the Spanish Civil War. For my purposes I am defining Black internationalism in the 1930s as a form of race-centred, anticolonial, anti-fascist, inter-racial class, politics.[8]

In this chapter I trace the American vector of black transnational politics through the frame of the local experiences of those African American radicals in and around the Left. Such a focus in no way denies the dynamic transnationalism which emerged in the US, Africa, the Caribbean and Europe between the wars. Indeed, historically the black radical imagination has precisely been marked by its internationalism where black activists transcended the local to provide powerful examples of forms of solidarity forged outside the limits of the nation state.[9] These subjects of racialisation and agents of an ambitious political imaginary were drawing upon a rich tradition of transnational connections. As C. L. R. James argued in 1939 the black transnational *tradition* rends asunder parochial histories going right back to the Haitian revolution:

> The continuous risings in Africa; the refusal of the Ethiopian warriors to submit to Mussolini; the American Negroes who volunteered to fight in Spain in the Abraham Lincoln Brigade, as Rigaud and Beauvais had volunteered to fight in America, tempering their swords against the enemy abroad for use against the enemy at home – these lightnings announce the thunder ... In Africa, in America, in the West Indies, on a national and international scale, the millions of Negroes will raise their heads, rise up from their knees, and write some of the most massive and brilliant chapters in the history of revolutionary socialism.[10]

For James and countless black radicals this tradition does not have a root so much as routes.[11] Those routes exist in the rich interconnections between the colonially oppressed and the wage labour exploited *and* the wage labour exploited colonially oppressed – the majority of the global working class throughout the history of capitalism. The commitment to international solidarity is indeed a radical political positioning for black communities in the US between the wars, when such envisionings often meant making connections with a variety of struggles whose relationship to the daily horrors of racism was on the face of it quite oblique. Irish independence for example is a focal point of interest in the black radical press of the 1920s.[12] That the Spanish Civil War became the site for the articulation of a race-conscious anti-fascism is in itself a testament to the radical vision of race/class politics inaugurated by African American and Caribbean writers and activists of the early twentieth century. Black radicals and Communists readily understood Jim Crow through an anti-fascist framework and the connections made between the war in Spain and racial conflict at home illuminated a range of unlaboured analogies which placed racialised oppression at the centre of both capitalism and fascism. It is within this context that I investigate articulations of African American anti-fascist discourses that emerged in the US in relation to the Spanish Civil war.

Anti-colonialism

> It is not only as an artist that I love the cause of democracy in Spain, but also as a Black. I belong to an oppressed race, discriminated against, one that could not live if fascism triumphed in the world.[13]

Paul Robeson famously supported the cause of Spain. He performed at many benefits to raise money for the International Brigades, visited the front in 1938 and after the war he was made a honorary member of the Abraham Lincoln Brigade.[14] His explicit rendering of an organic anti-fascism among African Americans was echoed by Thyra Edwards, an organiser for the Negro Committee to Aid Spanish Democracy. She told the *Daily Worker* from Spain that 'We would rather die in the ranks of the Loyalists than live in the slime of fascism'.[15] Edwards's wonderful ambiguity about where the 'slime of fascism' is located is left for the reader to decide. Edwards was a social worker from Chicago who travelled to Spain in October 1937 to link up with over 90 African Americans who joined the Abraham Lincoln Brigade to aid the Loyalists in an anti-fascist war against Franco.[16]

As many scholars of black Internationalism have noted, the black presence in the Abraham Lincoln Brigade cannot be understood without reference to the Italian fascist and colonial invasion of Ethiopia in 1935.[17] Indeed the anti-colonial nature of black radical anti-fascism can scarcely be accounted without reference to the impact of Mussolini's assault on Ethiopia. As stated in a 5 cent pamphlet about Salaria Kee, an African American nurse who travelled to Spain:

> The hundreds of Negro boys who had been prevented from going to Ethiopia understood the issues more clearly now. To them Spain was now the battlefield on which Italian fascism might be defeated.[18]

African Americans readily recognised the 'manifest racial character' of Mussolini's invasion.[19] In New York in particular, African Americans campaigned, rioted and organised boycotts of Italian business to both demand solidarity with the Ethiopian victims of fascist aggression and vent their frustrations at the inaction of the Western powers in the face of Mussolini's invasion.[20] Any potential volunteers from the US who wished to fight the fascists in Ethiopia were deterred by both Haile Selassie's compliance to US pressure not to recruit oversees and by the violation of a US law which would potentially see them stripped of citizenship.[21] The Spanish Civil war veteran James Yates told Cedric Robinson:

> We didn't get a chance to go to Ethiopia much as many of us would have like to have gone. But when Ethiopia was invaded and Italy overran it, those same troops left there and went to Spain. This was a time and a chance for especially the Blacks to volunteer and get back at the fascists that had invaded Ethiopia.[22]

While Yates here is echoing the famous dictum that Spain wasn't 'Ethiopia but it'll do' this is also the identification of a fascist *and* colonial threat that African Americans had a particular investment in opposing. Mussolini's invasion of Ethiopia was after all a colonial aggression and thus fascism and colonialism were understood as intimately and fatally connected to 'race.' Edward E Strong (head of the youth division the National Negro Congress) argued in *The Crisis* in 1936 that: 'A victory for the Spanish fascists would be a tremendous blow to the interests of dark people, colonial and semi-colonial nations the world over.'[23] For Strong as for the NNC more widely fascism and colonialism were thoroughly connected.[24] In July 1937 *Negro Worker* couldn't have been more explicit in its rendering of Spain as an anti-colonial struggle deeply entwined with Ethiopia's plight:

> Among these volunteers who have offered their lives in defence of Spain from fascist barbarism, are a number of Negroes and other colonials. These colonials, fighting in the ranks of the Government forces, realize that the fight for freedom in Spain is very closely connected with their own struggles against tyranny and the ever increasing world fascist menace. They realize further that a defeat of fascism in Spain, means not only a victory for the Spanish people, but a decisive curb to the fascist ambition of war for colonial annexation and a tremendous setback in Mussolini's attempt to consolidate his occupation of Abyssinia.[25]

Ethiopia is not the focus of this chapter but it forms a vital element of this story and is almost universally cited by African American volunteers as a motivating factor in their decision join the Abraham Lincoln Brigade.

Racism and the popular front

While Ethiopia is essential to understanding the anti-colonial politics which informed black anti-fascism there are also other reasons cited for going to Spain. Not least of these was the opportunity to escape US racism; as the volunteer Eluard Luchelle McDaniels put it, 'I would rather die here than be slaved any more'.[26] McDaniels here, in addition to calling upon the historical legacy of 'race' in the US, is echoing a sentiment expressed over 20 years earlier by Du Bois who remarked of the First World War: 'War is hell but there are things worse than hell, as every Negro knows.'[27] This 'opportunity' provided by war is also evoked by James Baldwin over 20 years after Spain in relation to the Second World War when he insists that the African American soldier 'is far freer in a strange land than he has ever been at home. Home! The very word begins to have a despairing and diabolical ring'.[28]

Relevant to this acknowledgement of dangers to black life in America is that the letters and memoirs of the African American volunteers in Spain insist is that fascism posed a *particular* threat to people of colour. Salaria Kee claimed: 'Surely Negro people will just as willingly give of their means to relieve the suffering of a people attacked by the enemy of all racial minorities – fascism.'[29] James Peck, a lieutenant in the Republican Army Air Force of Spain was quite clear that:

> what we were fighting for in Spain was a species of that thing which at home had kept me, a trained pilot, grounded, while keeping hundreds of thousands of other Negro youths from being what they wanted to be.[30]

This 'species of that thing' that Peck was fighting in Spain was a form of white supremacy that was readily evoked in fighting for the Republic. Identification of anti-fascism with the experience of living in racialised America was ubiquitous in the black radical press and among African American writers and activists. Of particular note here is the poet and activist Langston Hughes who visited Spain and covered the war for the Baltimore *Afro American* and the *Cleveland Call and Post* for over six months in 1937.[31] Hughes was crystal clear that African Americans were more poised to become anti-fascists because of their experiences of racism in the US. In the 1938 publication *Writers Take Sides* he stated: 'Of course I am against Fascism with its spread of color prejudice and race hatred and working class oppression. How could any sensible Negro be otherwise?'[32] In the same publication the African American journalist and poet Frank Marshall Davis insisted he was anti-fascist 'because Negroes would not only suffer the plight of white Americans but would also suffer especial terror aimed at minority groups'.[33]

Fascism is cited here and elsewhere as a particularly racialised form of oppression which African Americans are familiar with and are most threatened by its ascendancy. This commitment to fight against fascism as a particular form of racialised oppression is informed by the anti-colonial politics of black radicals of the period but for those African American Communists and fellow travellers who went to fight in

Spain the local expression of Communist praxis was also significant. During the Comintern directed Popular Front (1934–1939) anti-fascism and anti-racism in the US were linked in a variety of ways which attempted to mobilise African Americans as central to the articulation of a 'progressive' Americanism.[34] This had been unimaginable (theoretically if not in practice) during the so-called Third Period (1928–1934) where the war against the 'social fascism' of social democracy saw the black communist press concentrating on delineating an interracial class solidarity through a sectarian evisceration of the black middle class.[35] The Popular Front prioritised cross-class alliances in the fight against fascism at home and support to colonial nations like France and Britain in the fight against fascism abroad.[36]

As has been well documented, during the Cold War the relationship between black activists and US communism in the Depression era was mischaracterised as a form of racist realpolitik at the behest of a duplicitous white left, rather than one forged by active black subjects who shaped the contours and meaning of black freedom in relation to a version of Marxist politics.[37] African American activists and writers created their own interpretations of Comintern dictates in what Bill Mullen calls an 'improvisatory spirit'.[38] Internationally the Popular Front saw the deprioritisation of anti-colonial struggle through working with 'democratic' European *colonial* powers against fascism. As it was the Bolshevik commitment to anti-colonialism that had made such a deep impression on the African American and Afro-Caribbean activists in the early 1920s who had forged US Communist politics of race, this abandonment was not insignificant. But, as with all of this history, we are hampered in our understandings of the period if we do not understand the complex ways in which activists on the ground implemented and adapted the directives from Moscow at the local level.[39]

During the Popular Front period in the US internationalism was articulated predominantly in relation to forms of anti-fascism yet the black claim on these politics was precisely the expression of transnational anti-racism. As the African American brigadist Canute Frankson, wrote in a letter to home from Spain in 1937:

> If we crush Fascism here we'll save our people in America, and in other parts of the world from the vicious persecution, wholesale imprisonment and slaughter which the Jewish people suffered and are suffering under Hitler's Fascist heels … We will crush them. We will build us a new society – a society of peace and plenty. There will be no color line, no jim-crow trains, no lynching. That is why, my dear, I am here in Spain.[40]

The ambition of this vision is striking in its local and global horizons. The day-to-day experiences of racism inform the expressions of interracial internationalist solidarity. Indeed, as Benjamin Balthaser argues between the wars 'Race' in the US was understood as a 'transnational term, linking slavery, colonialism, Jim Crow and capitalism into a single frame of analysis'.[41] Notable here also is Frankson's evocation of Nazi anti-Semitism. African American radicals of this period made a powerful set of connections between US racism and anti-Semitism in Germany. W. E. B. Du

Bois, visited Germany in 1936 and wrote for the *Pittsburgh Courier* about 'The Present Plight of the German Jew' which made a set of connections between racialisation of German Jews and people of colour:

> There has been no tragedy in modern times equal in its awful effects to the fight on the Jew in Germany. It is an attack on civilization, comparable only to such horrors as the Spanish Inquisition and the African slave trade. It has set civilization back a hundred years, and in particular has it made the settlement and understanding of race problems more difficult and more doubtful ... The proof of this [war on Jews] is incontrovertible, and must comfort all those in any part of the world who depend on race hate as the salvation of men.[42]

Anti-Semitism in Germany was covered widely by the African American Press in the 1930s. As Paul Gilroy notes 'comparisons between the two differently racialized regimes in Germany and America had been routinely made by black Americans before the Nazi genocide was launched'.[43] As I argue below, the mobilisation of the language of anti-fascism in relation to Jim Crow was one which was highly attuned to the racial threat that fascism held, but without understating the complex historical relations between African Americans and other racialised subjects in the US, the black/Jewish relationship in the 1930s on the Left was primarily one of expressed solidarity. Leading African American Communist James W Ford argued that the fight against anti-Semitism was 'an integral part of our fight for a progressive America' and such a fight needed solidarity between Jews and 'all the forces within the camp of progress, particularly the Negro people'.[44] Certainly in relation to the Spanish Civil War both Jews and African Americans had particular investments in the conflict in relation to racialised oppression. As Paul Buhle and Robin Kelley argue:

> By defending the Spanish Republic, these volunteers were also avenging those Jews perishing in German concentration camps as well as those Ethiopians whose precious land Mussolini invaded in 1935. Despite pockets of anti-Semitism during the 1930s among a few isolated Black nationalist groups, the struggle against fascism strengthened the Black-Jewish bond within Communist circles.[45]

The black liberatory aspiration of the period also defied both spatial and temporal boundaries and the mobilisation of black histories and geographies permeates the black radical press in the 1930s. In the pre Popular Front black Communist newspaper the *Liberator/Negro Liberator* the history of rebellion against enslavement directly informs the contemporary black liberation struggle. Frederick Douglass, Toussaint L'Ouverture and Nat Turner are constantly celebrated in order, 'to revive the revolutionary traditions of the race and mobilize the Negro Workers to do honour to their revolutionary fighters and heroes'.[46] The routes of black struggle 'began by the brave slave insurrectionists' are reclaimed in a determined effort to construct a black radical tradition of militant self-defence.[47] Moreover this is a tradition which must be revived and rescued from those who 'do not wish the exploited Negro masses to have any traditions of revolt and struggle against their oppressors'.[48] The discursive battle over the meaning and custody of the black radical tradition inaugurated powerful models of black liberation which were marshalled in a myriad of ways by black activists between the wars.

Frankson's letter home in which black freedom is imagined in terms of a class-based transnational politics of solidarity which foregrounded questions of 'race' and race-making, is a powerful utterance of a very specific anti-fascist politics. Those interconnected traditions dominate leftwing black radicalism from the Bolshevik Revolution to the Spanish Civil War.[49] The salient point here is that the identification of anti-fascism with anti-racism was not some top-down implementation of a Popular Front directive. Frankson's vision is not a colour blind gesture to solidarity but the articulation of a race conscious anti-fascism which draws its power from the horrors of racism in the US:

> Since this is a war between whites who for centuries have held us in slavery, and have heaped every kind of insult and abuse upon us, segregated and jim-crowed us; Why I, a Negro who have fought through these years for the rights of my people, am here in Spain today? … We can but look back at the pages of American history stained with the blood of Negroes; stink with the burning bodies of our people hanging from trees; bitter with the groans of our tortured loved ones from whose living bodies ears, fingers, toes have been cut for souvenirs – living bodies into which red-hot pokers have been thrust. All because of a hate created in the minds of men and women by their masters who keep us all under their heels while they suck our blood, while they live in their bed of ease by exploiting us.[50]

The vampiric imagery in this graphic account of white supremacist violence makes a subtle distinction between the 'masters' of capitalism and their deluded, if homicidal, foot soldiers. It speaks to a nuanced raced politics of class while simultaneously bearing witness to the violence unleashed upon black bodies and black lives. What Frankson expresses in his personal correspondence is indicative of the wider race/class politics which structure more public annunciations of the nature of racialised capitalism.

What marks the diverse expressions of black anti-fascism between the wars is the attempt to make a myriad of connections between the status of African Americans, the colonially oppressed and Spanish workers. Langston Hughes was one among many African American voices who insisted that in Spain there was 'not the slightest trace of color-prejudice to be found'.[51] Indeed African Americans in Spain generally commented upon how liberating it was to be away from the dangers of US racism, not least in relation to the absence of Jim Crow laws dictating all social and sexual interaction. However Spain was not free of racism, even though the International Brigades themselves were multicultural and committed to a politics of anti-racism.[52] The Moroccan troops fighting for Franco were subject to vicious racist stereotyping by the Spanish Loyalists.[53] In addition to the racialising polemics against North Africans there were also rare but occasional racist undercurrents directed towards black brigadists among the white Volunteers.[54] The public utterances of the African American volunteers went out of their way to note the absence of racism in Spain, and although this is as much a pointed underlining of the extent of racism at home it also spoke to an experience of being among white Europeans and Americans who had 'come out of movements in which racism was simply not tolerated'.[55] The Abraham Lincoln Brigade sent Joe Louis a telegram after his victory over Max Schmeling in 1938 to become heavyweight champion; the telegram congratulated him for 'KAYOING MYTH OF ARYAN RACIAL SUPERIORITY'.[56] Peter Carroll notes that the group photographs sent from Spain were meticulously multicultural in order to underline 'a visible repudiation of fascist appeals to a master race'.[57]

The salient point here in relation to anti-racism and anti-fascism is not that some white anti-fascists were racist, but that it was black anti-fascists who were adamant that anti-fascism *was* anti-racism. During the McCarthyite witch hunt against veterans of the Abraham Lincoln Brigade in 1954 Crawford Morgan insisted that:

> Being aware of what the Fascist Italian government did to the Ethiopians, and also the way that I and all the rest of the Negroes in this country have been treated ever since slavery, I figured I had a pretty good idea of what fascism was.[58]

A varied set of connections were made through the frame of African American experience, but flexed towards a wider transnational politics of liberation. For decades the black radical press had prioritised transnational politics; not simply in terms of international *coverage* of events in African, India, Ireland and the Caribbean, but in the attempt to *link* the condition of African Americans to the transnational workings of global capitalism and imperialism. According to W. A. Domingo:

> Africans abroad can aid Africa by striving to the limit to break the system that is responsible for the present political degradation of Africa and their own oppression in the West Indies, Central and South America and the United States.[59]

Domingo's insistence in 1920 that fighting racism at home connects 'Africans Abroad' because they are oppressed by global racialised capitalism is relevant to a politics seventeen years later where fighting fascism abroad is envisioned as the key to dismantling racism at home. Writing from Spain during the autumn of 1937, in an article published in the *Negro Worker* and *The Crisis*, Langston Hughes insisted that African Americans had a special and inaugurating role to play in the fight against fascism. He makes reference to the Fascist invasion of Ethiopia but also to the wider context of racialised capitalism which oppresses African Americans. That racial oppression is delineated in a manner which ensures that African Americans are the vanguard of the fight against fascism at home and abroad. It is African Americans after all 'who have long known in actual practise the meaning of the word Fascism'.[60]

This stress on black agency was endemic to articulations of black liberation between the wars where African American activists rejected liberal politics which placed them in the role of objects of victimhood rather than subjects of rebellion. Liberals according to Domingo are those who 'seek to attain a position of angelic impartiality which is founded upon a just valuation of pure morals'.[61] In the earlier writings of Domingo, Cyril Briggs, Hubert Harrison and Claude McKay among many others there was a rejection of liberal paternalism and the insistence on an assertive politics of black self-defence in the face of white supremacist violence. As the African Blood Brotherhood had insisted, 'With the murderer clutching at our throats we cannot afford to choose our weapons, but must defend ourselves with what lies nearest, whether that be poison, fire or what.'[62]

In the context of these earlier formulations Hughes' articles on Spain are not unusual in his consistent foregrounding of the racial threat of fascism, the African American claim on recognising fascism's particular character and the necessity for active black resistance:

> Those who have already practiced bombing the little villages of Ethiopia and now bomb Guernica and Madrid. The same Fascists who forced Italian peasants to fight in Africa now force African Moors to fight in Europe … Race means nothing when it can be turned to Fascist use. And yet race means everything when the Fascists of the world use it as a bugaboo and a terror to keep the working masses from getting together … And the old myths of race are kept alive to hurt and impede the rising power of the working class. But in America, where race prejudice is so strong, already we have learned what the lies of race mean – continued oppression and poverty and fear …[63]

Hughes interest here in the use of Moroccan troops by Franco during the civil war is echoed also by the African American Communist Louise Thompson who told Richard Wright in the *Daily Worker* that she 'wanted to see with my own eyes the difference between these two dark-skinned people fighting on opposite sides of the struggle'.[64] Wright himself insisted that the fascists had 'duped and defrauded a terribly exploited people'.[65] Silent on the racist constructions of the Moroccans by the Loyalists, but also evading such racist constructions themselves, the consensus among black Communists was that Franco's Moroccan troops had been tricked into fighting against the Spanish Republic.[66] The ex-Communist George Padmore took a rather more pointed approach to the 'duping' of North Africans by Franco. Padmore insisted that the use of Moroccan troops had been facilitated precisely by the refusal of the Spanish Republicans to relinquish their colonial territories. Writing in 1937 Padmore notes:

> it is so regrettable that democratic Spain, by failing to make an anti-imperialist gesture to the Moors, played into the hands of Franco. This should be a reminder to the European workers that: 'No people who oppress another people can themselves be free.'[67]

For Padmore anti-fascism had to be anti-colonial *in practice*, not merely in its rhetorical flourishes and he famously broke with Communism over what he saw as the betrayal of the anti-colonial struggle instituted by Popular Frontism.[68] Both his work and the work of C. L. R. James in this period provides us with a powerful anti-Stalinist black internationalism which is ruthlessly critical of the role of the Soviet Union in relation to both Ethiopia and Spain *while at the same time* recognising the valuable contribution of the African diaspora in Communist led anti-colonial and anti-fascist struggles.[69]

Jim Crow and 'domestic' fascism

For the writers and activists at the centre of this study there is little said of the betrayals of the anti-colonial (and indeed anti-fascist) cause by Soviet realpolitik. It is the *activities* of anti-fascists and anti-racists which informs their visions of trans-national solidarity, a solidarity which is mobilised through an unerring focus on race. Hughes locates fascism in the oppression and exploitation of African Americans and makes links between them and the war that Franco is waging on Spanish workers and peasants:

> Fascists know that we long to be rid of hatred and terror and oppression, to be rid of conquering and of being conquered, to be rid of all the ugliness of poverty and imperialism that eat away the heart of life today. *We represent the end of race.* And the Fascists know that when there is no more race, there will be no more capitalism, and no more war, and no more money for the munition makers because the workers of the world will have triumphed.[70]

This sophisticated argument for the centrality of race to capitalism and fascism, is the prioritisation of race as a structuring element of capitalism and the identification of fascism with imperialism. The language of anti-fascism in the 1930s thus was imbued with a particular purchase for racialised subjects: as Hughes's 'Letters from Spain' poems in the *Daily Worker* succinctly asserted, 'Fascists is Jim Crow peoples, honey / And here we shoot 'em down.'[71] This ability to fight fascism by any means necessary was attractive to more than one volunteer. Louise Thompson insisted that African Americans in Spain were far 'luckier' than those at home because:

> Here we have been able to strike back in a way that hits at those who for years have pushed and pulled us from pillar to post. I mean this – actually strike back at the counterparts of those who have been grinding us down back home.[72]

In relation to Peck's 'species of thing' that fascism conjured, Spain offered an opportunity for armed resistance. Crawford Morgan who articulated why as an African American he 'knew' fascism also summed up the attraction of Spain as 'I got a chance to fight it there with bullets'.[73]

The language of anti-fascism more generally in the Popular Front era in the US constantly refers to Jim Crowism as 'home-grown fascism'. Indeed the comparisons between the Southern States and Nazi Germany were ubiquitous in the African American press more widely.[74] In the Communist press, the 'fascist drive' of the Southern ruling class is often cited with reference to 'book burnings' and 'would be Hitlers'.[75] In *Southern Worker* racial terror in the South is compared to Nazi anti-Semitism in the 1930s: 'No story out of Hitler's Germany is more terrible than the night executions carried out by the Black Legion.'[76] The prolific black journalist J. A. Rodgers wrote an article for the *Pittsburgh Courier* in October 1936 entitled 'Hitler Could Have Copied System from Our Southern States'. Nazism was so indebted to Jim Crow laws he argued it was probable that Hitler could have 'saved time and copied them'. Thus 'Negroes, as the chief victims of Fascism' had a particular role to play in ensuring its defeat.[77] Hughes makes the connection baldly in relation to fascism in Spain:

> Give Franco a hood and he would be a member of the Ku Klux Klan, a Kleagle. Fascism is what the Ku Klux Klan will be when it combines with the Liberty League and starts using machine guns and airplanes instead of a few yards of rope.[78]

As Brian Dolinar has noted Hughes was 'articulating an argument for "double victory" several years before WWII'.[79] However this connection between fascism and Jim Crowism was not quite the same as the 'double victory' call during the Second World War. The 'Double V' slogan was an important and ambitious anti-racist slogan launched by the *Pittsburgh Courier* in 1942 which 'indicated that black Americans were fighting simultaneously for victory over totalitarianism abroad and victory over racial discrimination on the home front'.[80] Thus are many similarities to be seen in relation to the Double V campaign and the anti-fascism of pre-Second World War African American radicals. The Double V Campaign was a broad-based anti-racist initiative and there were various radical purchases upon its meaning, not least in the black press.[81] Yet in relation to *transnational* anti-fascism there are also significant differences, not least in the experience of black combatants in Spain as opposed to the US army. As Ruth Wilson Gilmore has noted in relation to the Second World War, 'the war against racism was also a racist war, in that it renovated the US racial state on several fronts'.[82] While the US fought Hitler its own army was notoriously institutionally racist. The Abraham Lincoln Brigade however was not the segregated US army where black soldiers were excluded from combat roles, it was a 'people's army' in which African Americans had military positions which put them in charge of white volunteers.[83] Moreover as Helen Graham has argued about the Spanish Civil war more widely:

> In racial and cultural as well as political terms, then, the heterogeneity of the Brigades made them a living form of opposition to the principles of purification and brutal categorization espoused by fascism and, above all, by Nazism ... this was not just about doing battle with European demons.[84]

The African American Soldiers who fought in the Second World War fought in a Jim Crow army and this was of primary importance in the Double V campaign. Indeed many of African American volunteers who fought in Spain and went to fight in the Second World War found the entrenched racialised hierarchies of the army hard to bear. After being assigned 'trash disposal' duties, the veteran James Bernard Rucker wrote angrily to his wife of the 'reactionary affront to just plain common sense' this represented to a man who had fought against fascism on the frontline in Spain.[85]

Double V was a call to fight fascism abroad *and* racism at home.[86] For Hughes and his contemporaries what was foregrounded in relation to Spain was the characterisation of Jim Crowism *as a form* of fascism, a form of fascism which linked the oppressed of the world. This formulation was shared by many African Americans in relation to the Double V campaign, but it was not the primary mobilisation of the term which was to use 'the contradictions of American democracy' to force the US government to deliver civil rights.[87] Moreover as Dayo F. Gore has argued 'within more mainstream African American politics the "Double V" campaign often operated to buttress American nationalism'.[88] In going to fight in Spain the volunteers were breaking US law and their relationship to the nation state was explicitly a hostile one. The brigadists were 'premature anti-fascists' who were breaking US neutrality by volunteering to fight in Spain.[89] Despite Soviet influence in defence of its own national interests, black anti-fascism in the 1930s was expressed as a cause which drew together the globally oppressed across the boundaries of the nation state. This cause was championed by African American activists before the advent of the Popular Front. The *Programme for Negro Liberation*, a pamphlet published by the League of Struggle for Negro Rights, insisted in 1933 that:

> The Negro problem in the United States is closely related to the problems of the Negro people and other peoples oppressed by imperialism throughout the world ... Thus a common bond of interest is established for the Negro people all over the world in the fight against their oppressors.[90]

Explicitly in terms of black anti-fascism and the Spanish civil war, the relationship between fascism and Jim Crow is cited by many of the African American volunteers in their reasons for travelling to Spain.[91] Dedicated Party member and member of the Abraham Lincoln Brigade Harry Haywood proclaimed that African Americans were in Spain to fight 'lynch-loving Hitlers'.[92] This purposeful conjoining of homegrown racialised murder and Nazism drew upon a powerful register of black experience of white supremacy in the fight against fascism. As Hughes expressed in the *Baltimore Afro-American*: 'Fascism preaches the creed of Nordic supremacy and a world for whites alone.'[93]

The point here is not that Jim Crow South was necessarily a fascist state in the classical sense of the term.[94] But rather that the racial terror of the state was foregrounded as 'fascist' by black radicals as a way to underline the structural racial violence that was normalised in the everyday lexicons of American democratic discourse. Jim Crow was not lamented as a blot on America's democracy but castigated as emblematic of US race hatred. This was a repudiation of American liberal race politics. As Erik S Gellman argues black radical activists 'envisioned the vanquishing of Jim Crow not as a moral dilemma but as an economic-based struggle to transform America into the democratic nation it had never been'.[95] Here, as in countless other black radical struggles, the puny vision of 'freedom' offered by liberal democracy was replaced with a far-reaching and ambitious aim to transform racial capital in its entirety.[96] As Paul Robeson noted African Americans had been a long time 'yearning for freedom from an oppression that predated fascism'.[97] The anti-fascist struggle was a dialectical one in relation to the radical black tradition of internationalism and anti-colonialism. 'Fascism' was not used as a random political swear word by African American radicals, it was mobilised to highlight the horrors of a racialised capitalism in the US. This was a politics which placed black subjects at the core of anti-fascist struggle. According to the veteran Walter Garland:

> We cannot forget for one minute that the oppression of the Negro is nothing more than a very concrete form, the clearest expression of fascism … in other words, what we saw in Spain … those who chain us in America to cotton fields and brooms.[98]

More than just a comparator to Jim Crow, fascism here is welded to race hatred. A race hatred which in its 'concrete form' controls and diminishes black life in a direct reference to slavery, field and house, man and woman. As Glenda Gilmore incisively notes, 'African Americans compared Jim Crow with Nazi oppression to unsettle white supremacy's place in a democratic system'. This endeavour was not only salient but effective as by '1938 African American anti-Fascism had stripped off the South's veil to reveal a modern monster'.[99] Thus Jim Crow was demystified as a place of revered Southern 'tradition' and presented as a vicious homicidal modern racist state.

While the period of the Popular Front marked the apex of these comparisons, as early as 1923 *The Messenger* had argued that 'Fascism like Ku Kluxism is the white guard of plutocracy – two brokers of unspeakable terrorism.'[100] The attempt to make interconnections between European fascism and American racism was part of a larger transnational project which placed race at the centre of anti-capitalist and anti-colonial politics. The characterisation of Jim Crow as domestic fascism was not just a neat analogy with which to shame the American State, it cast African Americans as the advanced troops of the international fight against fascism. Their intimate knowledge of the experience of white supremacy, their double investment in anti-fascism and their potential fate in terms of fascist victory all worked to invest them with a historic role in transnational anti-fascism.

Our understanding of the anti-fascism which inspired African Americans to fight in Spain is limited if we concentrate only on the terrain of US Communist historiography. Indeed much of the race/class politics that dominated CPUSA anti-racism between the wars emerged from the internationalism of Caribbean migrants to the US in the early years of the century. Of particular note here are the African Blood Brotherhood whose esoteric and blistering politics of black liberation were indebted to Marxism, black nationalism, anti-colonialism and migratory experience in the US.[101] These transnational subjects created a particular set of paradigms through which to understand racism in the US as the manifestation of global racialised capitalism that we can see in the African American approach to the Spanish Civil war. As Kelley notes 'the particular historical road that African Americans had to travel before arriving on Spanish soil gave them a unique vantage point'.[102]

The startling moment of solidarity with Spain is best understood through its prehistory rather than in the post-war assessments of the limits of the Stalinised Comintern and indeed the CPUSA's de-prioritisation of anti-colonialism during the Popular Front and anti-racism during the Second World War.[103] It is the construction of class politics as multi-racial and internationalist with a particular vanguard role for the African dispora. As David Featherstone has argued, for black radicals in this period 'it was impossible to understand fascism without relating it directly to colonial practices and imaginaries'.[104] While we don't get here Aime Cesaire's full throated indictment of colonialism as the necessary precursor to fascism and the corresponding indictment of liberal humanism, we do find a pointed critique of fascism in relation to the democratic racialised state.[105] As Robeson put it at a fundraiser for Spain in London in 1937 'I have made my choice, I had no alternative. The history of the capitalist era is characterised by the degradation of my people'; thus, 'the liberation of Spain from oppression of fascist reactionaries is not a private matter of the Spaniards, but the common cause of all advanced and progressive humanity'.[106]

This is not the expression of a facile colour blind plea for universalism but an insistence on a commonality of interests where anti-fascism and anti-racism coalesce in a transnational politics of liberation. The same sentiment is expressed a year earlier by Edward Strong in *The Crisis* where the link to Jim Crowism is particularly pointed:

> The objectives of the Spanish fascists and the southern landlords in our own country are identical – to keep the masses of underprivileged peasants tied to the soil in complete subjugation and ignorance… It can no longer be maintained that the Spanish conflict is one that concerns only the Spanish people, for questions are involved that have long since transcended the boundaries of the country and are of vital concern to the entire world and to the American Negro in particular.[107]

In the writings of African American radicals fascism was represented as intimately connected to questions of race and colonialism and, as such, prefigures the erudite work of the post-war Pan-African and Negritude formulations which broadened the understanding of the term to include the race policies of empire and the interconnections between fascism and racialised capitalism.[108] Spain, 'the Front of the world'[109] for radical African American activists and writers, was part of a powerfully expressed transnational solidarity which had routes in black radical history, contemporary articulation in the language of anti-racism and influence on the anti-colonial struggles to come.

Notes

1 'Charlottesville Vice-Mayor: "Call Them White Supremacists"', BBC, 13 August 2017, online at www.bbc.co.uk/news/av/world-us-canada-40918604/charlottesville-vice-mayor-call-them-white-supremacists (accessed 7 May 2018).
2 Patrick Strickland, 'Alt-Right Rally: Charlottesville Braces for Violence', Al Jazeera, 11 August 2017, online at www.aljazeera.com/indepth/features/2017/08/alt-rally-charlottesville-braces-violence-170810073156023.html (accessed 6 June 2018).
3 Robin Kelley, *Race Rebels: Culture, Politics & the Black Working Class* (New York: Free Press, 1996), pp. 123–160; David Featherstone, *Solidarity: Hidden Histories and Geographies of Internationalism* (London: Zed Books, 2012), pp. 99–127; Peter N. Carroll & Fraser Ottanelli, *Letters from the Spanish Civil War* (Kent, OH: Kent State University Press, 2013); Erik. S. McDuffie, *Sojourning for Freedom: Black Women, American Communism and the Making of Black Left Feminism* (Durham, NC: Duke University Press, 2011), pp. 104–111; Danny Duncan Collum & Victor A. Berch (eds), *African Americans in the Spanish Civil War: 'This ain't Ethiopia, but it'll Do'* (New York: G. K. Hall, 1992).
4 Kelley, *Race Rebels*, p.132.
5 Todd Vogle (ed.), *The Black Press New Literary and Historical Essays* (New Brunswick, NJ: Rutgers University Press, 2001), p. 152.
6 Erik S. Gellman, *Death Blow to Jim Crow: The National Negro Congress and the Rise of Militant Civil Rights* (Chapel Hill, NC: University of North Carolina Press, 2012), p. 5.
7 See for example Paul Gilroy, *The Black Atlantic: Modernity and Double Consciousness* (London: Verso, 1993); Featherstone, *Solidarity*; Brent Hayes Edwards, *The Practice of Diaspora. Literature, Translation, and the Rise of Black Internationalism* (Cambridge, MA: Harvard University Press, 2003); Benjamin Balthaser, *Anti-Imperialist Modernism: Race and Transnational Radical Culture from the Great Depression to the Cold War* (Ann Arbor, MI: University of Michigan Press, 2016).
8 Cathy Bergin, *African American Anti-Colonial Thought, 1917–1937* (Edinburgh: Edinburgh University Press, 2016) pp.1–22.
9 Minkah Makalani, *In the Cause of Freedom: Radical Black Internationalism from Harlem to London, 1917–1939* (Chapel Hill, NC: University of North Carolina Press, 2011); Jonathan Derrick, *Africa's 'Agitators': Militant Anti-Colonialism in Africa and the West, 1918–1939* (London: Hurst, 2008); Michelle Stephens, *The Black Empire: The Masculine Global Imaginary of Caribbean Intellectuals in the United States 1914–1962* (Durham, NC: Duke University Press, 2005).
10 'The Revolution and the Negro', *New International*, Volume V, December 1939, pp. 339–343.
11 Gilroy, *The Black Atlantic*, p. 133.
12 Bergin, *African American Anti-Colonial Thought*, pp. 58–79
13 Nicolás Guillén interview 1938 cited in Martin Duberman, *Paul Robeson: A Biography* (New York: New Press, 1989), p. 216.

14 Lindsey R. Swindall, *Paul Robeson: A Life of Activism and Art* (Plymouth: Rowman & Littlefield, 2013), pp. 84–86.
15 Thyra Edwards to Richard Wright in *Daily Worker*, 12 November 1937.
16 Greg Andrews, *Thyra Edwards: Black Activist in the Global Freedom Struggle* (Columbia, MO: University of Missouri Press, 2011), pp. 100–104.
17 Kelley, *Race Rebels*, pp. 131–134; Cedric Robinson, *Black* Marxism (London: Zed Press, 1983) p.396; Featherstone, *Solidarity*, pp. 112–113.
18 'A Negro Nurse in Republican Spain – Negro committee to Aid Spain', (1938), in Collum & Berch, *Africans in the Spanish Civil War*, p. 124.
19 Brenda Gayle Plummer, *Rising Wind: Black Americans and U.S. Foreign Affairs, 1935–1960* (Chapel Hill, NC: University of North Carolina Press, 1996), p. 42.
20 The Communists created Provisional Committee for the Defense of Ethiopia attempted to 'redirect antiwhite anti-Italian sentiment towards antifascism', but these efforts were scuppered by the Soviet Union's passivity in relation to condemning the invasion and their trading with Italy. See Kelley, *Race Rebels*, p. 17.
21 Robin Kelley, introduction in Collum & Berch, *Africans in the Spanish Civil War*, p. 17.
22 Robinson, *Black Marxism*, p. 397.
23 Strong, 'I Visited Spain', *The Crisis*, December 1936.
24 Gellman, *Death Blow to Jim Crow*, p. 11.
25 *Negro Worker*, July 1937.
26 Peter N. Carroll, *The Odyssey of the Abraham Lincoln Brigade* (Stanford, CA: Stanford University Press, 1994), p. 133.
27 W. E. B. Du Bois, *The Crisis*, December 1916, p. 59.
28 James Baldwin, 'Letter from a Region in My Mind', *The New Yorker*, 9 November 1962.
29 Collum & Berch, *Africans in the Spanish Civil War*, pp. 123–134.
30 Carroll, *The Odyssey of the Abraham Lincoln Brigade*, pp. 133–134.
31 Maurice Orlando Wallace, *Langston Hughes: The Harlem Renaissance* (New York: Marshall Cavendish, 2008) p. 54.
32 Langston Hughes in League of American Writers, *Writers Take Sides: Letters about the War in Spain from 418 American Writers* (New York: The League of American Writers, 1938), p. 31.
33 Frank Marshall Davis in League of American Writers, *Writers Take Sides*, p. 18.
34 Michael Denning, *The Cultural Front: The Laboring of American Culture in the Twentieth Century* (London: Verso, 1997), p. 316.
35 Cathy Bergin, *Bitter with the Past but Sweet with the Dream* (Chicago, IL: Haymarket Books, 2016), pp. 49–65.
36 Nikhil Pat Singh, *Black is a Country: Race and the Unfinished Struggle for Democracy* (Cambridge MA: Harvard University Press, 2005), pp. 109–111.
37 Bergin, *African American Anti-Colonial Thought*, pp. 1–20; Mark Naison, *Communists in Harlem During the Depression* (New York: Grove Press, 1985); Mark Solomon Mark, *The Cry Was Unity: Communists and African Americans, 1917–1936* (Jackson, MS: University Press of Mississippi, 1998); Robin Kelley, *Hammer and Hoe: Alabama Communists during the Great Depression* (Chapel Hill, NC: University of North Carolina Press, 1990).
38 Bill Mullen, *Popular Fronts: Chicago and African-American Cultural Politics* (Urbana, IL: University of Illinois Press, 1999), p. 10.
39 Jacob Zumoff, 'The American Communist Party and the "Negro Question"', *Journal for the Study of Radicalism*, Vol. 6, No. 2, 2012, pp. 53–89.
40 Cary Nelson & Jefferson Hendricks (eds), *Madrid 1937: Letters of the Abraham Lincoln Brigade from the Spanish Civil War* (New York: Routledge, 1996), pp. 33–34.
41 Balthaser, *Anti-Imperialist Modernism*, p. 16.
42 Du Bois cited in David Levering Lewis, *W. E. B Du Bois: A Reader* (New York: Henry Holt & Co, 1995), pp. 81–82.
43 Paul Gilroy, *Against Race: Imagining Political Culture beyond the Color Line* (Cambridge, MA: Harvard University Press, 2000), pp. 294, 310; for a more detailed account of

some of the tensions of African American/Jewish relations of this period see Plummer, *Rising Wind*, pp. 67–68.

44 James W. Ford, *Anti-Semitism and the Struggle for Democracy* (New York: National Council of Jewish Communists, 1939), p. 11.
45 Paul Buhle & Robin Kelley, 'Allies of a Different Sort' in Jack Salzman & Cornel West (eds), *Struggles in the Promised Land: Toward a History of Black-Jewish Relations in the United States* (Oxford: Oxford University Press, 1997), p. 208.
46 *Liberator*, 15 February 1930.
47 *Liberator*, 14 March 1931.
48 *Liberator*, 6 June 1931.
49 Bergin, *African American Anti-Colonial Thought.*
50 Nelson & Hendricks (eds), *Madrid 1937*, pp. 33–34.
51 Brian Dolinar, *The Black Cultural Front: Black Writers and Artists of the Depression Generation* (Jackson, MS: University of Mississippi Press, 2012), p. 92.
52 Featherstone, *Solidarity*, pp. 121–123.
53 Christian Høgsbjerg, '"The Fever and the Fret": C. L. R. James, the Spanish Civil War and the Writing of The Black Jacobins', *Critique*, Vol. 44: No. 1–2, 2016, pp. 171–173.
54 Robin Kelley, introduction in Collum & Berch, *Africans in the Spanish Civil War*, pp. 31–34.
55 Ibid., p. 34.
56 Carroll, *The Odyssey of the Abraham Lincoln Brigade*, p. 133.
57 Ibid., p. 15.
58 Collum & Berch, *Africans in the Spanish Civil War*, p. 175.
59 W. A. Domingo, *The Emancipator*, 27 March 1920, p. 1.
60 Langston Hughes, 'Too Much of Race', *The Crisis*, September 1937, p. 272.
61 *The Emancipator*, 10 April 1920, p. 1.
62 *The Crusader*, January 1921, p. 1.
63 Hughes, 'Too Much of Race'.
64 *Daily Worker*, 29 September 1937, cited in Collum & Berch, *Africans in the Spanish Civil War*, p. 119.
65 Ibid., p. 121.
66 For a discussion of 'Franco's Moors' see Derrick, *African's 'Agitators'*, pp. 361–371.
67 George Padmore in 'Authors Take Sides on the Spanish Civil War', *Left Review* (1937) cited in Featherstone, *Solidarity*, p. 102.
68 Ibid., pp. 103–104.
69 Høgsbjerg, 'The Fever and the Fret', pp. 161–177.
70 Hughes, 'Too Much of Race'. My emphasis.
71 *The Daily Worker*, 23 January 1938.
72 Louise Thompson, in Nelson & Hendricks, *Madrid 1937*, p. 120.
73 Collum & Berch, *Africans in the Spanish Civil War*, p. 176.
74 Glenda Elizabeth Gilmore, *Defying Dixie: The Radical Roots of Civil Rights, 1919–1950* (New York: W. W. Norton & Company, 2008), pp. 168–171.
75 *Southern Worker*, December 1934, p. 4; July 1937, p. 7.
76 Ibid., June 1936, p. 8.
77 J. A. Rodgers cited in Clayton Vaughn-Roberson, 'The "Jewish Question" in the Black Mind: The Image of World Jewry in African American Socialism', *Journal of Civil and Human Rights*, Vol. 3, No. 2, 2017, p. 69; Gilmore, *Defying Dixie*, p. 193.
78 Hughes, 'Soldiers from Many Lands United in Spanish Fight', *Afro American*, 18 December 1937, cited in Christopher C. De Santis (ed.), *The Collected Works of Langston Hughes*, Vol. 9 (Columbia, MO: University of Missouri Press, 2003), p. 178.
79 Dolinar, *The Black Cultural Front*, p. 87.
80 Sherie Mershon & Steve Schlossman, *Foxholes and Color Lines: Desegregating the US Armed Forces* (Baltimore, MD: Johns Hopkins University, 2003), pp. 96–97.
81 Penny M. von Eschen, *Race against Empire: Black Americans and Anticolonialism, 1937–1957* (Ithaca, NY: Cornell University Press, 1997), p. 33.

82 Ruth Wilson Gilmore, 'Fatal Couplings of Power and Difference: Notes on Racism and Geography', *The Professional Geographer*, Vol. 54, No. 1, 2002, p. 18.
83 Peter N. Carrol, Michael Nash & Melvin Small, *The Good Fight Continues: World War II Letters from the Abraham Lincoln Brigade* (New York: New York University Press, 2006), p. 116.
84 Helen Graham, *The Spanish Civil War: A Very Short Introduction* (Oxford: Oxford University Press, 2005), p. 44.
85 Carrol, Nash & Small, *The Good Fight Continues*, pp. 130–131.
86 Notably the Communist Party was against the Double V because of its deprioritisation of African American struggles after the entry of the Soviet Union into the war. See C. L. R. James et al., *Fighting Racism in World War II* (New York: Pathfinder, 1980), pp. 157–158.
87 Earnest L. Perry Jr., 'It's Time to Force a Change: The African-American Press' Campaign for a True Democracy during World War II', *Journalism History*, Vol. 28, No. 2, 2008, p. 94.
88 Dayo F. Gore, *Radicalism at the Crossroads: African American Women Activists in the Cold War* (New York: NYU press, 2011), p. 4.
89 John Gerassi, *The Premature Antifascists: North American Volunteers in the Spanish Civil War, 1936–39: An Oral History* (Westport, CT: Praeger, 1986), p. 14.
90 League of Struggle for Negro Rights, *Programme for Negro Liberation* (Harlem, New York City, 1933), p. 17.
91 Collum & Berch, *Africans in the Spanish Civil War*, pp. 175–176.
92 Carroll, *The Odyssey of the Abraham Lincoln Brigade*, p. 135.
93 'Hughes Finds Moors being used as pawns by Fascists in Spain', *Baltimore Afro-American*, 30 October 1937.
94 Gilmore, *Defying Dixie*, p. 160.
95 Gellman, *Death Blow to Jim Crow*, p. 264.
96 Robin Kelley, *Freedom Dreams: The Black Radical Imagination* (Boston, MA: Beacon Press, 2002), pp. 6–7.
97 Robeson, cited in von Eschen, *Race against Empire*, p. 41.
98 Collum & Berch, *Africans in the Spanish Civil War*, p. 31.
99 Gilmore, *Defying Dixie*, pp. 160–161.
100 'The Fascisti in America', *The Messenger*, June 1923.
101 Makalani, *In the Cause of Freedom*, pp. 45–71; Cathy Bergin, '"Unrest among the Negroes": The African Blood Brotherhood and the Politics of Resistance', *Race and Class*, Vol. 57, No. 3, 2016, pp. 45–58; Jacob Zumoff, *The Communist International and US Communism, 1919–1929* (Leiden: Brill, 2014), pp. 298–301.
102 Kelley, *Race Rebels*, p. 157.
103 Maurice Isserman, *Which Side Were You On? The American Communist Party During the Second World War* (Middletown, CT: Wesleyan University Press, 1982), pp. 117–119.
104 Featherstone, *Solidarity*, p. 108.
105 Aimé Césaire, *Discourse on Colonialism* (New York: Monthly Review Press, 2001), p. 36.
106 *Daily Worker*, 4 November 1937, cited in Philip Foner, *Paul Robeson Speaks* (New York: Citadel Press, 1978), pp. 118–119.
107 Edward E. Strong, 'I Visited Spain', *The Crisis*, December 1936.
108 Gary Wilder, *Freedom Time: Negritude, Decolonization, and the Future of the World* (Durham, NC: Duke University Press, 2014), pp. 1–5.
109 Langston Hughes, 'To a Poet on his Birthday Edwin Rolfe' (1937) in Cary Nelson, *Revolutionary Memory: Recovering the Poetry of the American Left* (London: Routledge, 2002), p. 111.

14

'A GREAT EXAMPLE OF INTERNATIONAL SOLIDARITY'

Cuban medical volunteers in the Spanish Civil War

Ariel Mae Lambe

Alongside tens of thousands of international combat volunteers who travelled to Spain during the Civil War to aid the Spanish Republic – over 1,000 of them Cuban – came a much smaller number of equally important individuals: men and women who gave medical aid. The Non-Intervention Agreement (1936) that complicated combat volunteers' journeys to Spain did not prohibit humanitarian efforts; therefore, some international supporters 'chose to express their solidarity with the Republicans by raising funds for medical aid or by going to Spain themselves to provide it'.[1] Medical volunteers from around the world served both with the Republican army and with the International Brigades.[2] Some were medical professionals prior to the trip, while others were limited to the role upon arrival by their capacity or gender, and still others found their calling when they were assigned to work in medical support after spending time injured or ill in Republican military hospitals. As analysis of Cuban medical volunteers in this chapter demonstrates, a complex combination of humanitarian, political, and personal motivations caused people to travel to Spain to offer medical aid to the Republic.

A very few of the medical volunteers were Cuban. Though their number was small, an unusually rich set of source material allows us to study their diversity and glimpse their complex motivations for risking the trip. Due to the research efforts of US nurse, Spanish Civil War volunteer, and author Fredericka 'Freddie' Martin, there exists in New York City an intriguing archive of materials concerning Cuban medical volunteers in Spain. During the war, Martin served as head nurse for US medical volunteers. She began work with the newly formed American Medical Bureau to Aid Spanish Democracy (AMB) at the urging of a fellow member of her union and went on to serve in Spain from January 1937 to February 1938.[3] In 1950 Martin moved to Cuernavaca, Mexico, home to many fellow US expatriates as well as Spanish exiles. There, between 1967 and 1982, she researched extensively for a book she wished to write on medical volunteers during the war, corresponding with hundreds of people around the world and soliciting historical source materials. She relied on strong interpersonal connections with others who had volunteered in Spain and with those who had an interest in the subject. Martin struggled with her own economic and health challenges and confronted frustrating political realities – including the US embargo against Cuba – as she sought and ultimately failed to complete and publish the work. The fruits of her labours comprise the Fredericka Martin Papers in the Abraham Lincoln Brigade Archives at the Tamiment Library.[4] This collection provides valuable resources for the study of Cuban medical volunteers in Spain.

It is fitting to arrive at a study of the Cuban medical volunteers through a US archive because of the close connection many (though importantly not all) Cuban volunteers had with US volunteers and organisations. The AMB, for example, was responsible for the recruitment of some Cuban volunteers in New York City and, as Martin's story suggests, US and Cuban volunteers worked closely together in Spain. They built transnational solidarity around shared anti-fascism, but also around longstanding cultural and migratory connections between the United States and Cuba. Cuba's neocolonial position relative to the United States following US intervention in the Cuban War of Independence (1895–1898) was highly problematic for Cubans, but it did result in a significant degree of familiarity between the two countries. For example, many Cuban volunteers had the experience of living in the United States prior to serving in Spain. Familiarity with both their country's neocolonial power, the United States, and also its former colonial power, Spain, allowed some Cuban volunteers to act as highly valuable linguistic and cultural translators during their service for the Spanish Republic, as some of the individual stories in this chapter demonstrate.

Cubans did not need US inspiration to want to serve in Spain, however. Anti-fascist Cubans who volunteered were part of a vibrant Cuban anti-fascist movement that was both transnational and deeply rooted in Cuba's domestic political fights. Many Cuban anti-fascists were longstanding activists who, following the lead of prominent student leader and Cuban Communist Party co-founder Julio Antonio Mella, began during the 1920s to define Cuban anti-fascism as encompassing their domestic struggles against US imperialism and strongman dictatorship, as well as for economic and social justice and some form of revolution and/or democracy. Cuba's domestic activists included Cuban nationalists/anti-imperialists with a range of ideological stances, anarchists (past their peak in Cuba but still influential), Communists (newly established but rapidly ascendant), and Trotskyists (significant disproportionate to their small number in part due to their ties to nationalists), men and women, black (some pan-Africanist) and white. Their diversity meant that their movement included many different perspectives and goals and struggled to achieve unity. Nevertheless, they enjoyed notable success when they helped trigger the downfall of president-turned-dictator Gerardo Machado and toppled his US-backed replacement in the Revolution of 1933. After strongman Fulgencio Batista's destruction early in 1934 of the revolutionary government established in 1933, and especially after his brutal suppression of Cuba's largest-ever general strike in March 1935, Cuban activists frustrated by failure and repression increasingly redefined their domestic fight as anti-fascist. By doing so, they broadened their political arena from national to global. Transnational identities and experiences allowed these Cuban anti-fascists – diverse both in terms of their identities and their politics – to keep up their domestic fight despite severe repression and, eventually, to exert pressure on Batista that contributed to his 'populist turn' of the late 1930s and early 1940s. This chapter examines the transnational identities and experiences of a few Cuban anti-fascists, and shows the ways in which these individuals embodied key characteristics of Cuban anti-fascism.[5]

Although the *New York Times* reported that all aboard were US citizens,[6] at least one Cuban travelled to Spain with Fredericka Martin as part of the first AMB group that departed New York in January 1937: Dr Eduardo Odio Pérez. Odio Pérez may have become a US citizen prior to his departure for Spain,[7] or the *Times* report could exemplify the notable tendency of US sources to count Cuban volunteers as US volunteers. Their identities – as immigrants, exiles, and frequent transnational migrants – were complex, and aloof US observers seem to have struggled with accounting for this complexity. Martin, a lifelong migrant herself, did not, instead interpreting their identities through the lens of interpersonal connection – national borders and identities seemed real to her only in so far as they were inevitable. The embargo against Cuba by the United States, for example, confronted her with a harsh and undeniable reality that disturbed her deeply, for it denied her most dearly held beliefs about the universality of the human community. With wistful frustration, she wrote Odio Pérez in 1970, 'I hope someday it will be possible for me to visit you but the roads are blocked now … we must just m[a]nage to live a long time.'[8]

She had reconnected with Odio Pérez, whom she considered a dear friend, in the late 1960s and shared an affectionate correspondence with him.[9] She solicited information about him and other Cubans, including: Dulcea Hernaiz, 'the Cuban nurse who went from the States to Spain with one of our AMB groups',[10] and Hernaiz's husband Arturo Corona (often written incorrectly as Coruña) who was a combat volunteer; Oscar Soler, who had been a patient at her hospital and then took a job as a medical assistant; and Dr Luis Díaz Soto and his companion Pía Mastellari Maecha who volunteered in Spain as a nurse. This chapter examines the experiences of these six Cuban men and women.[11] Their diversity – in terms of background, beliefs, and behaviour – as well as that which they shared in common makes this group a valuable case study. Exploring the stories of these individuals and couples demonstrates that no one simple narrative can encapsulate Cuban anti-fascism or the Cuban volunteer experience in Spain.

Dr Eduardo Odio Pérez

Eduardo Odio Pérez was born in Santiago de Cuba in 1893.[12] He called his parents 'anti-fascists', while the book *Cuba y la defensa de la República Española (1936–1939)* – the collection of documents and biographical sketches of Cuban volunteers published in 1981 by the Cuban Institute of History – called them 'petit-bourgeois'.[13] Like many Cubans of his era, Odio Pérez lived a transnational life starting at an early age. He attended primary school in Santiago de Cuba and secondary school in Far Rockaway, New York, then pursued medical training at the University of Havana, Loyola University (1917), and Chicago Memorial Hospital, earning an MD. He married a Cuban woman named Antonia Elena Muñiz in 1919.[14] Dr Odio Pérez, an AMB press release stated, 'was chief of the Disinfection and Sanitation Health Department in Havana from 1933 to 1935'.[15] A biographical survey he completed in Spain in 1938 confirms his employment as 'head of disinfection' in Havana.[16]

The press release described the doctor's politics, stating that he 'was forced to flee his native land because of his political activity'.[17] His interest in activism began in 1927 during 'political revolutions in Cuba'. He went into political exile twice before Machado's downfall, in 1930 and 1932, the latter time in Central America.[18] In February 1930 a group of doctors protested a planned homage to Machado. The event divided the Federación Médica Cubana (Cuban Medical Federation), with some members supporting it and others vehemently opposed. Odio Pérez was one of the leaders of the latter group, helping to organise a protest letter to the Federation's executive. An editorial in the New York City Spanish-language press on 15 February 1930 concluded that, though the tribute event would take place despite the protest, the Cuban people would know that 'honorable doctors' did not support it.[19] Odio Pérez noted with pride that he 'renounced Cuban Medical Federation with other companions for giving this homage to tyrant Machado'. In 1938 he remembered the date of this event as 1929. The doctor stood before trial courts in Havana in 1929 and 1930, accused of conspiracy and illegal publication. Declared a rebel, he spent three days in jail before being freed on bail. He received amnesty in 1932.[20] In June of that year secret police agents foiled a plot by 'Dr Eduardo Odio, revolutionary by profession', and others to stage an armed expedition from Honduras to Cuba. The group planned to land in Pinar del Río and join forces with troops led by General Mario García Menocal (1866–1941) against Machado, an article in *La prensa* of San Antonio, Texas reported on 9 June 1932. Members of the failed mission including Colonel Carlos Mendieta (1873–1960), the report stated, were imprisoned on the Isle of Pines.[21] A few years later Mendieta would be among those the doctor opposed.

With a wife and three children, Dr Odio Pérez found himself in exile again in 1935 in New York City because of his participation in anti-dictator activism including the March 1935 general strike.[22] He remembered attending May Day celebrations in the city that spring.[23] In October Odio Pérez, identified in his capacity as a representative of Cuba's Partido Agrario Nacional (National Agrarian Party, or PAN), spoke at a city meeting of Cuban exiles and their supporters against the 'government of Caffery-Batista-Mendieta', a triumvirate of US ambassador, strongman, and puppet president identified as 'traitorous to Cuban nationalism and an instrument of Yankee imperialism'. The doctor argued that the 'lands of the *guajiro*', or Cuban peasant, had been 'robbed by the North American companies'. Members of various political groups including Joven Cuba (Young Cuba), the Partido Revolucionario Cubano – Auténticos ('Authentic' Cuban Revolutionary Party), the Organización Revolucionaria Cubana Anti-imperialista (Cuban Revolutionary Anti-imperialist Organization, or ORCA), and Nacionalista Puertorriqueño (the Puerto Rican nationalism movement) attended the meeting, held at a dancehall at 146th Street and Broadway. Odio Pérez spoke alongside prominent Cuban anti-fascists such as Pablo de la Torriente Brau and Joaquín Ordoqui.[24]

The doctor remembered attending an exposition of ambulances and information about the Spanish Civil War at Madison Square Garden.[25] The gathering he recalled was probably the reception for Spanish Republican Ambassador Fernando de los Ríos, which took place on 4 January 1937. The *New York Times* reported that approximately 16,000 people attended the meeting organised by the 'United Spanish Societies, an organization of fraternal and benevolent groups in the Spanish colonies of the metropolitan area'. At the meeting, the AMB presented four ambulances 'to the Spanish Leftist government', AMB members pushing two of the vehicles into the hall amid applause.[26] 'I could appreciate it was a serious and strong organization', the Cuban doctor noted, and so he applied to volunteer with the first AMB group to leave for Spain.[27] They left twelve days later.

When asked by Martin in 1968 to give his motives for going to Spain, Odio Pérez listed 'humanitarian' reasons and 'political awareness'. Elaborating, he wrote that his political motive was that 'we could not do much in Cuba or in USA, helping to win the war in Spain, it was much easi[e]r [than] to knock down Machado'. Given the chronology of events, Odio Pérez likely meant to write Batista here rather than Machado, whom he had helped to pressure out of office in 1933. Additionally, the doctor remembered that he was in a very bad economic situation at the time, trying to support his wife and three children. This final stated motive suggests that the doctor received payment, compensation, and/or support for his family in exchange for his AMB service. For these various reasons, he volunteered to go to Spain. The ship carrying the first AMB group arrived in Paris, and the doctor crossed the border at Port Bou in an automobile, then continued on, also by car, to Barcelona.[28] Following his stay in Barcelona, he travelled around some and spent a time at the battlefront of Jarama before settling in at Villa Paz, Saelices.[29] Saelices is a very small town near Tarancón to the southeast of Madrid and 'Villa Paz' was the name of the Saelices estate in which the AMB hospital was housed.[30]

In answer to the question, 'Are you known as a Communist in your country?' put to him by the Communist Party of Spain in March 1938, Odio Pérez called himself a 'sympathizer'.[31] Records in the doctor's personnel file from the Comintern archives show an interesting series of events regarding his membership in the Communist Party of Spain and his proposed promotion in the Sanitation Service of the International Brigades – and evidently a connection between the two. Odio Pérez's superiors proposed a promotion to the rank of captain for him early in the autumn of 1937, to no avail; a letter from the doctor's supervisor, Commander Dr

Edward Barsky, begins: 'Several months ago recommendations were made to you that Dr Odio Perez receive the rank of captain. However, up until now we have received no official confirmation that this advance in rank has been granted.'[32] In the midst of this wait for response regarding promotion, in November 1937, Odio Pérez applied for membership in the Spanish Communist Party, his card signed by a US volunteer as a witness.[33] The request moved up the chain of command: 'Please kindly name to the rank of Captain comrade Lieutenant Dr Eduardo Odio Pérez …'.[34] Another US volunteer posted in an administrative role[35] signed a short report on Dr Odio Pérez supportive of his promotion, stating that the Cuban doctor 'acted as responsible in the absence of Dr Edward Barsky', and calling him a '[v]ery good anti-fascist'. A handwritten response on the report in German, though very difficult to read in its entirety, appears to lay out a rather complicated set of bureaucratic instructions to facilitate promotion. However, written across the top of the same document in what appears to be identical handwriting, except this time in French, are the words: 'It is not possible.'[36] Dr Odio Pérez's Comintern personnel file concludes without any confirmation of a promotion. The final document leaves open the question of whether or not the doctor's politics played a role in the consideration of his rank. An undated, unsigned note addressed to US volunteer Jim Bourne – an adjutant-commissar of the 15th International Brigade responsible for reporting on the politics of volunteers[37] – stated somewhat ominously in Spanish: 'We have a particular interest in knowing everything possible about Eduardo Odio Perez, and so please send us reports from responsible comrades who have known him here, in Cuba, or in the US.'[38]

Despite whatever concerns the Communists had about the Cuban doctor, Odio Pérez served in Spain for fourteen months and then continued his work for the AMB and the Republican cause back in the United States on a publicity and fundraising tour. He spoke on behalf of the AMB in cities and towns of New York and Pennsylvania, and gave interviews to the press.[39] A form press release intended for use by local sponsoring committees advertising the presentations emphasised the doctor's political credentials gained through participation in Cuban struggles and exaggerated the length of his service in Spain, claiming he had been there for eighteen months.[40] An ambulance machine-gunned in the war accompanied the doctor on the speaking tour. Many years later he remembered fondly that the ex-Governor of Pennsylvania, with assistance from some workers' organisations, had hosted a grand reception in Philadelphia for his talk.[41]

Also upon his return to the United States, Dr Odio Pérez ran into trouble with immigration officials, who sent him to Ellis Island for deportation back to Cuba. He stood trial before a federal jury, and the AMB helped to appeal the jury's decision to deport him. He recalled that the Bureau had paid his expenses in New York 'for some time'.[42] A letter from an attorney to the Bureau dated 21 July 1939 requested payment for legal services regarding immigration and medical practice rendered on behalf of Odio Pérez.[43] It is unclear from the records Martin compiled whether or not the lawyers ever collected their fee, but their work on behalf of the Cuban doctor failed. 'In 1939', he wrote to Martin in 1975, 'I returned to Cuba', and he had never since been to visit the United States.[44] A faint recollection about his deportation recorded by Odio Pérez in the questionnaire he prepared for Martin sheds light on his connection to larger networks and with one US figure of particular importance to New York City's Cuban exiles: 'My expenses from New York to Cuba I really do not know because I spoke about it to the negroe [*sic*] leader of the communist party of New York, I think his name was Ford.'[45] African-American Communist leader James W. Ford served as an central point of connection between Cubans and the US Communist Party, especially during the 1930s. Despite any troubles his lack of Communist Party membership may have caused him in Spain, Odio Pérez nevertheless received assistance from the CPUSA.

Dr Eduardo Odio Pérez's trajectory from Cuban political activism during the struggle against Machado to the March 1935 general strike through exile in New York City, participation in Spain, and eventual return to Cuba is in many ways exemplary of the Cuban Spanish Civil War volunteer experience. Odio Pérez lived a migratory life from an early age. He was a professional family man and a non-Communist who was nevertheless a militant activist in Cuba, jailed and exiled for his political work. He did not shy away from working with Communists or accepting assistance from the Communist Party. He went to Spain at the age of 44 for a combination of political, humanitarian, and pragmatic reasons, the latter including financial need and a perceived inability to direct his efforts more effectively toward Cuban domestic issues. He took pride in his work in Spain. He stayed in Cuba after the Cuban Revolution of 1959, though he kept a low profile as a Spanish Civil War volunteer relative to many others. His remembrance was featured in Cuba's official history of the effort, but he did not receive the kind of extensive and longstanding public commemoration in Cuba that a number of his fellow veterans of Spain enjoyed, probably at least in part because he was not a Communist.

Nurse Dulcea Hernaiz and her husband Arturo Corona

'About her there is something mysterious', Martin commented about Cuban nurse Dulcea Hernaiz.[46] AMB records from early 1937 provide basic information about the Cuban nurse. She was 21 years old at the time and married with no children. She was living in New York City, but listed as her 'responsible relative' an aunt in Havana. She was a Cuban citizen and spoke only Spanish. She attended high school in Havana and earned a bachelor's degree from the University of Havana. She stated that she received professional training at the Reina Mercedes Hospital in Havana, having served there as an emergency nurse during a large strike in Havana in 1934. Though she was not employed as a nurse at the time of the survey, she claimed her experience during this strike as 'military medical experience', asserting that it was equivalent. Further qualifications for volunteer work in Spain, she suggested, included her level-headedness in emergencies, her strength and good health, and her ability to work long hours without sleep. To the question of motivation, she replied: 'It is the duty of all who have the proper professional training to help the Loyalists in Spain.' She would be willing to serve there indefinitely, she stated.[47] She left for Spain in March 1937.[48]

Dulcea Hernaiz's husband was combat volunteer Arturo Corona, who left for Spain from the United States as part of the second major group of US volunteers in January 1937 on the same ship voyage as Martin, Odio Pérez, and the rest of the AMB group. Martin recalled that after a few months with the AMB in Spain, Hernaiz 'abandoned' the group to go with Corona when he left the Lincoln Battalion for a Spanish unit in late spring or early summer 1937 and 'enticed her away'. Martin never saw Hernaiz again.[49]

Dr Odio Perez believed that Corona, whom he called Coruña, was 'not very straight'.[50] Corona was indeed a suspicious character. His personnel file in the Comintern archives contains two documents, both of which raise questions. A document in English dated 7 April 1937 begins by stating that Corona is Cuban, age 36, a member of the Communist Party of Cuba, First Lieutenant of the 17th Battalion of the 15th International Brigade (which was the US Lincoln Battalion), and 'Commander of Second Company up to Feb. 27'. It notes that he was, as of early April, at Villanueva, and that Comrades Walsh and Suarez investigated him there the week of 1 April. Their findings were as follows. Corona 'passed himself as battalion commander when he arrived in Villanueva ten days ago. Corona assigned one comrade Delgado, Albert, to be an adjutant and courier to one Doctor Fogarty, now residing in Villanueva'. The report stated that this Dr Fogarty carried a letter signed by Corona which he showed to Walsh, and that the letter was marked, under Corona's signature, 'ACOLB', for American Commandant of Lincoln Battalion. The report mentioned that Corona claimed he possessed a special pass from the International Brigades allowing him free movement, as well as 'a Packard and a late model Ford motor car to drive around in, one of which was burnt up'. The report noted also that Corona wore three wide stripes on his hat and one on his sleeve, and that a man named Pablo, currently in Hospital Number 2 in Albacete, could give further information about him. A handwritten note at the top of the report reads, 'Place on his record card', though unfortunately the file contains no such card.[51] A document in French, which is undated, states that its information is based on a report from Cuban volunteer Florentino Alejo. The document accuses Corona of stealing 3,000 pesos from the Cuban Communist Party, and also notes that he was a deserter in Spain.[52] Clearly, officials had their eyes on Corona, and did not think favourably of him.

Corona made himself infamous back in the United States as well, or as Martin put it in one letter, he 'turned out badly'.[53] Upon her return to New York, Martin learned that Corona had run a scam in which he solicited money from US families of volunteers reported missing, ostensibly to support search and recovery efforts, and then vanished with the money and fled back to Cuba.[54] Martin lamented never having been able to find Hernaiz again. Since 1939, she wrote, she and other nurses had searched for news of her, and her memory haunted Martin. 'Sometimes I dreamed of her – nightmares, not dreams – remembering Arturo's bad deeds in New York', she wrote.[55] Believing that her friend might have been one more victim of Corona's cons made her angry. 'Dr Odio thinks he was in US Army and killed in the Pacific', Martin wrote of Corona, and conjectured bitterly: 'I'd bet [he] is sitting easy somewhere.'[56]

Tales of this corrupt individual illustrate several important points about Cuban volunteers in Spain. It is essential to note that actors could be both politically motivated and ruthlessly opportunistic. Corona may have been a genuine believer in Communism led astray by personal greed, or he may have joined the Party simply to benefit from the opportunities for theft and cons with which Party membership presented him. These opportunities, in Corona's case, extended to the battlefronts of Spain where reports indicate the volunteer was unscrupulous and devious, dishonestly gaining in the process not only money but also power. In Spain Corona showed that he had an inflated sense of his own grandeur by bragging about his status and showing off the trappings of his alleged rank. These behaviours suggest that the volunteer may have sought adventure and glory as well as money and power in Spain. Finally, the variety of reports about Corona stealing money and fleeing across national borders demonstrate that transnational movement did not always result from political ideals or honest economic necessity; the clichéd example of the criminal crossing a border to escape justice applied as well. Meanwhile, the haunting Hernaiz, who appears to exist only in Martin's archive and even there only in fragments, illustrates the anonymity of so many Cuban anti-fascists – surely many more are lost to history altogether.

Oscar Soler

Oscar Soler was born in Cuba in 1893 and was 43 or 44 years old when he travelled to Spain. He may have been a US citizen, and was certainly a US resident. His address prior to departure for Europe was on West 112th Street in New York City. Documents refer to him as both Cuban and American. Though trained as a nurse with a diploma in nursing and 15 years of experience practicing in the medical field (possibly in neurology), he reported having been self-employed in New York selling items on commission.[57]

Upon his arrival in Spain on 27 January 1937 Soler enrolled in the International Brigades as a member of the US Lincoln Battalion. Over the course of 1937 and 1938, Soler took part in multiple military operations, including Jarama, Brunete, Belchite, Aragon, and Ebro. He was wounded several times and received treatment at multiple hospitals, including Villa Paz/Saelices, Murcia, and Moià.[58] Convalescing in the hospital at Villa Paz/Saelices, Soler met members of the AMB including Martin. Once he recuperated, he joined the hospital staff as an interpreter, clerk, and orderly. 'Since he was not well – or became so useful – he remained with us as interpreter-orderly', Martin stated, and wrote, 'we attached him to the staff of Villa Paz as clerk and interpreter'. She called him 'our valiant interpreter and nurse'.[59] Martin clearly valued his role as interpreter. He is one of many examples of Cubans who, having lived in the United States prior to the war, became vital intermediaries between Spaniards and US volunteers, acting as cultural and linguistic translators, even language tutors. In a 1939 letter to Martin, Soler told her that he wrote in Spanish because he had been her 'Spanish professor'. He admonished her affectionately, 'since I suppose you will not have forgotten it, I want, when you reply to me, that you do so in Spanish'.[60]

Conflicting documents from the Comintern archives make analysis of Soler's politics difficult. The list 'Characteristics of the Cuban Communists', dated 21 November 1938, assessed politically a number of Communist volunteers, placing each in one of five categories: leader, good, average, weak, or bad. The list ranked Soler as 'Good'.[61] Another document in the same file – this one handwritten and undated – lists Soler among seven 'Bad and Suspicious Cubans'.[62] Soler's own personnel file contains similar contradictions. An evaluation by the Communist Party of Spain dated 9 November 1938 commended his conduct as 'good', assessed his work as 'quite effective', noted that he was a member of the Party, and called him an 'old militant'.[63] However, a political appraisal by the Medical Service dated both August 1938 and 5 October 1938 evaluated him negatively: 'Politically not organised. Indifferent, inactive. Bad antifascist. … His expulsion from Spain has been proposed. He should be repatriated.' Beneath these notes typed in Spanish, someone handwrote in English: 'Check: Oscar Soler (suspect).'[64]

Oscar himself had an opportunity to state his political beliefs in the Autumn of 1938 when he completed a survey for the Comisariado de Guerra de las Brigadas Internacionales (War Commission of the International Brigades). Statements of opinion made about him may have been conflicting, but no such contradictions appeared in Soler's written assessments of the Communist Party and the International Brigades in 1938. His written answers were unabashedly pro-Communist. The Popular Front, he asserted, was a 'good and just policy'. It had 'united all people in a single slogan Unity and this will win the war'. The International Brigades, he wrote, had 'demonstrated that of which the world proletariat is capable'. The Brigades had taught him and his fellow volunteers 'many lessons' both political and military. To Spain, he believed, they had 'given a great example of international solidarity'. They were 'always occupying the dangerous posts and always willing to sacrifice'. And they would remain 'an example for the future'.[65] Either he genuinely believed in Communist anti-fascism, or he felt it opportune to emphatically state that he did in the survey (or perhaps both). The timing of the survey's administration to Soler raises the possibility that the Cuban volunteer knew he was considered suspect by some and wished to prove his true loyalty. It is also possible that he wrote such high praise in a cynical attempt to stay out of trouble and get back to New York safely at the war's impending end.

Letters Soler wrote to Martin in 1939, however, show he was not able to travel back to New York as he wished, and like many of his countrymen, struggled for a time to leave Europe. Writing in June from Camp de Gurs in the region of Aquitaine in southwestern France, he stated to Martin, 'You know already that I am a *guest* of the French government and that they take very good care of me.' He composed the letter in rambling Spanish prose dotted with English words (italicised):

> It is very difficult to explain it because I am in this concentration camp but they say that love is the bread of life but how this too is difficult to explain but who knows if some time we will encounter each other *in dear old USA*. I could describe to you all my adventures and as they are very numerous to describe I will hope that we encounter each other in person.

At this time, it seems, he still had hope that he would travel to the United States after leaving the camp. By the time he composed his next letter to Martin in August, however, he was in Havana. His situation, he told her, had been terrible since his arrival. 'I never know where I'm going to eat or where I'm going to sleep', he wrote. No one – no group – in Cuba could assist him, he stated, because the 'organizations are all broke + the Party can not [*sic*] render any help as the Party is without funds'.[66] This claim raises suspicion, as the Cuban Communist Party was at the time enjoying new legal status, newly-cemented control over Cuban organised labour, and an increasingly favourable relationship with the country's strongman leader, Batista. Nevertheless, Soler wrote to Martin again in October from Havana, stating: 'I'm trying very hard to get out of here + get back to the United States but somehow I can never get enough money together for the fare.'[67] Far from Dr Odio Pérez's experience of going on a high-profile fundraising tour for Republican Spain, Soler was merely seeking travel funds sufficient to return home.

In Europe Oscar had married a Spanish woman named Pepita, 'one of the two nurses we acquired at Romeral from among the Madrid refugees and whom we trained', Martin recalled. Martin lamented the fact that Pepita was left behind in a French concentration camp after the war when Soler was repatriated to Cuba. 'I am haunted by what happened to her … and other girls whom we were unable to help', she wrote to Odio Pérez.[68] In his August letter from Havana Soler referenced having asked Martin to 'raise amongst my friends in the USA enough money to bring my wife here'. Since then, though, he had been informed by the Cuban Department of State that the government would bring his wife to Cuba 'on or about the 26 or 28 of this month. That is she will sail from France on that date.'[69] However, Pepita was still in Europe and still Oscar's main preoccupation when he wrote to Martin two months later in October. 'I've been worrying a lot about my wife who is still in France as there is not a way to get her here on account of the war', he confided to Martin. The Cuban government, he now believed, was working to arrange for some US ships to take Cubans stuck in France to the United States and then on to Cuba, and his wife might be included in this group, but it would probably take a long time and 'nothing effective' had yet been done. Winter approached, he lamented, and his wife was 'in a very cold region of France' and probably lacked 'the necessary things to protec[t] her from the cold'. He asked Martin if any organisation could offer assistance, and what might be done to obtain winter garments for her. He felt at a loss and pleaded for help. 'In hopes that you will write to me this time', he concluded, 'I remain as ever yours: Oscar.'[70] Of this final letter Martin noted:

'Perhaps it was not my final letter from him but it is the last I have. If I remember correctly, he did not answer a letter of mine but when? I do not remember.'[71]

Soler's story illustrates the vital role bilingual and bicultural Cubans could play in Spain as translators and interpreters. It also demonstrates the political complexity of even those individuals who were avowed members of a particular political ideology or party, in Oscar's case, the Communist Party. Though he was a Party member and dutifully gave the Party line when asked, some officials suspected him of bad politics. Finally, Soler's experience upon his departure from Spain, his time spent in a French concentration camp and his subsequent hardships after crossing the Atlantic back to Cuba, show the ways in which many international veterans of the war suffered in the aftermath of Republican defeat, especially those who were neither wealthy nor members of the professional class.

Dr Luis Díaz Soto and Pía Mastellari Maecha

The son of a public employee and a teacher, Dr Luis Díaz Soto earned his medical degree at the University of Havana. He was an activist in the university student struggles between 1923 and 1929, the year of his graduation. He joined the Cuban Communist Party early in 1934 – 'observing discipline and fulfilling efficiently all the tasks entrusted to him' – and worked as a leftist organiser in the field of medicine, taking leadership positions in strikes by medical personnel during the mid-1930s. In 1938 Cuban Communist Party official Ramón Nicolau González called him 'one of the most beloved and considerate intellectuals' of the Party at that time.[72]

Traveling from Cuba by way of New York, he arrived in Spain in the summer of 1937.[73] He joined the International Brigades in August, serving first briefly as a soldier in the Canadian Mackenzie-Papineau Battalion before his incorporation into the US Lincoln Battalion as its medic. He served the Lincoln Battalion from August 1937 through February 1938, at which time he became medical director for the 15th International Brigade. He was 33 years old as of March 1938 and listed as unmarried, though he did have a female companion sometimes referred to as his wife. Nurse Pía Mastellari Maecha also took part in Cuba's political struggles of the 1930s as a member of the medical community and also served in Spain.

Two photographs taken by the Photographic Unit of the 15th International Brigade show Díaz Soto in December 1937. In one he poses with an ambulance donated by the AMB.[74] These photographs show a thin man with sunken cheeks. Nicolau González noted that though the Party's Central Committee had 'accepted this comrade's trip to Spain' believing that he would offer both a political and medical benefit, due to the doctor's 'not being a person of a sufficiently strong constitution', the Committee agreed that his stay abroad should be limited to six months. Dr Díaz Soto first became seriously ill in Spain during November 1937 and was sent to Villa Paz/Saelices Hospital for three days. On Christmas Eve, he suffered an acute appendicular attack. Then, on 25 January in Teruel, he developed a pulmonary condition, possibly pneumonia, for which he spent three days in the Mora de Rubielos Hospital in a small town east of Madrid. He continued to suffer from fevers but took on leadership of medical services for the 15th International Brigade through the end of the Segura Offensive, at which time he received permission to travel to Barcelona for treatment. At the time of his writing, Nicolau González noted in March 1938, Dr Díaz Soto had already remained in Spain eight or nine months, despite the Party's initial recommendation that he stay only six. 'I believe it opportune', he concluded, 'to request and to prepare for his immediate return to Cuba.'[75]

A couple of weeks later, on 24 March, Mastellari wrote a letter from Barcelona requesting assistance from the Communist Party of Spain. She had entered Spain using a Spanish passport and now wished to leave with a Spanish passport. She came as a nurse, she stated, because her 'companion' was in the International Brigades, but she fell ill upon her arrival. She received treatment, she wrote, and the doctor forbade her from work until she had recovered fully. Then, during the time of her rehabilitation, she stated, 'my companion has had to leave, and under these conditions we have decided that I too should leave given the state of health in which I remain'. In support of her request, she chronicled her political credentials for Communist officials. 'I participated in the organization of the Union of Clinics, Convalescent Homes, and Hospitals (Worker Confederation of Cuba) in the place where I worked: the Fortun-Souza Clinic, in 1933 …' She became responsible for union work as a delegate and served as a member of strike committees during the 'national movement of medics and sanitary workers' in 1934 and the general strike of 1935. In addition to her union work, she noted her affiliation with Communist groups in Cuba as an 'organizing member of the National Union of Women (P.C.) and of the legal political party Revolutionary Union Party (P.C.)'.[76] The state of her health, her partner's departure, her past political work, and her history with the Communist Party, she hoped, would incline Party officials to grant her leave and provide her with a Spanish passport.

Like many of her contemporaries, Mastellari had a complex transnational identity. Her father was Italian, and she was born in Zaragoza, Mexico. She moved to Cuba with her family when she was a child and became a citizen upon reaching adulthood. Her complicated nationality caused logistical difficulties for Mastellari as she prepared to travel to Europe. She had great trouble obtaining the necessary documentation because her Italian father had not completed the work of declaring his citizenship. For this reason, 'the means of traveling as a Spanish woman was facilitated for me'. For her new Spanish identity, she adopted the pseudonym María García. In April 1938, Cuban Communist official Nicolau González assisted in evacuating Díaz Soto to France 'at the request of the Cuban Communist Party'. Mastellari, however, remained due to the fact that she did not have 'documents with which to obtain a legal passport', and therefore the consulate refused to issue her one. She was delayed 'until the situation with the passport was clarified', but was able to reunite with Díaz Soto in Paris on 30 April. They returned to Cuba shortly thereafter.[77]

This couple's story demonstrates the limits personal matters could set on the political work of individuals and families. Though devoted Communists and anti-fascist activists, Díaz Soto and Mastellari could not remain in Spain due to poor health. Also, in the case of Mastellari it illustrates the way in which Cubans' complex transnational identities and experiences might interact with certain transnational networks, such as international Communism. Communist officials were able to render Mastellari Spanish for the sake of facilitating her transportation to Spain, though this power was somewhat limited as illustrated by the delay in her exit from the country.

Though the six individuals examined in this chapter all shared the desire to work for the Republic and the experience of volunteering in Spain, they constituted a diverse group. Men and women of different ages, civil statuses, and stations in life, diverse in their motivations, political backgrounds, and ideological beliefs, they offer us one small view of the broad spectrum of Cuban anti-fascism. Like other Cuban volunteers in Spain and other Cuban anti-fascists more generally, these six embodied key characteristics of Cuban anti-fascism: the significance of Cubans' transnational identities and experiences in their anti-fascist work, the way in which they situated their anti-fascism in Cuban domestic politics, the nature of their connections to the international left, and in some cases the ambivalence of their politics and character. Their human stories – and Fredericka Martin's role in bringing these stories to us – also highlight the interconnectedness of global anti-fascism, created in large part through interpersonal contacts and relationships, and offer a glimpse of the significance of Cubans' role in this transnational movement.

Notes

1 Martin F. Shapiro, 'Medical Air to the Spanish Republic during the Civil War (1936–1939)', *Annals of Internal Medicine*, Vol. 97, 1982, p. 120.
2 Nicholas Coni, 'Medicine and the Spanish Civil War', *Journal of the Royal Society of Medicine*, Vol. 95, March 2002, p. 147.
3 Michael D'Ambrosio, Gail Malmgreen, Jennifer Waxman, & Jessica Weglein, archivists, 'Guide to the Fredericka Martin Papers ALBA (ALBA 001): Historical/Biographical Note', Tamiment Library, New York University, New York.
4 Michael Nash, 'The Abraham Lincoln Brigade Archives at New York University's Tamiment Library', *Science & Society*, Vol. 68, No. 3, 2004, pp. 358–359; D'Ambrosio et al., 'Guide to the Fredericka Martin Papers'.
5 Ariel Mae Lambe, *No Barrier Can Contain It: Cuban Antifascism and the Spanish Civil War* (Chapel Hill, NC: University of North Carolina Press, 2019).
6 'Medical Unit Here Ready to Aid Spain', *New York Times*, 15 January 1937.
7 Eduardo Odio Pérez, 'Biografía de Militantes', 5 March 1938, Comintern Archives, Russian State Archive of Socio-Political History, Moscow, Russia (hereafter RGASPI), 545/6/598 fond/opis/delo). Fond 545 contains the records of the International Brigades. RGASPI has also been translated as the 'Russian Center for the Preservation and Study of Recent History'. All historical source material must be approached with caution, but the Comintern archives warrant a particularly critical eye. Communist obsession with collecting biographical and autobiographical information provides us with rich historical source material, but we must interpret these sources with an understanding of the highly politicised context in which they were created. As Brigitte Studer reminds us,

Comintern records are 'integral elements of complex bureaucratic and political practices' and 'based on a co-production between authority and individual'. Brigitte Studer, *The Transnational World of the Cominternians* (Basingstoke: Palgrave Macmillan, 2015) pp. 16–17, see also: pp. 73–82. In other words, the information extracted from these files in this chapter – offered by the individual in question and/or filtered through officials or informants – simply cannot be taken at face value. I interpret it accordingly in the text, with commentary on the specific source when possible, and otherwise conjecture on how political motivations may have coloured personnel assessments.

8 Martin to Odio Pérez, 6 June 1970, Folder 4, Box 2, Fredericka Martin Papers, ALBA 001, Tamiment Library, New York University, New York (hereafter FMP-ALBA) (ellipsis in original).

9 Correspondence between Martin and Odio Pérez can be accessed in Folder 4: Cuba: Doctors & Nurses undated, 1968–1981' and Folder 5: Cuba: Odio Pérez, Eduardo 1968–1981, Box 2, FMP-ALBA.

10 Martin to Louis [probably Louis Miller], 29 April & 5 May 1970, Folder 4, Box 2, FMP-ALBA.

11 The six described in this chapter were not the only Cuban medical volunteers in Spain. Martin lists also Dr Rafael de la Vega, Dr Benigno Sauza, Dr [Humberto] Sinobas [del Olmo], Lieutenant José Campos Cuina, and Lieutenant Mario Sánchez Díaz. Martin appears to have been less interested in these individuals because she had not personally met them in Spain.

12 Odio Pérez, 'Solicitud de Paso o Ingreso en el Partido Comunista Español (Sección de la Internacional Comunista)', 9 November 1937, RGASPI, 545/6/598; Dr Oscar Telge to Comarade Commandant de la Base, 8 December 1937, RGASPI, 545/6/598; Odio Pérez, 'Biografía de Militantes', 5 March 1938, RGASPI, 545/6/598; Odio Pérez, 'Biographical Statistics of the Personnel of the American Medical Bureau and Co-Workers', survey sent by Martin, 1968, Folder 5, Box 2, FMP-ALBA. The last of these sources is undated, but correspondence indicates that Martin sent the blank survey to Odio Pérez in October 1968 and the doctor returned it completed to her in December of the same year.

13 Odio Pérez, 'Biografía de Militantes', 5 March 1938, RGASPI, 545/6/598; Odio Pérez, 'La batalla duró diez días', Instituto de Historia del Movimiento Comunista y de la Revolución Socialista de Cuba, *Cuba y la defensa de la República Española (1936–1939)* (Havana: Editora Política, 1981) p. 115.

14 Odio Pérez, Biografía de Militantes, 5 March 1938, RGASPI, 545/6/598; Odio Pérez, 'Biographical Statistics',1968, Folder 5, Box 2, FMP-ALBA.

15 American Medical Bureau, press release, undated, Folder 5, Box 2, FMP-ALBA.

16 Odio Pérez, 'Biografía de Militantes', 5 March 1938, RGASPI, 545/6/598.

17 American Medical Bureau, press release, undated, Folder 5, Box 2, FMP-ALBA.

18 Odio Pérez, 'Biografía de Militantes', 5 March 1938, RGASPI, 545/6/598.

19 'Se oponen al homenaje a Machado', *Gráfico* (New York, New York), 15 February 1930.

20 Odio Pérez, 'Biografía de Militantes', 5 March 1938, RGASPI, 545/6/598.

21 United Press, 'Se preparaba una expedición armada a Cuba', *La Prensa* (San Antonio, Texas), 9 June 1932.

22 Odio Pérez, 'Biographical Statistics', 1968, Folder 5, Box 2, FMP-ALBA; Odio Pérez, 'La batalla duró diez días', *Cuba y la defensa*, p. 115.

23 Odio Pérez, 'Biografía de Militantes', 5 March 1938, RGASPI, 545/6/598.

24 R. Zubaran Capmany, 'Oratoria Tropical en Nueva York', *La Prensa* (San Antonio, Texas), 10 October 1935.

25 Odio Pérez, 'Biographical Statistics', 1968, Folder 5, Box 2, FMP-ALBA; Odio Pérez, 'La batalla duró diez días', *Cuba y la defensa*, 111.

26 'Recruiting Denied by Spanish Envoy', *New York Times*, 5 January 1937.

27 Odio Pérez, 'Biographical Statistics', 1968, Folder 5, Box 2, FMP-ALBA.

28 Ibid.

29 Odio Pérez, 'La batalla duró diez días', *Cuba y la defensa*, 111–112; Odio Pérez to Martin, 4 December 1968, Folder 5, Box 2, FMP-ALBA.
30 D'Ambrosio et al., 'Guide to the Fredericka Martin Papers'.
31 Odio Pérez, 'Biografía de Militantes', 5 March 1938, RGASPI, 545/6/598.
32 Edward Barsky to Oscar Telge, 8 December 1937, RGASPI, 545/6/598.
33 Odio Pérez, 'Solicitud de Paso o Ingreso', 9 November 1937, RGASPI, 545/6/598.
34 Oscar Telge to Camarade Commandant de la Base, 8 December 1937, RGASPI, 545/6/598.
35 Arthur H. Landis, *The Abraham Lincoln Brigade* (New York: The Citadel Press, 1967) p. 338.
36 Sol Rose, 'Perez, Odio (Doctor)', 10 December 1937, RGASPI, 545/6/598.
37 Landis, *The Abraham Lincoln Brigade*, pp. 351, 354–355.
38 'Comision de Extranjeros, Al camarada Jim BOURNE', RGASPI, 545/6/598.
39 American Medical Bureau and North American Committee to Aid Spanish Democracy Executive Board Minutes, 24 March 1938, Folder 5, Box 2, FMP-ALBA; Odio Pérez to Martin, 4 December 1968, Folder 5, Box 2, FMP-ALBA; Odio Pérez, 'Biographical Statistics', 1968, Folder 5, Box 2, FMP-ALBA.
40 American Medical Bureau, press release, Folder 5, Box 2, FMP-ALBA.
41 Odio Pérez to Martin, 7 July 1975, Folder 5, Box 2, FMP-ALBA; Odio Pérez, 'La batalla duró diez días', *Cuba y la defensa*, 115.
42 Odio Pérez, 'Biographical Statistics', 1968, Folder 5, Box 2, FMP-ALBA.
43 Sam S. Kaplan to John Sherman, Medical Bureau to Aid Spanish Democracy, New York, New York, 21 July 1939, Folder 5, Box 2, FMP-ALBA.
44 Odio Pérez to Martin, 7 July 1975, Folder 5, Box 2, FMP-ALBA.
45 Odio Pérez, 'Biographical Statistics', 1968, Folder 5, Box 2, FMP-ALBA.
46 Martin to Sociedad de Amistad Cubana-Española, 6 June 1970, Folder 4, Box 2, FMP-ALBA.
47 American Medical Bureau, survey entitled 'American Medical Corps.', 15 January 1937, Folder 11, Box 9, FMP-ALBA.
48 Folder 11, Box 9, FMP-ALBA.
49 Martin to Louis [probably Louis Miller], 29 April 1970 & 5 May 1970, Folder 4, Box 2, FMP-ALBA; Martin to Sociedad de Amistad Cubana – Española, 6 June 1970, Folder 4, Box 2, FMP-ALBA.
50 Rosa Hilda Zell to Martin, 26 September 1968, Folder 4, Box 2, FMP-ALBA; Odio Pérez to Martin, 4 December 1968, Folder 5, Box 2, FMP-ALBA.
51 Servicio de Cuadros, Base de la Brigadas Internacionales to the Control Commission, 7 April 1937, RGASPI, 545/6/598; 'Report sur le camarade Corona', undated, RGASPI, 545/6/598.
52 'Report sur le Camarade Corona', undated, RGASPI, 545/6/598.
53 Martin to John Martinez, 28 July 1977, Folder 11, Box 19, FMP-ALBA.
54 Martin to Sociedad de Amistad Cubana – Española, 6 June 1970, Folder 4, Box 2, FMP-ALBA.
55 Martin to Alberto Pena, 22 February 1978, Folder 4, Box 2, FMP-ALBA.
56 Martin to Louis [probably Louis Miller], 29 April 1970 & 5 May 1970, Folder 4, Box 2, FMP-ALBA.
57 Comisariado de Guerra, Servicio Sanitario Internacional, 'Apreciación política del camarada', dated both August 1938 and 5 October 1938, RGASPI, 545/6/601; Oscar Soler, survey administered by Comisariado de Guerra de las Brigadas Internacionales, 31 October 1938, RGASPI, 545/6/601; Carles Hervás i Puyal, 'La Clínica Militar núm. 5: Un hospital de les Brigades Internacionals a Santa Coloma de Farners (1938–1939)', *Quaderns de la Selva*, 20, 2008, p. 182. Carles Hervás i Puyal does not give a specific citation for the information on Soler, but the source materials for the whole article are from: El fons documental del Balneari Termes Orion de Santa Coloma de Farners (1906–1975), l'Arxiu Comarcal de la Selva, Santa Coloma de Farners, Catalunya.

58 Oscar Soler, survey, 31 October 1938, RGASPI, 545/6/601; Odio Pérez to Martin, 4 December 1968, Folder 5, Box 2, FMP-ALBA; Comisariado de Guerra, Servicio Sanitario Internacional, 'Apreciación política del camarada', dated both August 1938 and 5 October 1938, RGASPI, 545/6/601; Hervás i Puyal, 'La Clínica Militar núm. 5', p. 182.
59 Martin to Odio Pérez, 31 October 1968, Folder 5, Box 2, FMP-ALBA; Martin to Louis [probably Louis Miller], 29 April 1970 & 5 May 1970, Folder 4, Box 2, FMP-ALBA; Martin to Sociedad de Amistad Cubana – Española, 6 June 1970, Folder 4, Box 2, FMP-ALBA.
60 Soler to Martin, 21 June 1939, Folder 6, Box 2, FMP-ALBA.
61 'Características de los comunistas cubanos', Barcelona, 21 November 1938, File 585, RGASPI.
62 'Cubanos Malos y sospechosos', undated, RGASPI, 545/6/585.
63 Comité Central, Partido Comunista de España, conduct assessment form, 9 November 1938, File 601, RGASPI. This document is signed by Jim Bourne, A. Donaldson, and a third person whose signature is illegible (it appears to begin M. del).
64 Comisariado de Guerra, Servicio Sanitario Internacional, 'Apreciación política del camarada', dated both August 1938 and 5 October 1938, RGASPI, 545/6/601.
65 Soler, survey, 31 October 1938, RGASPI, 545/6/601.
66 Soler to Martin, 11 August 1939, Folder 6, Box 2, FMP-ALBA.
67 Soler to Martin, 11 October 1939, Folder 6, Box 2, FMP-ALBA.
68 Martin to Odio Pérez, 31 October 1968, Folder 5, Box 2, FMP-ALBA.
69 Soler to Martin, 11 August 1939, Folder 6, Box 2, FMP-ALBA.
70 Soler to Martin, 11 October 1939, Folder 6, Box 2, FMP-ALBA.
71 Martin, 'Buscando informes o direcciones', Folder 29, Box 22, FMP-ALBA.
72 Ramón Nicolau González, 'Memorandum', 11 March 1938, RGASPI, 545/6/590.
73 Nicolau González states that Díaz Soto arrived in Spain on 8 July 1937, having embarked in June. The undated document 'Solicitación de permiso (para el extranjero)', however, records his date of arrival as 26 August, RGASPI, 545/6/590.
74 Photographic Unit of the Fifteenth International Brigade, 'Dr Luis Diaz Soto, Lincoln-Washington medical staff Dec 1937', 11–0665 Photo Unit #: B140 and 11–0666 Photo Unit #: B141, Harry Randall Fifteenth International Brigade Photograph Collection (ALBA PHOTO 011), Tamiment Library, New York University, New York.
75 Nicolau González, 'Memorandum', 11 March 1938, RGASPI, 545/6/590.
76 Pía Mastellari Maecha to Camarada Minor, 24 March 1938, RGASPI, 545/6/597. 'P.C.' here stands for Partido Comunista, or Communist Party.
77 'Solicitación de permiso (para el extranjero)', undated, RGASPI, 545/6/590; Nicolau González, 'Memorandum', 11 March 1938, RGASPI, 545/6/590; Pía Mastellari Maecha to Camarada Minor, 24 March 1938, RGASPI, 545/6/597; Obituary: 'Dr Eloesser is Dead', *The Volunteer* (December 1976) p. 3; Mastellari, 'El pueblo español', in *Cuba y la defensa*; Nydia Sarabia, 'Guerra Civil Española: Cubanos contra el fascismo', *Mujeres con historia*, no. 106 (18 October 2002).

Acknowledgements

Adapted from *No Barrier Can Contain It: Cuban Antifascism and the Spanish Civil War* by Ariel Mae Lambe. Copyright © 2019 by the University of North Carolina Press. Used by permission of the publisher.

INDEX

For Product Safety Concerns and Information please contact our EU representative GPSR@taylorandfrancis.com
Taylor & Francis Verlag GmbH, Kaufingerstraße 24, 80331 München, Germany

www.ingramcontent.com/pod-product-compliance
Lightning Source LLC
Chambersburg PA
CBHW050334270326
41926CB00016B/3457
* 9 7 8 1 1 3 8 3 5 2 1 9 3 *